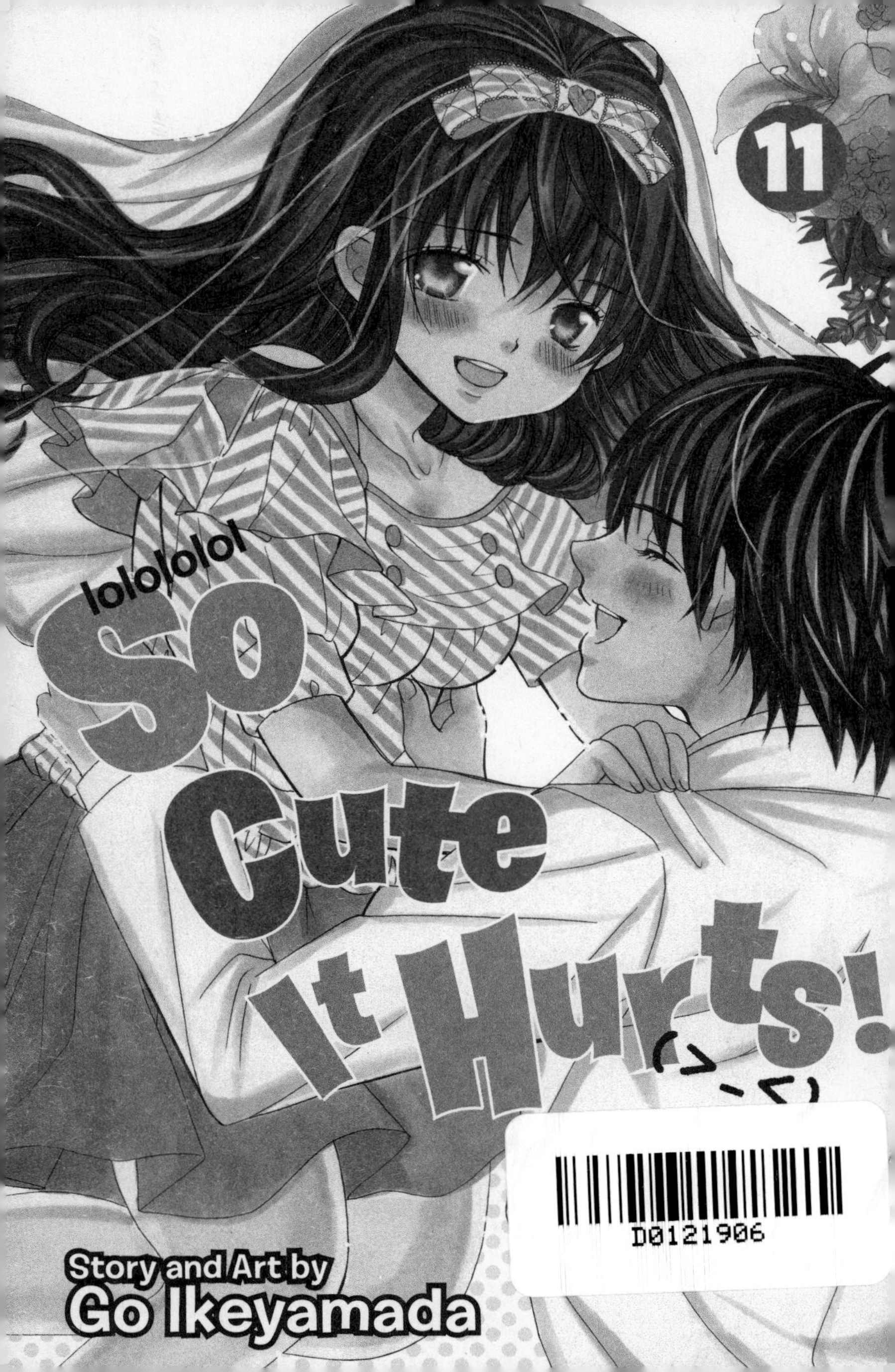
11
So Cute It Hurts!
Story and Art by
Go Ikeyamada

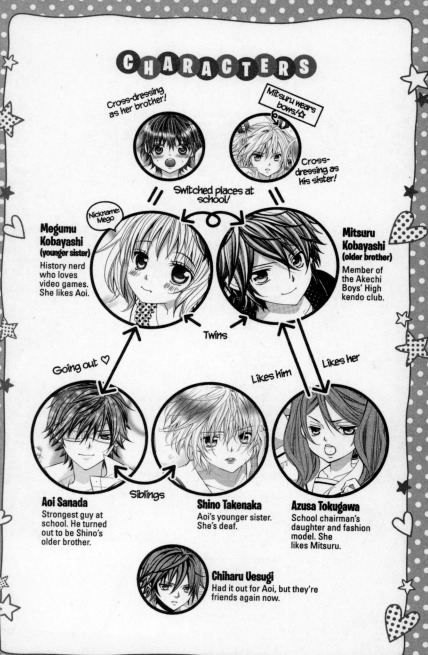

CHARACTERS

Cross-dressing as her brother!

Mitsuru wears bows! ☆

Cross-dressing as his sister!

== Switched places at school! ==

Nickname: Mego

Megumu Kobayashi (younger sister)
History nerd who loves video games. She likes Aoi.

Mitsuru Kobayashi (older brother)
Member of the Akechi Boys' High kendo club.

Twins

Going out ♡

Likes him

Likes her

Aoi Sanada
Strongest guy at school. He turned out to be Shino's older brother.

Siblings

Shino Takenaka
Aoi's younger sister. She's deaf.

Azusa Tokugawa
School chairman's daughter and fashion model. She likes Mitsuru.

Chiharu Uesugi
Had it out for Aoi, but they're friends again now.

S T O R Y

★ Mitsuru and Megumu are twins. One day they switch places and go to each other's school for a week! That's when Megumu falls in love with Aoi and Mitsuru falls in love with Shino. When the week is over, Megumu declares her love for Aoi, and they start dating. But Aoi is so uncomfortable around women that he faints when he touches one.

★ One day while Aoi is protecting Megumu, his eye patch falls off and exposes scars from a burn he suffered when he was a child. Aoi is about to retreat into his shell when Megumu kisses his scar. Her kiss heals his psychological wounds, and the two are finally able to touch! Meanwhile, Azusa confesses her love for Mitsuru and declares that she will make him fall in love with her! Mitsuru finds himself becoming attracted to the headstrong Azusa.

★ A magazine article exposes that Azusa's parents are both having affairs. Mitsuru heads to Tosho High because he's worried about Azusa, and he ends up learning something shocking from Aoi. Shino was the product of an affair, and she and Azusa have the same father, Shuichi Tokugawa! Their father loves Shino but doesn't care much about Azusa. When Mitsuru finds out about Azusa's past and realizes how lonely she's been all her life, he announces that he'll make sure she's always happy now!

C O N T E N T S

So Cute It Hurts!! (ﾉ-ω-)

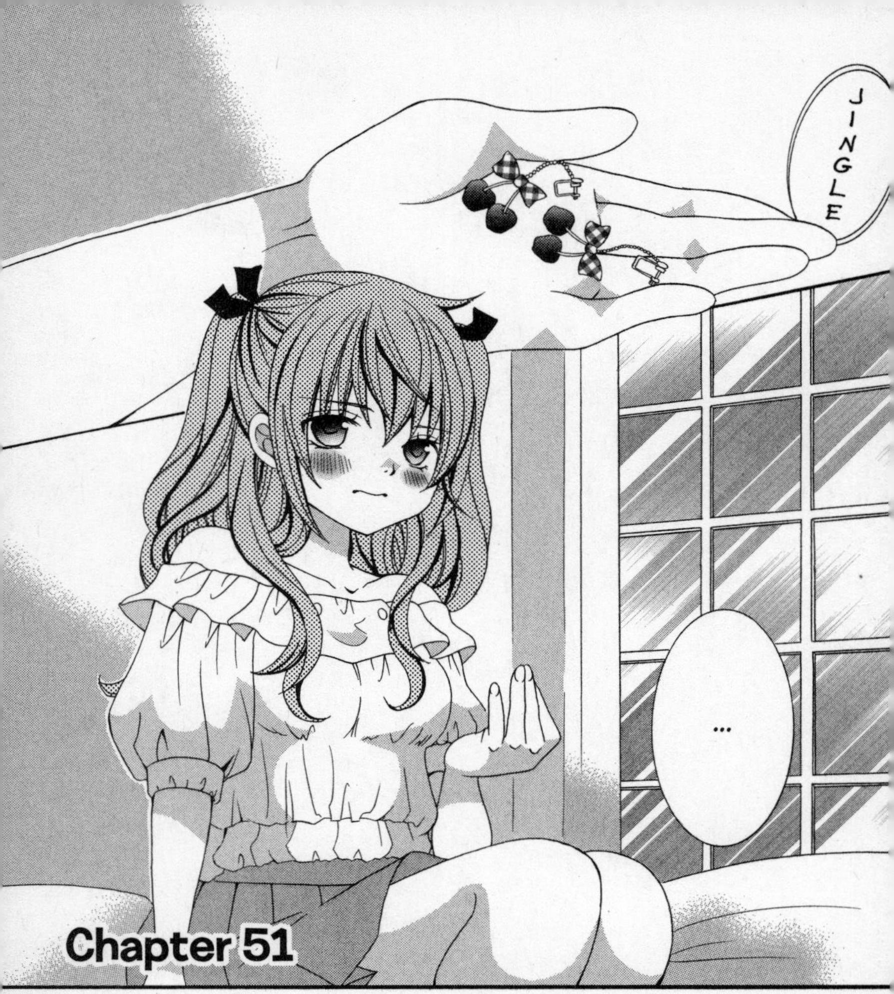
JINGLE
...

Chapter 51

NICE TO MEET YOU AND HELLO. ♡ I'M GO IKEYAMADA. THANK YOU FOR PICKING UP MY 54TH BOOK!! THIS IS VOLUME 11 OF *SO CUTE IT HURTS!!* I WAS SO HAPPY ABOUT THE HUGE REACTION VOLUME 10 RECEIVED. (ToT) VOLUME 11 BEGINS WITH AZUSA AND MITSURU. WHY IS AZUSA WEARING A WEDDING DRESS ON THE COVER?! I'VE BEEN REALLY LOOKING FORWARD TO DRAWING CHAPTER 51, SO I HOPE YOU ALL LOVE IT!! (ToT) (^o^)

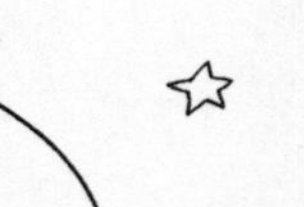

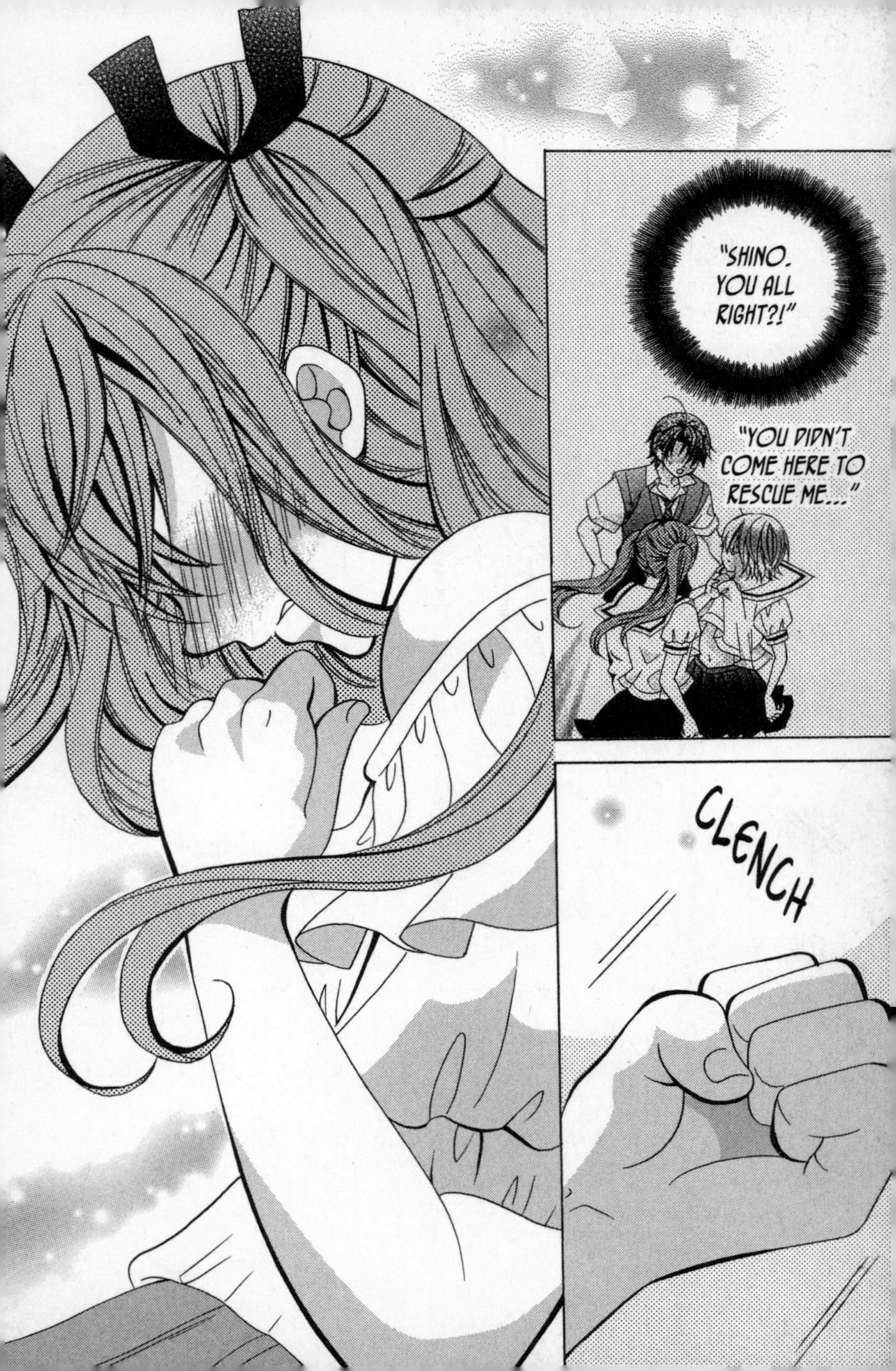
"SHINO. YOU ALL RIGHT?!"
"YOU DIDN'T COME HERE TO RESCUE ME..."
CLENCH

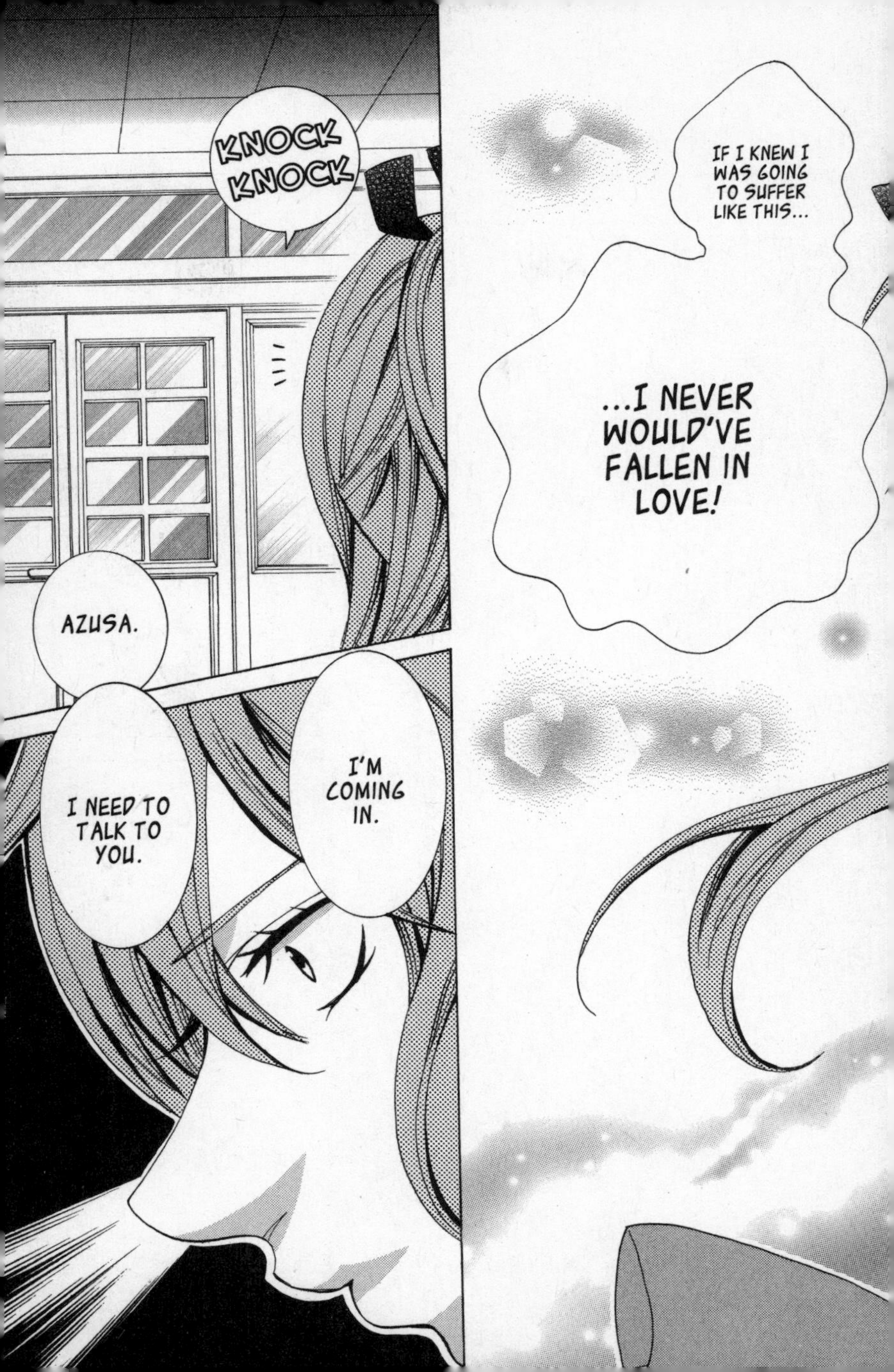
IF I KNEW I WAS GOING TO SUFFER LIKE THIS...
...I NEVER WOULD'VE FALLEN IN LOVE!
KNOCK KNOCK
AZUSA.
I NEED TO TALK TO YOU.
I'M COMING IN.

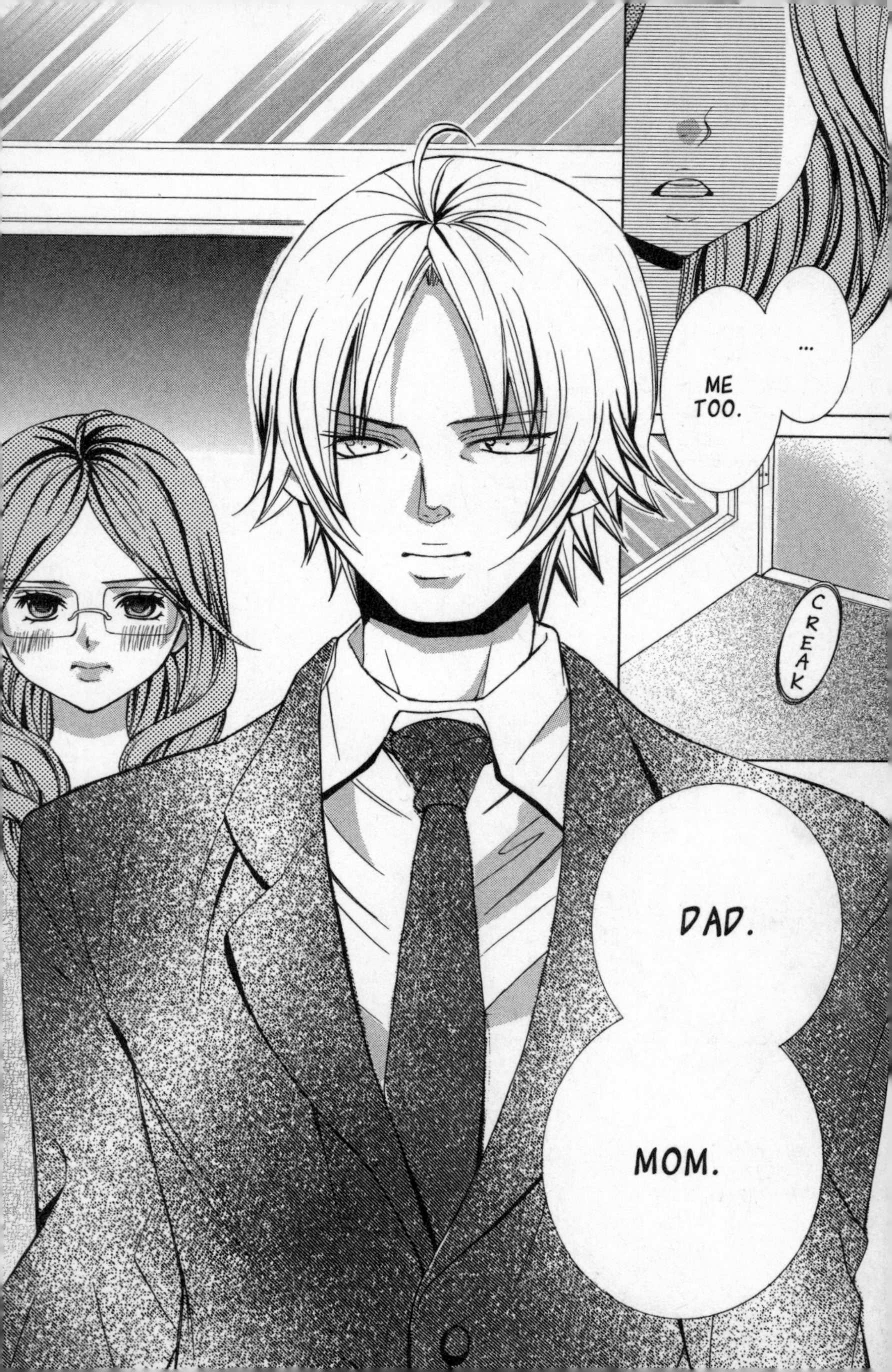
...
ME TOO.
CREAK
DAD.
MOM.

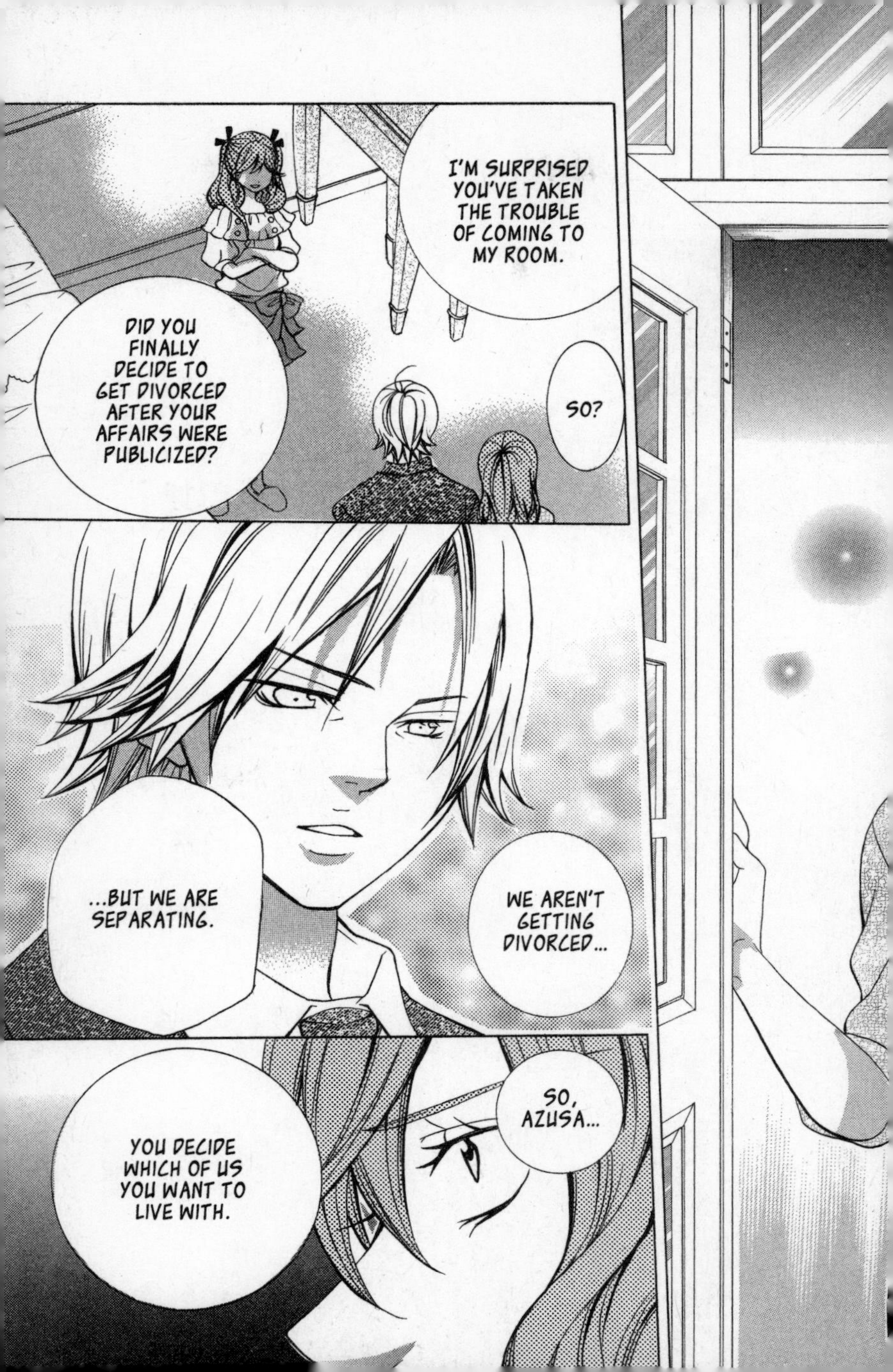
I'M SURPRISED YOU'VE TAKEN THE TROUBLE OF COMING TO MY ROOM.
SO?
DID YOU FINALLY DECIDE TO GET DIVORCED AFTER YOUR AFFAIRS WERE PUBLICIZED?
WE AREN'T GETTING DIVORCED...
...BUT WE ARE SEPARATING.
SO, AZUSA...
YOU DECIDE WHICH OF US YOU WANT TO LIVE WITH.

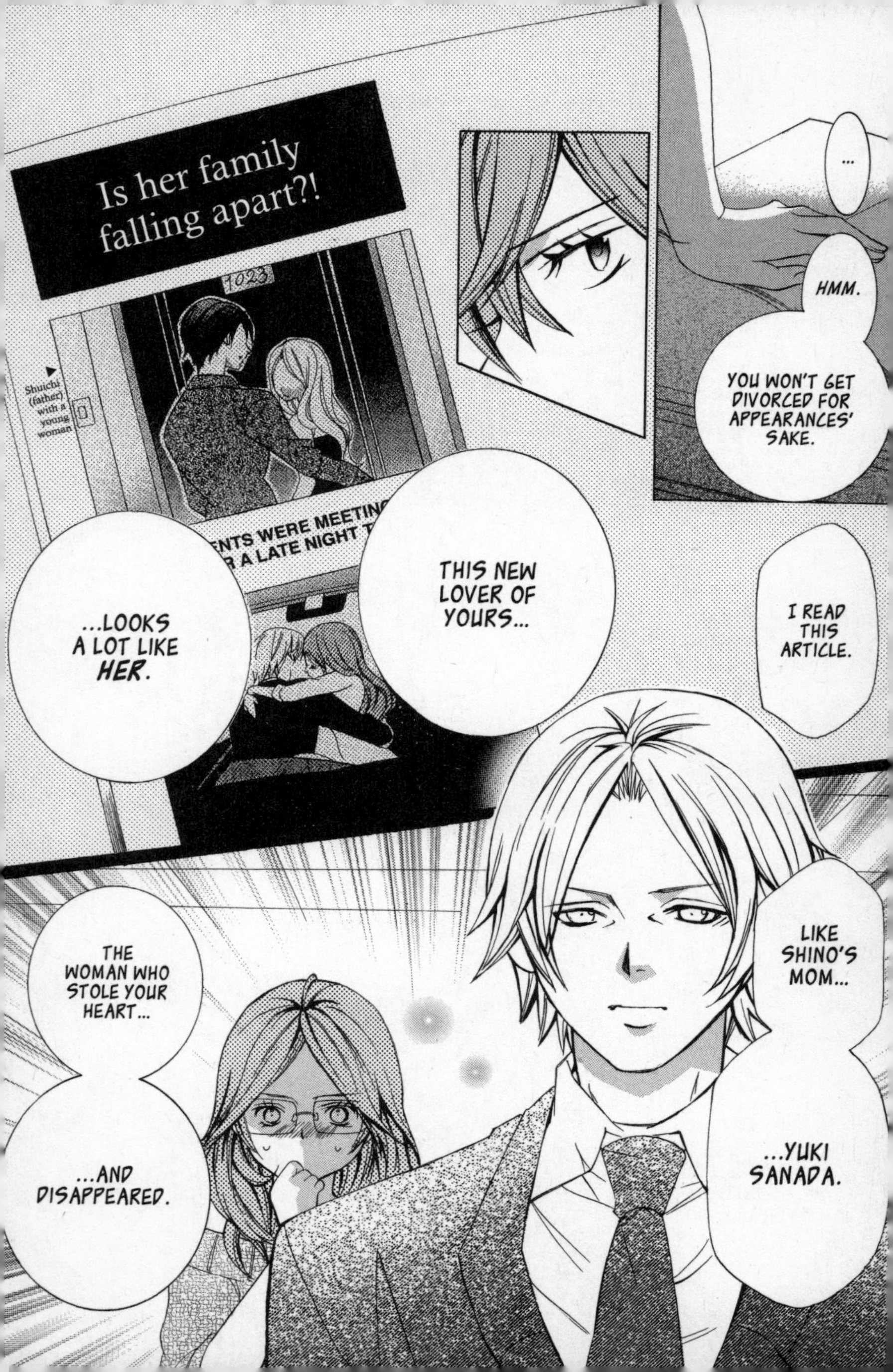
...
HMM.
YOU WON'T GET DIVORCED FOR APPEARANCES' SAKE.
Is her family falling apart?!
Shuichi (father) with a young woman
I READ THIS ARTICLE.
THIS NEW LOVER OF YOURS...
...LOOKS A LOT LIKE HER.
LIKE SHINO'S MOM...
...YUKI SANADA.
THE WOMAN WHO STOLE YOUR HEART...
...AND DISAPPEARED.

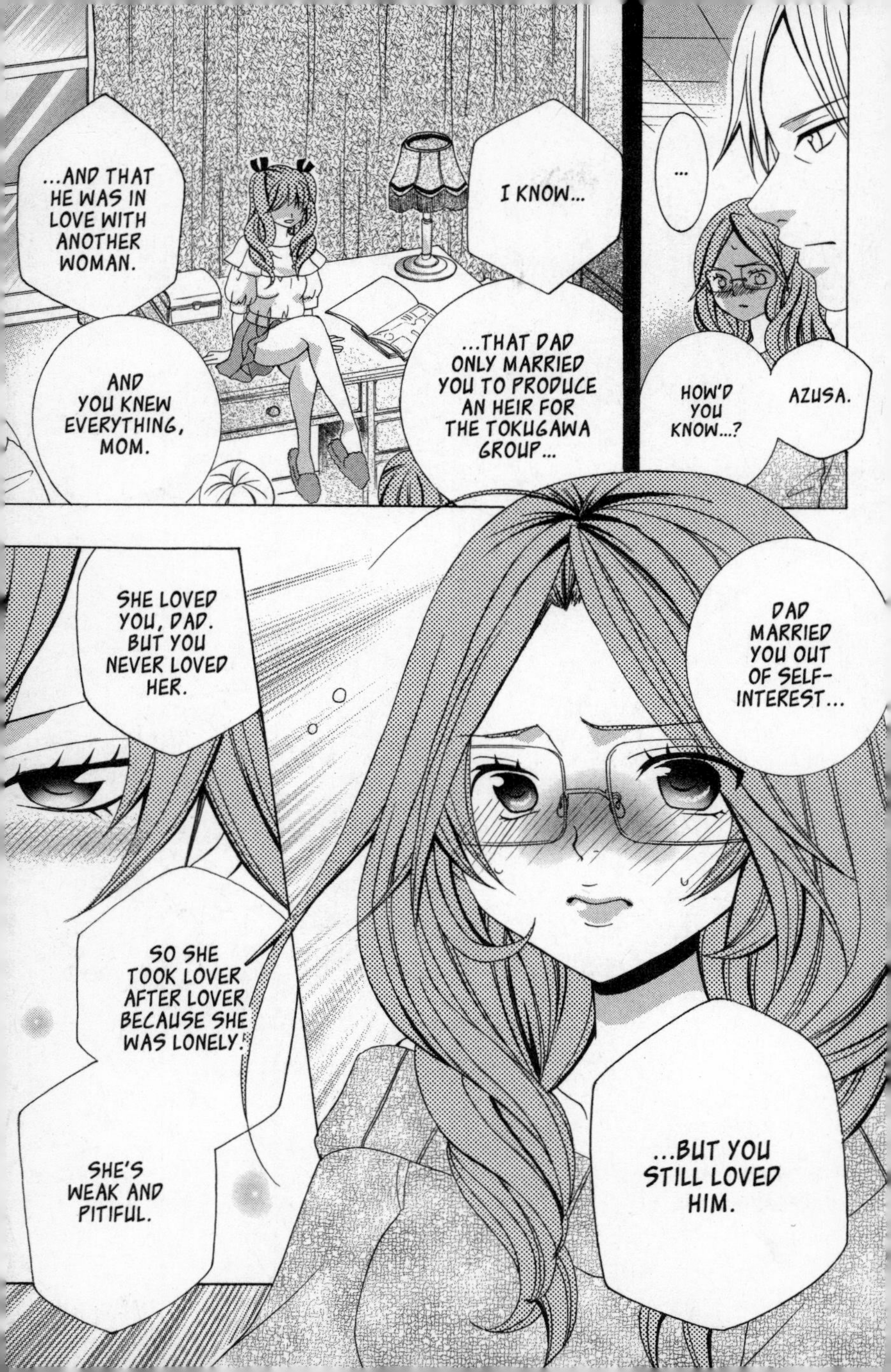
...
AZUSA.
HOW'D YOU KNOW...?
I KNOW...
...THAT DAD ONLY MARRIED YOU TO PRODUCE AN HEIR FOR THE TOKUGAWA GROUP...
...AND THAT HE WAS IN LOVE WITH ANOTHER WOMAN.
AND YOU KNEW EVERYTHING, MOM.
DAD MARRIED YOU OUT OF SELF-INTEREST...
SHE LOVED YOU, DAD. BUT YOU NEVER LOVED HER.
SO SHE TOOK LOVER AFTER LOVER BECAUSE SHE WAS LONELY.
...BUT YOU STILL LOVED HIM.
SHE'S WEAK AND PITIFUL.

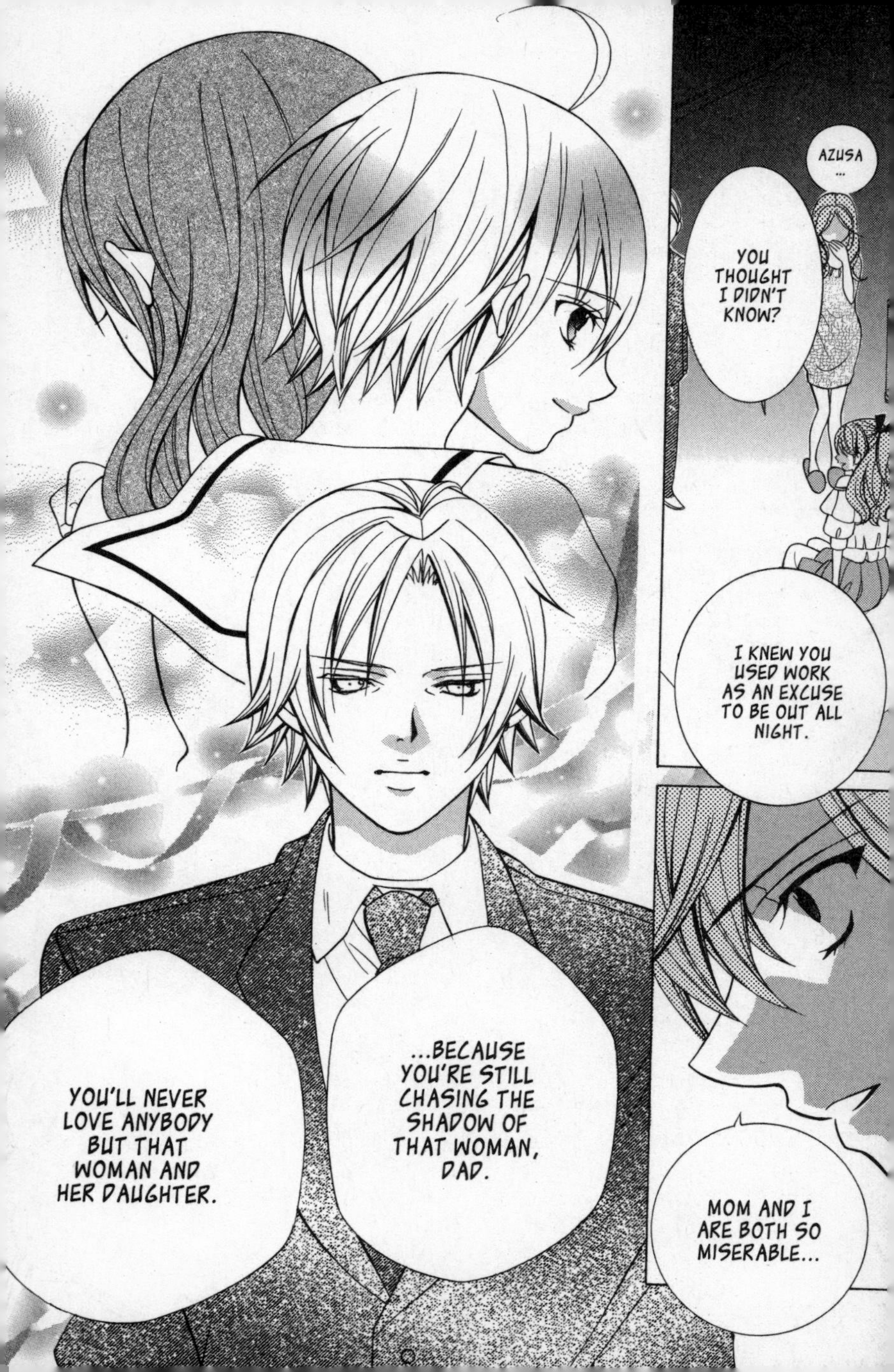
AZUSA ...
YOU THOUGHT I DIDN'T KNOW?
I KNEW YOU USED WORK AS AN EXCUSE TO BE OUT ALL NIGHT.
MOM AND I ARE BOTH SO MISERABLE...
...BECAUSE YOU'RE STILL CHASING THE SHADOW OF THAT WOMAN, DAD.
YOU'LL NEVER LOVE ANYBODY BUT THAT WOMAN AND HER DAUGHTER.

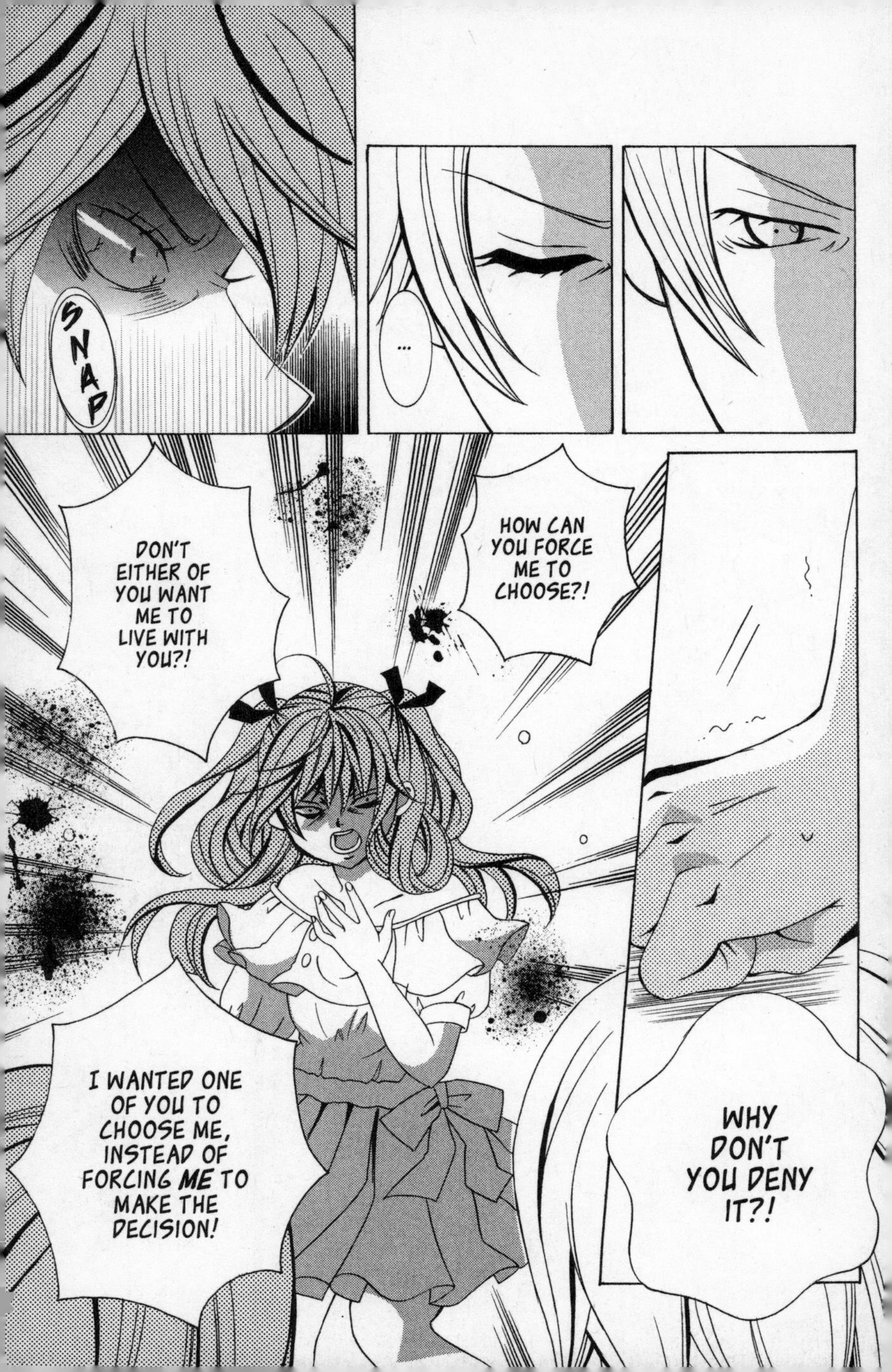
...
SNAP
WHY DON'T YOU DENY IT?!
HOW CAN YOU FORCE ME TO CHOOSE?!
DON'T EITHER OF YOU WANT ME TO LIVE WITH YOU?!
I WANTED ONE OF YOU TO CHOOSE ME, INSTEAD OF FORCING *ME* TO MAKE THE DECISION!

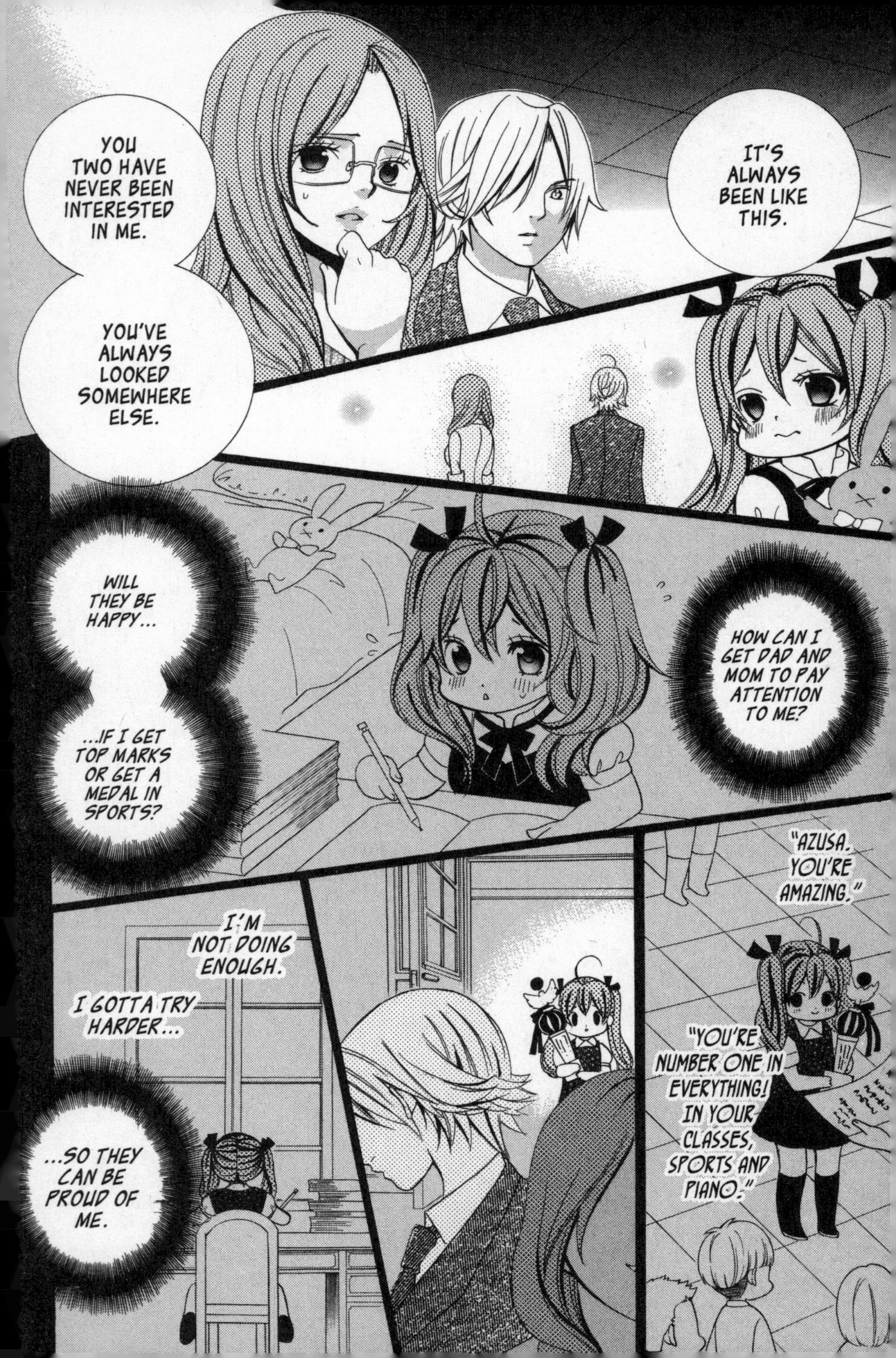
IT'S ALWAYS BEEN LIKE THIS.
YOU TWO HAVE NEVER BEEN INTERESTED IN ME.
YOU'VE ALWAYS LOOKED SOMEWHERE ELSE.
HOW CAN I GET DAD AND MOM TO PAY ATTENTION TO ME?
WILL THEY BE HAPPY...
...IF I GET TOP MARKS OR GET A MEDAL IN SPORTS?
"AZUSA. YOU'RE AMAZING."
"YOU'RE NUMBER ONE IN EVERYTHING! IN YOUR CLASSES, SPORTS AND PIANO."
I'M NOT DOING ENOUGH.
I GOTTA TRY HARDER...
...SO THEY CAN BE PROUD OF ME.

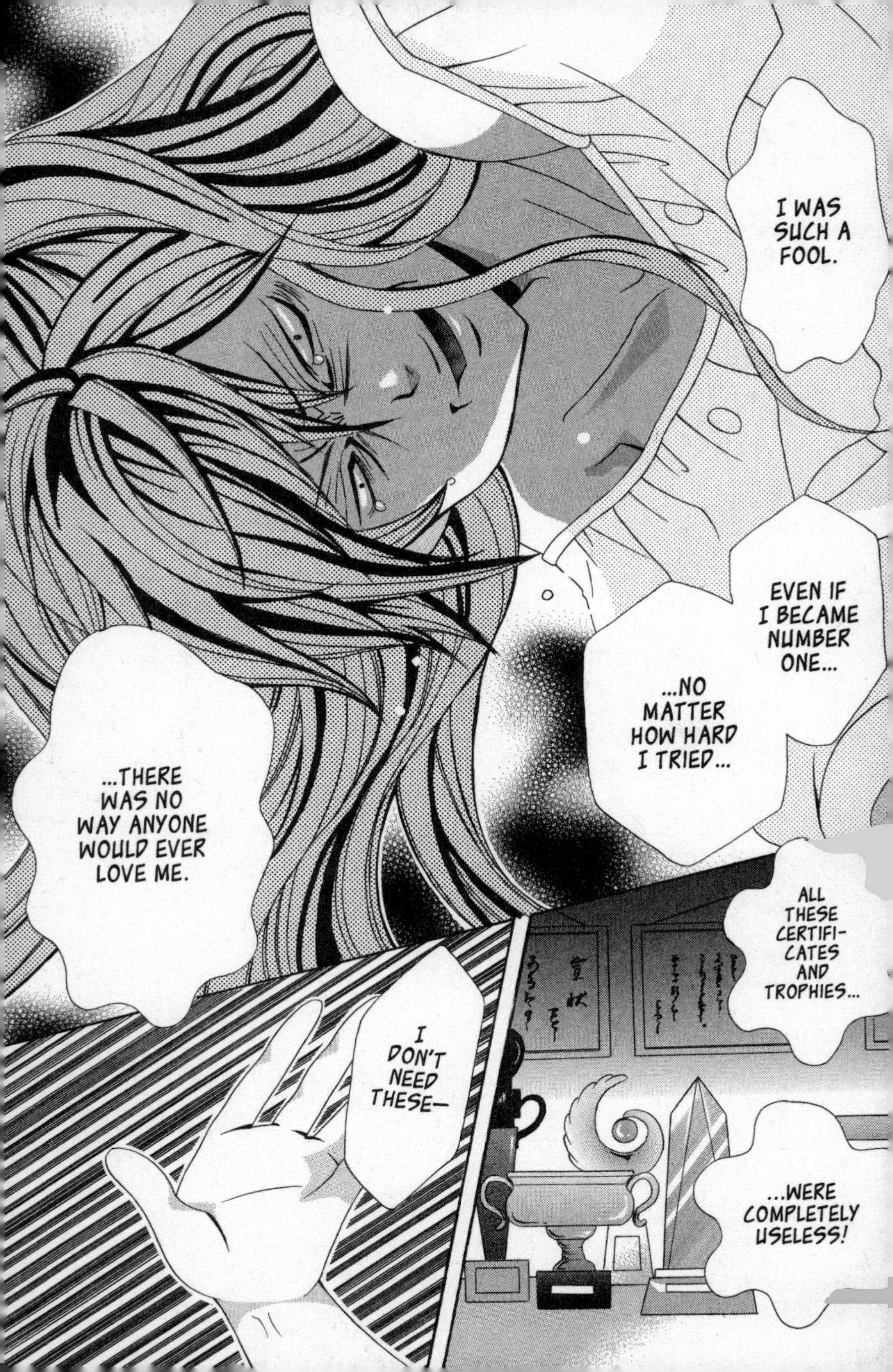
I WAS SUCH A FOOL.
EVEN IF I BECAME NUMBER ONE...
...NO MATTER HOW HARD I TRIED...
...THERE WAS NO WAY ANYONE WOULD EVER LOVE ME.
ALL THESE CERTIFICATES AND TROPHIES...
...WERE COMPLETELY USELESS!
I DON'T NEED THESE—

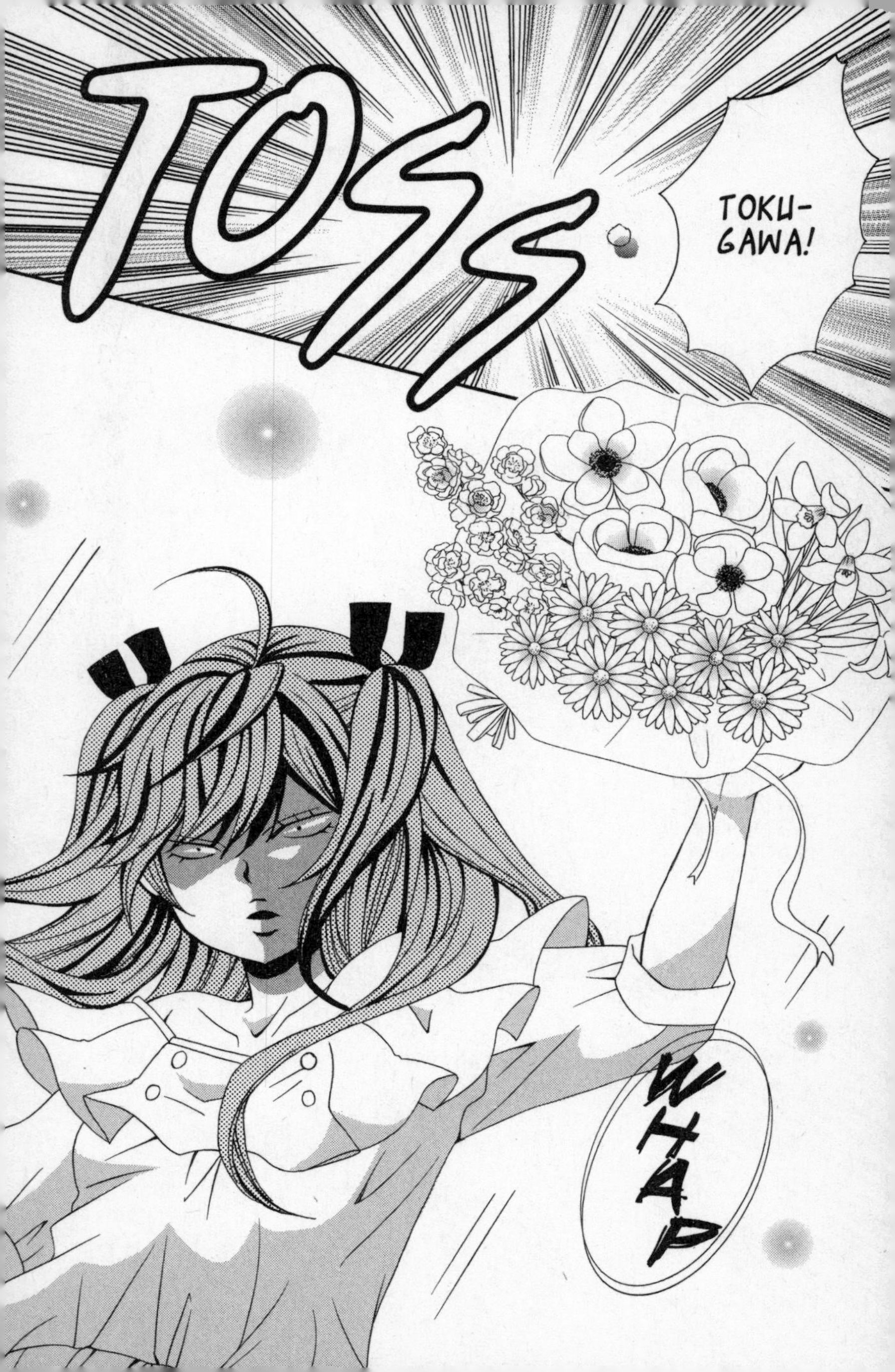

TOKU-GAWA!
TOSS
WHAP

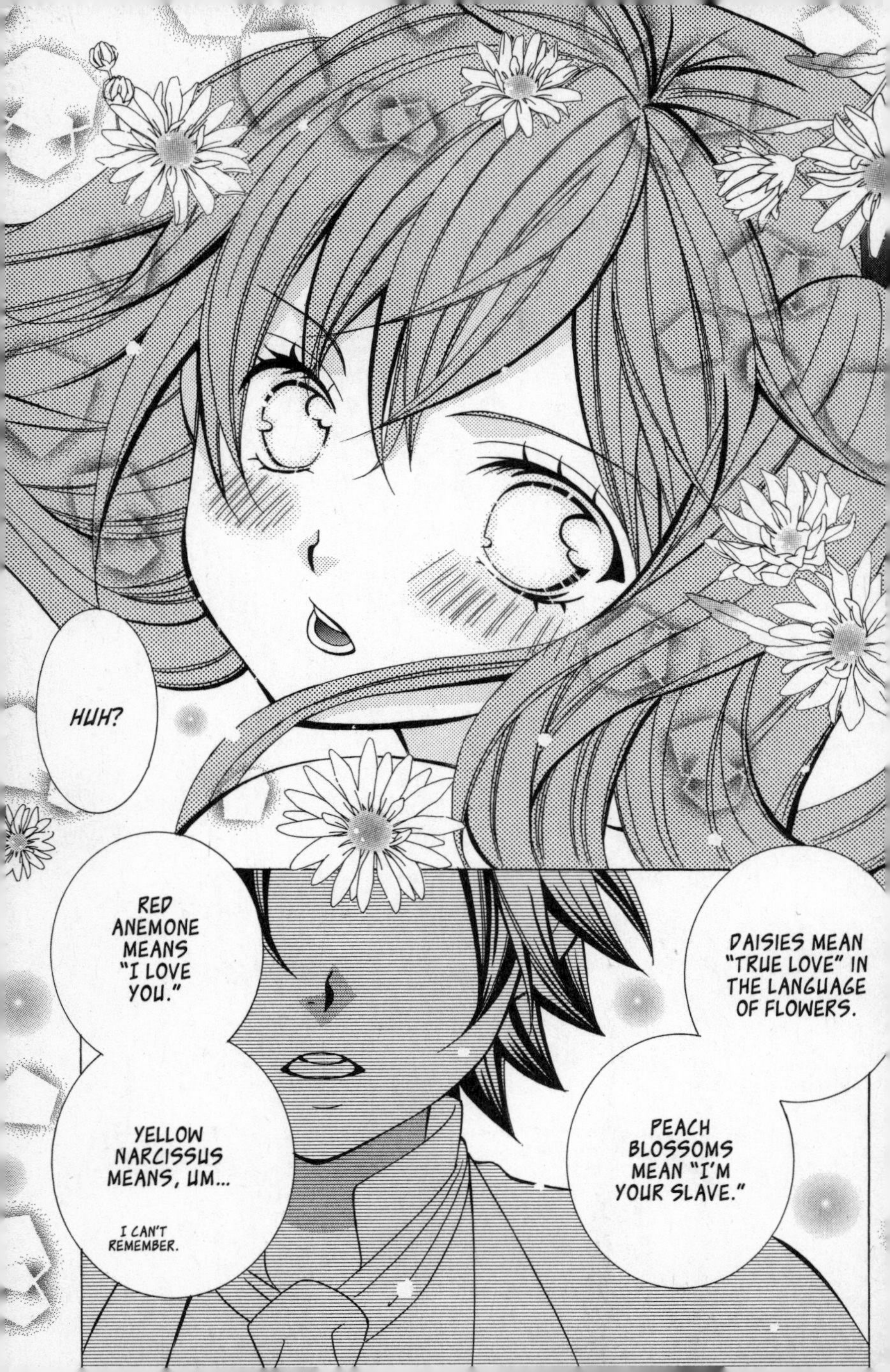
HUH?
DAISIES MEAN "TRUE LOVE" IN THE LANGUAGE OF FLOWERS.
PEACH BLOSSOMS MEAN "I'M YOUR SLAVE."
RED ANEMONE MEANS "I LOVE YOU."
YELLOW NARCISSUS MEANS, UM...
I CAN'T REMEMBER.

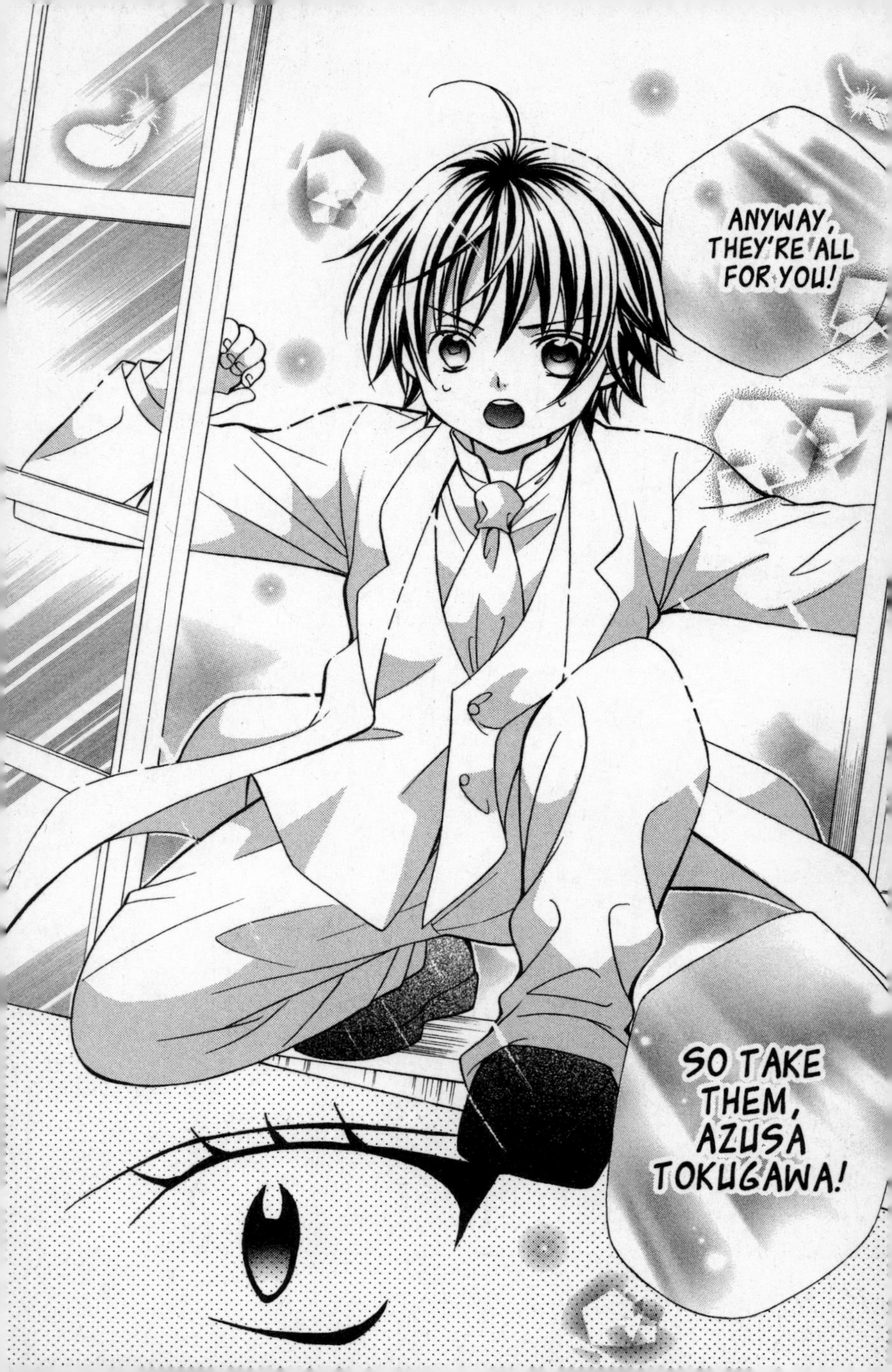
ANYWAY, THEY'RE ALL FOR YOU!
SO TAKE THEM, AZUSA TOKUGAWA!

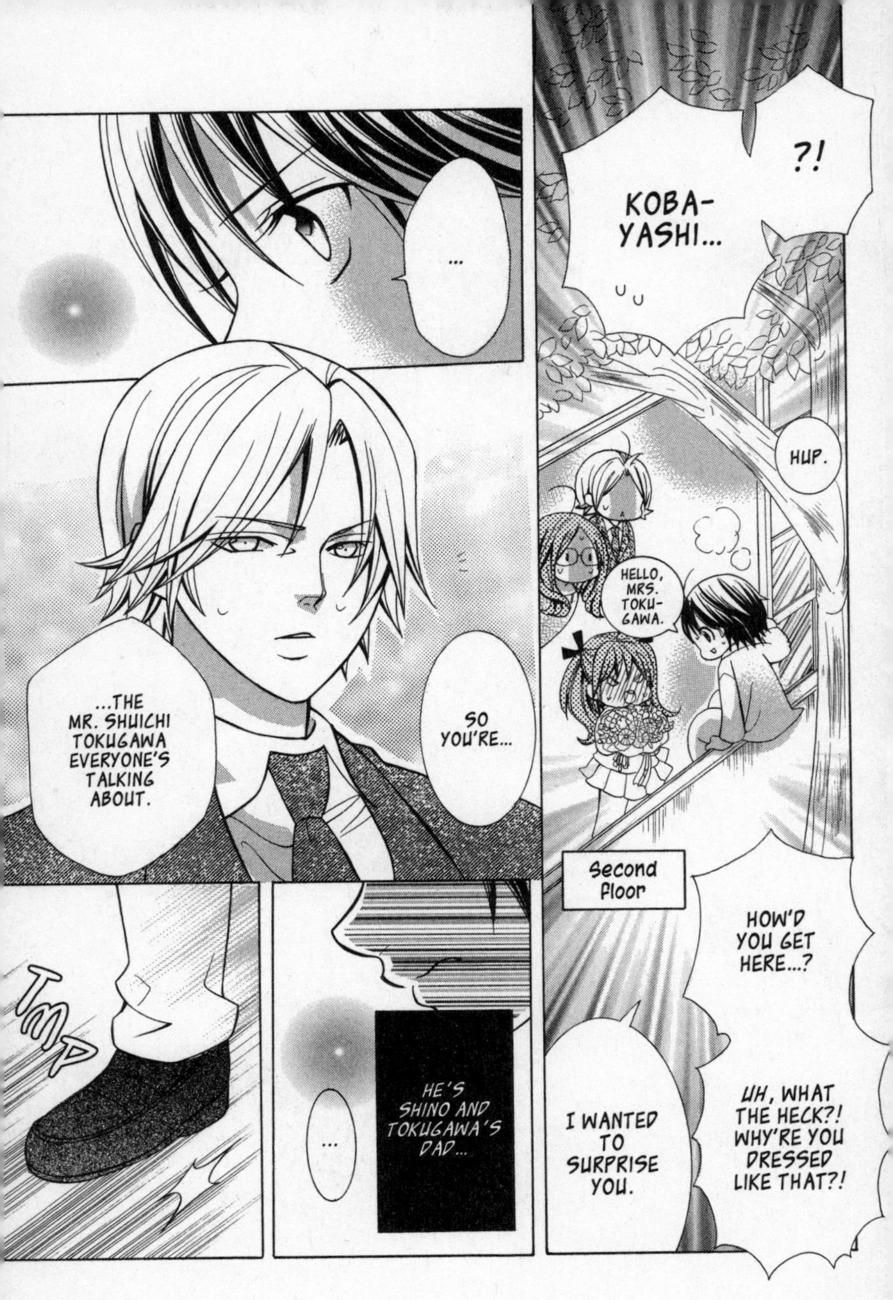
?!
KOBA-YASHI...
HUP.
HELLO, MRS. TOKU-GAWA.
Second floor
HOW'D YOU GET HERE...?
UH, WHAT THE HECK?! WHY'RE YOU DRESSED LIKE THAT?!
I WANTED TO SURPRISE YOU.
...
SO YOU'RE...
...THE MR. SHUICHI TOKUGAWA EVERYONE'S TALKING ABOUT.
HE'S SHINO AND TOKUGAWA'S DAD...
...
TMP

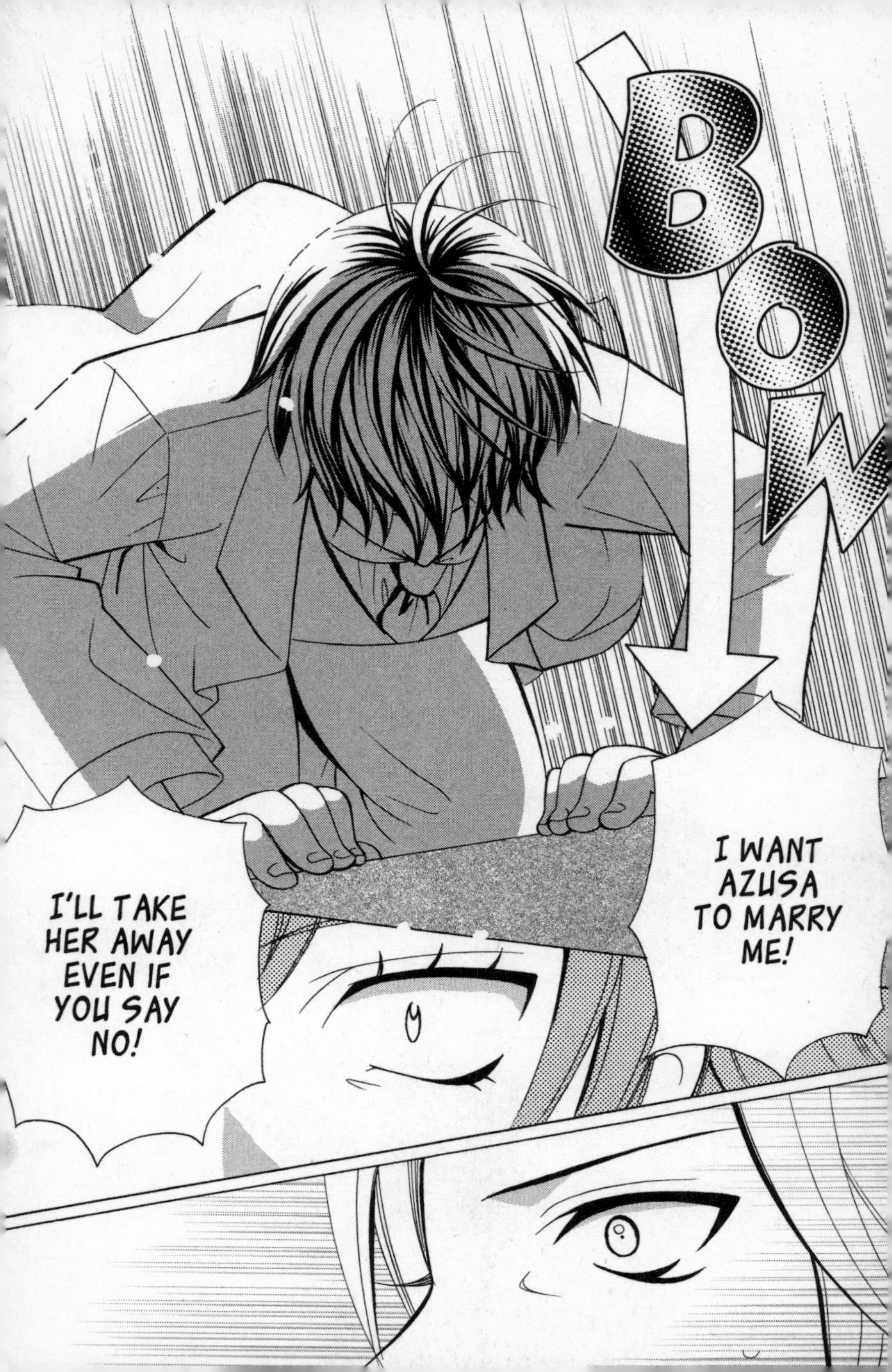
BOW
I WANT AZUSA TO MARRY ME!
I'LL TAKE HER AWAY EVEN IF YOU SAY NO!

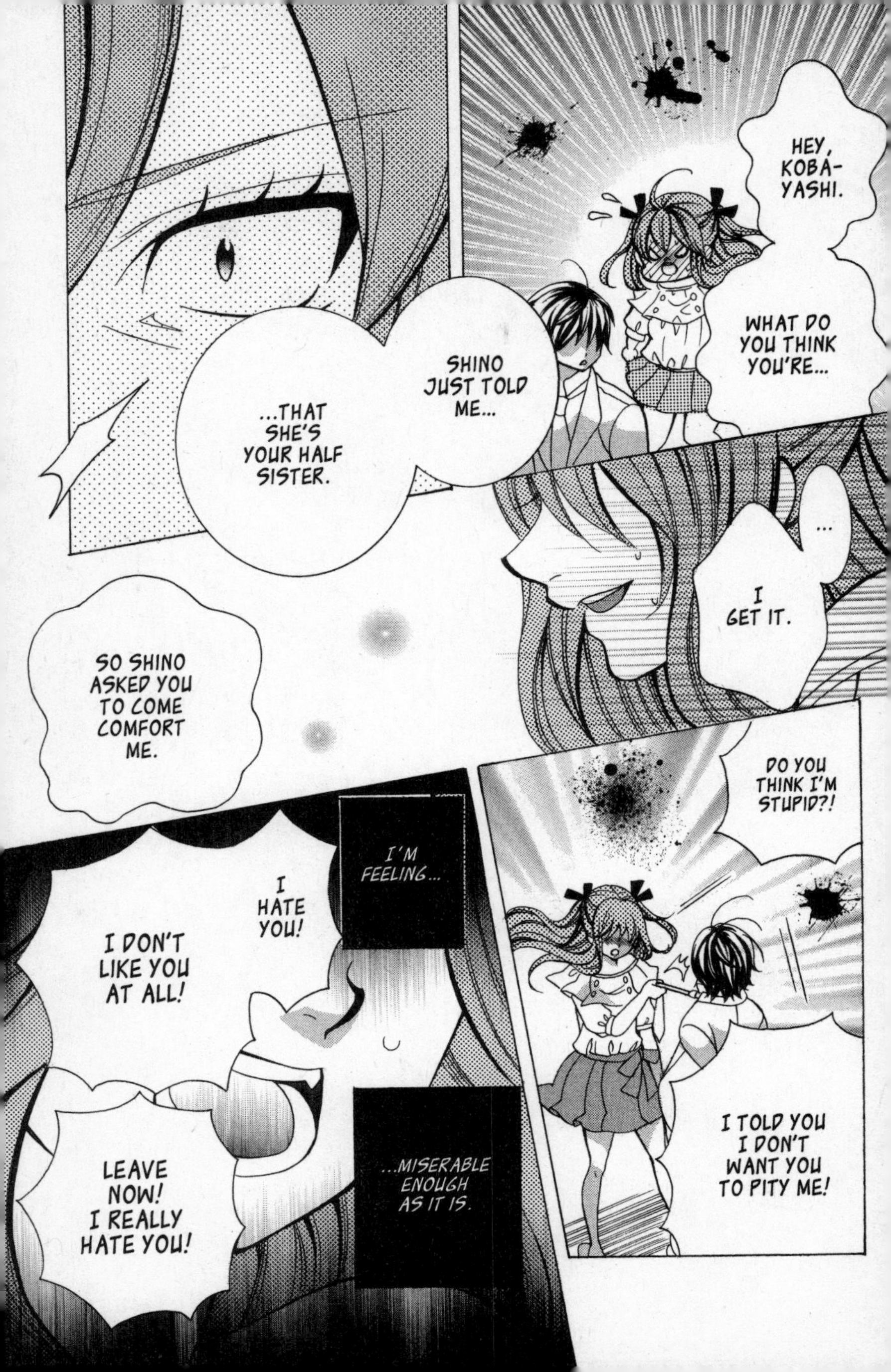
HEY, KOBA-YASHI.
WHAT DO YOU THINK YOU'RE...
SHINO JUST TOLD ME...
...THAT SHE'S YOUR HALF SISTER.
...
I GET IT.
SO SHINO ASKED YOU TO COME COMFORT ME.
DO YOU THINK I'M STUPID?!
I TOLD YOU I DON'T WANT YOU TO PITY ME!
I'M FEELING...
I HATE YOU!
I DON'T LIKE YOU AT ALL!
...MISERABLE ENOUGH AS IT IS.
LEAVE NOW! I REALLY HATE YOU!

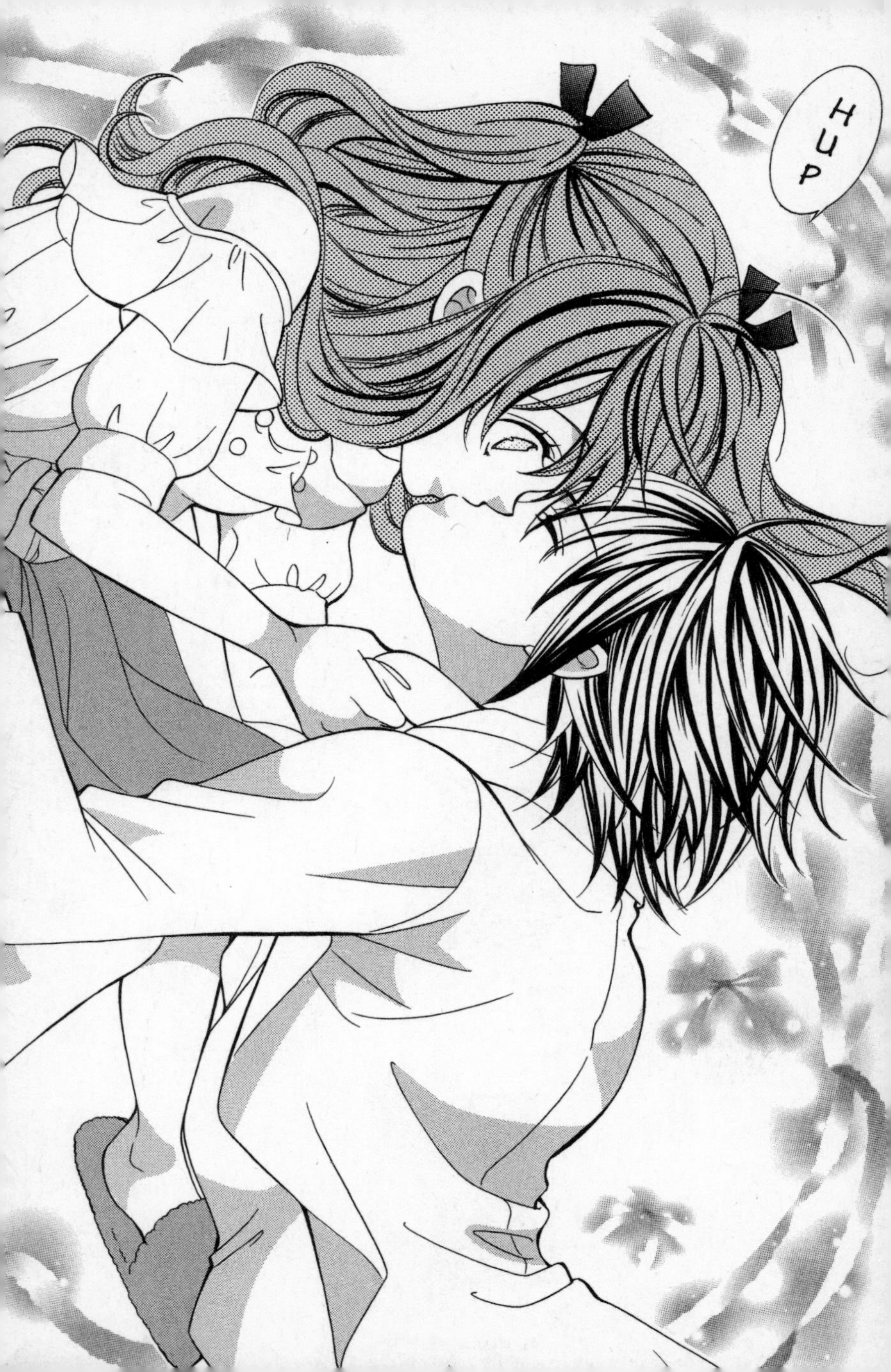
HUP

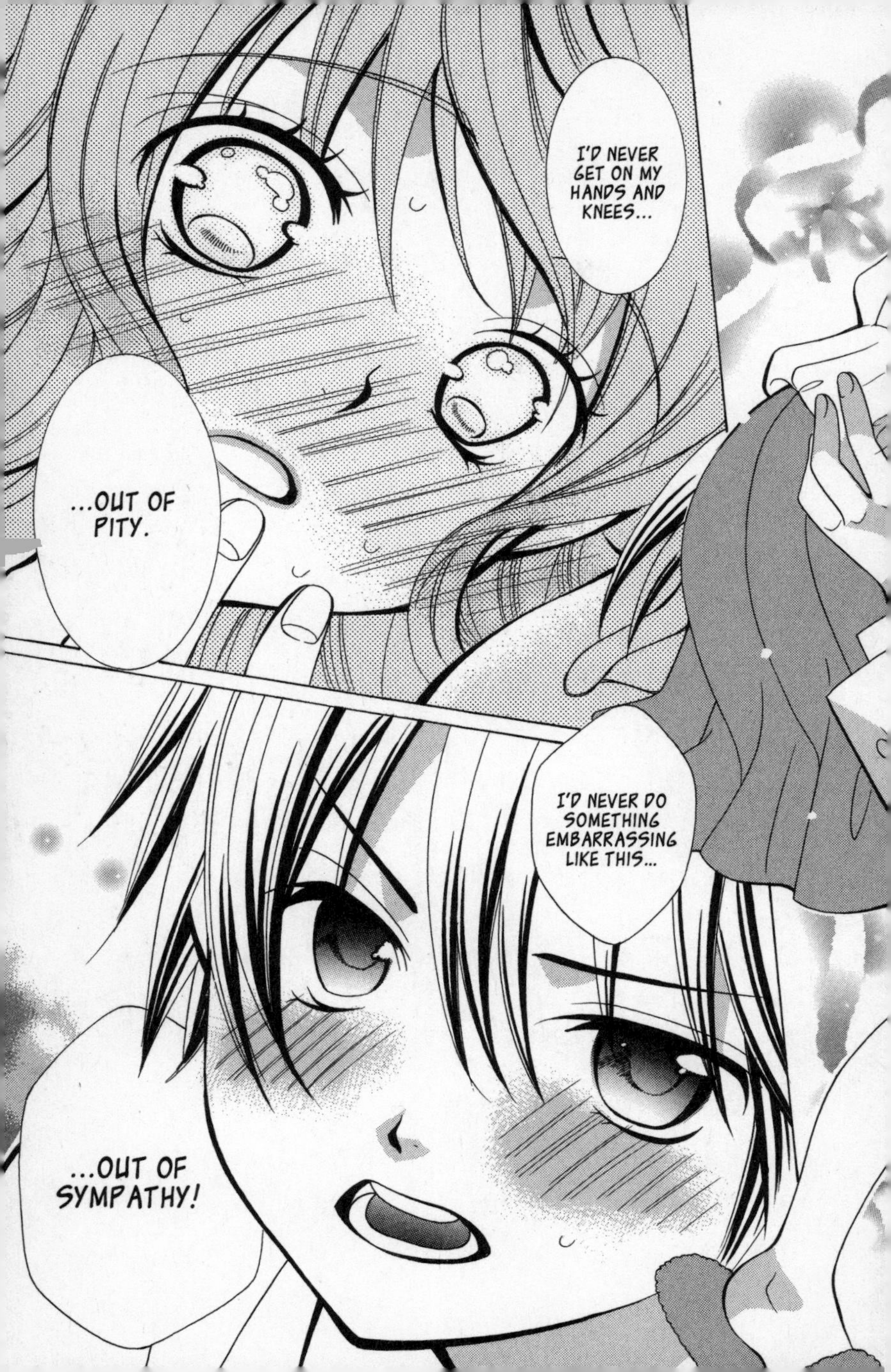
I'D NEVER GET ON MY HANDS AND KNEES...
...OUT OF PITY.
I'D NEVER DO SOMETHING EMBARRASSING LIKE THIS...
...OUT OF SYMPATHY!

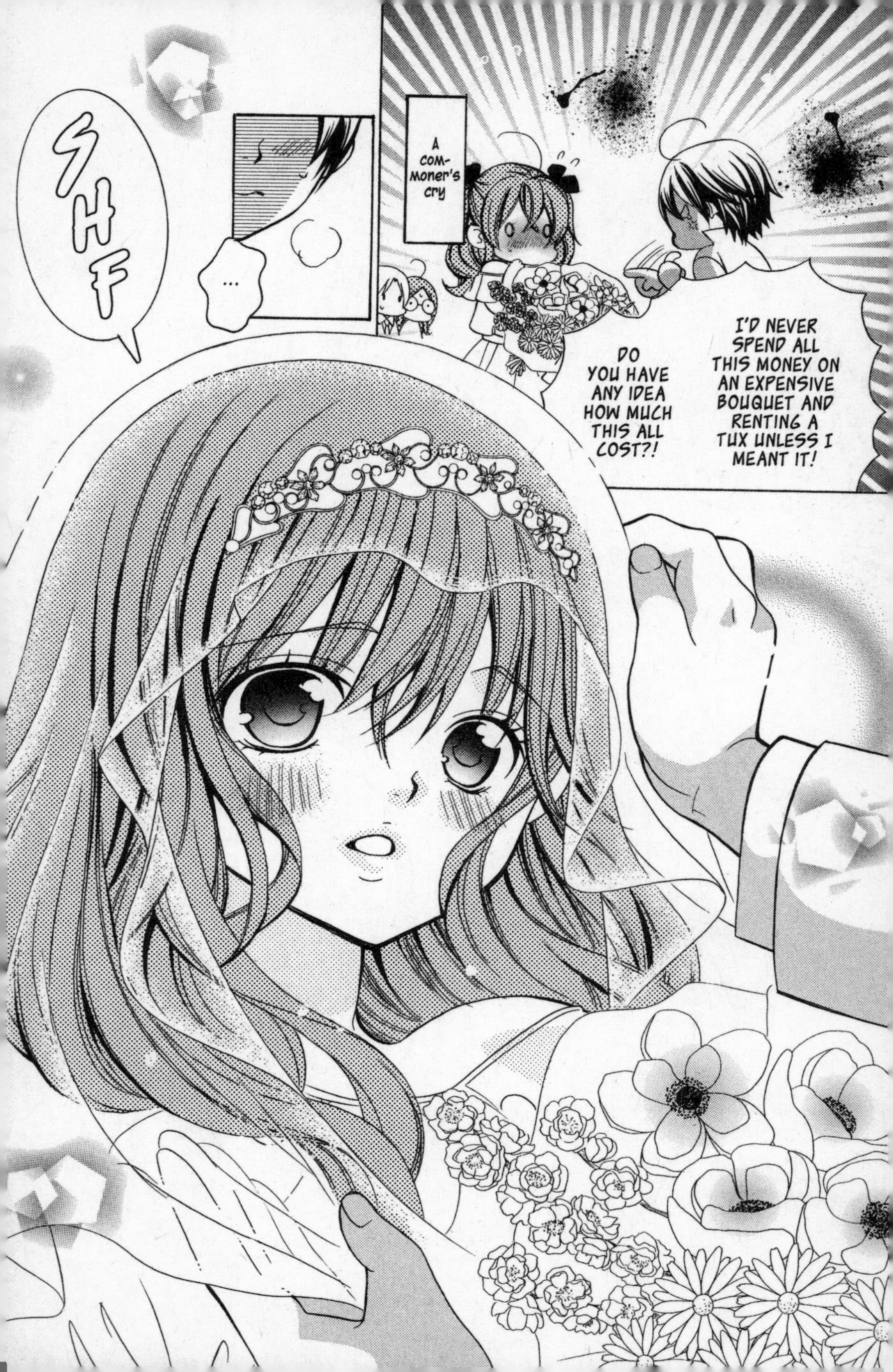
I'D NEVER SPEND ALL THIS MONEY ON AN EXPENSIVE BOUQUET AND RENTING A TUX UNLESS I MEANT IT!
DO YOU HAVE ANY IDEA HOW MUCH THIS ALL COST?!
A com-moner's cry
...
SHF

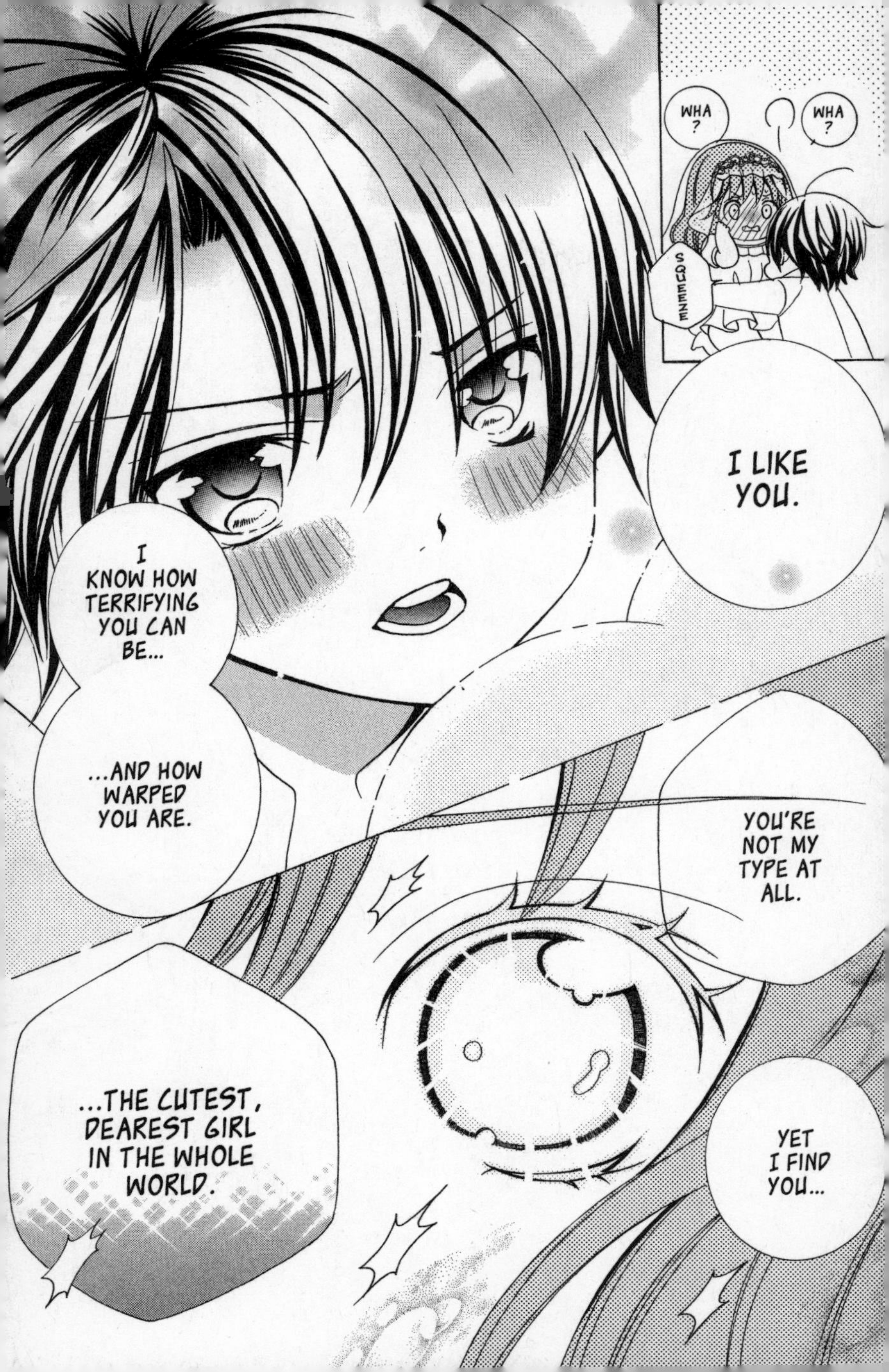
WHA ?
WHA ?
SQUEEZE
I LIKE YOU.
I KNOW HOW TERRIFYING YOU CAN BE...
...AND HOW WARPED YOU ARE.
YOU'RE NOT MY TYPE AT ALL.
YET I FIND YOU...
...THE CUTEST, DEAREST GIRL IN THE WHOLE WORLD.

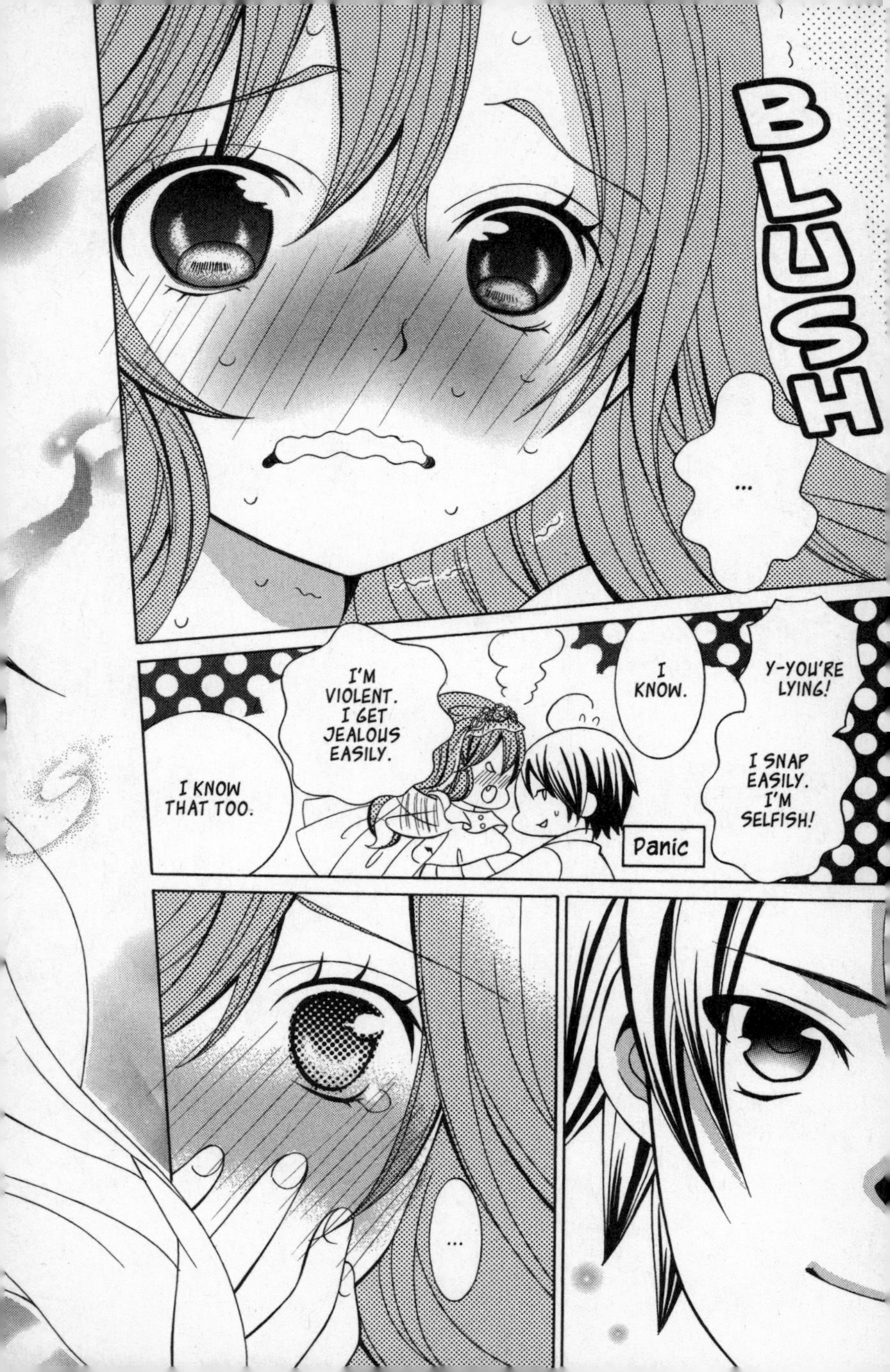
BLUSH
...
Y-YOU'RE LYING!
I SNAP EASILY. I'M SELFISH!
I KNOW.
I'M VIOLENT. I GET JEALOUS EASILY.
Panic
I KNOW THAT TOO.
...

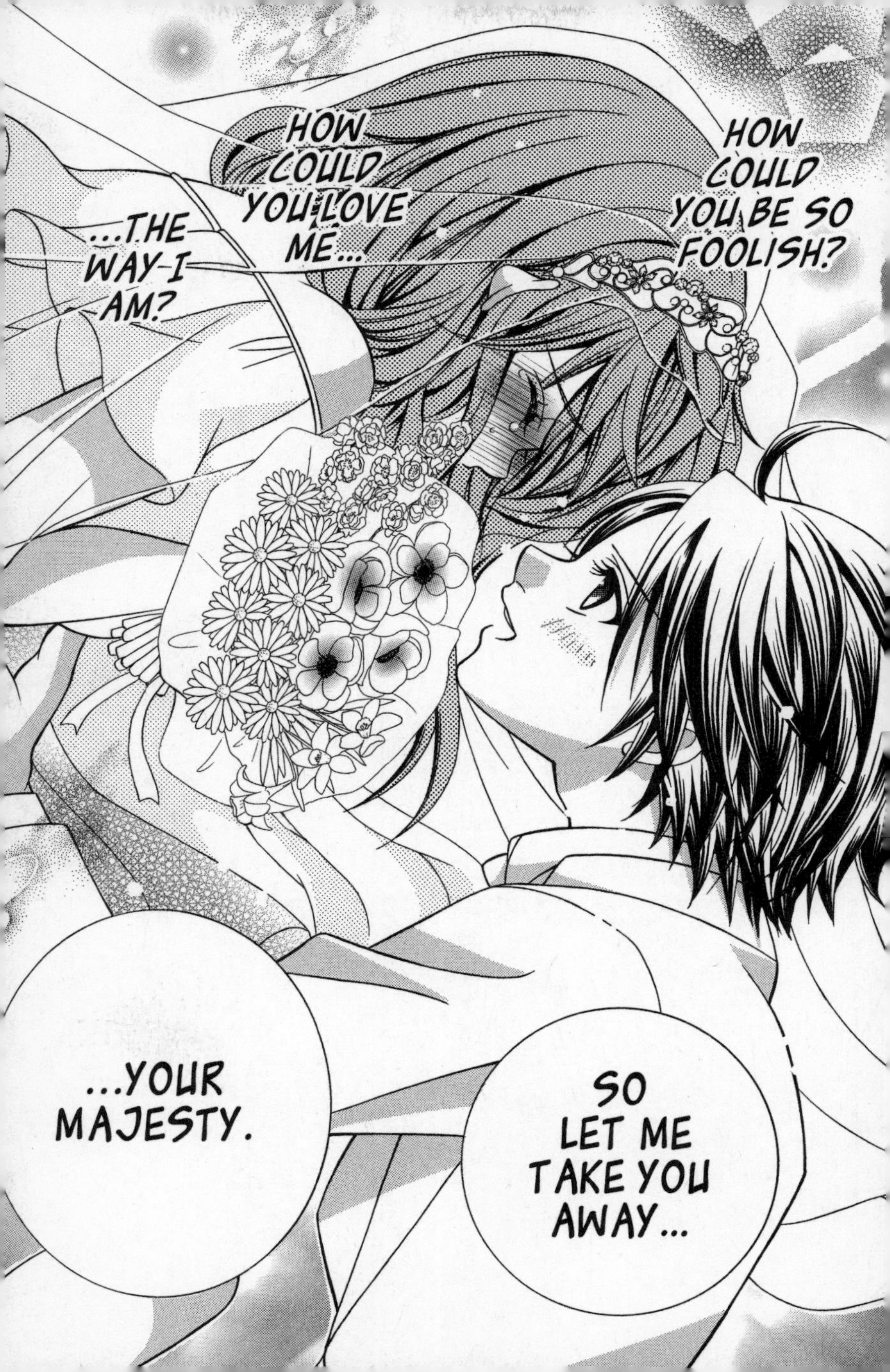
HOW COULD YOU BE SO FOOLISH?
HOW COULD YOU LOVE ME...
...THE WAY I AM?
SO LET ME TAKE YOU AWAY...
...YOUR MAJESTY.

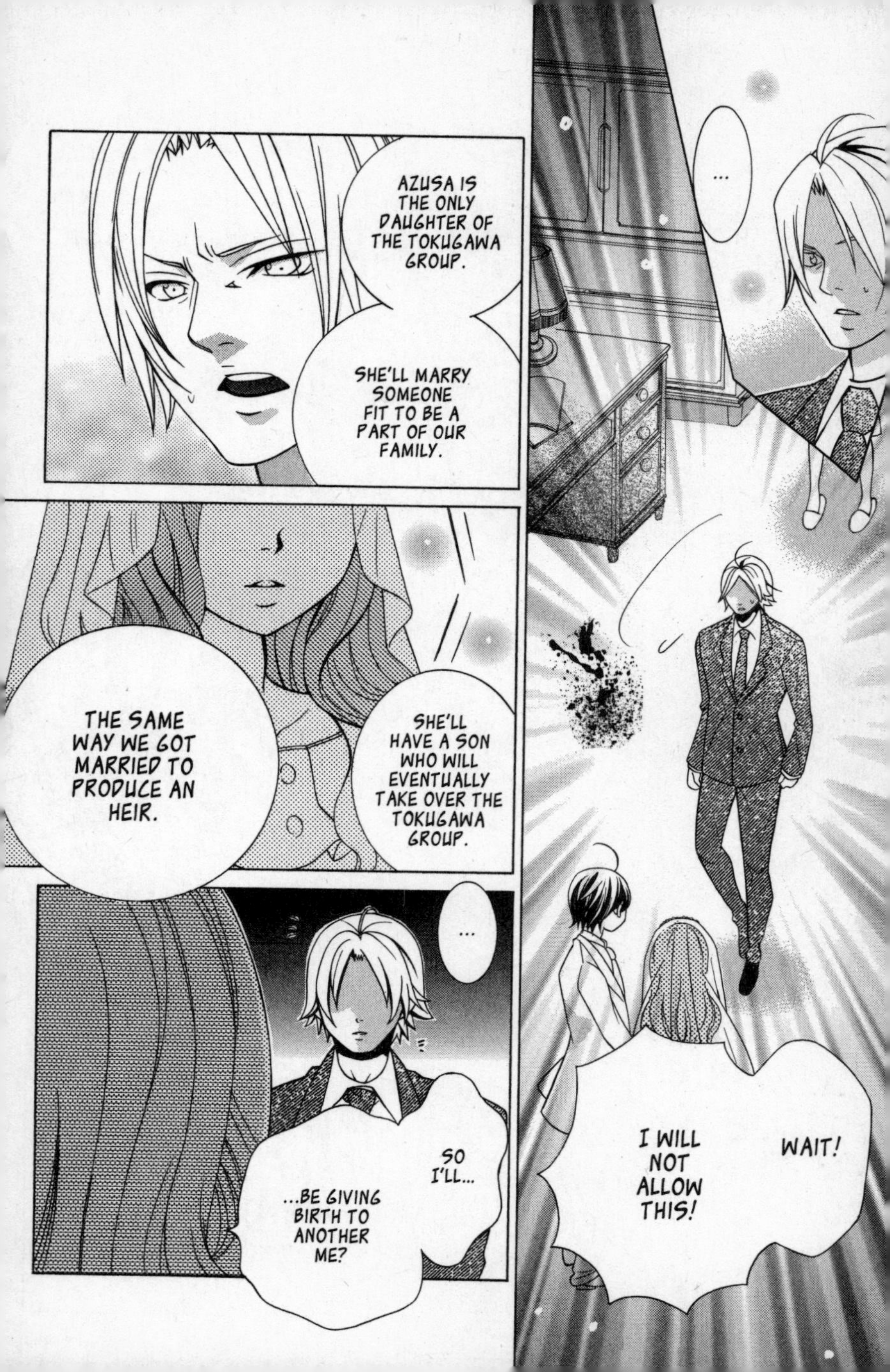
...
WAIT!
I WILL NOT ALLOW THIS!
AZUSA IS THE ONLY DAUGHTER OF THE TOKUGAWA GROUP.
SHE'LL MARRY SOMEONE FIT TO BE A PART OF OUR FAMILY.
SHE'LL HAVE A SON WHO WILL EVENTUALLY TAKE OVER THE TOKUGAWA GROUP.
THE SAME WAY WE GOT MARRIED TO PRODUCE AN HEIR.
...
SO I'LL...
...BE GIVING BIRTH TO ANOTHER ME?

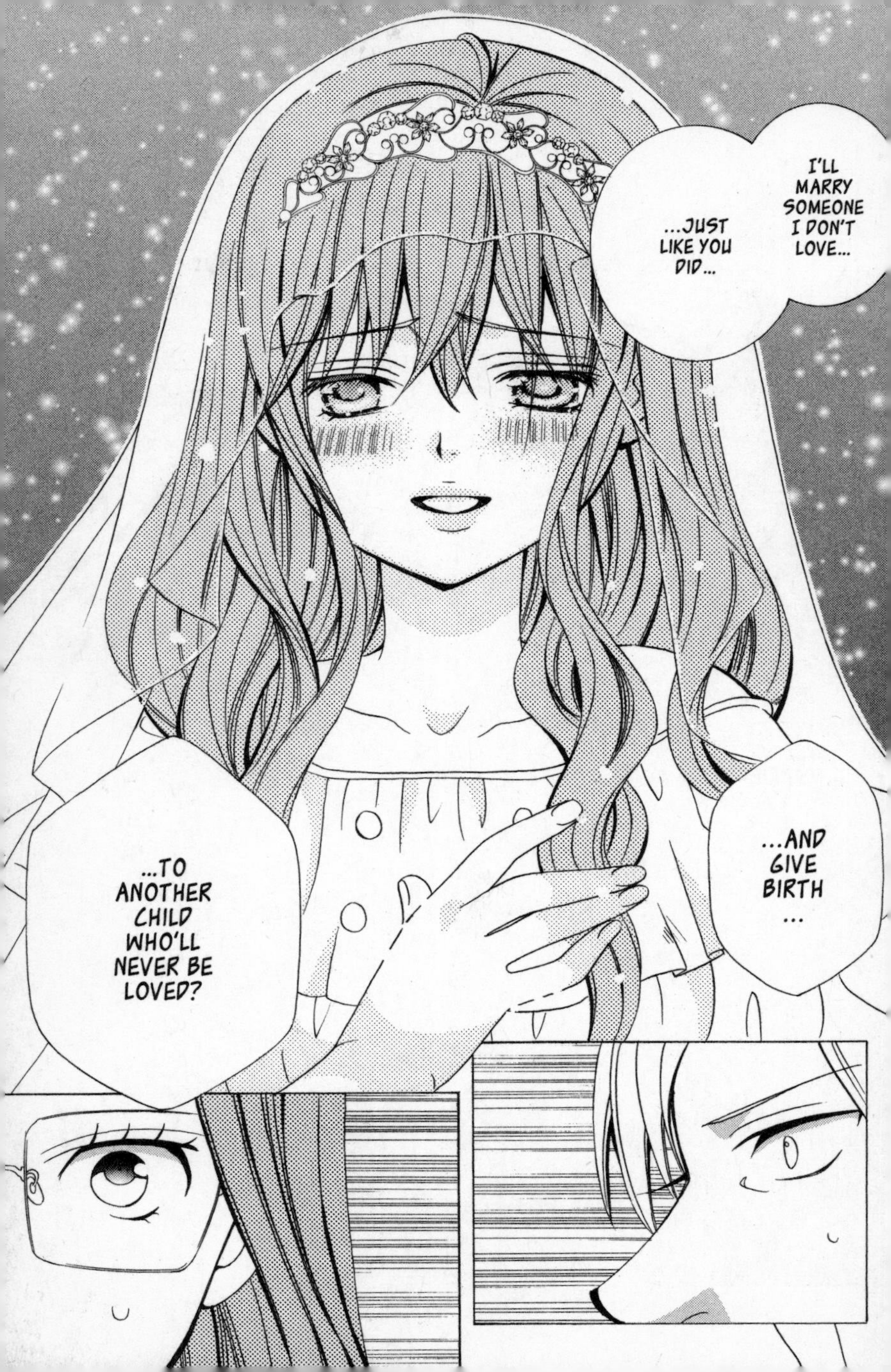
I'LL MARRY SOMEONE I DON'T LOVE...
...JUST LIKE YOU DID...
...AND GIVE BIRTH...
...TO ANOTHER CHILD WHO'LL NEVER BE LOVED?

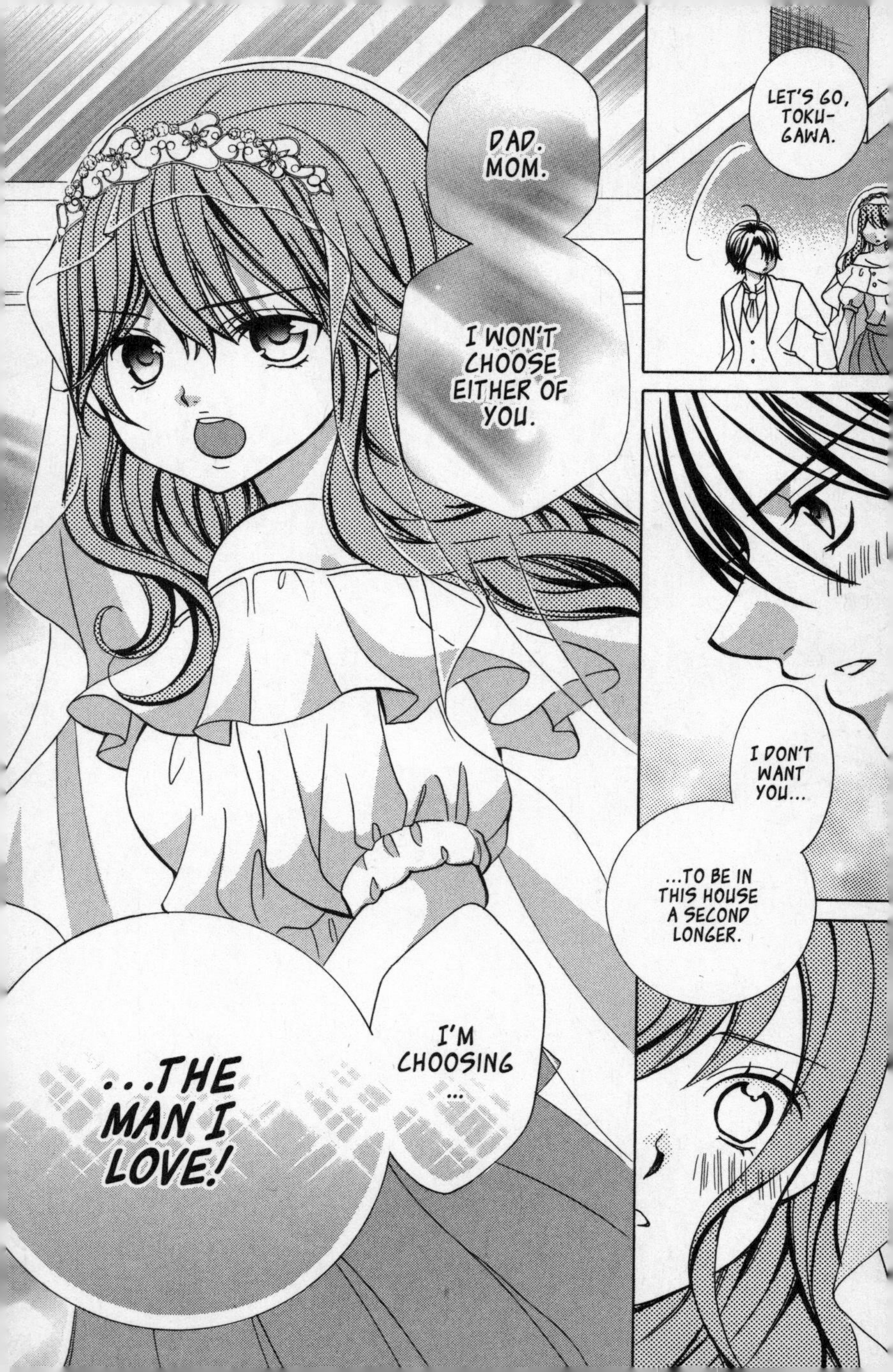
LET'S GO, TOKU-GAWA.
I DON'T WANT YOU...
...TO BE IN THIS HOUSE A SECOND LONGER.
DAD. MOM.
I WON'T CHOOSE EITHER OF YOU.
I'M CHOOSING ...
...THE MAN I LOVE!

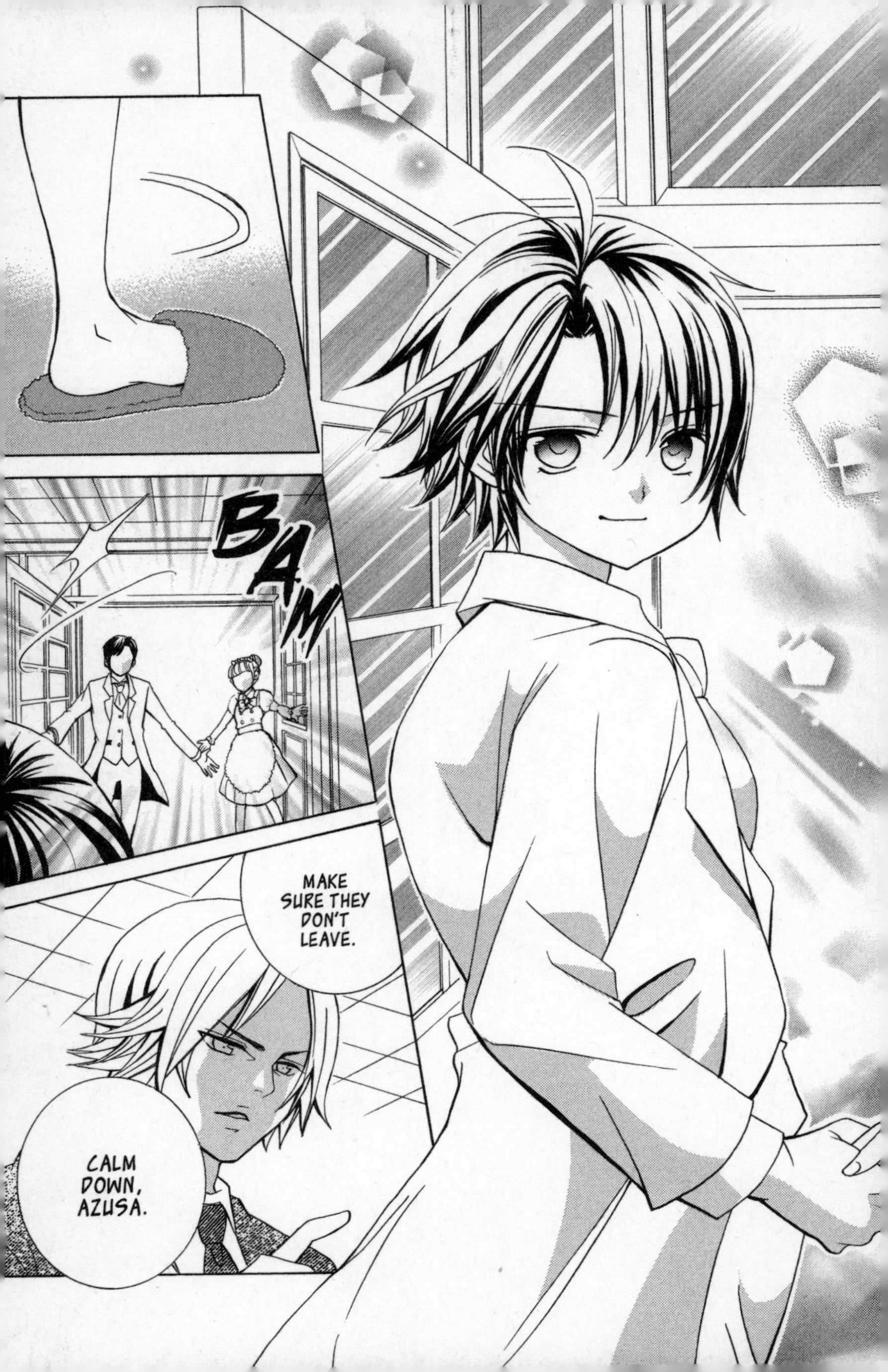
BAM
MAKE SURE THEY DON'T LEAVE.
CALM DOWN, AZUSA.

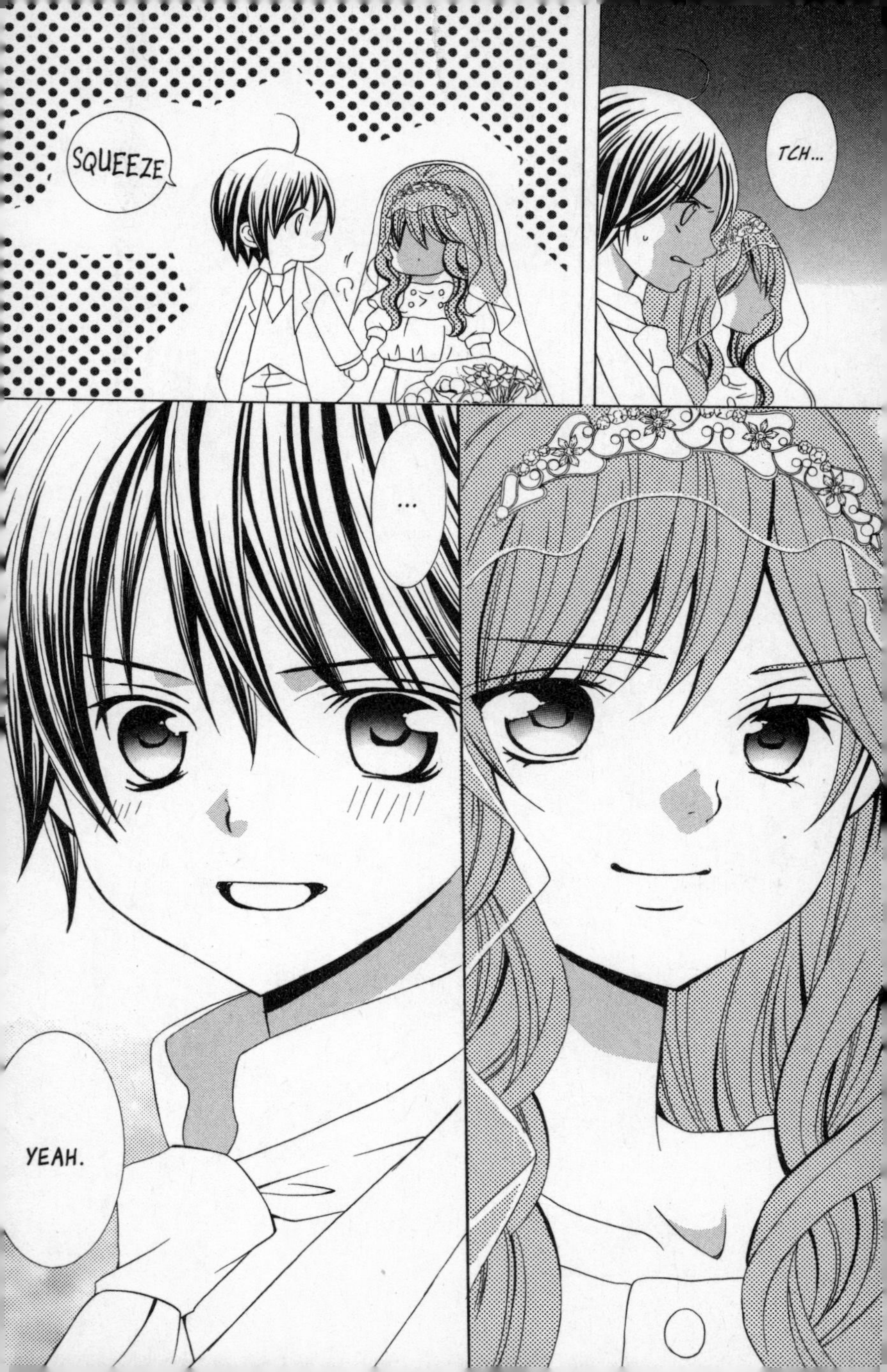
TCH...
SQUEEZE
...
YEAH.

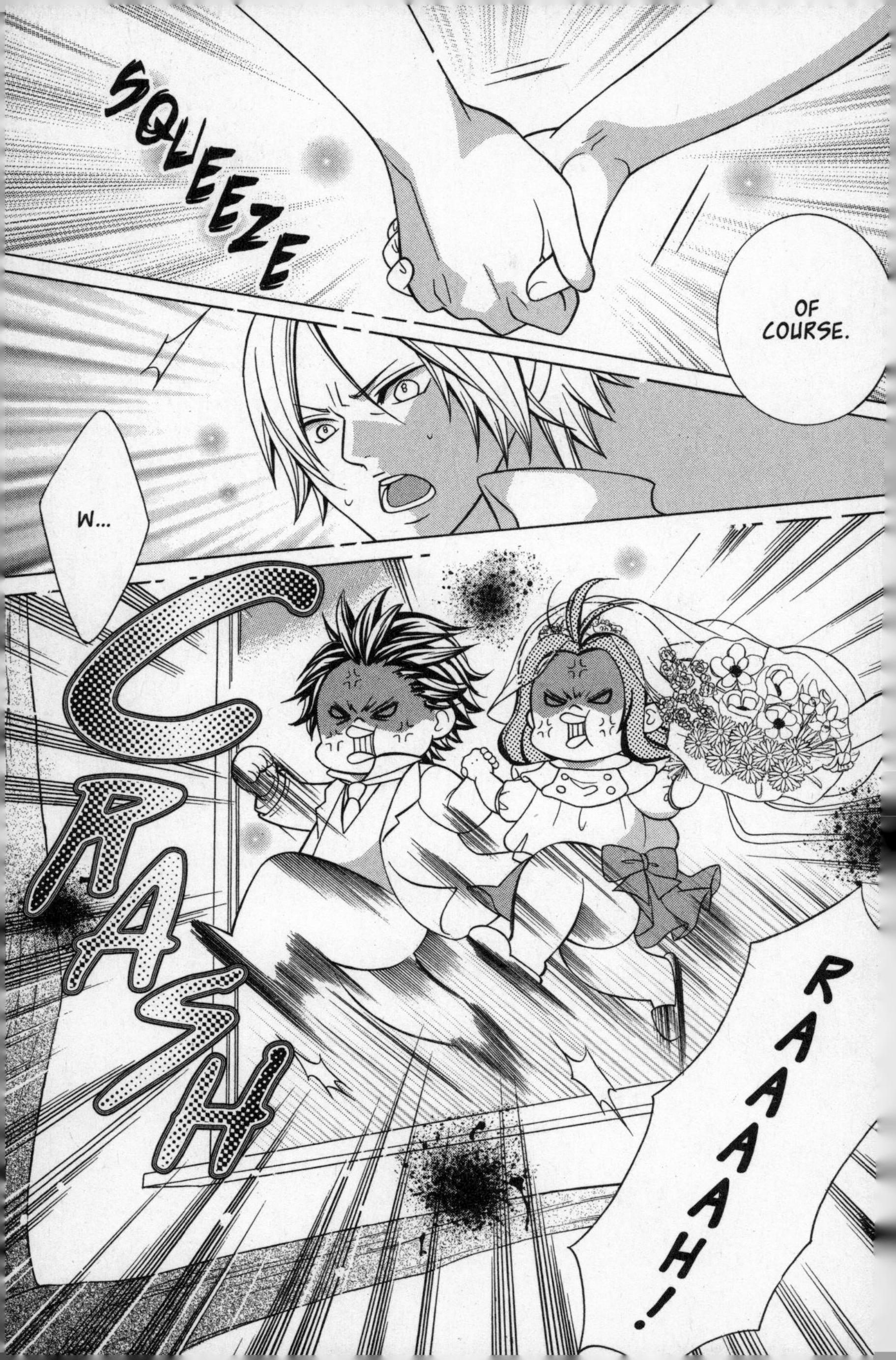
SQUEEZE
OF COURSE.
W...
CRASH
RAAAAAH!

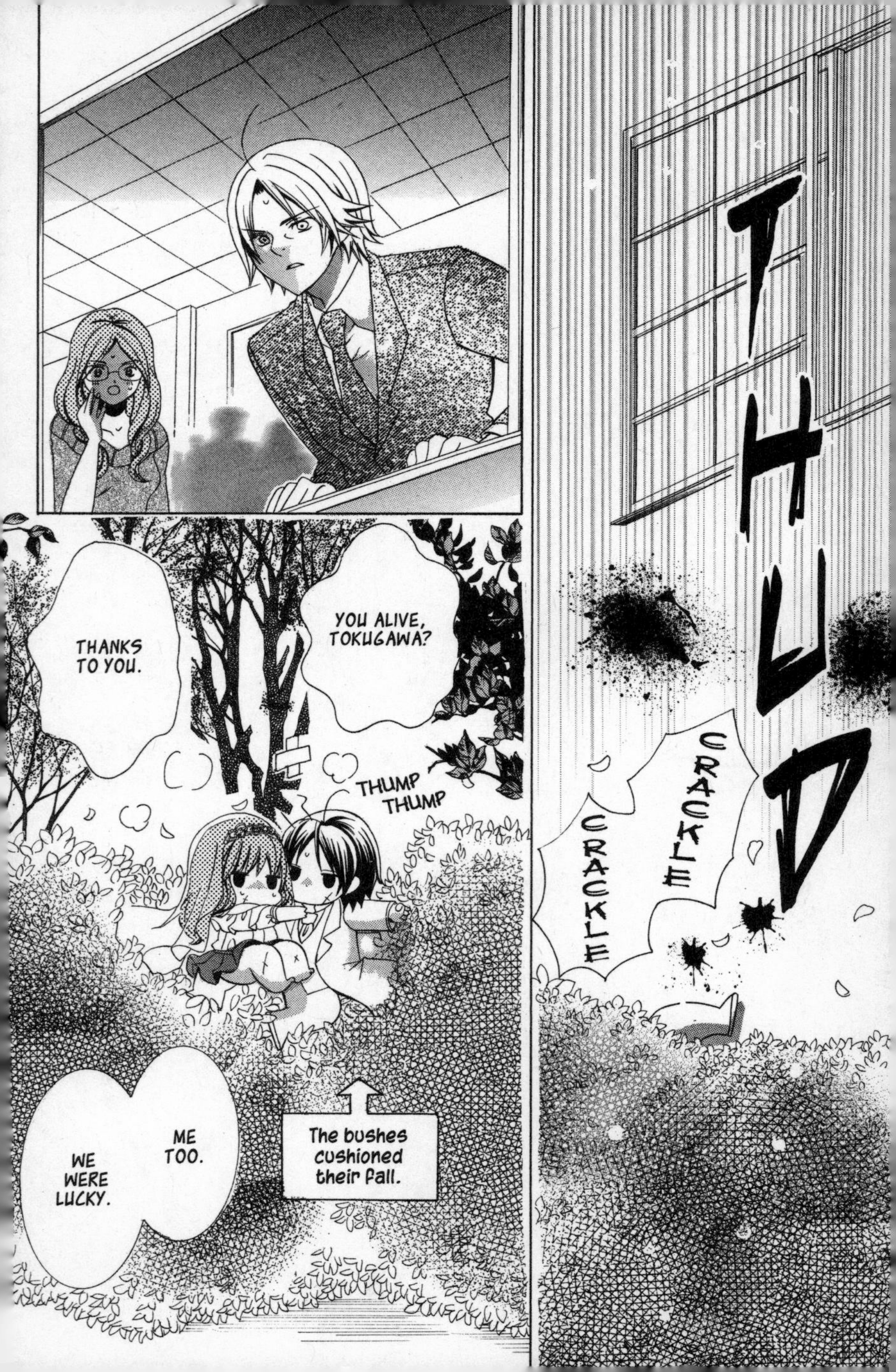
THUD
CRACKLE
CRACKLE
YOU ALIVE, TOKUGAWA?
THANKS TO YOU.
THUMP THUMP
The bushes cushioned their fall.
ME TOO.
WE WERE LUCKY.

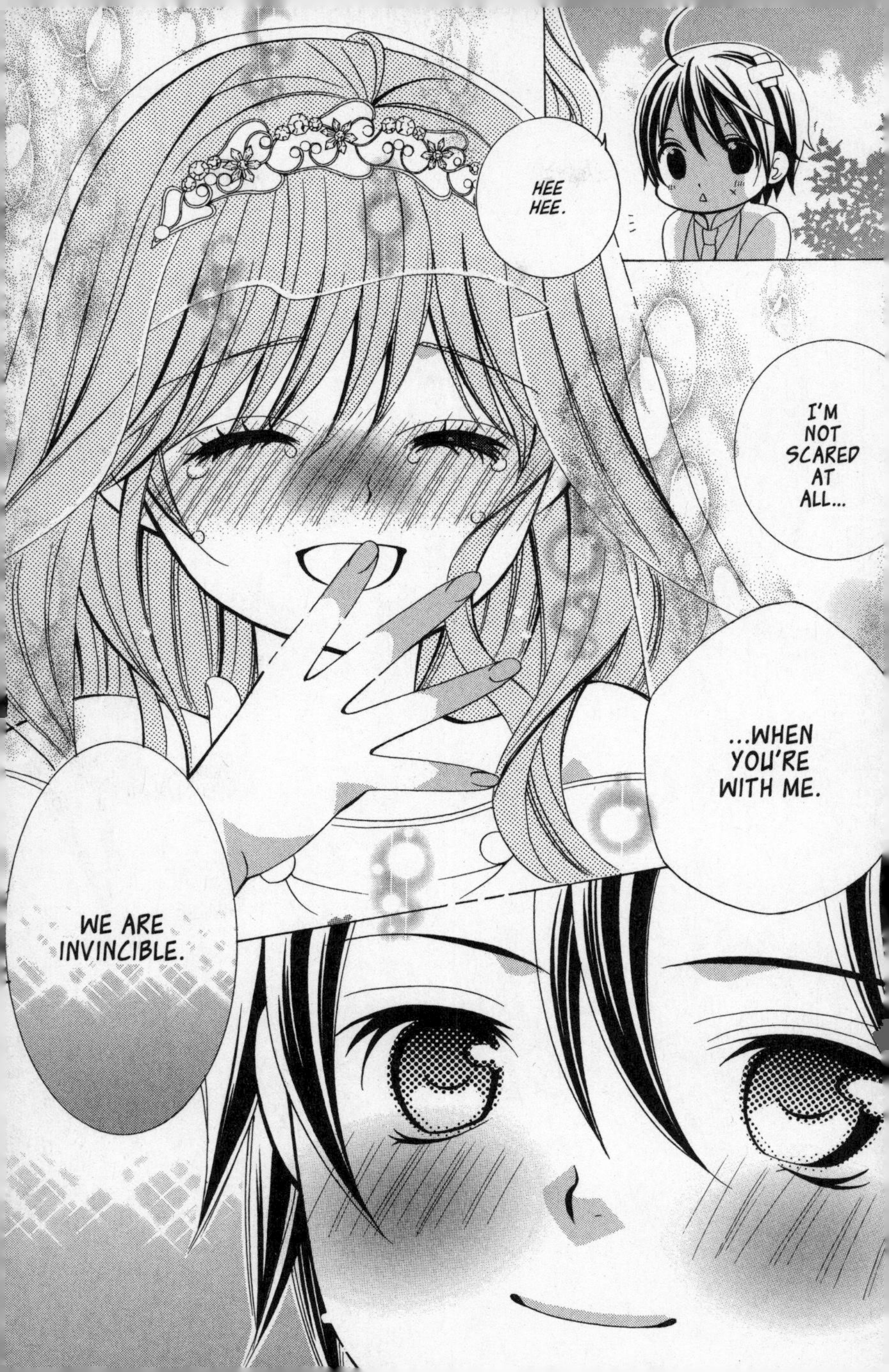
HEE HEE.
I'M NOT SCARED AT ALL...
...WHEN YOU'RE WITH ME.
WE ARE INVINCIBLE.

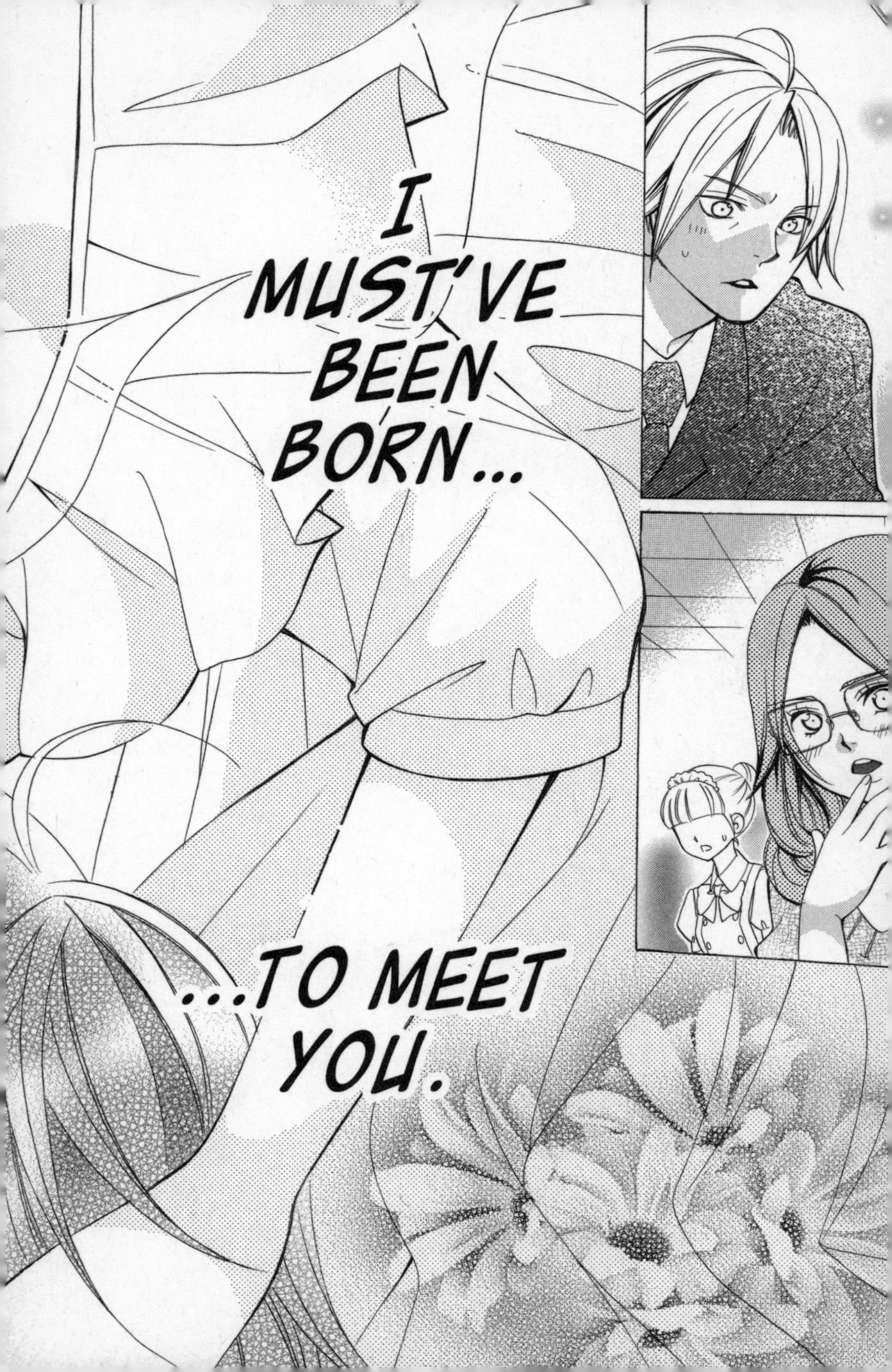
I MUST'VE BEEN BORN...
...TO MEET YOU.

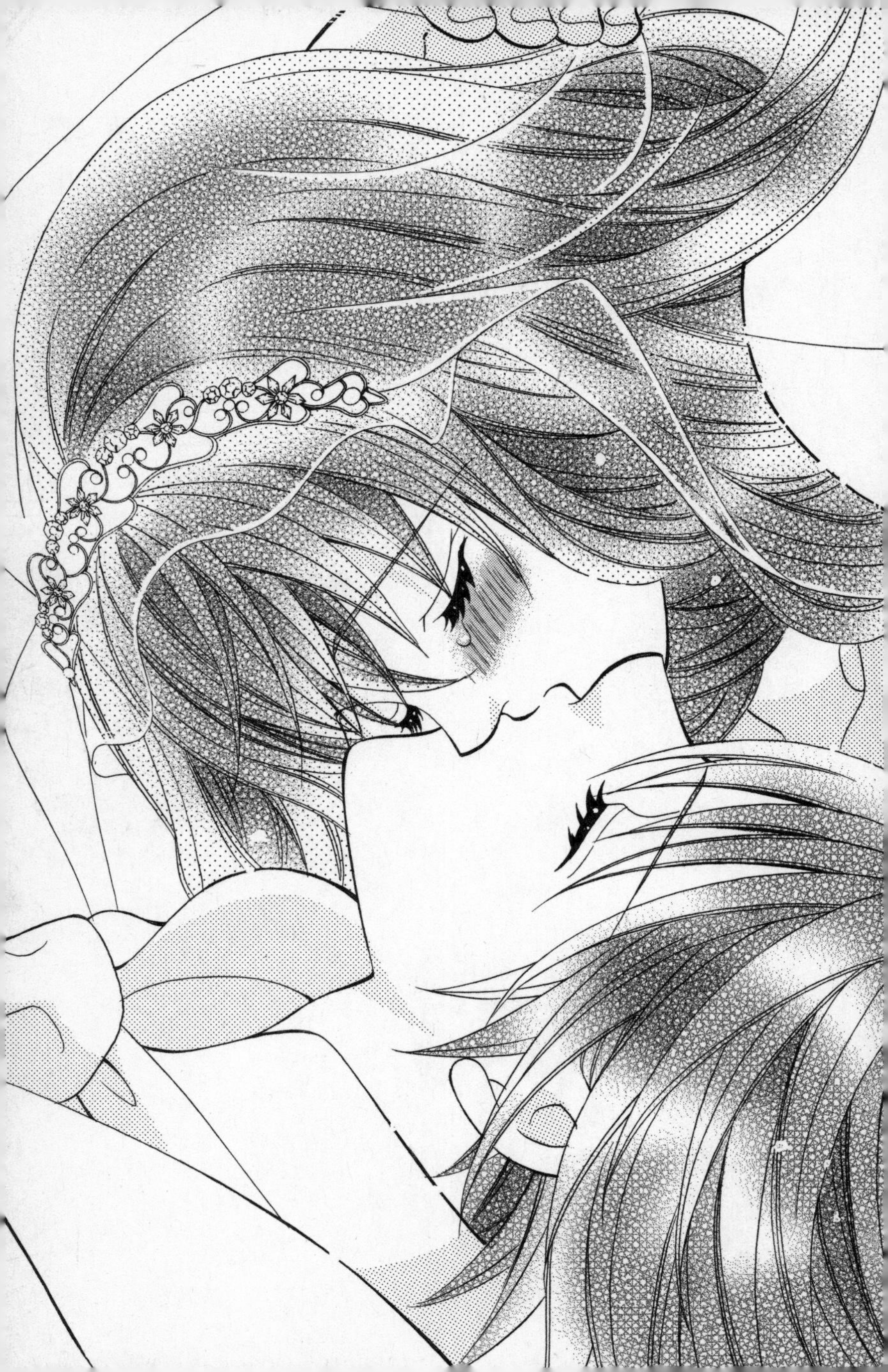

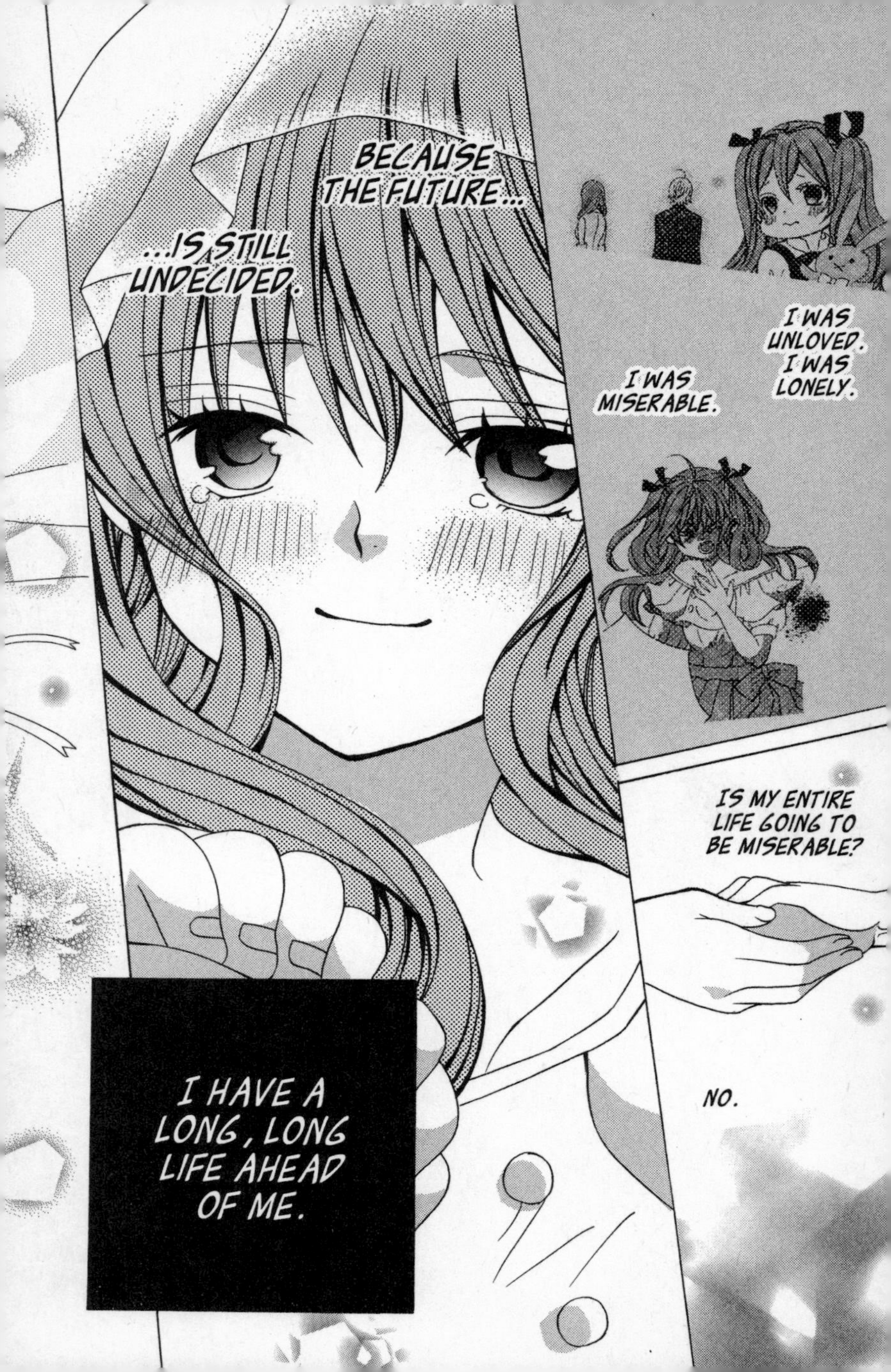
I WAS UNLOVED. I WAS LONELY.
I WAS MISERABLE.
IS MY ENTIRE LIFE GOING TO BE MISERABLE?
NO.
BECAUSE THE FUTURE...
...IS STILL UNDECIDED.
I HAVE A LONG, LONG LIFE AHEAD OF ME.

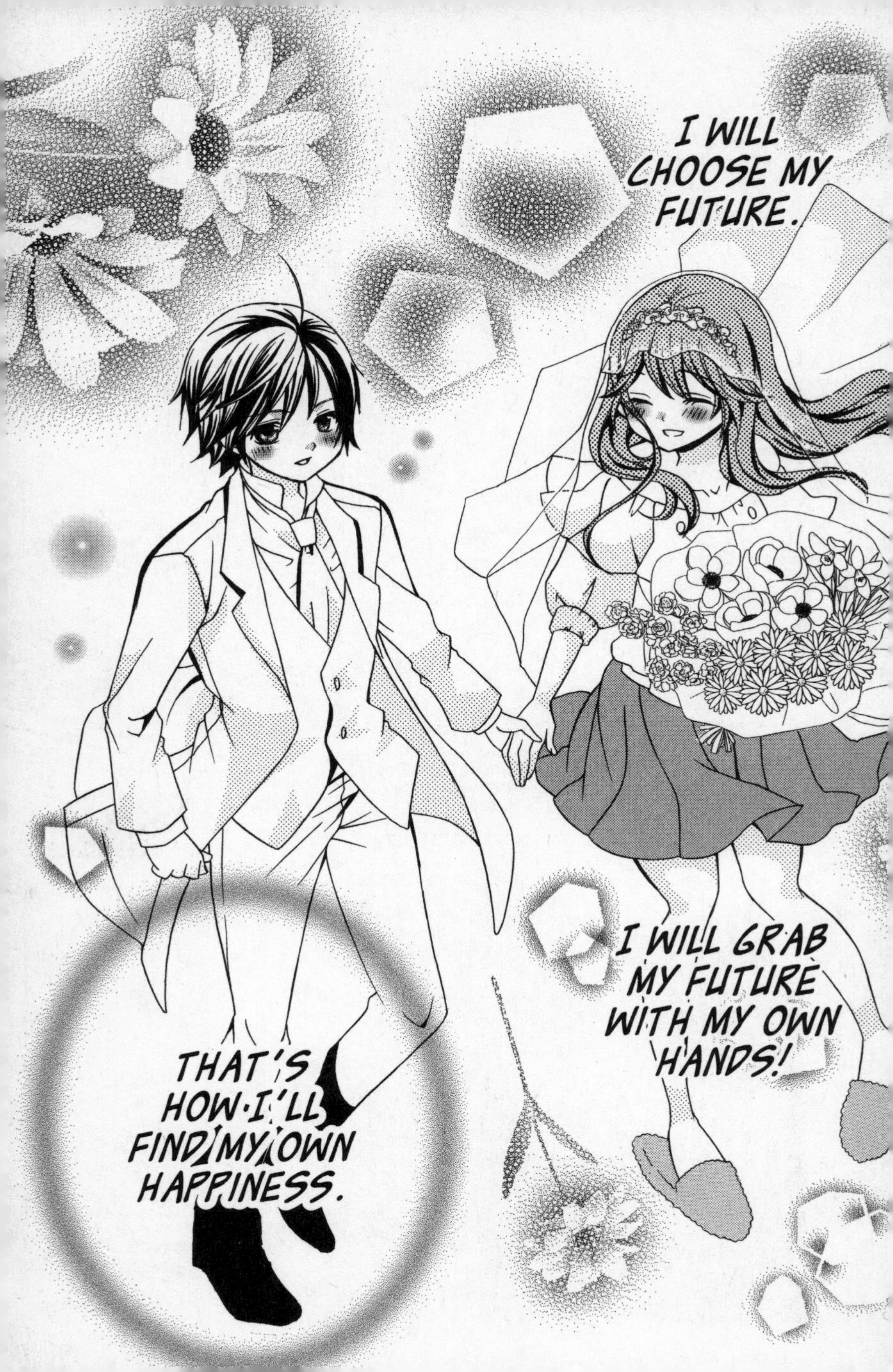
I WILL CHOOSE MY FUTURE.
I WILL GRAB MY FUTURE WITH MY OWN HANDS!
THAT'S HOW I'LL FIND MY OWN HAPPINESS.

So Cute! Fan Art Feature ♥

EVERYONE'S DRAWINGS ARE SO CUTE, THEY HURT!!

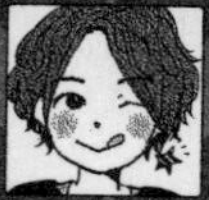

Shoji

Editor Shoji has commented on each one this time!!

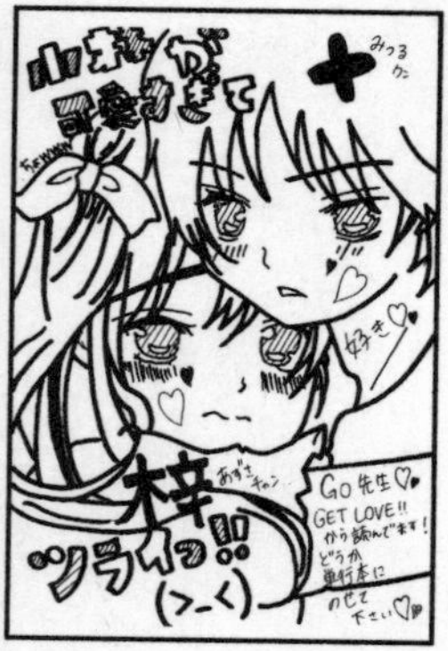

GO先生♡
GET LOVE!!
から読んでます！
どうか
単行本に
のせて
下さい♡

Omurice (Nara) ←
Ed.: I love the blushing Azusa!!

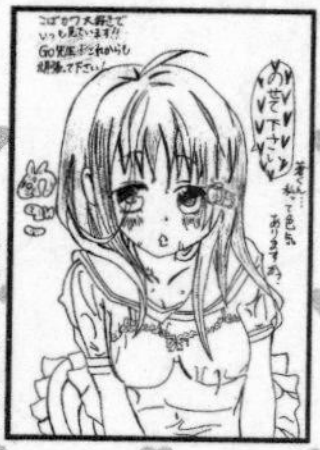

Do-S (Akita) →
Ed.: She's so, so sexy!!!

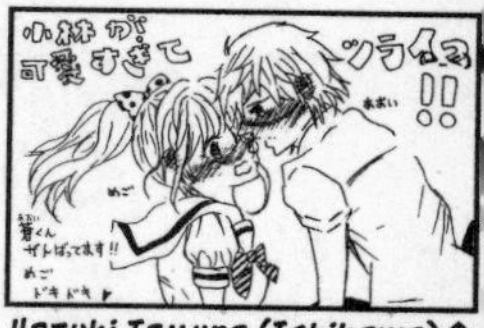

Hazuki Tamura (Ishikawa) ↑
Ed.: Aoi's doing his best, and Mego's heart flutters. ♥

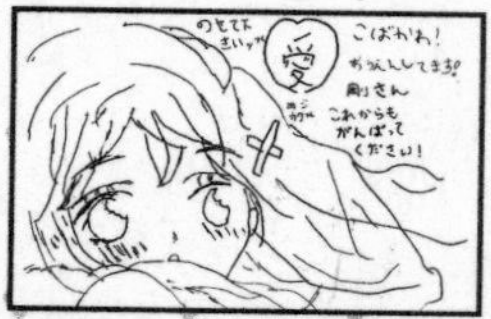

Haru Ichinose (Hokkaido) ↑
Ed.: Mego's becoming more and more beautiful...

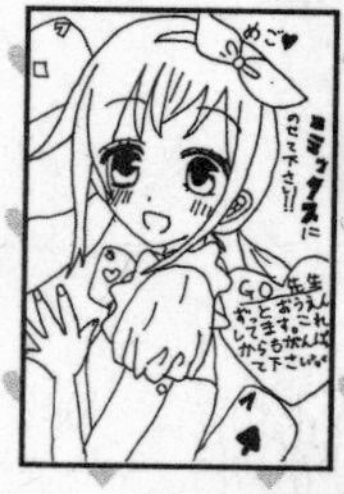

Ed.: I love the pure Mego too. ♥ Munch munch...

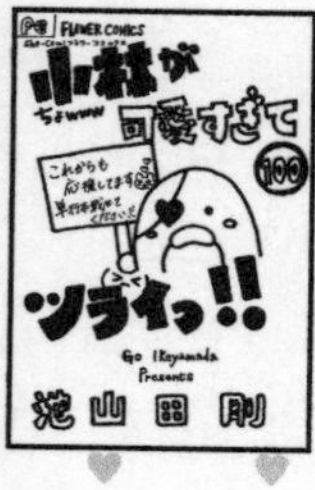

Kana Kitagawa (Gifu) ←
Ed.: 100... 100 volumes?! And the penguin's on the cover...

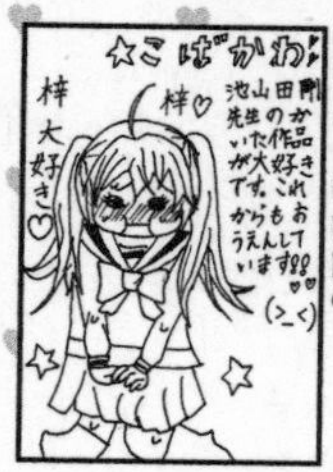

Rina Watanabe (Miyazaki) ←
Ed.: I wanna poke Azusa's pouting cheeks!!

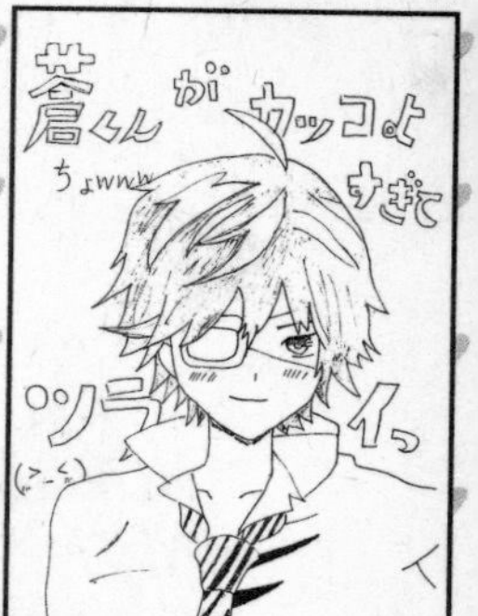

Setsuna (Fukuoka) ↑
Ed.: Even guys fall in love with his coolness!!

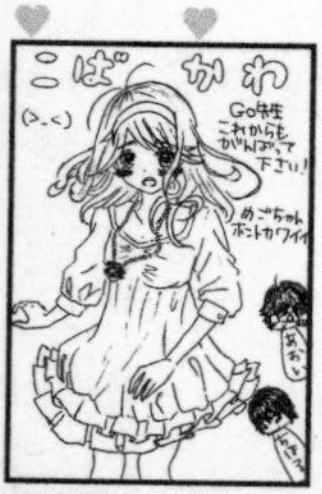

Mina Shoji (Hokkaido) ↑
Ed.: Both Aoi and Chiharu love Mego. ♥

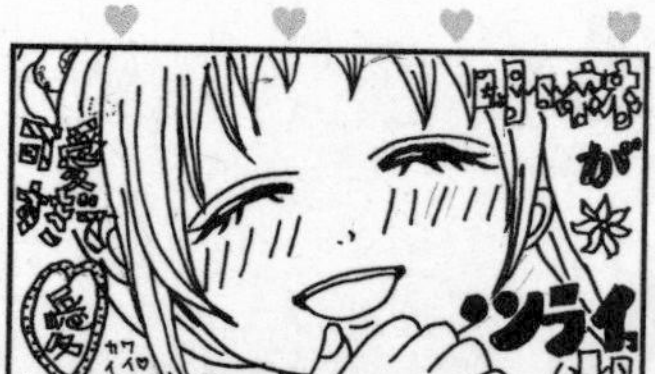

CAT ♥ (Aichi) ↑
Ed.: Mego's smile totally makes me smile!!

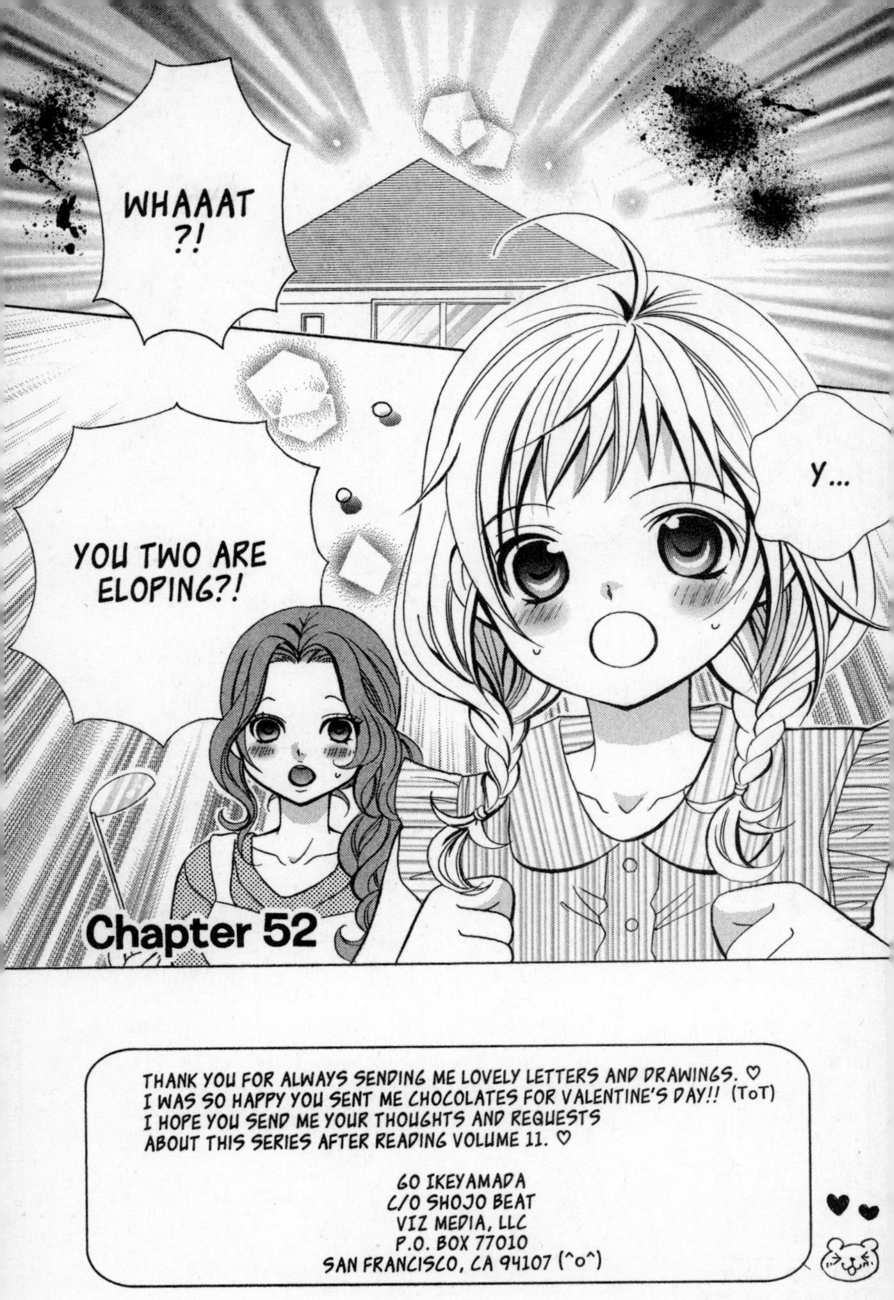
Y...
YOU TWO ARE ELOPING?!
WHAAAT ?!

Chapter 52

THANK YOU FOR ALWAYS SENDING ME LOVELY LETTERS AND DRAWINGS. ♡
I WAS SO HAPPY YOU SENT ME CHOCOLATES FOR VALENTINE'S DAY!! (ToT)
I HOPE YOU SEND ME YOUR THOUGHTS AND REQUESTS
ABOUT THIS SERIES AFTER READING VOLUME 11. ♡

GO IKEYAMADA
C/O SHOJO BEAT
VIZ MEDIA, LLC
P.O. BOX 77010
SAN FRANCISCO, CA 94107 (^o^)

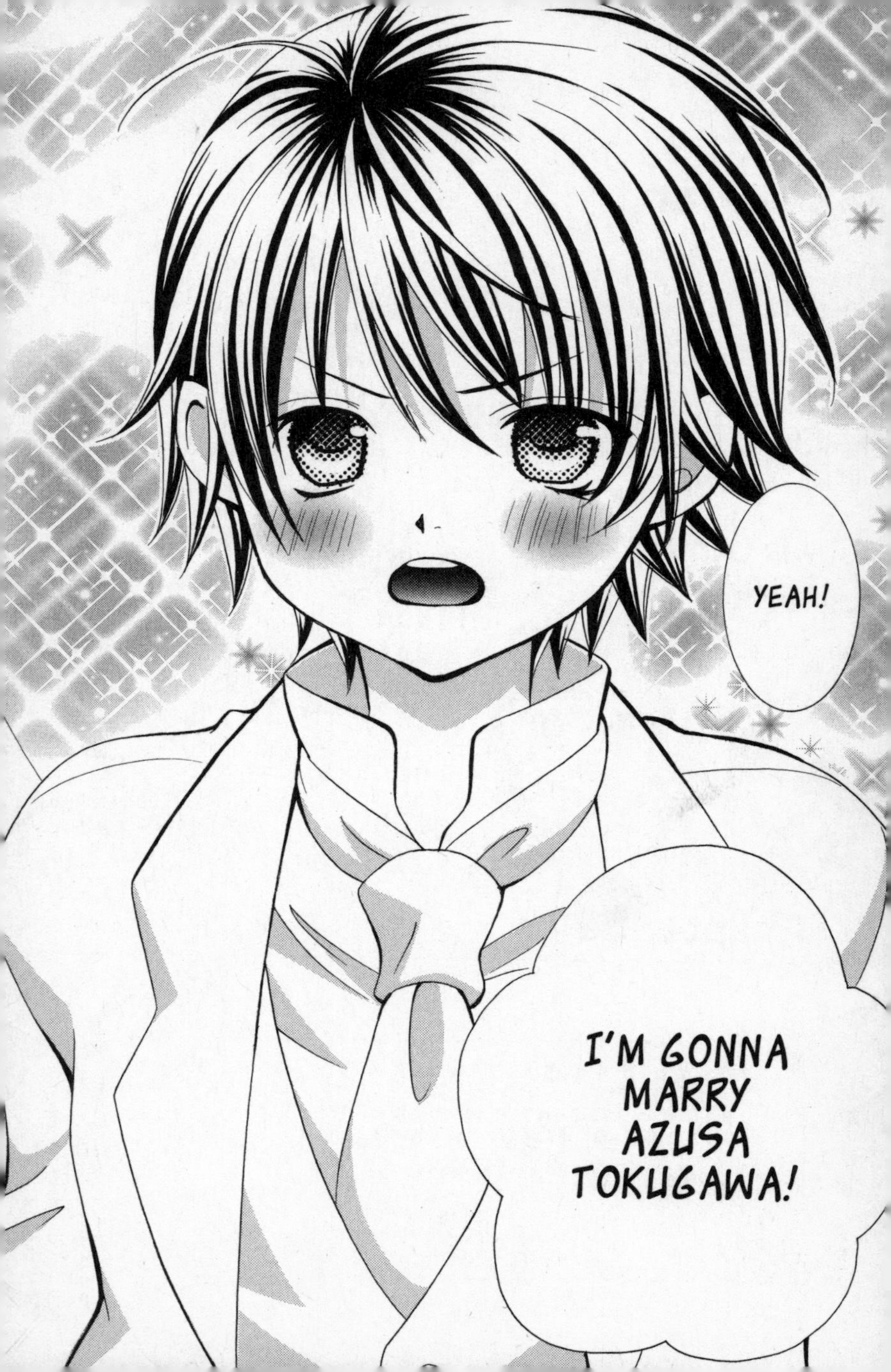
YEAH!
I'M GONNA MARRY AZUSA TOKUGAWA!

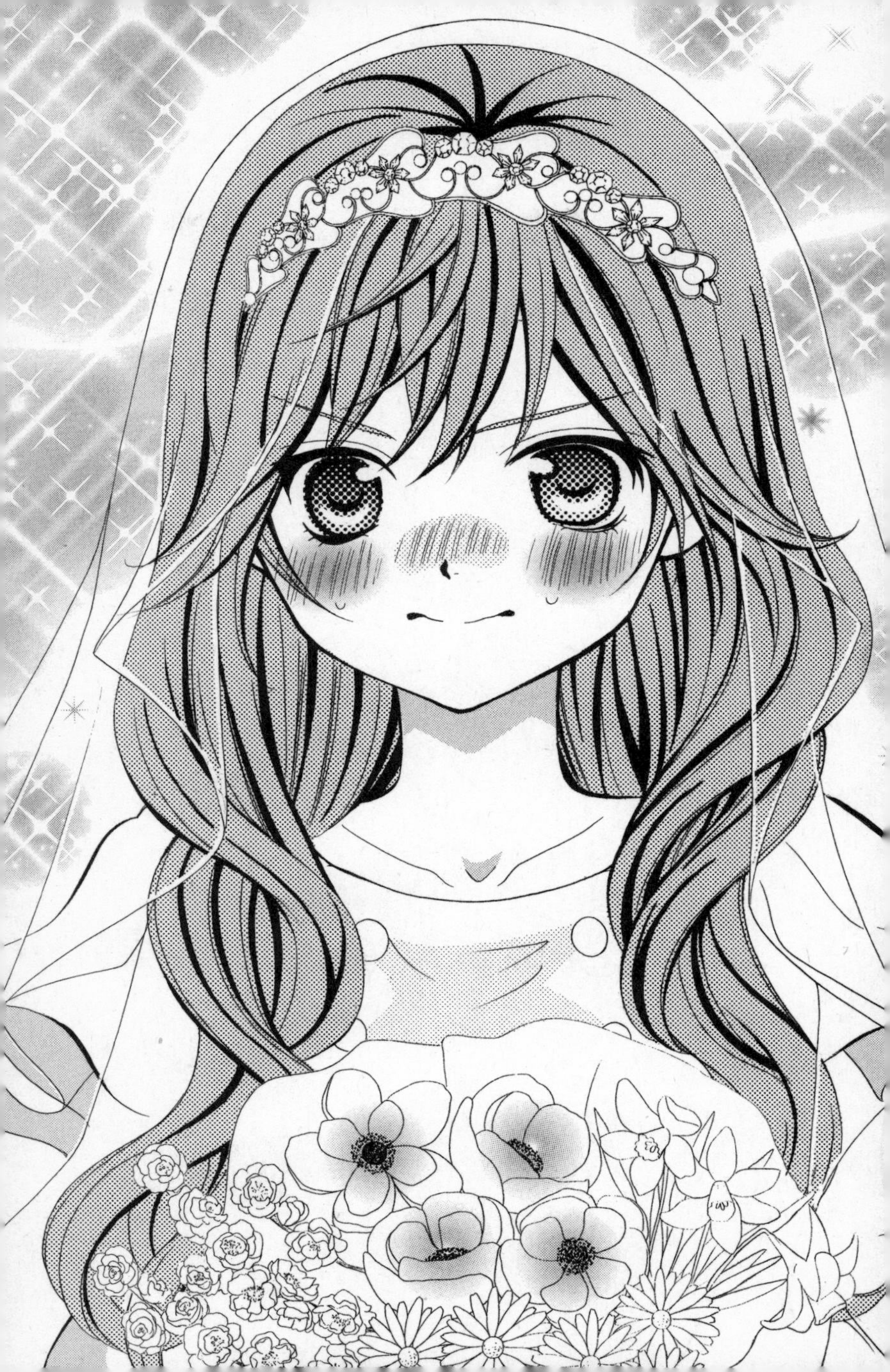

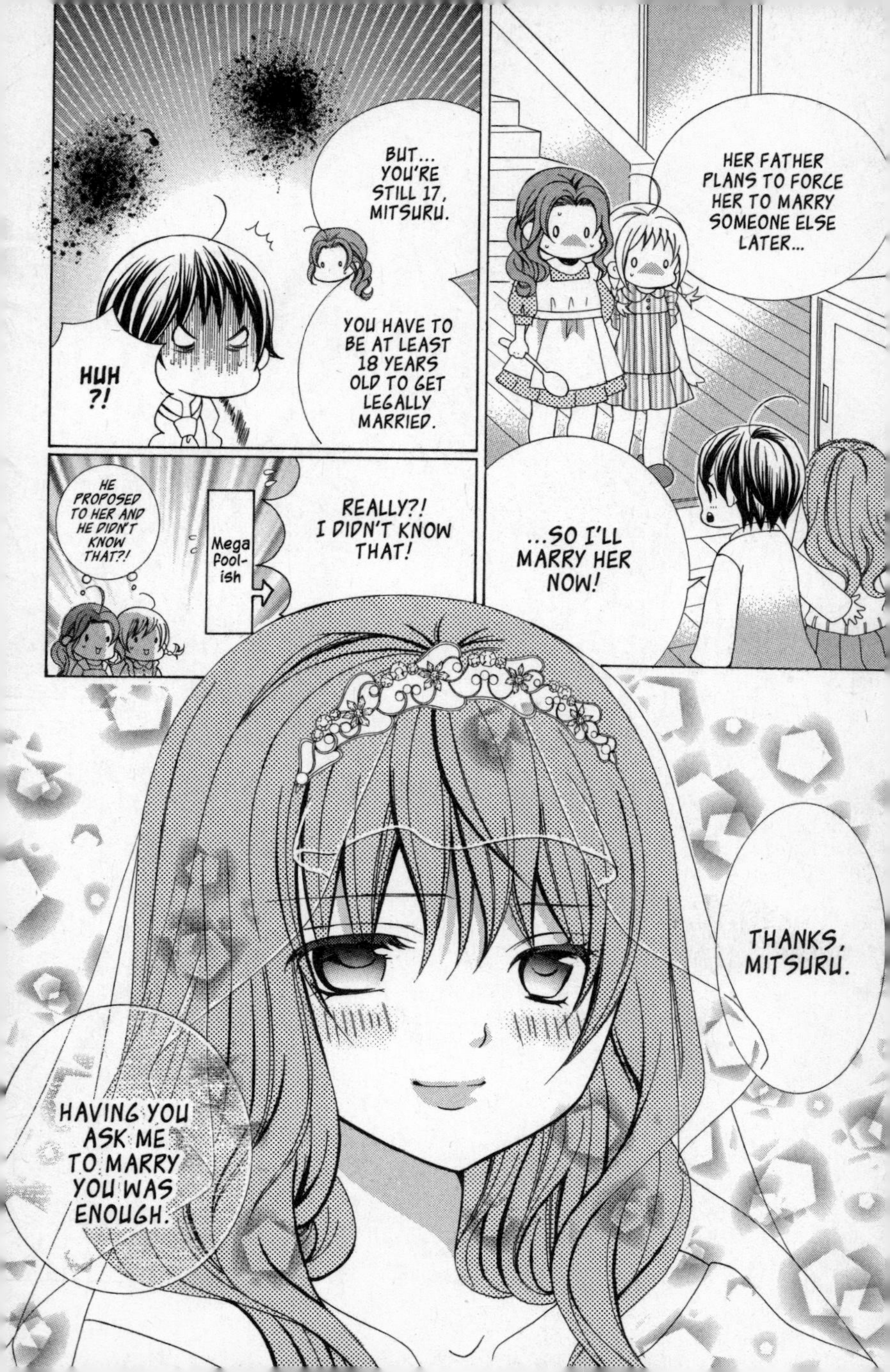
HER FATHER PLANS TO FORCE HER TO MARRY SOMEONE ELSE LATER...
...SO I'LL MARRY HER NOW!
BUT... YOU'RE STILL 17, MITSURU.
YOU HAVE TO BE AT LEAST 18 YEARS OLD TO GET LEGALLY MARRIED.
HUH?!
REALLY?! I DIDN'T KNOW THAT!
HE PROPOSED TO HER AND HE DIDN'T KNOW THAT?!
Mega fool-ish
THANKS, MITSURU.
HAVING YOU ASK ME TO MARRY YOU WAS ENOUGH.

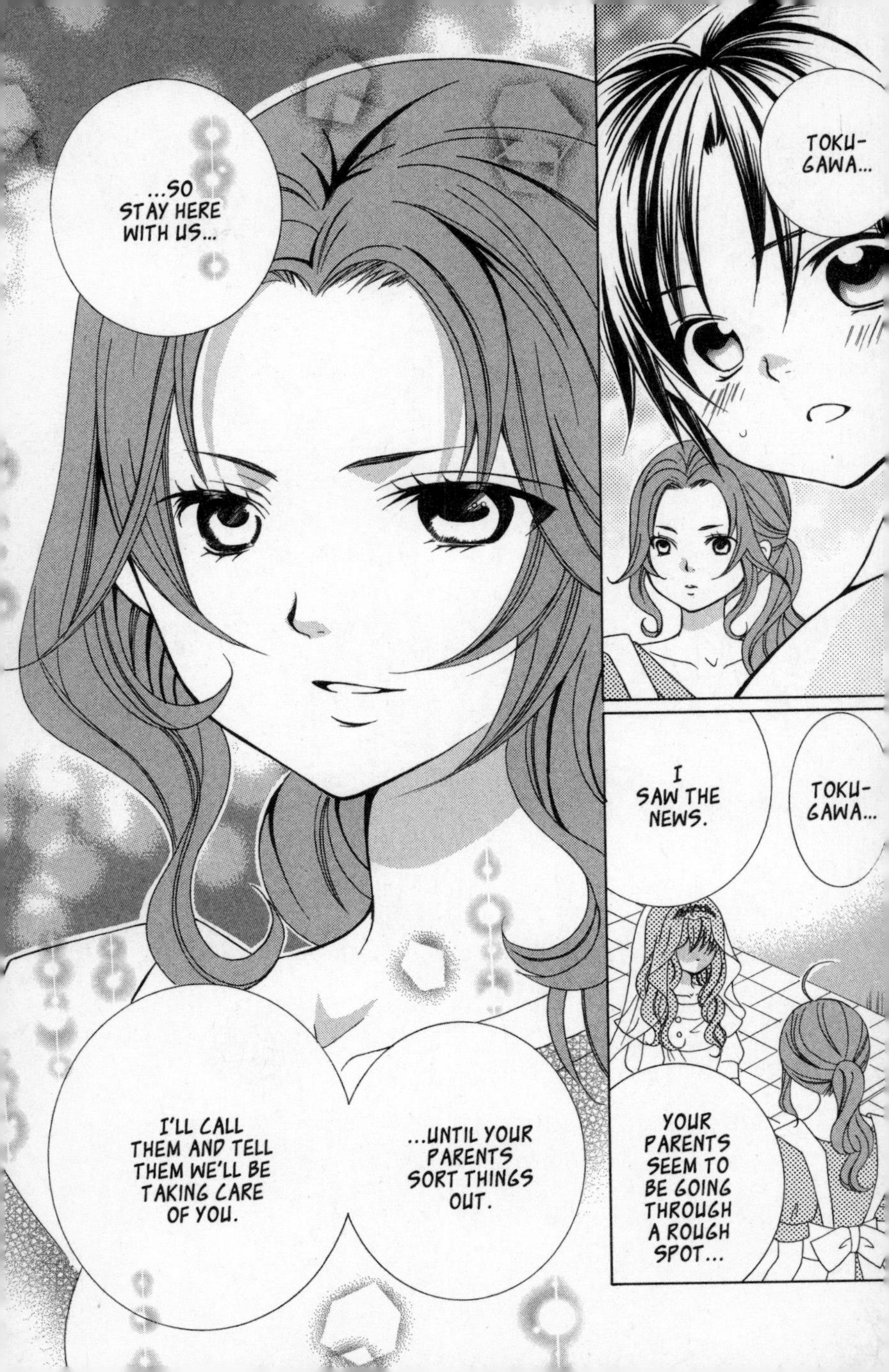
TOKU-GAWA...
TOKU-GAWA...
I SAW THE NEWS.
YOUR PARENTS SEEM TO BE GOING THROUGH A ROUGH SPOT...
...SO STAY HERE WITH US...
...UNTIL YOUR PARENTS SORT THINGS OUT.
I'LL CALL THEM AND TELL THEM WE'LL BE TAKING CARE OF YOU.

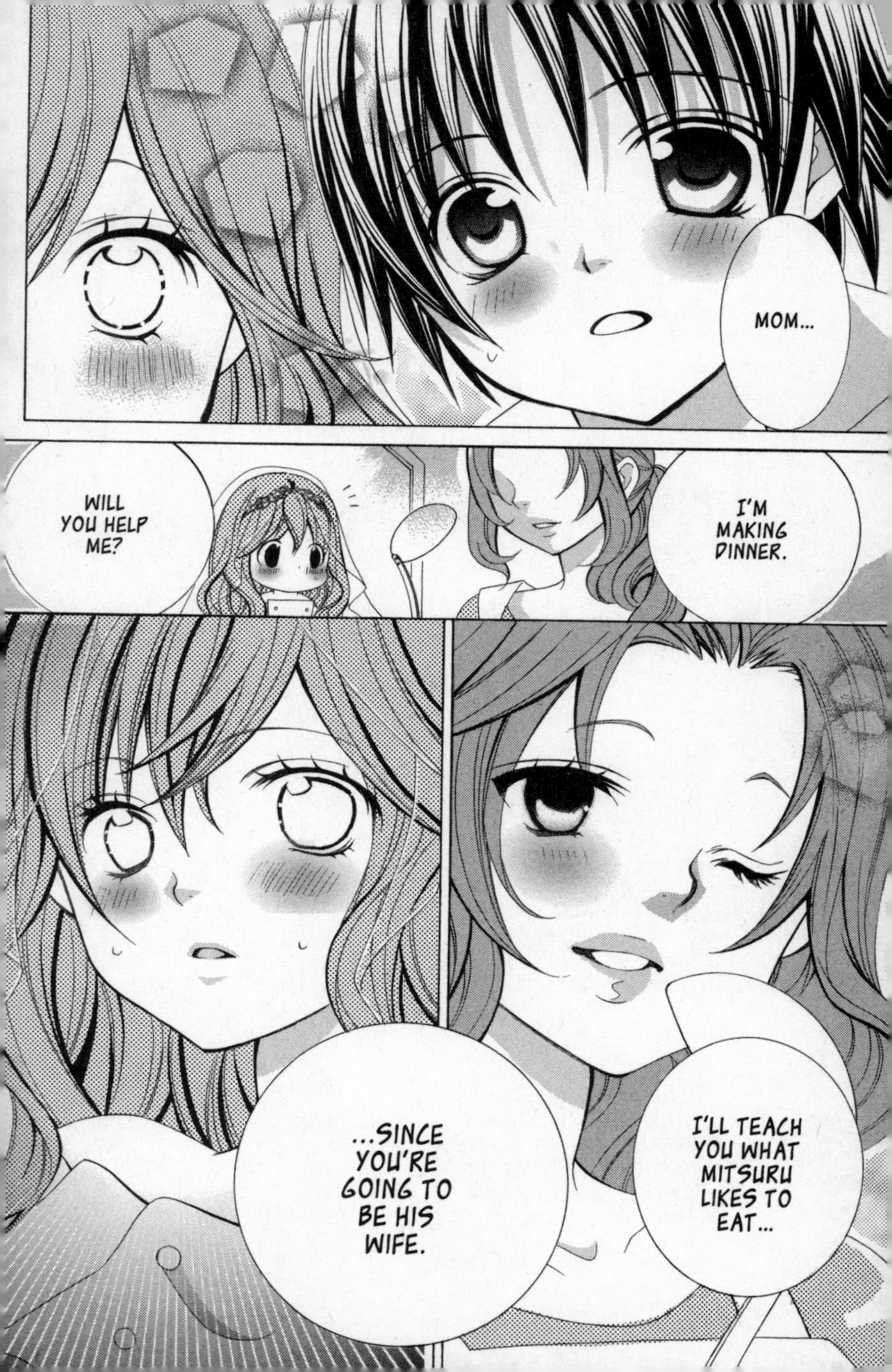
MOM...
I'M MAKING DINNER.
WILL YOU HELP ME?
I'LL TEACH YOU WHAT MITSURU LIKES TO EAT...
...SINCE YOU'RE GOING TO BE HIS WIFE.

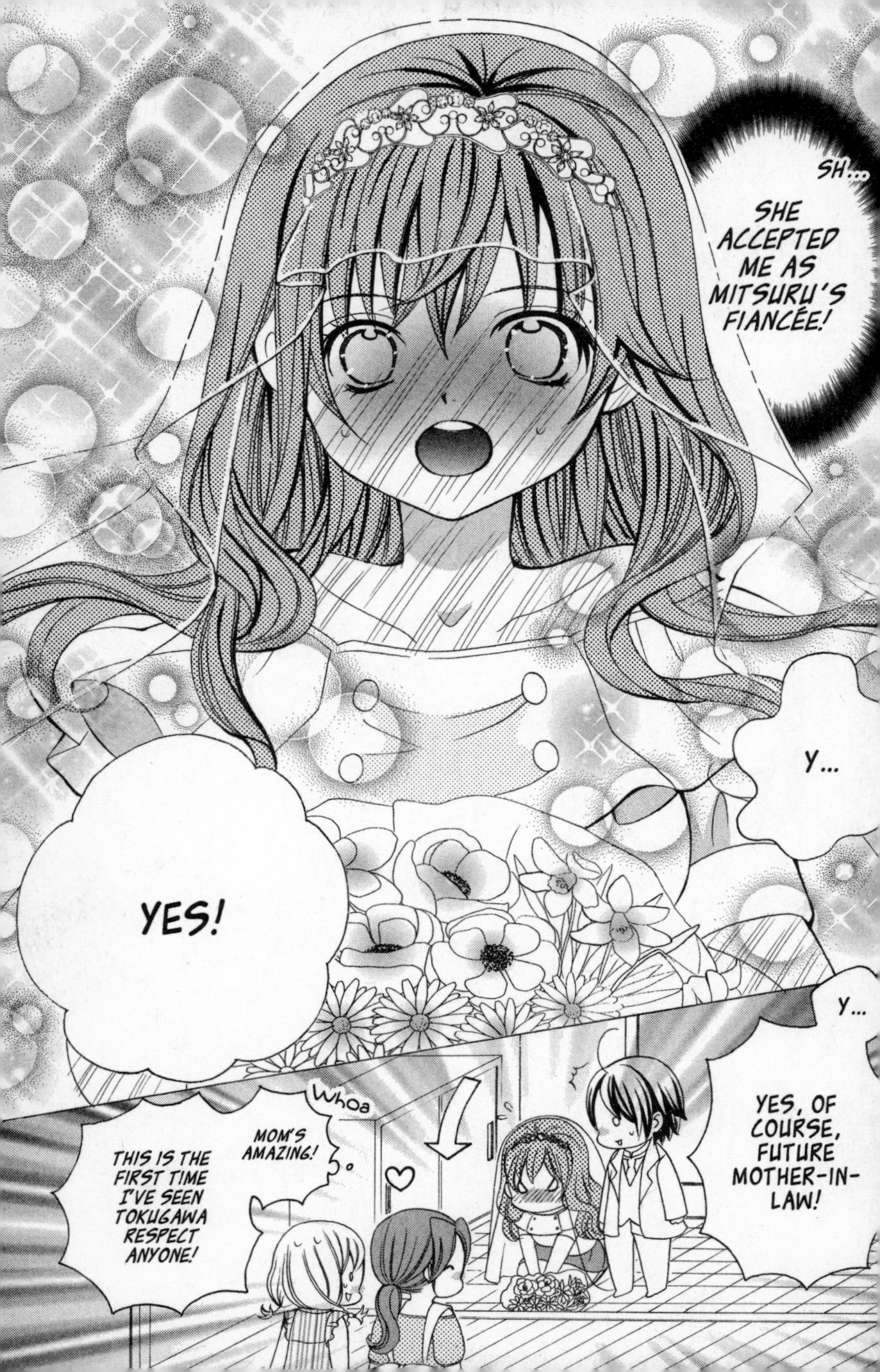
SH...
SHE ACCEPTED ME AS MITSURU'S FIANCÉE!
Y...
Y...
YES!
YES, OF COURSE, FUTURE MOTHER-IN-LAW!
Whoa
MOM'S AMAZING!
THIS IS THE FIRST TIME I'VE SEEN TOKUGAWA RESPECT ANYONE!

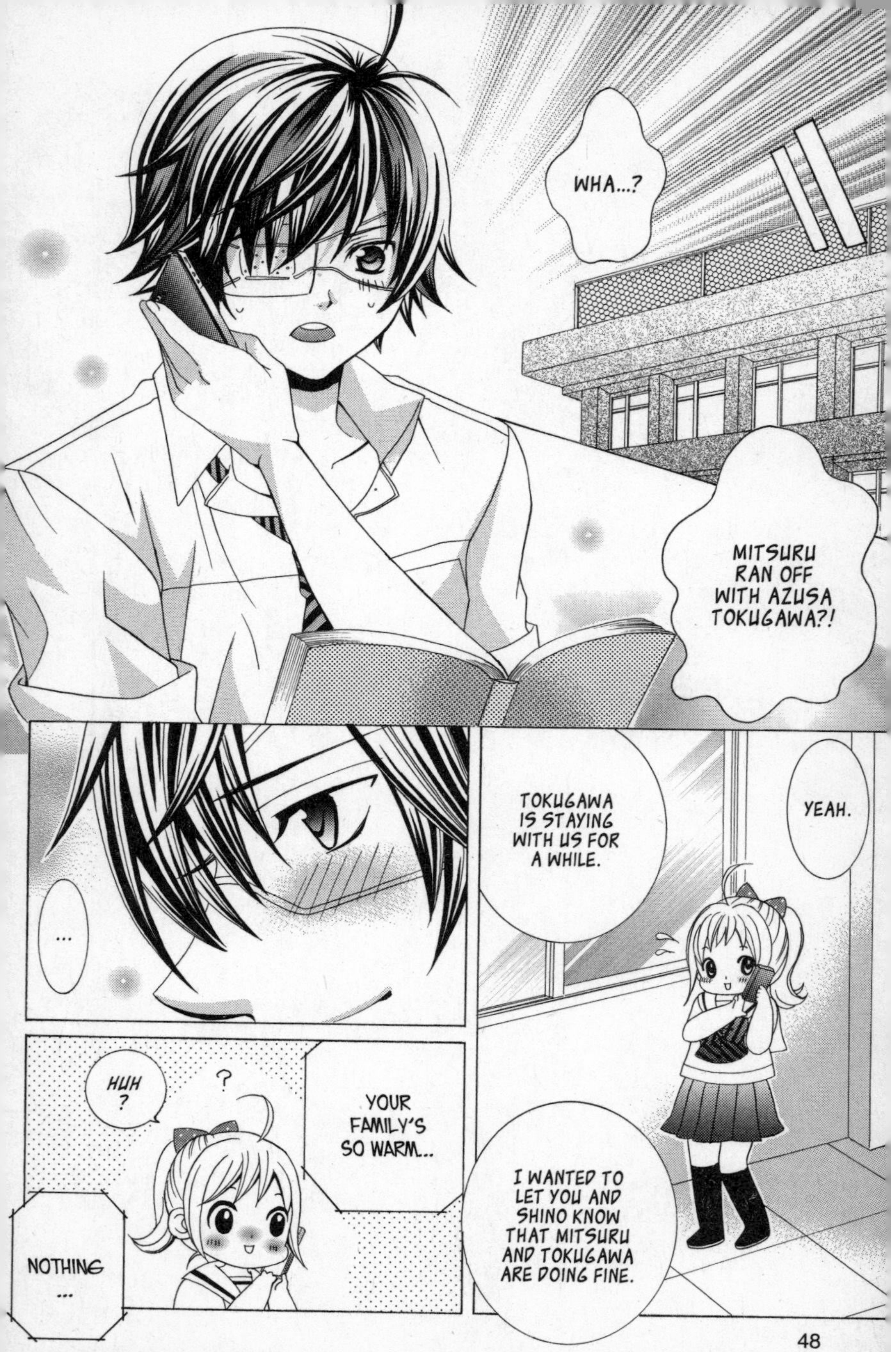
WHA...?
MITSURU RAN OFF WITH AZUSA TOKUGAWA?!
YEAH.
TOKUGAWA IS STAYING WITH US FOR A WHILE.
I WANTED TO LET YOU AND SHINO KNOW THAT MITSURU AND TOKUGAWA ARE DOING FINE.
...
YOUR FAMILY'S SO WARM...
HUH ?
?
NOTHING ...

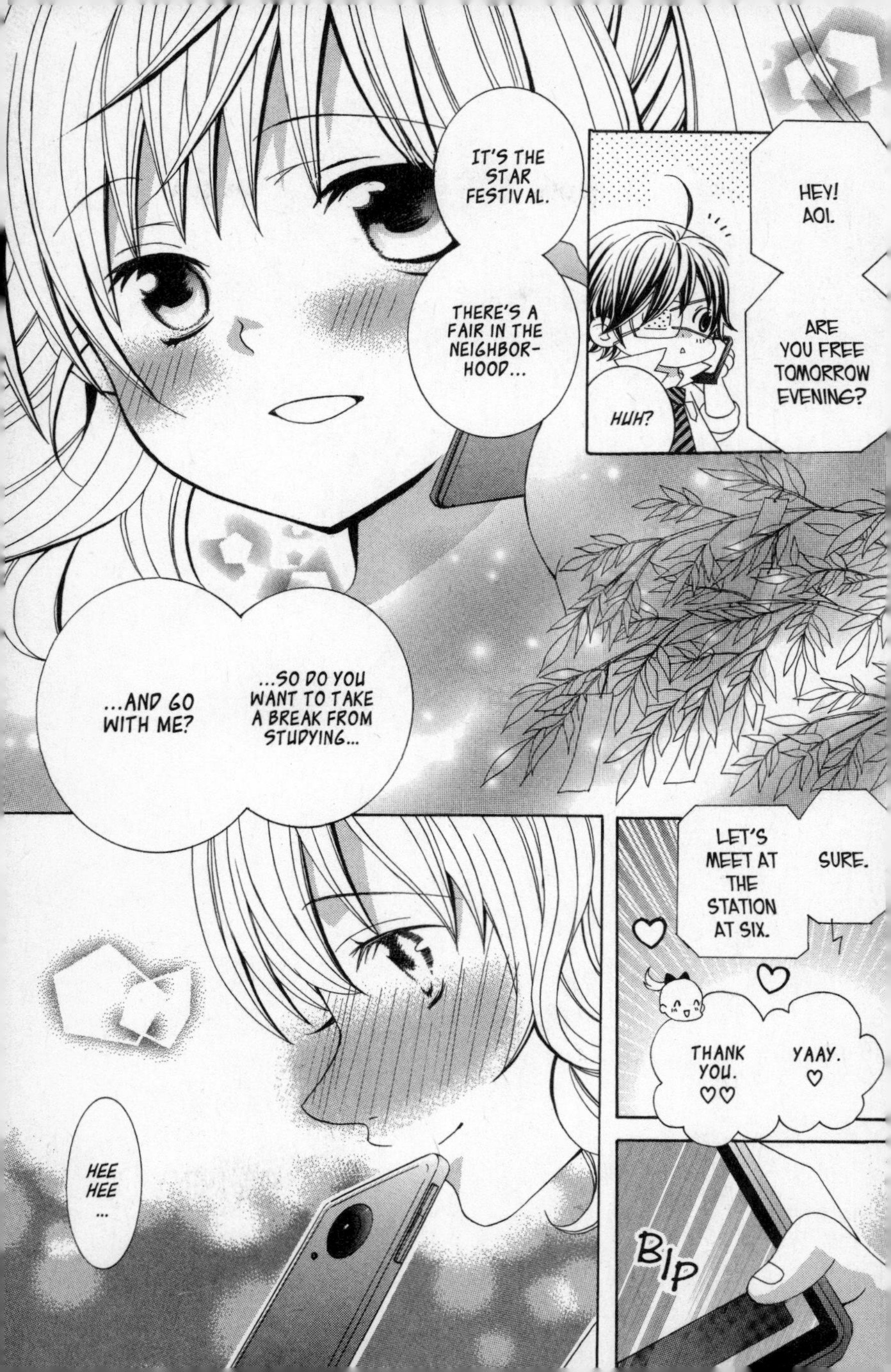
HEY! AOI.
ARE YOU FREE TOMORROW EVENING?
HUH?
IT'S THE STAR FESTIVAL.
THERE'S A FAIR IN THE NEIGHBOR-HOOD...
...SO DO YOU WANT TO TAKE A BREAK FROM STUDYING...
...AND GO WITH ME?
SURE.
LET'S MEET AT THE STATION AT SIX.
YAAY. ♡
THANK YOU. ♡♡
BLIP
HEE HEE ...

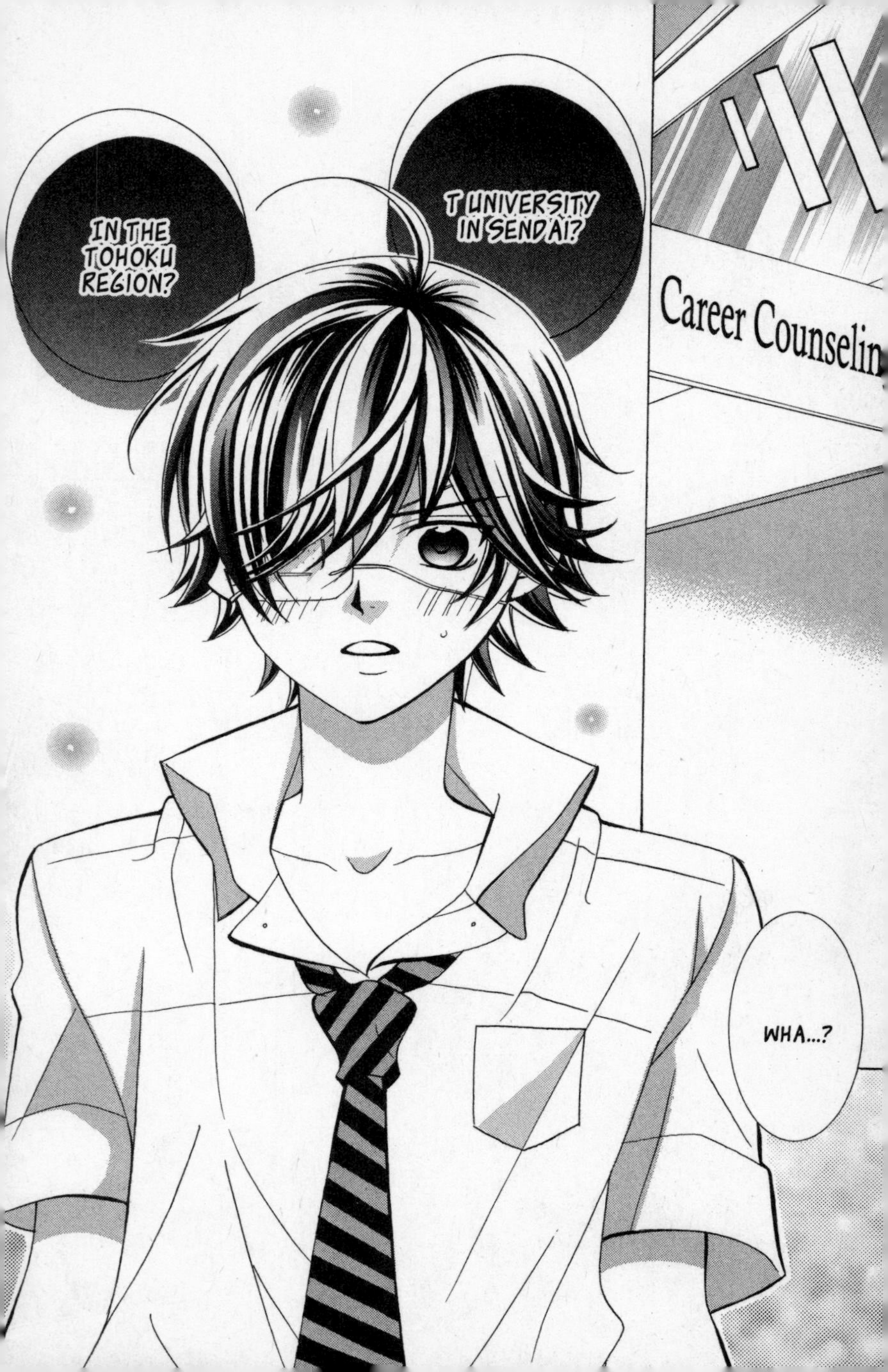
T UNIVERSITY IN SENDAI?
IN THE TOHOKU REGION?
Career Counselin
WHA...?

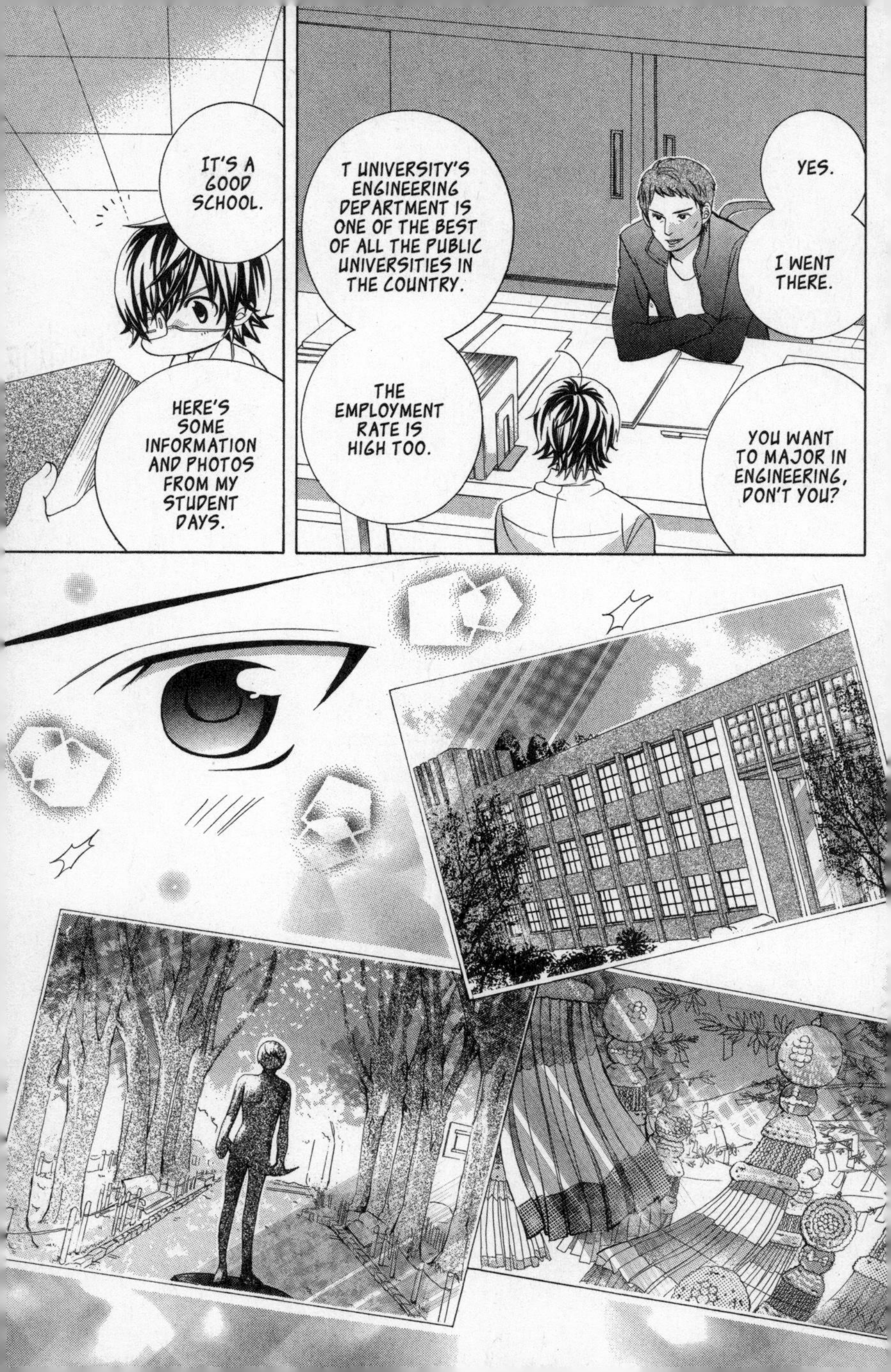
YES.
I WENT THERE.
T UNIVERSITY'S ENGINEERING DEPARTMENT IS ONE OF THE BEST OF ALL THE PUBLIC UNIVERSITIES IN THE COUNTRY.
THE EMPLOYMENT RATE IS HIGH TOO.
YOU WANT TO MAJOR IN ENGINEERING, DON'T YOU?
IT'S A GOOD SCHOOL.
HERE'S SOME INFORMATION AND PHOTOS FROM MY STUDENT DAYS.

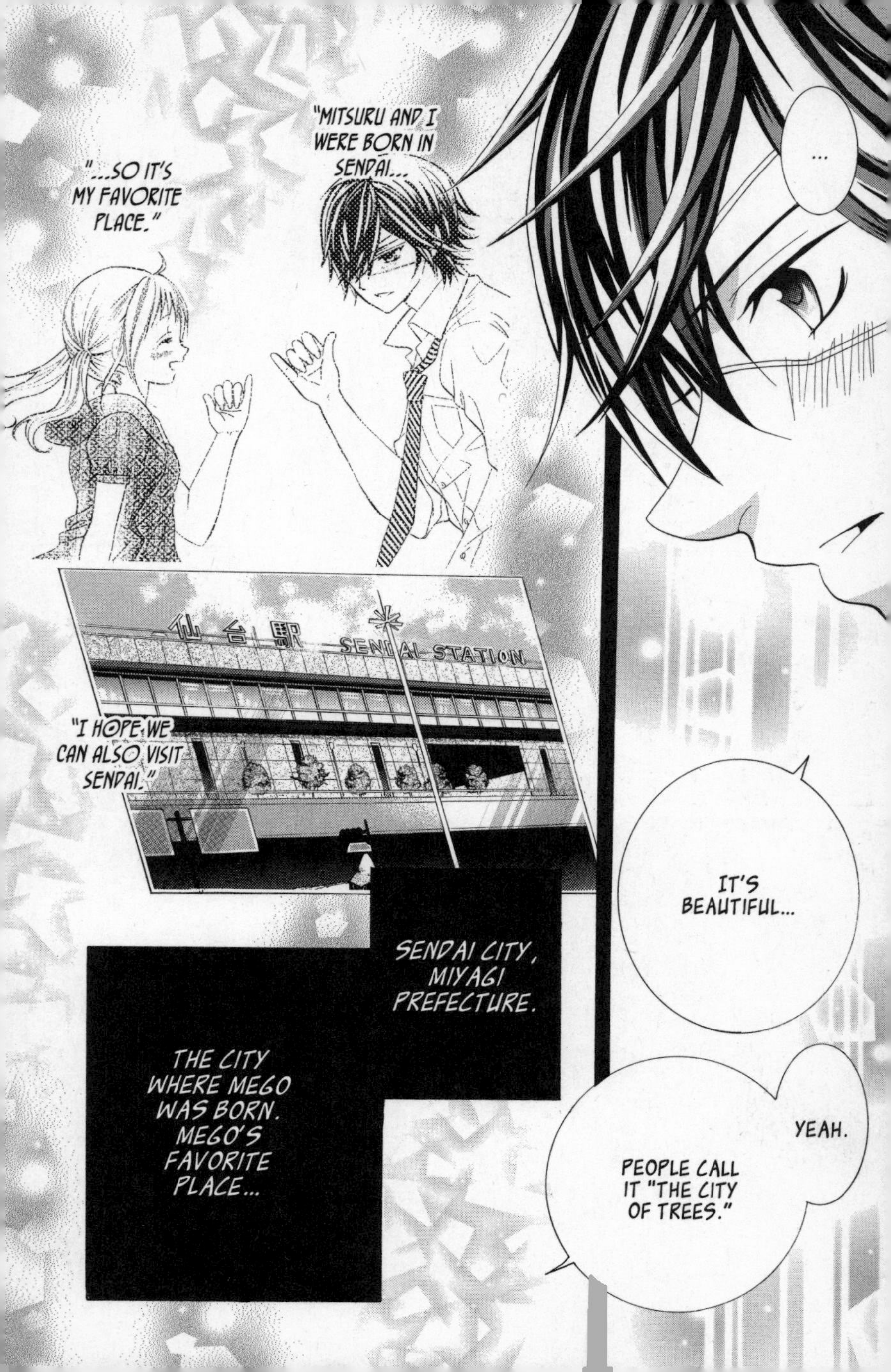
...
IT'S BEAUTIFUL...
YEAH.
PEOPLE CALL IT "THE CITY OF TREES."
"MITSURU AND I WERE BORN IN SENDAI...
"...SO IT'S MY FAVORITE PLACE."
仙台駅 SENDAI STATION
"I HOPE WE CAN ALSO VISIT SENDAI."
SENDAI CITY, MIYAGI PREFECTURE.
THE CITY WHERE MEGO WAS BORN. MEGO'S FAVORITE PLACE...

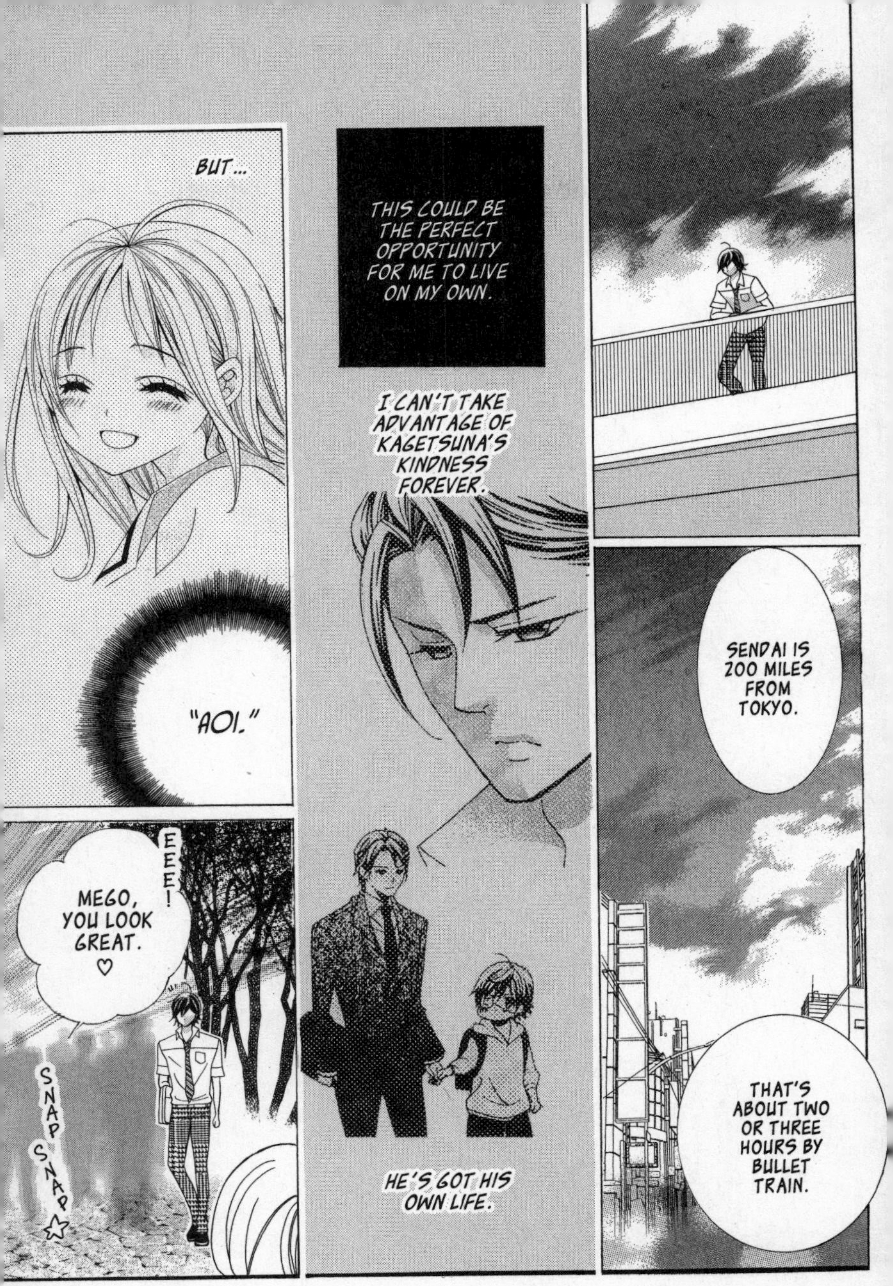
SENDAI IS 200 MILES FROM TOKYO.
THAT'S ABOUT TWO OR THREE HOURS BY BULLET TRAIN.
THIS COULD BE THE PERFECT OPPORTUNITY FOR ME TO LIVE ON MY OWN.
I CAN'T TAKE ADVANTAGE OF KAGETSUNA'S KINDNESS FOREVER.
HE'S GOT HIS OWN LIFE.
BUT...
"AOI."
EEE!
MEGO, YOU LOOK GREAT. ♡
SNAP SNAP ☆

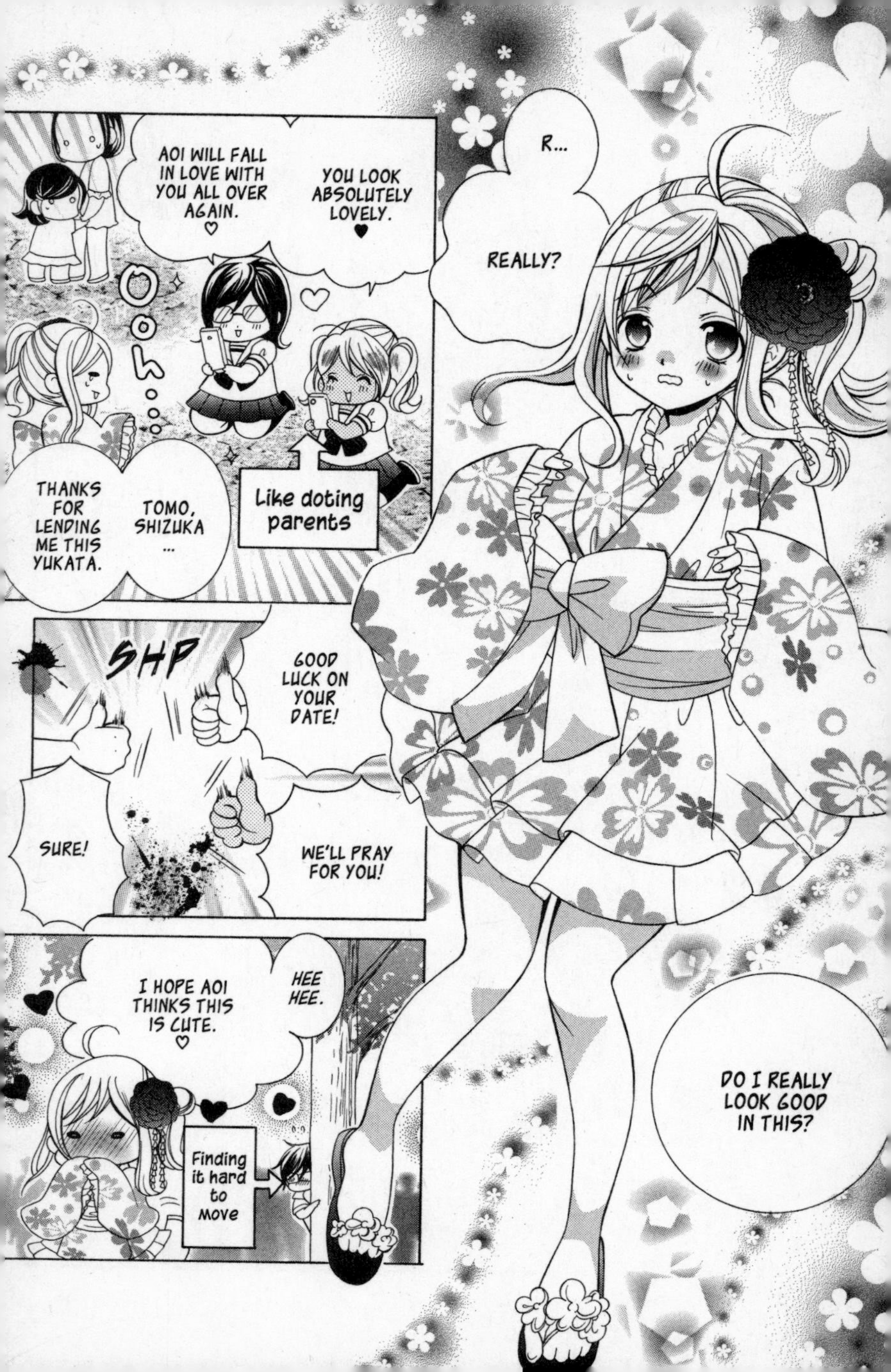
R...
REALLY?
DO I REALLY LOOK GOOD IN THIS?
YOU LOOK ABSOLUTELY LOVELY. ♥
AOI WILL FALL IN LOVE WITH YOU ALL OVER AGAIN. ♡
Ooh...
Like doting parents
TOMO, SHIZUKA...
THANKS FOR LENDING ME THIS YUKATA.
GOOD LUCK ON YOUR DATE!
SHP
WE'LL PRAY FOR YOU!
SURE!
HEE HEE.
I HOPE AOI THINKS THIS IS CUTE. ♡
Finding it hard to move

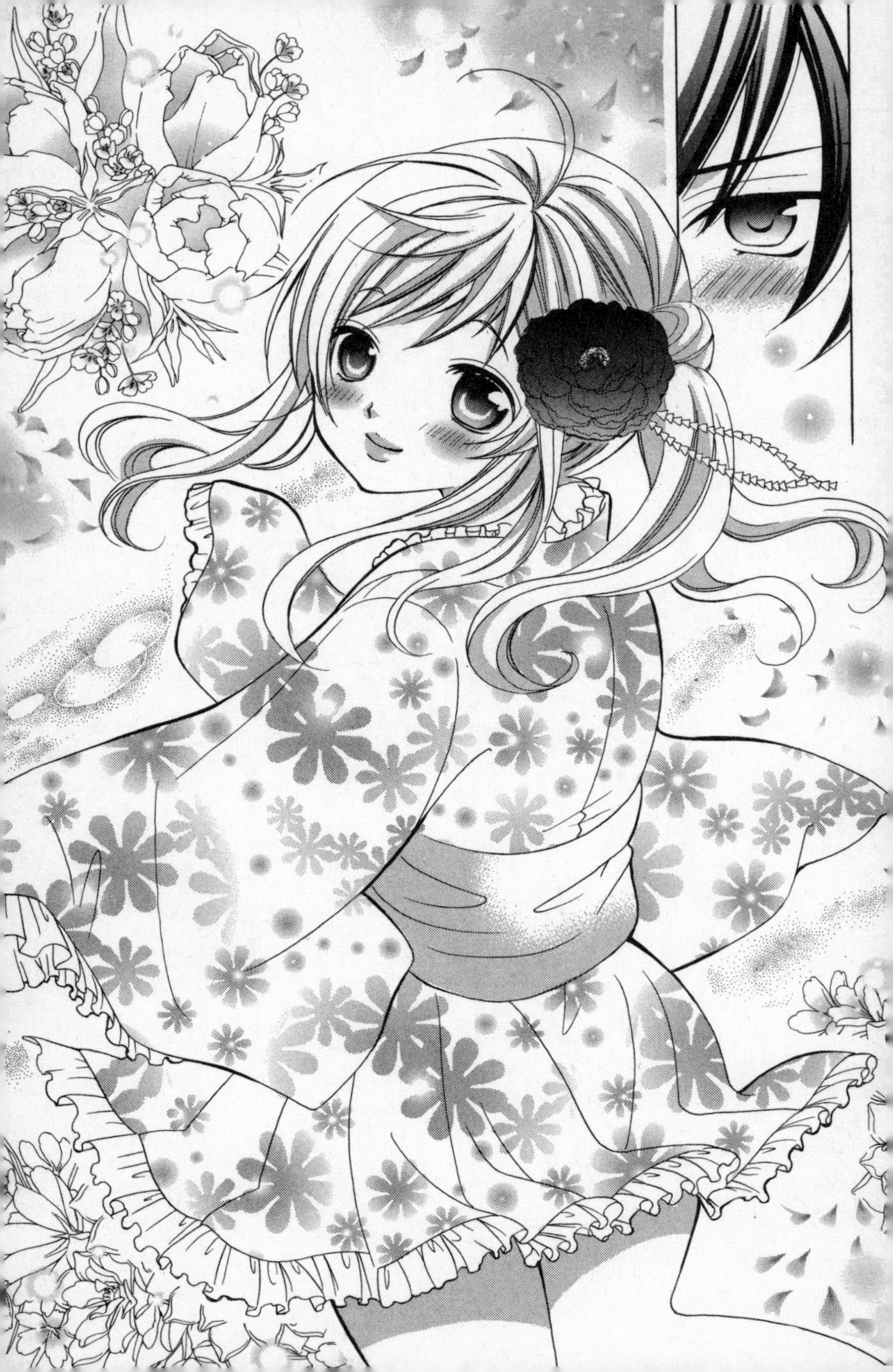

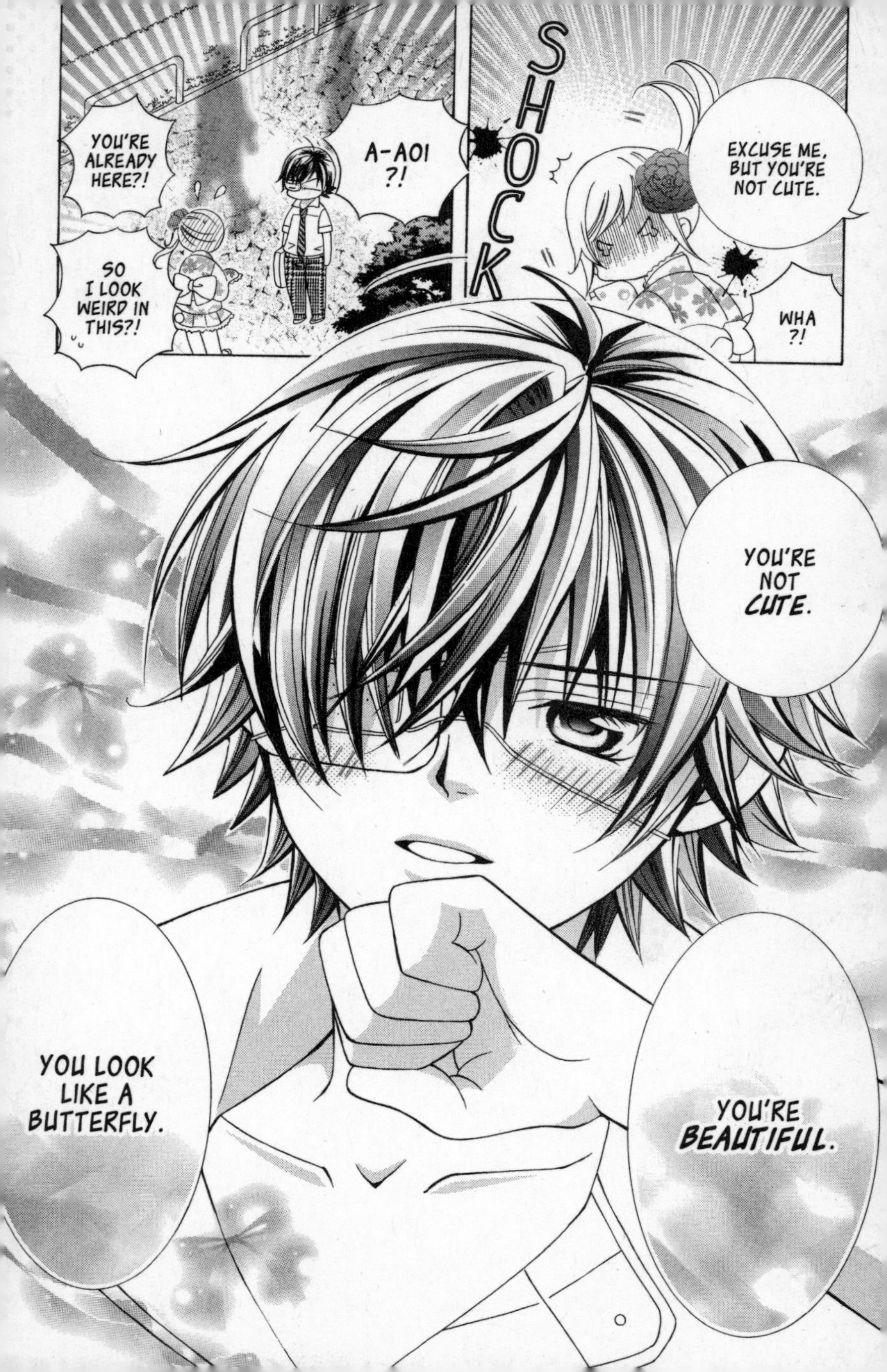
EXCUSE ME, BUT YOU'RE NOT CUTE.
SHOCK
WHA ?!
A-AOI ?!
YOU'RE ALREADY HERE?!
SO I LOOK WEIRD IN THIS?!
YOU'RE NOT CUTE.
YOU'RE BEAUTIFUL.
YOU LOOK LIKE A BUTTERFLY.

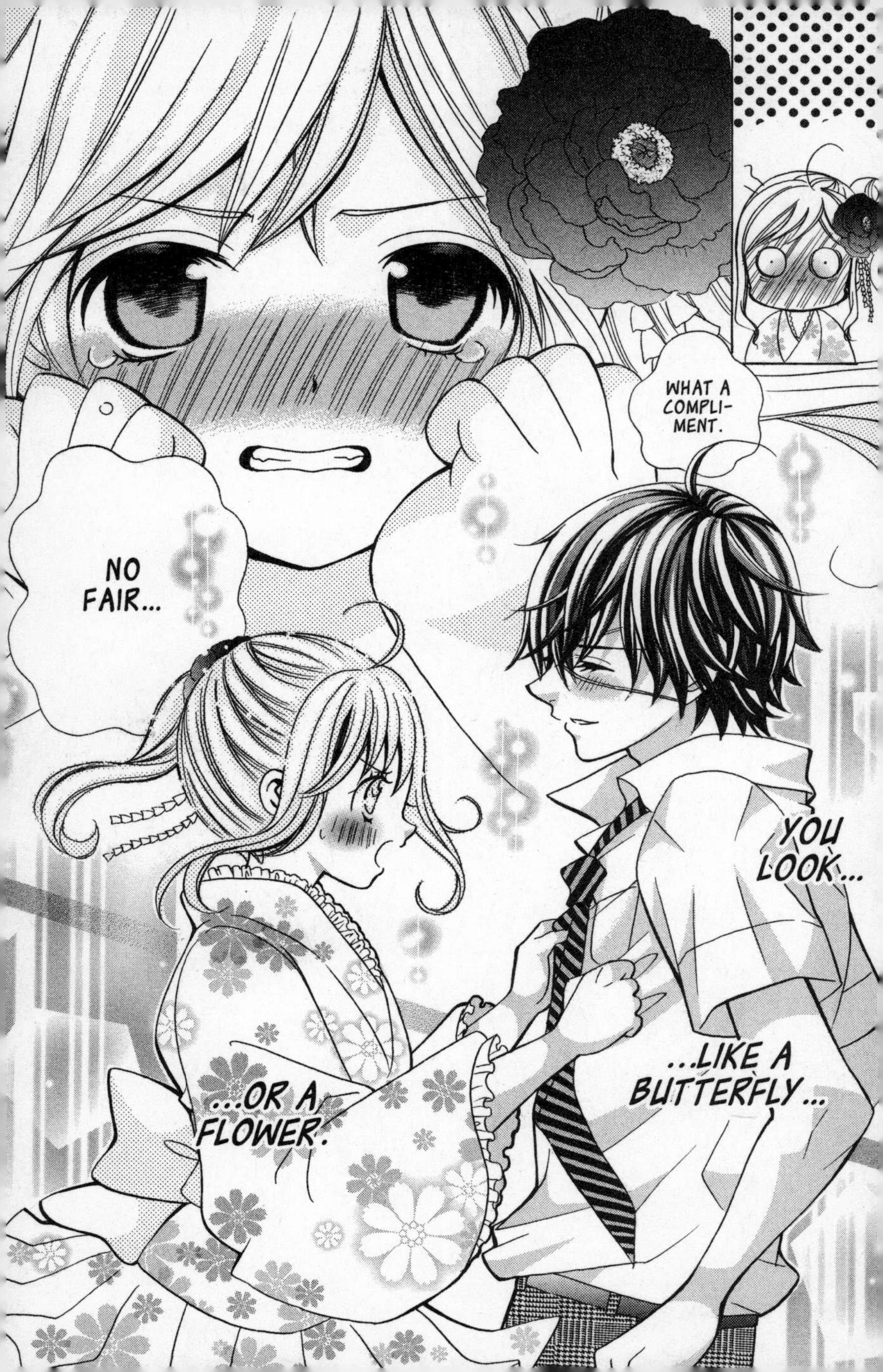
WHAT A COMPLIMENT.
NO FAIR...
YOU LOOK...
...LIKE A BUTTERFLY...
...OR A FLOWER.

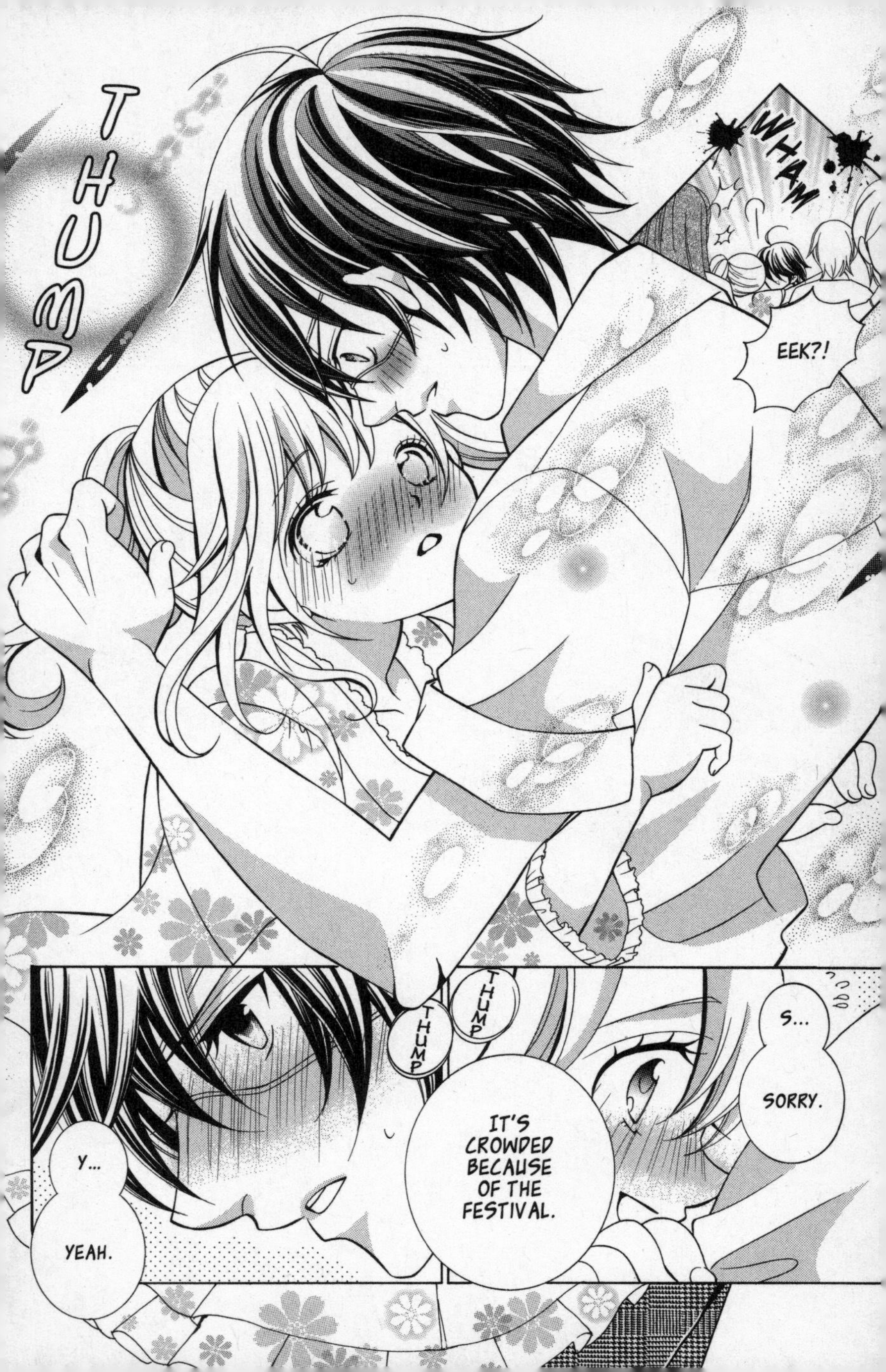
WHAM
EEK?!
THUMP
S...
SORRY.
THUMP
THUMP
IT'S CROWDED BECAUSE OF THE FESTIVAL.
Y...
YEAH.

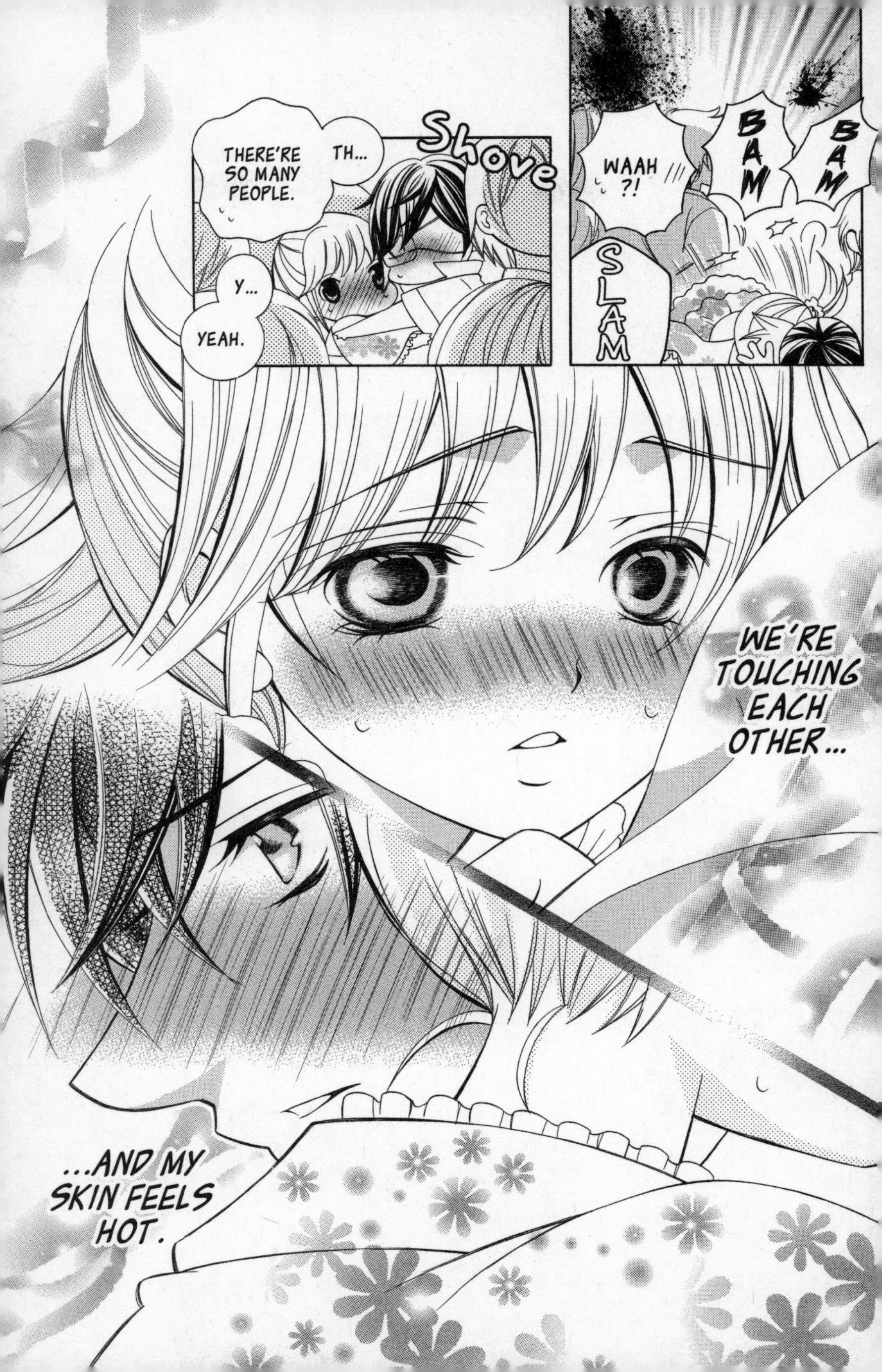

BAM
BAM
WAAH ?!
SLAM
Shove
TH...
THERE'RE SO MANY PEOPLE.
Y...
YEAH.
WE'RE TOUCHING EACH OTHER...
...AND MY SKIN FEELS HOT.

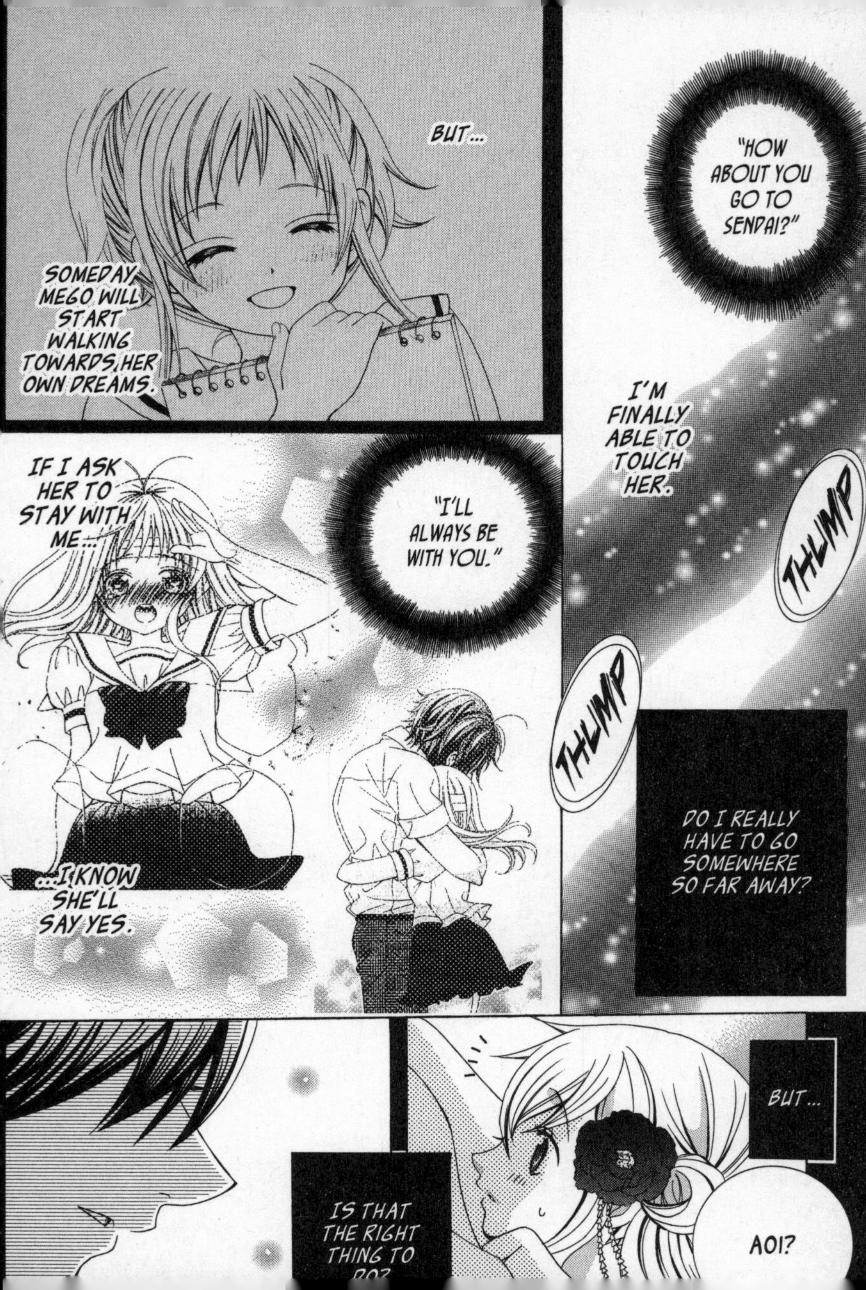
"HOW ABOUT YOU GO TO SENDAI?"
I'M FINALLY ABLE TO TOUCH HER.
THUMP
THUMP
DO I REALLY HAVE TO GO SOMEWHERE SO FAR AWAY?
BUT...
SOMEDAY MEGO WILL START WALKING TOWARDS HER OWN DREAMS.
"I'LL ALWAYS BE WITH YOU."
IF I ASK HER TO STAY WITH ME...
...I KNOW SHE'LL SAY YES.
BUT...
AOI?
IS THAT THE RIGHT THING TO DO?

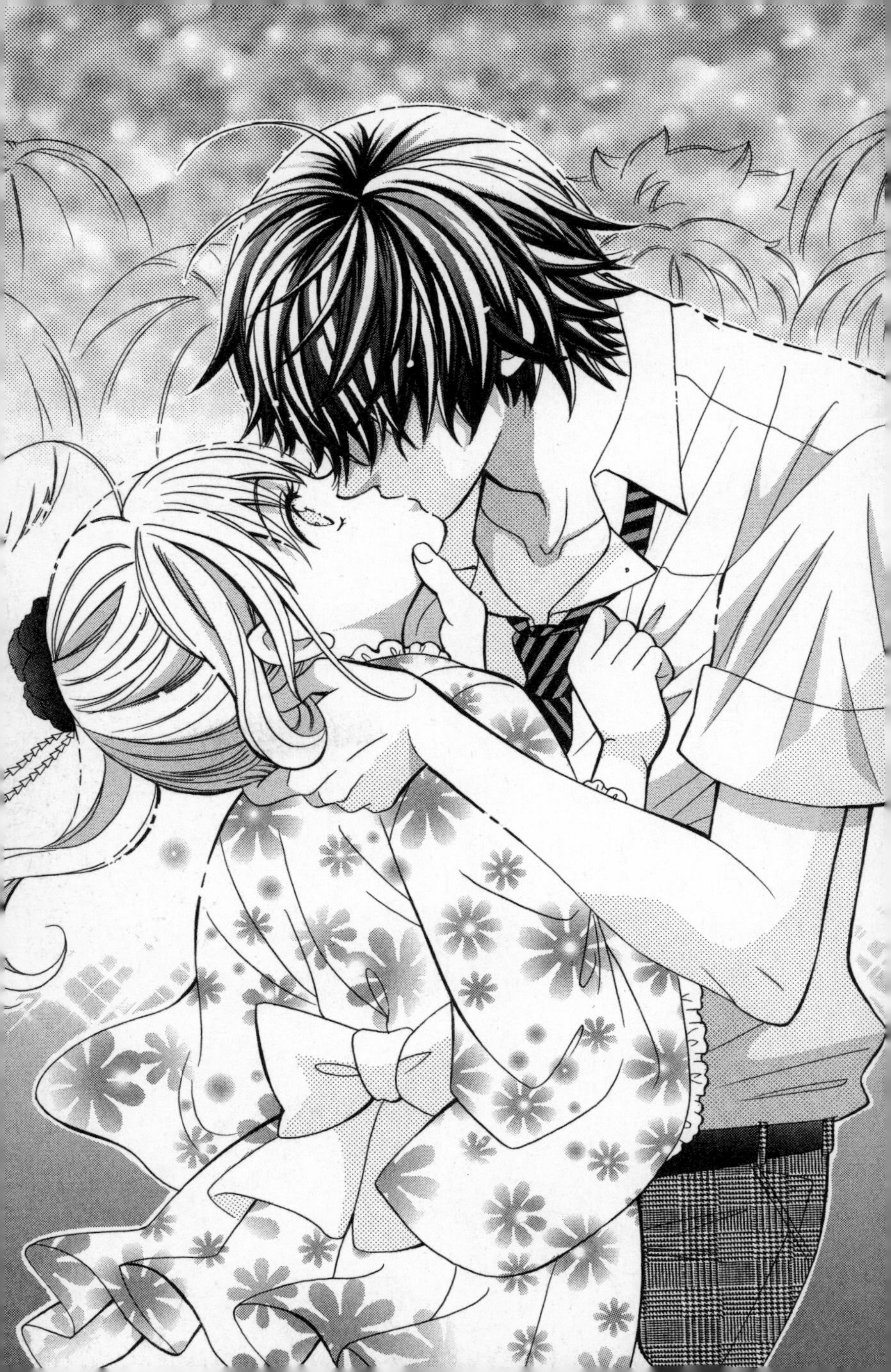

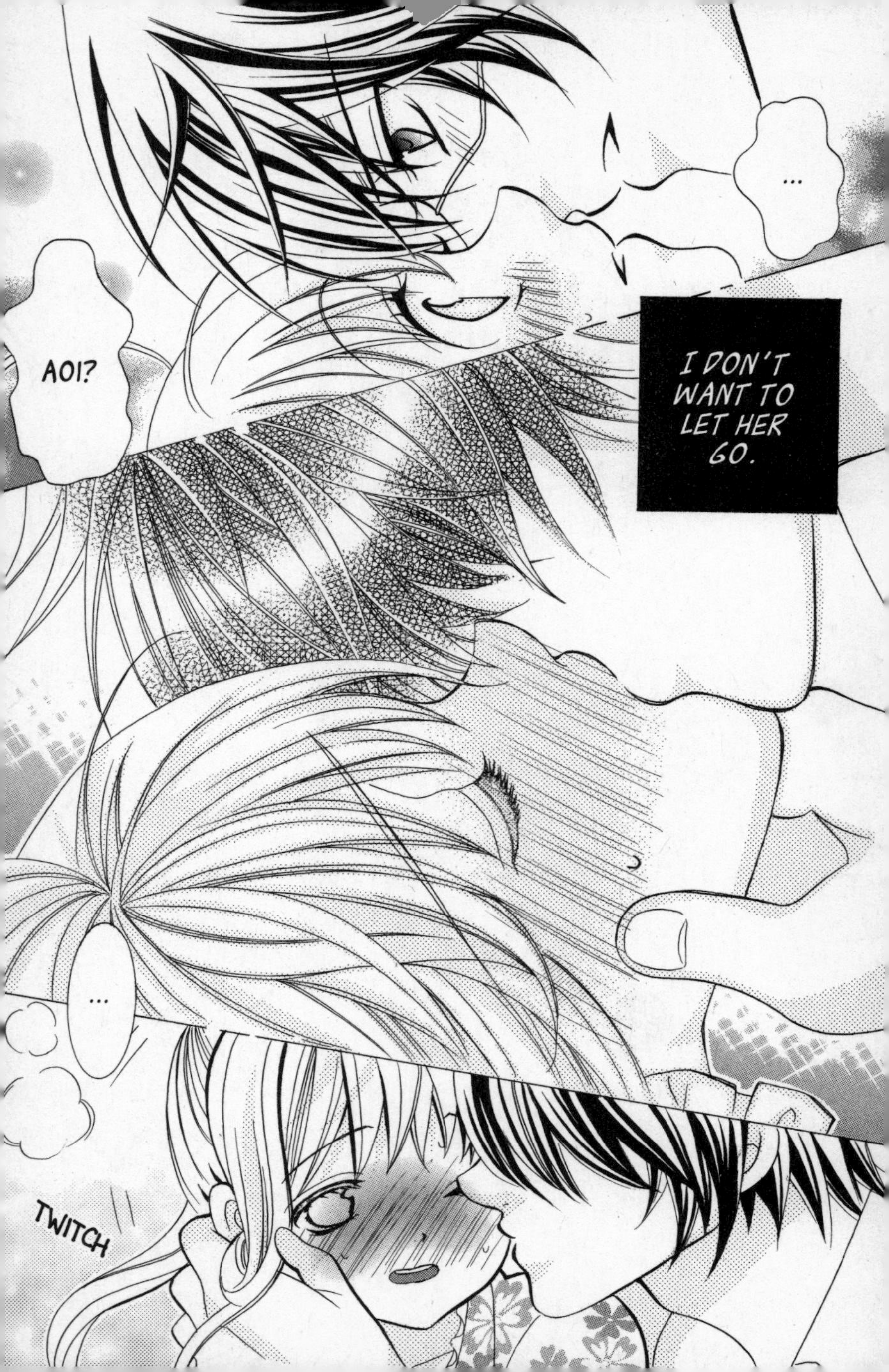
...
I DON'T WANT TO LET HER GO.
AOI?
...
TWITCH

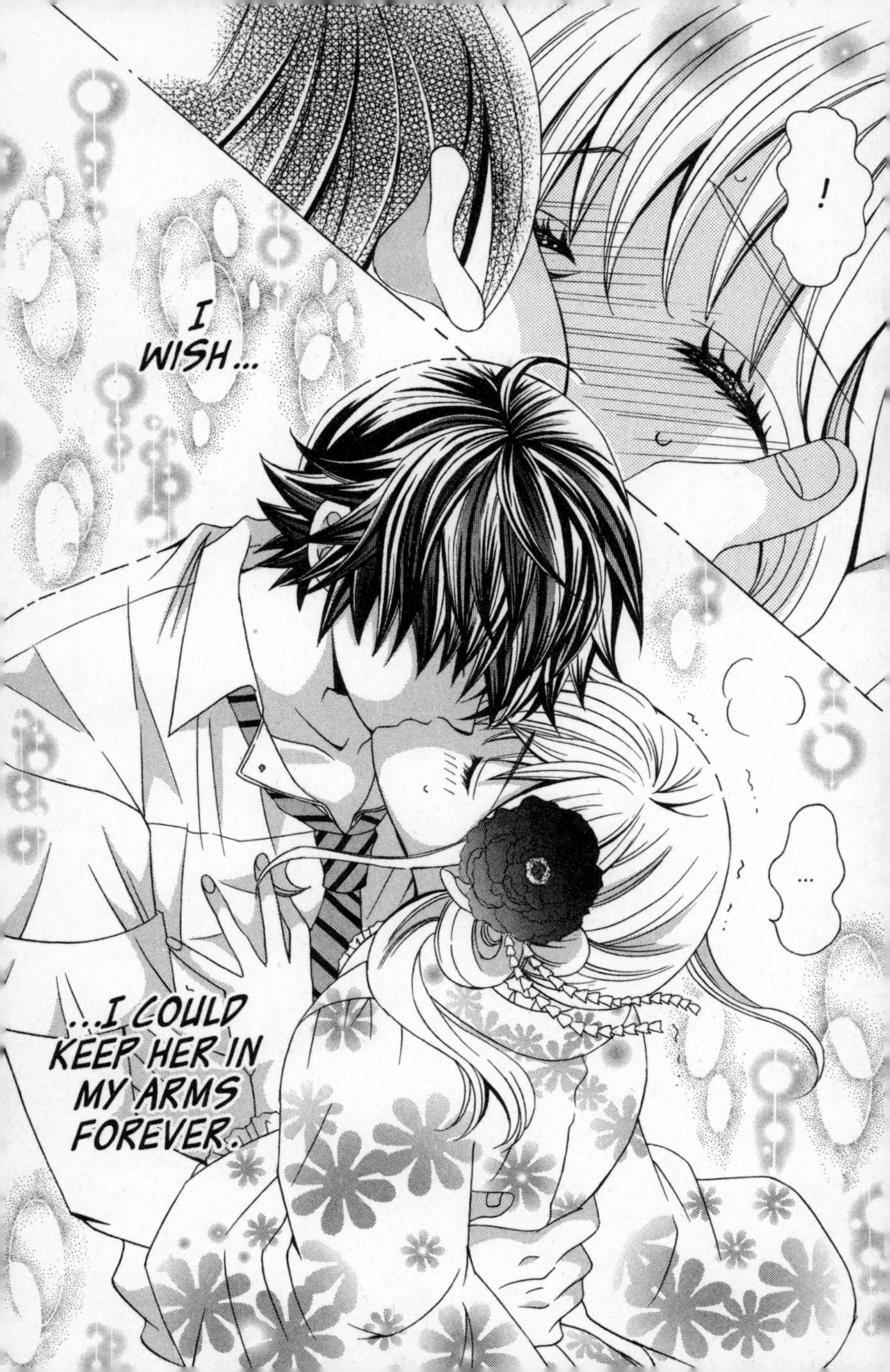
!
I WISH...
...
...I COULD KEEP HER IN MY ARMS FOREVER.

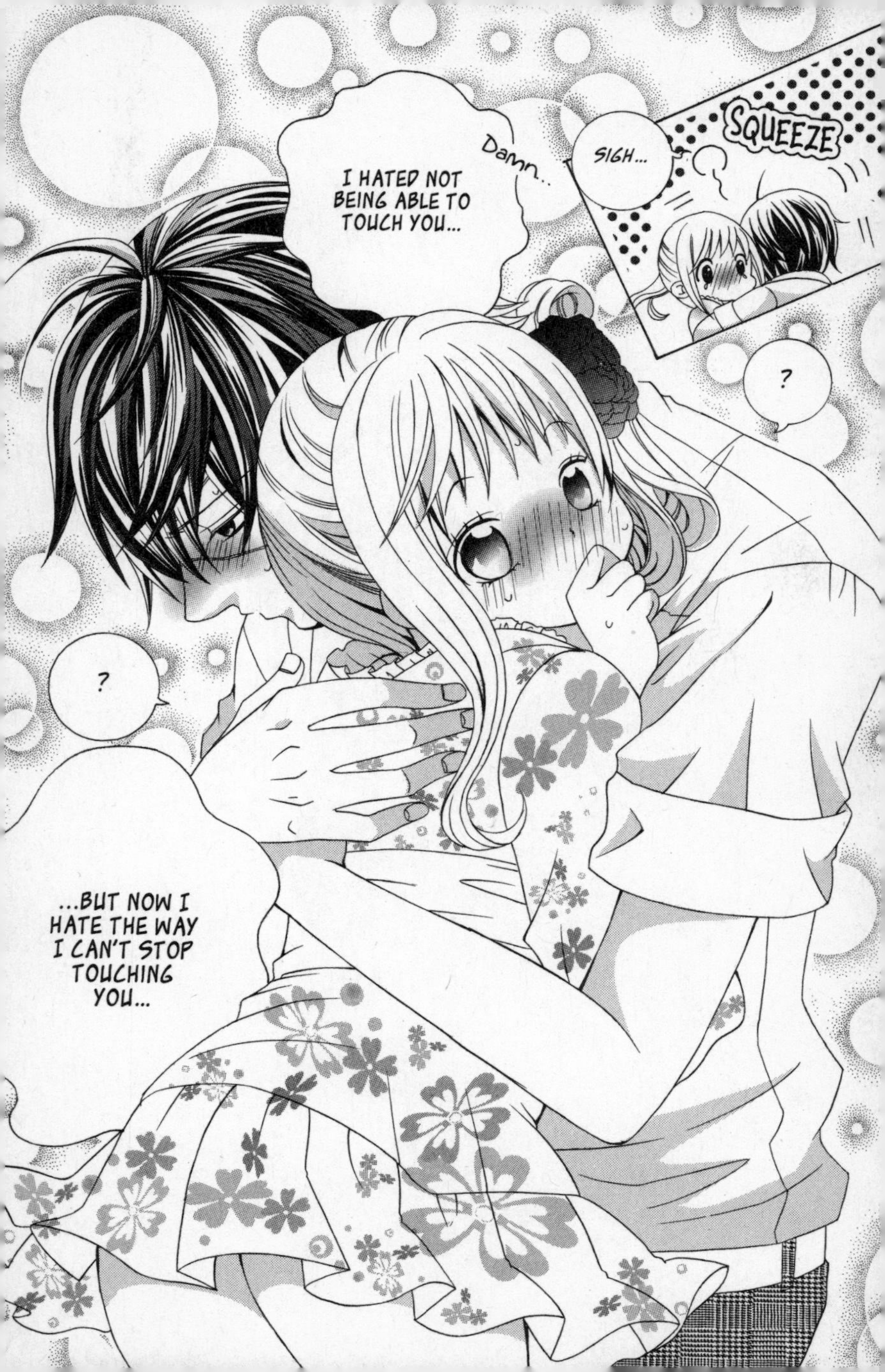
SQUEEZE
SIGH...
Damn...
I HATED NOT BEING ABLE TO TOUCH YOU...
?
?
...BUT NOW I HATE THE WAY I CAN'T STOP TOUCHING YOU...

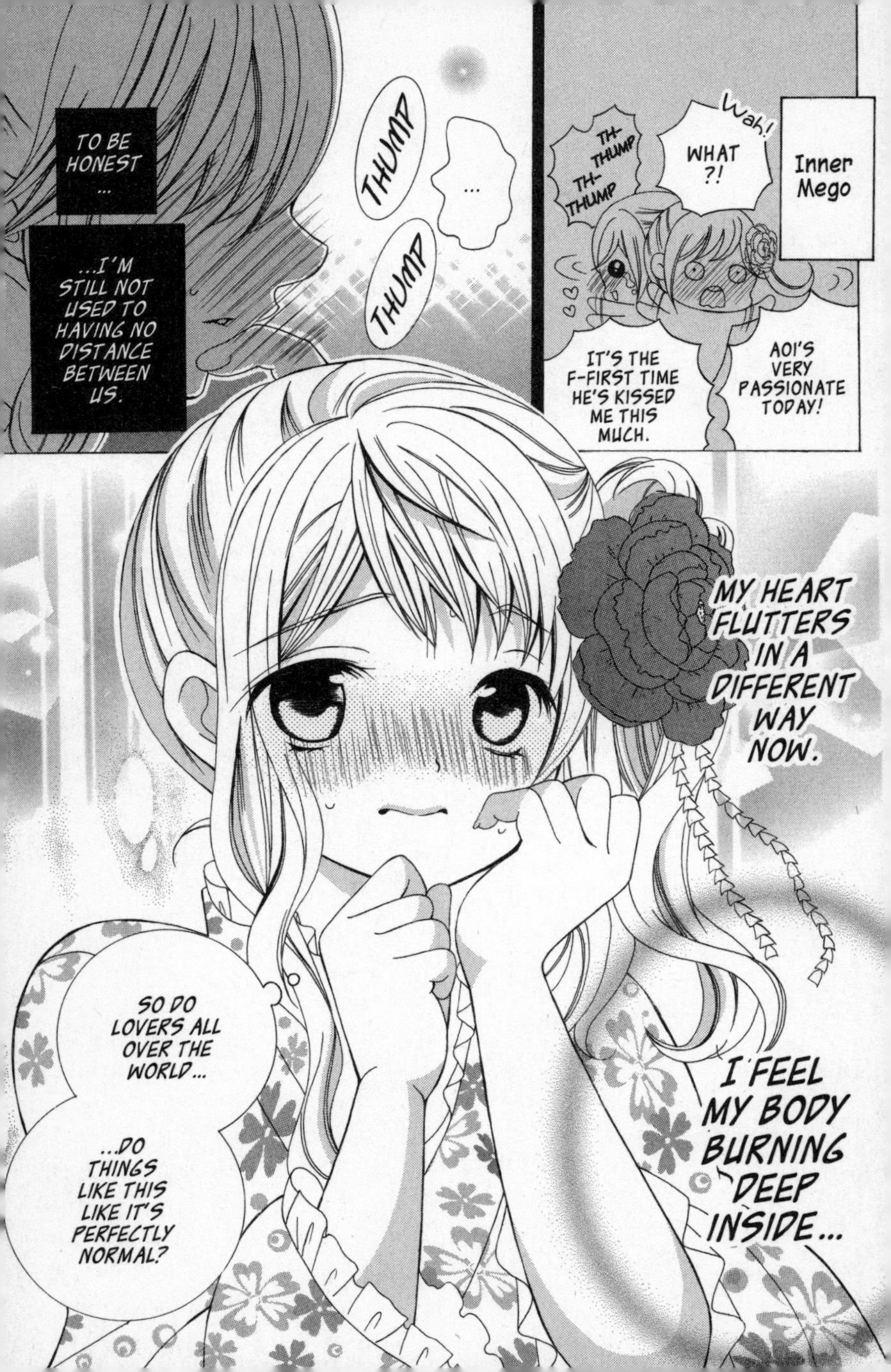
Inner Mego
Wah!
WHAT ?!
TH-THUMP TH-THUMP
AOI'S VERY PASSIONATE TODAY!
IT'S THE F-FIRST TIME HE'S KISSED ME THIS MUCH.
THUMP
...
THUMP
TO BE HONEST ...
...I'M STILL NOT USED TO HAVING NO DISTANCE BETWEEN US.
MY HEART FLUTTERS IN A DIFFERENT WAY NOW.
I FEEL MY BODY BURNING DEEP INSIDE...
SO DO LOVERS ALL OVER THE WORLD...
...DO THINGS LIKE THIS LIKE IT'S PERFECTLY NORMAL?

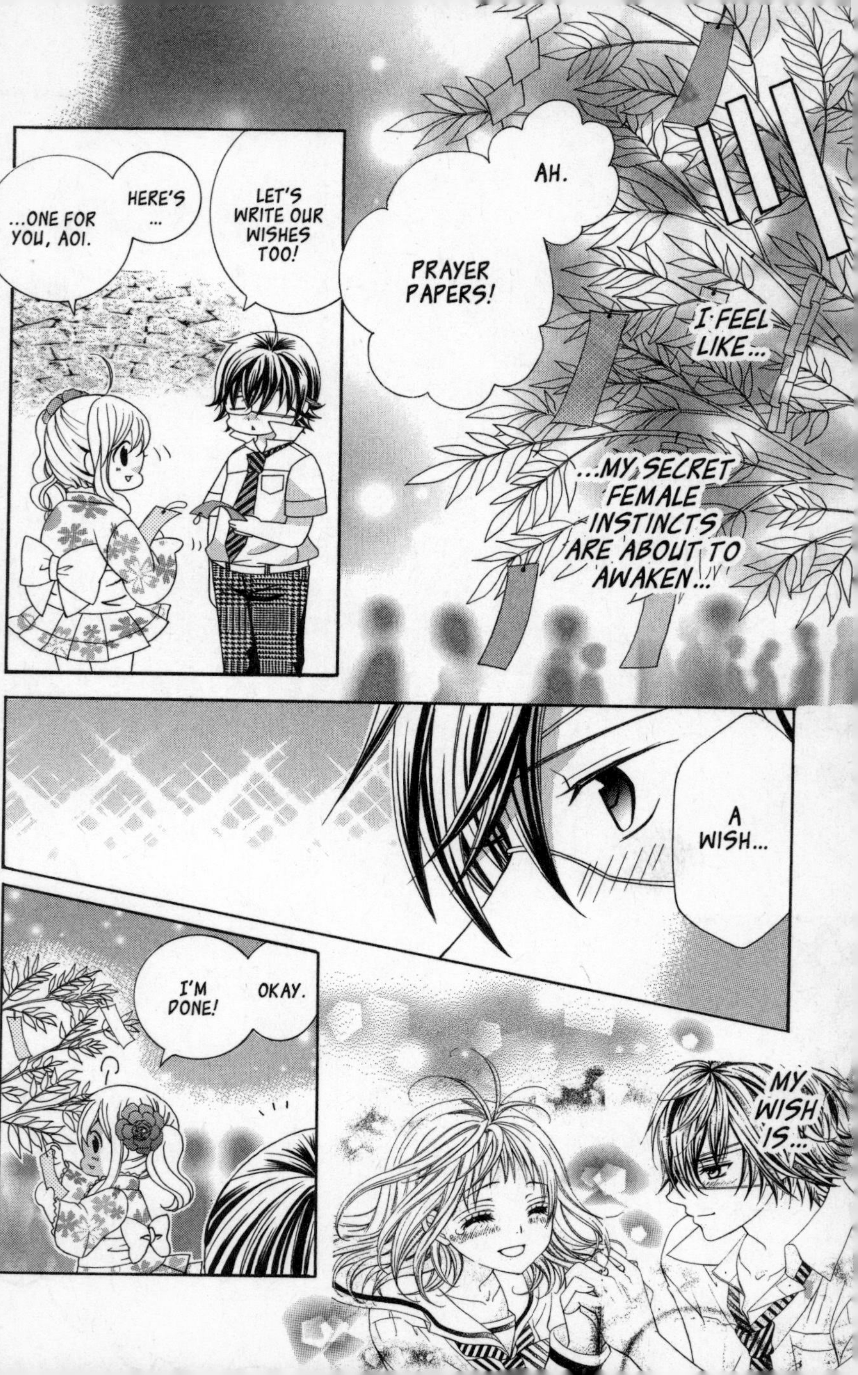

AH. PRAYER PAPERS!
I FEEL LIKE...
...MY SECRET FEMALE INSTINCTS ARE ABOUT TO AWAKEN...
LET'S WRITE OUR WISHES TOO!
HERE'S ... ...ONE FOR YOU, AOI.
A WISH...
MY WISH IS...
I'M DONE! OKAY.

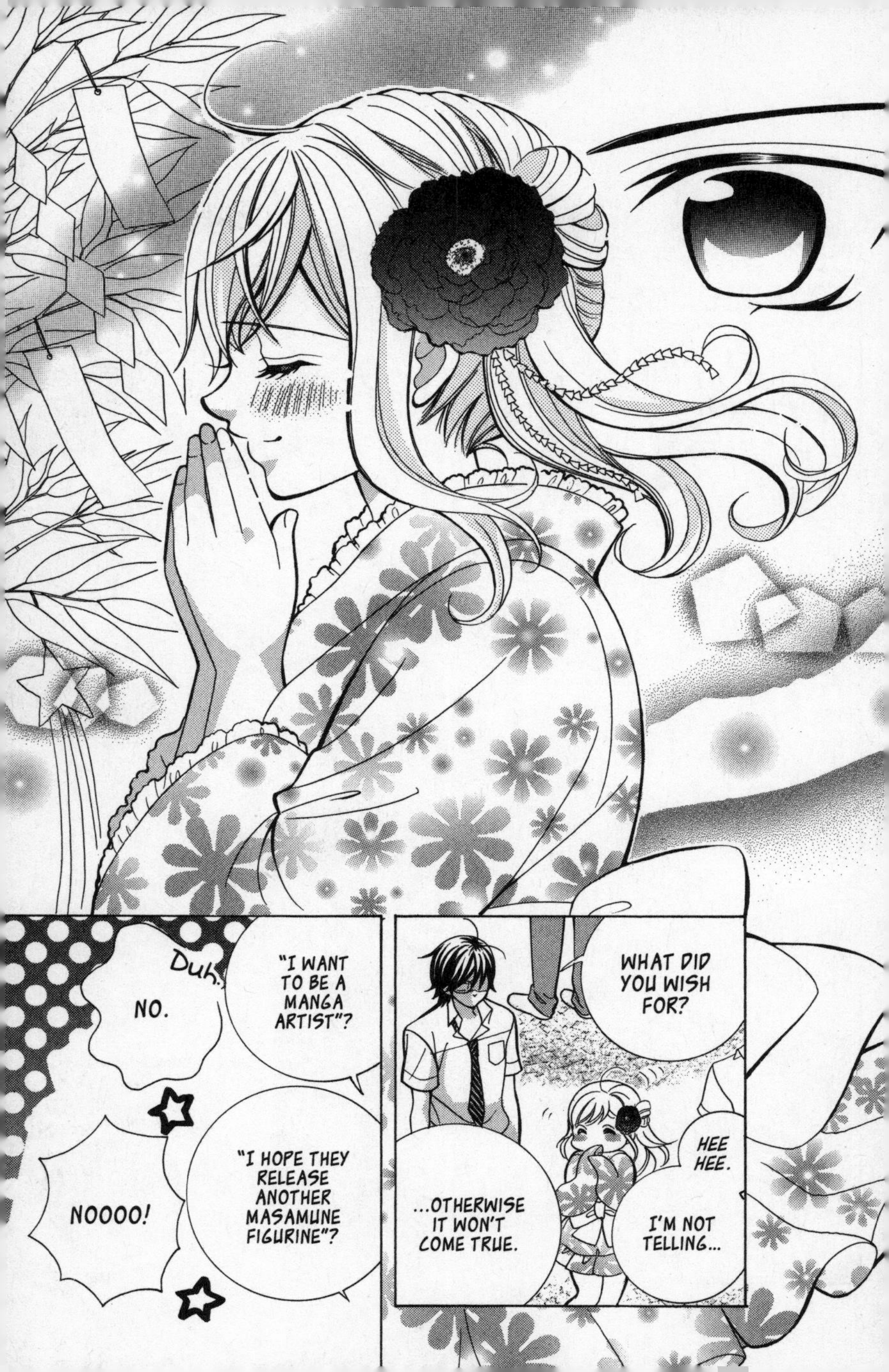
WHAT DID YOU WISH FOR?
HEE HEE.
I'M NOT TELLING...
...OTHERWISE IT WON'T COME TRUE.
"I WANT TO BE A MANGA ARTIST"?
Duh.
NO.
"I HOPE THEY RELEASE ANOTHER MASAMUNE FIGURINE"?
NOOOO!

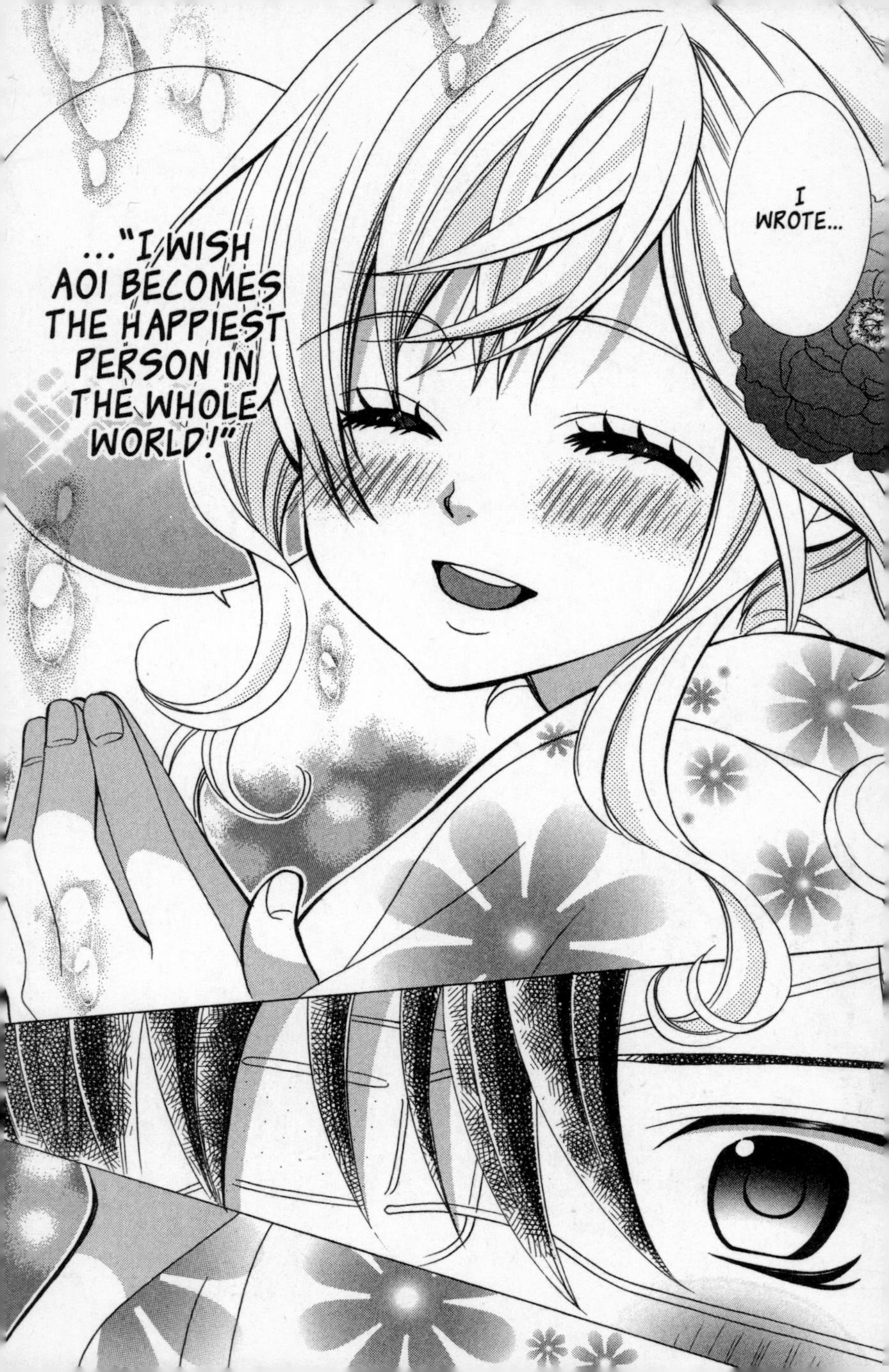
I WROTE...
..."I WISH AOI BECOMES THE HAPPIEST PERSON IN THE WHOLE WORLD!"

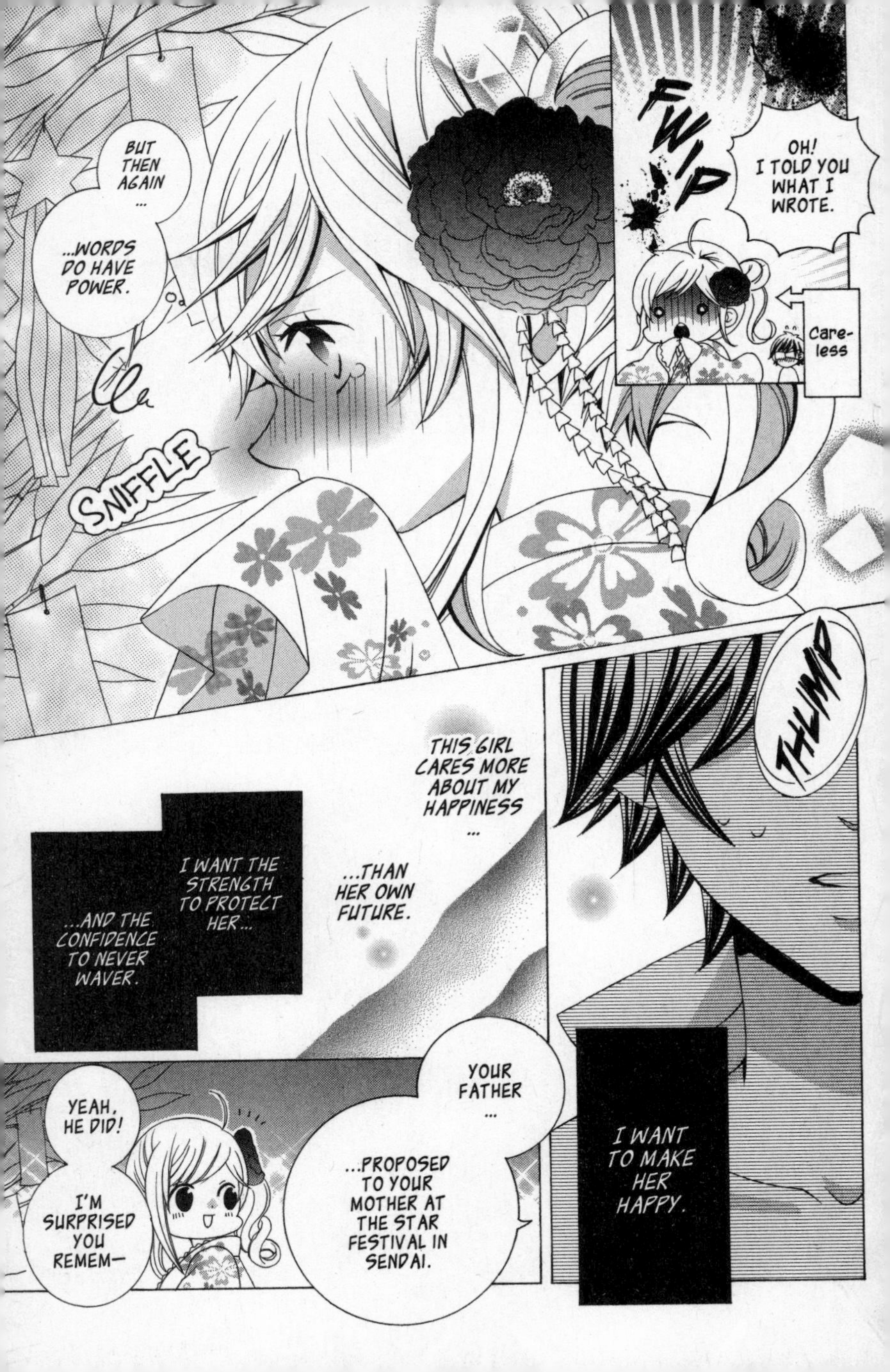
FWIP
OH! I TOLD YOU WHAT I WROTE.
Care-less
BUT THEN AGAIN ...
...WORDS DO HAVE POWER.
SNIFFLE
THUMP
I WANT TO MAKE HER HAPPY.
THIS GIRL CARES MORE ABOUT MY HAPPINESS ...
...THAN HER OWN FUTURE.
I WANT THE STRENGTH TO PROTECT HER...
...AND THE CONFIDENCE TO NEVER WAVER.
YOUR FATHER ...
...PROPOSED TO YOUR MOTHER AT THE STAR FESTIVAL IN SENDAI.
YEAH, HE DID!
I'M SURPRISED YOU REMEM—

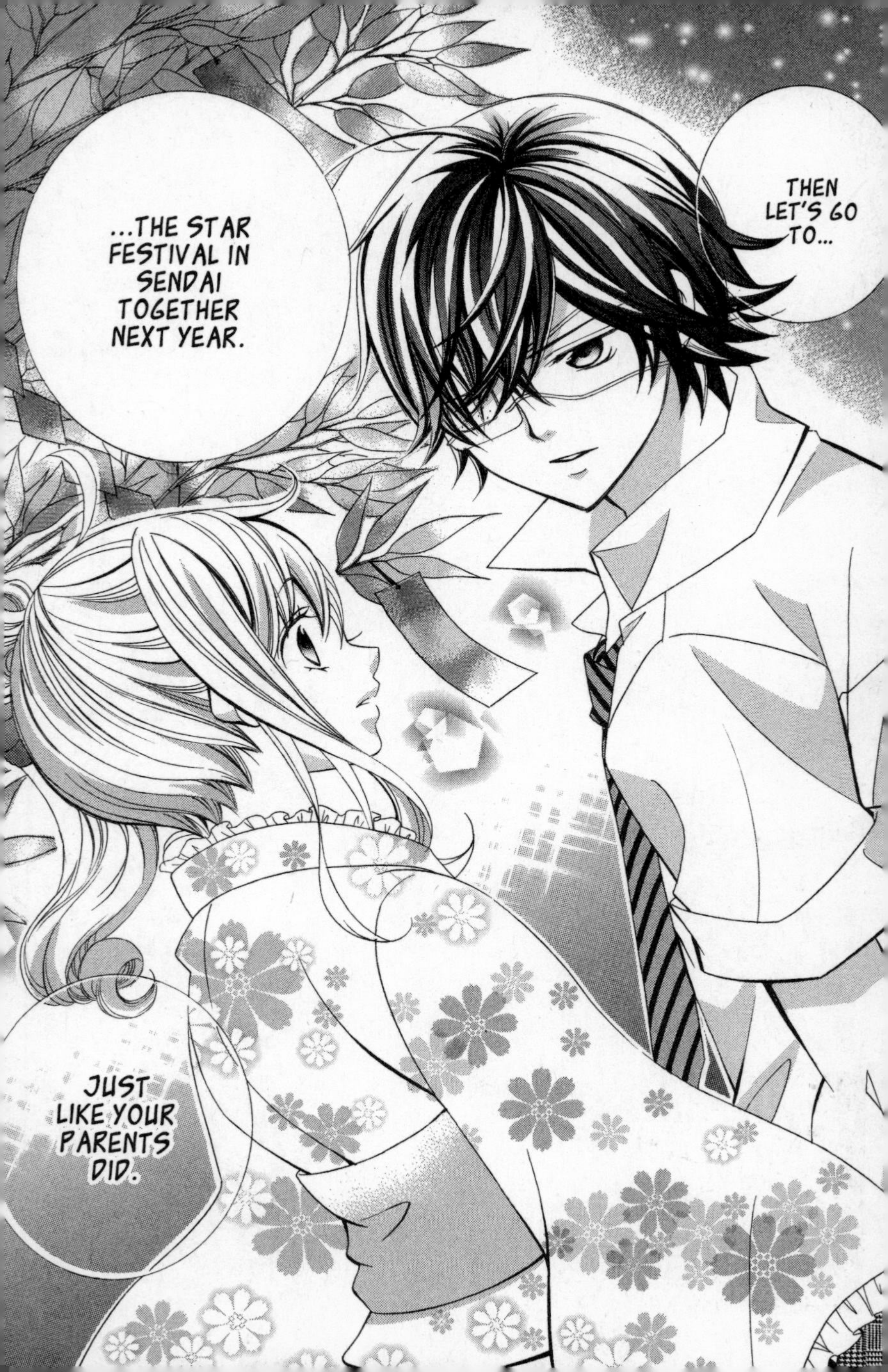
THEN LET'S GO TO...
...THE STAR FESTIVAL IN SENDAI TOGETHER NEXT YEAR.
JUST LIKE YOUR PARENTS DID.

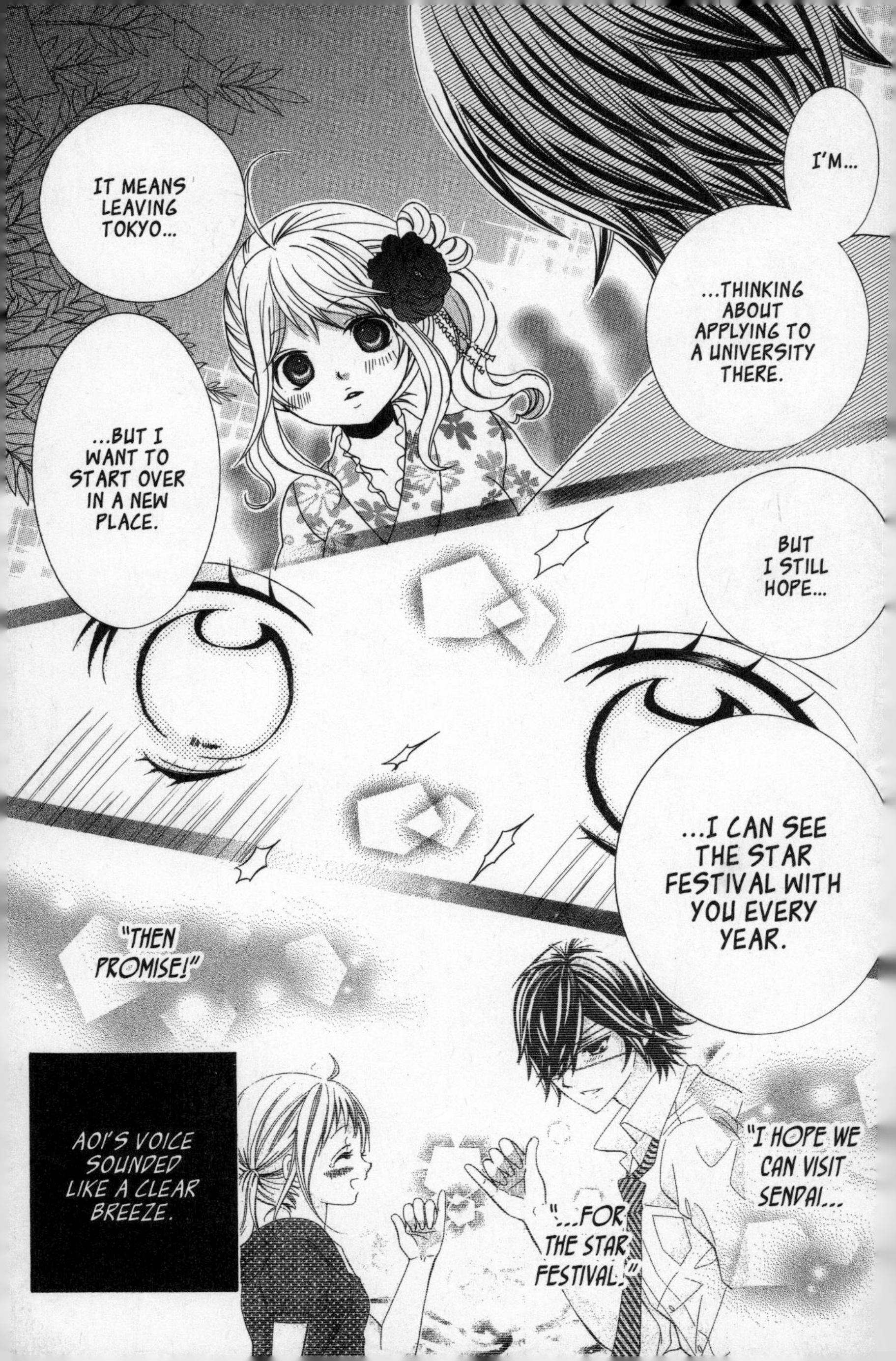
I'M...
...THINKING ABOUT APPLYING TO A UNIVERSITY THERE.
IT MEANS LEAVING TOKYO...
...BUT I WANT TO START OVER IN A NEW PLACE.
BUT I STILL HOPE...
...I CAN SEE THE STAR FESTIVAL WITH YOU EVERY YEAR.
"THEN PROMISE!"
"I HOPE WE CAN VISIT SENDAI...
"...FOR THE STAR FESTIVAL."
AOI'S VOICE SOUNDED LIKE A CLEAR BREEZE.

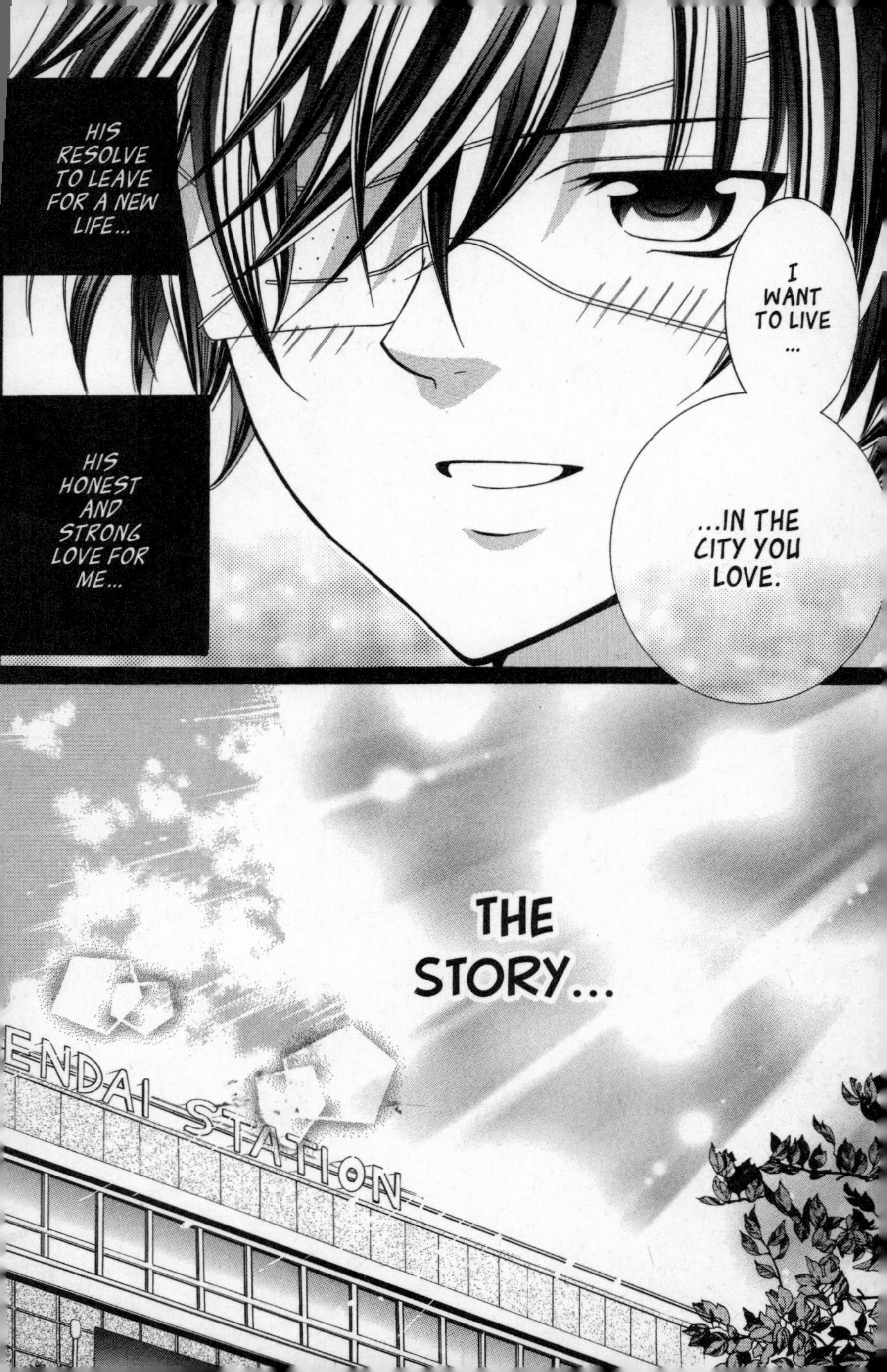
I WANT TO LIVE ...
...IN THE CITY YOU LOVE.
HIS RESOLVE TO LEAVE FOR A NEW LIFE...
HIS HONEST AND STRONG LOVE FOR ME...
THE STORY...
ENDAI STATION

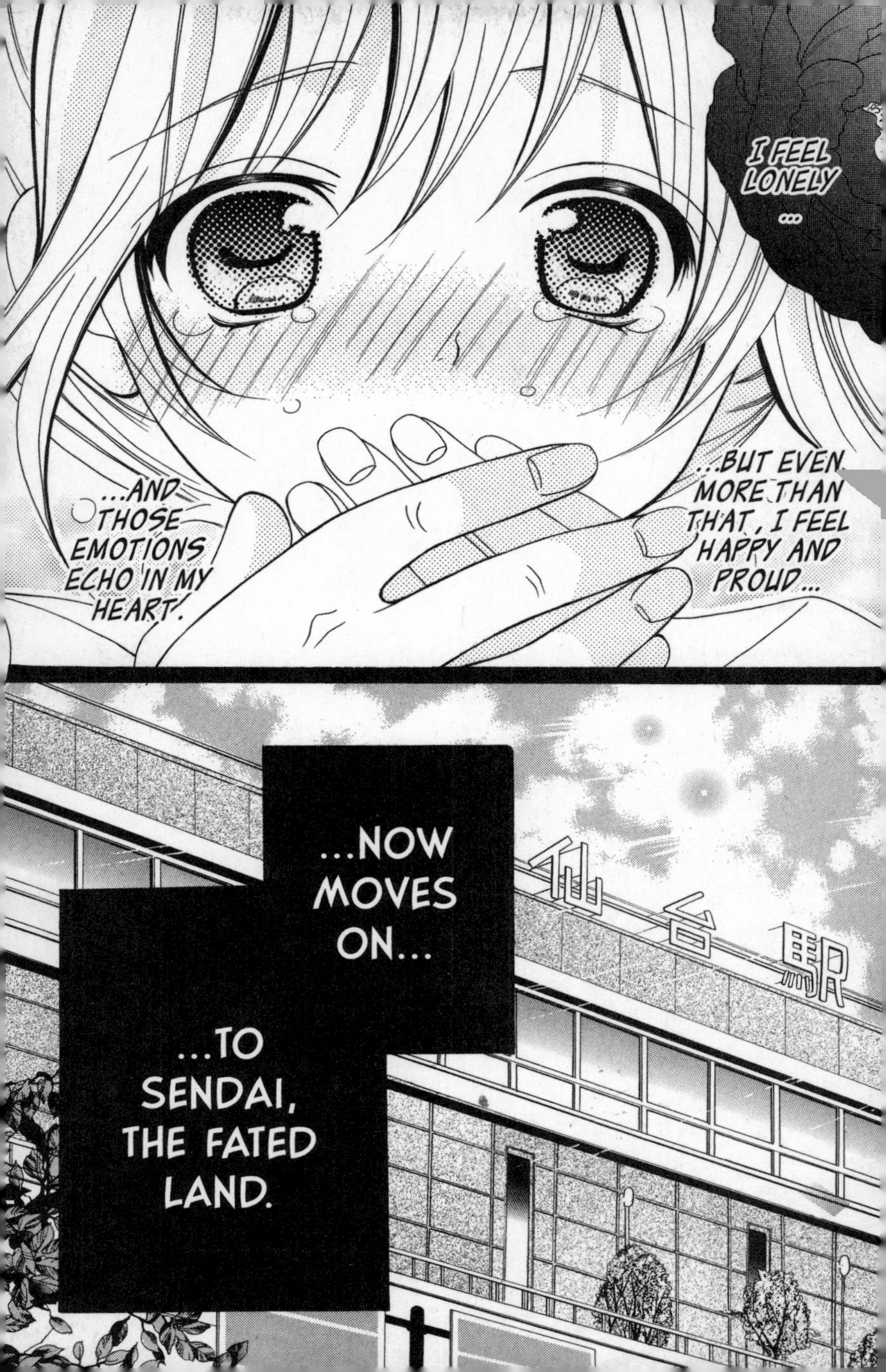
I FEEL LONELY ...
...BUT EVEN MORE THAN THAT, I FEEL HAPPY AND PROUD...
...AND THOSE EMOTIONS ECHO IN MY HEART.
...NOW MOVES ON...
...TO SENDAI, THE FATED LAND.
仙台駅

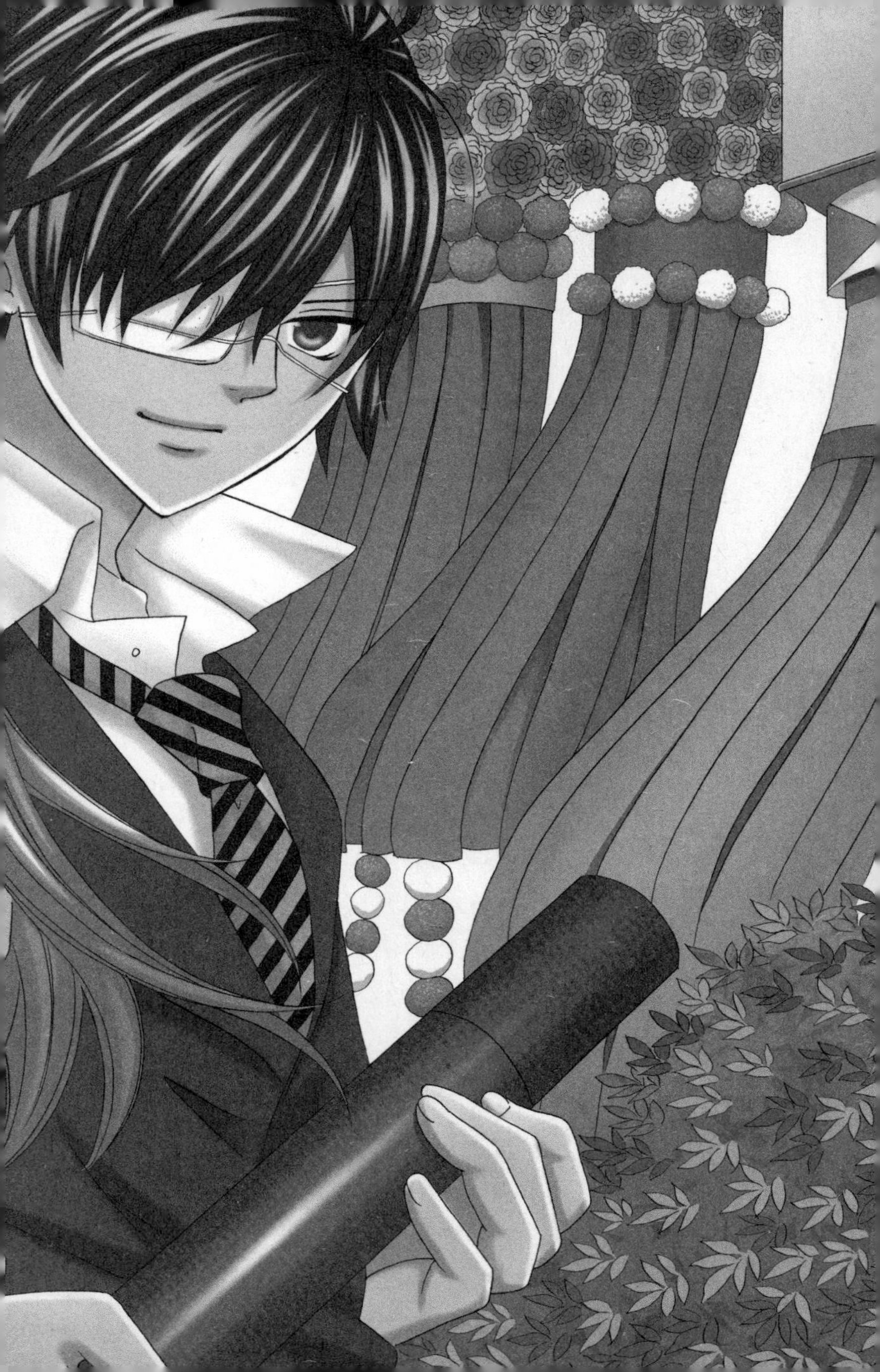

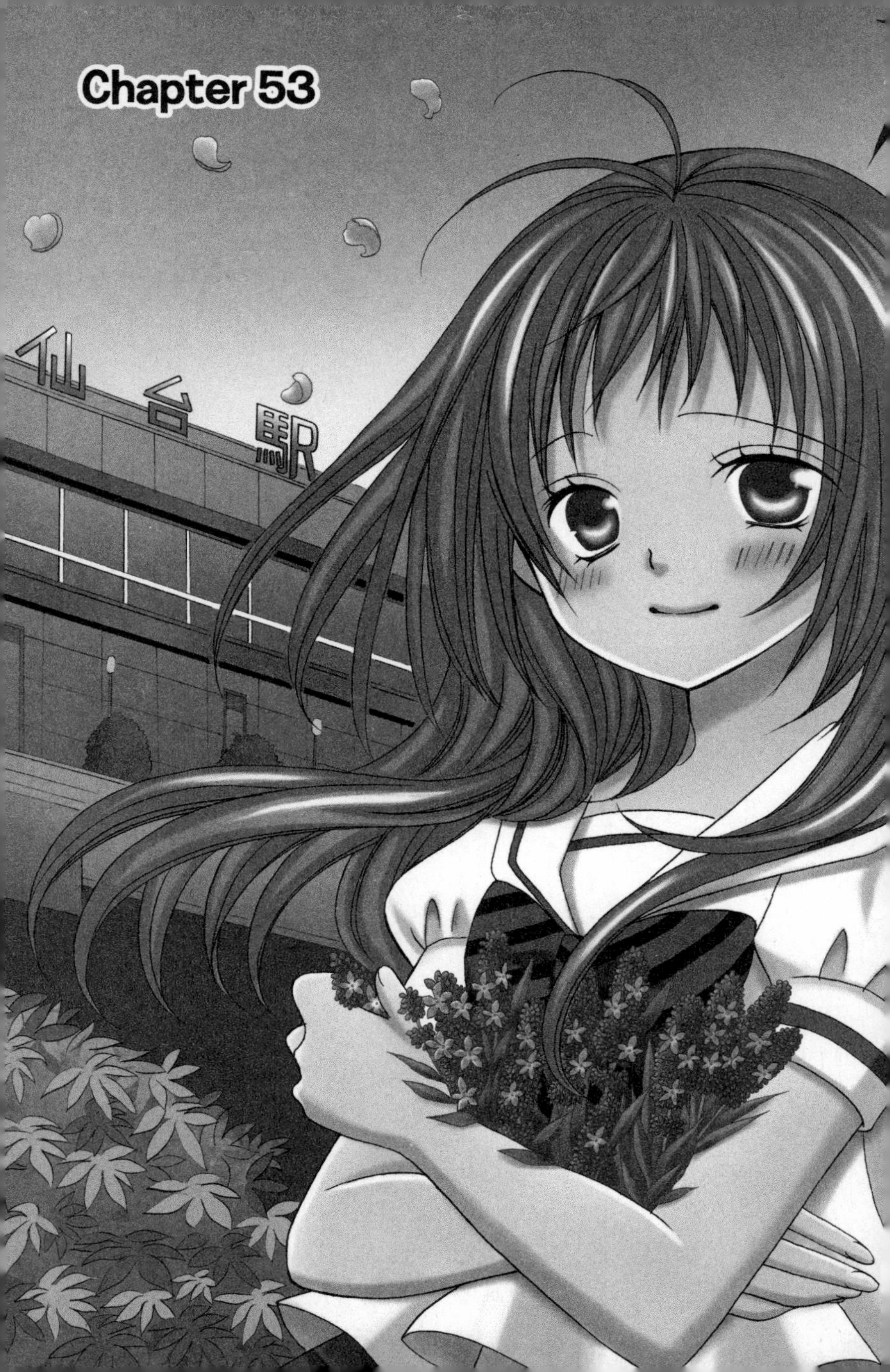
Chapter 53
仙台駅

So Cute It Hurts !! (⁊-ᴗ)

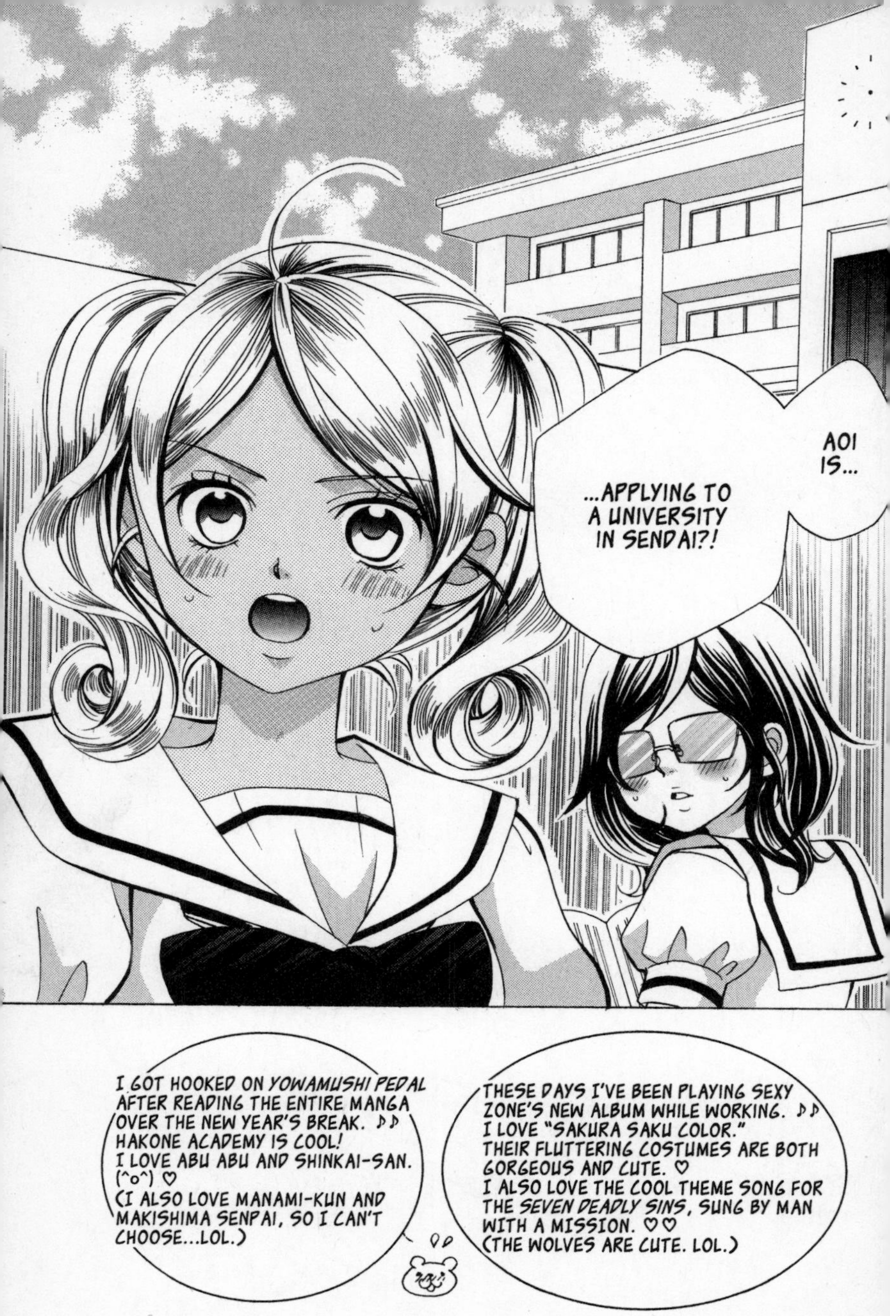
AOI IS...
...APPLYING TO A UNIVERSITY IN SENDAI?!

THESE DAYS I'VE BEEN PLAYING SEXY ZONE'S NEW ALBUM WHILE WORKING. ♪♪
I LOVE "SAKURA SAKU COLOR."
THEIR FLUTTERING COSTUMES ARE BOTH GORGEOUS AND CUTE. ♡
I ALSO LOVE THE COOL THEME SONG FOR THE *SEVEN DEADLY SINS*, SUNG BY MAN WITH A MISSION. ♡♡
(THE WOLVES ARE CUTE. LOL.)

I GOT HOOKED ON *YOWAMUSHI PEDAL* AFTER READING THE ENTIRE MANGA OVER THE NEW YEAR'S BREAK. ♪♪
HAKONE ACADEMY IS COOL!
I LOVE ABU ABU AND SHINKAI-SAN. (^o^) ♡
(I ALSO LOVE MANAMI-KUN AND MAKISHIMA SENPAI, SO I CAN'T CHOOSE...LOL.)

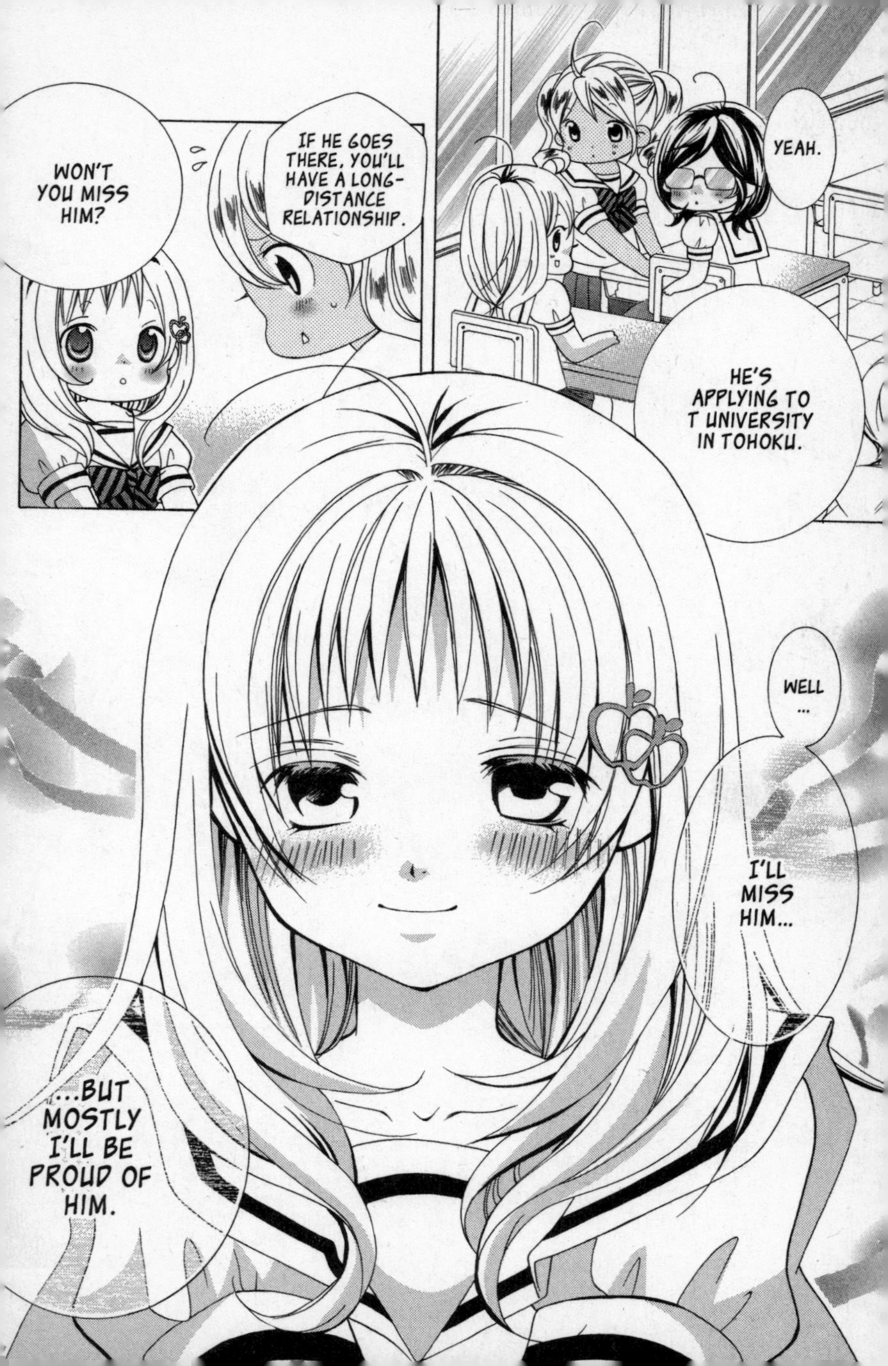
YEAH.
HE'S APPLYING TO T UNIVERSITY IN TOHOKU.
IF HE GOES THERE, YOU'LL HAVE A LONG-DISTANCE RELATIONSHIP.
WON'T YOU MISS HIM?
WELL ...
I'LL MISS HIM...
...BUT MOSTLY I'LL BE PROUD OF HIM.

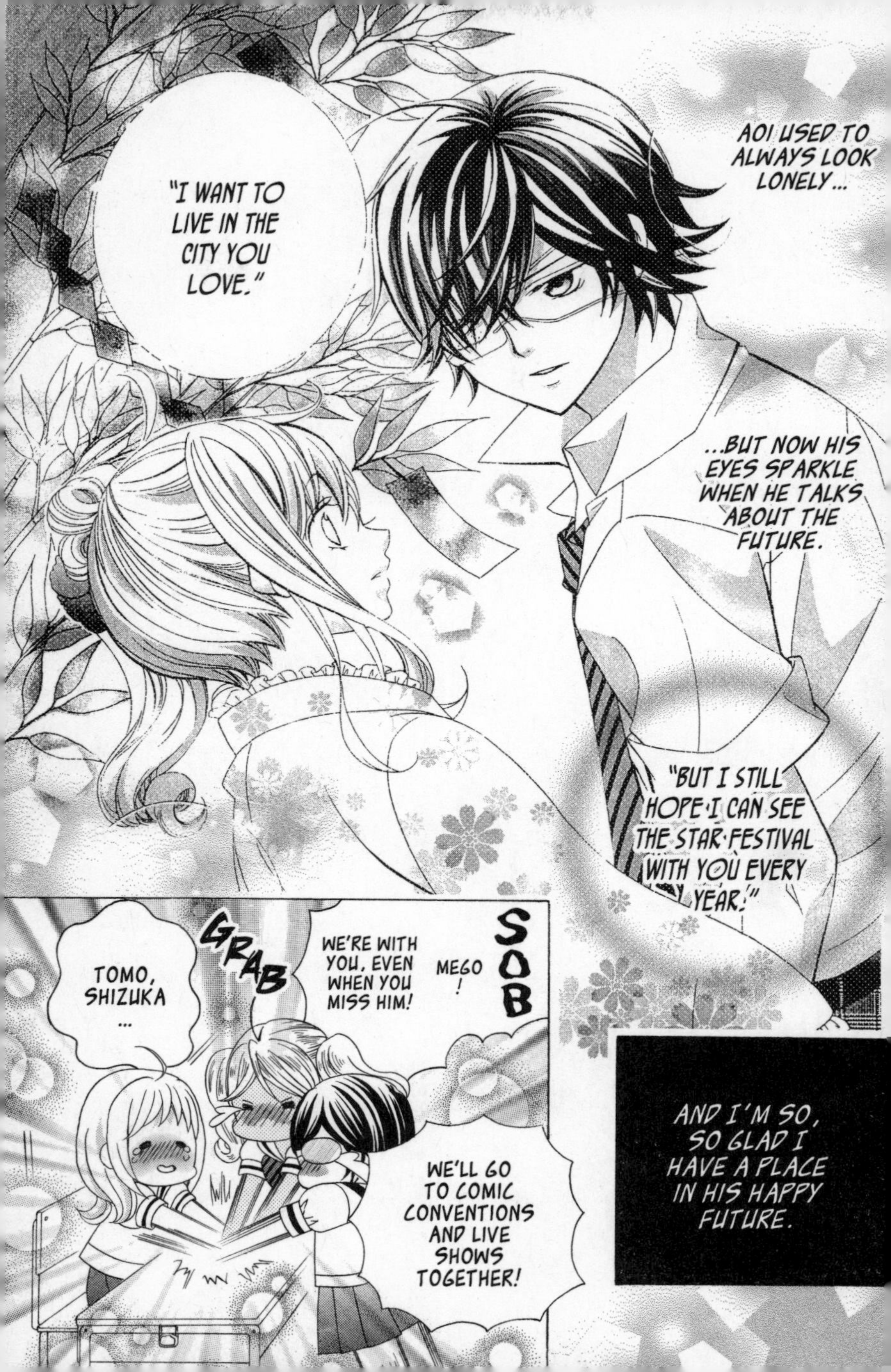
AOI USED TO ALWAYS LOOK LONELY...
"I WANT TO LIVE IN THE CITY YOU LOVE."
...BUT NOW HIS EYES SPARKLE WHEN HE TALKS ABOUT THE FUTURE.
"BUT I STILL HOPE I CAN SEE THE STAR FESTIVAL WITH YOU EVERY YEAR."
AND I'M SO, SO GLAD I HAVE A PLACE IN HIS HAPPY FUTURE.
SOB
MEGO!
WE'RE WITH YOU, EVEN WHEN YOU MISS HIM!
GRAB
TOMO, SHIZUKA...
WE'LL GO TO COMIC CONVENTIONS AND LIVE SHOWS TOGETHER!

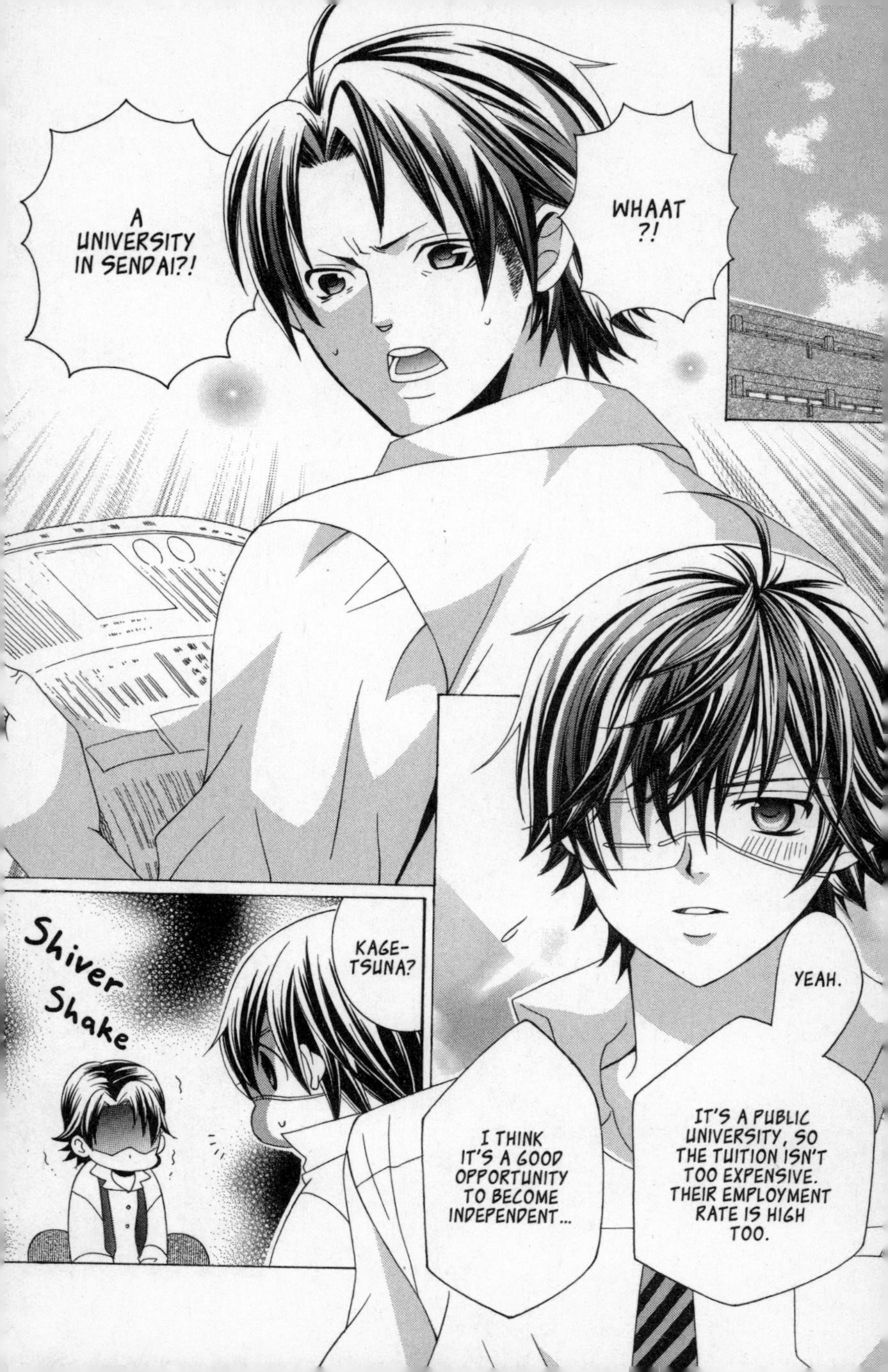
WHAAT ?!
A UNIVERSITY IN SENDAI?!
YEAH.
IT'S A PUBLIC UNIVERSITY, SO THE TUITION ISN'T TOO EXPENSIVE. THEIR EMPLOYMENT RATE IS HIGH TOO.
I THINK IT'S A GOOD OPPORTUNITY TO BECOME INDEPENDENT...
KAGE-TSUNA?
Shiver Shake

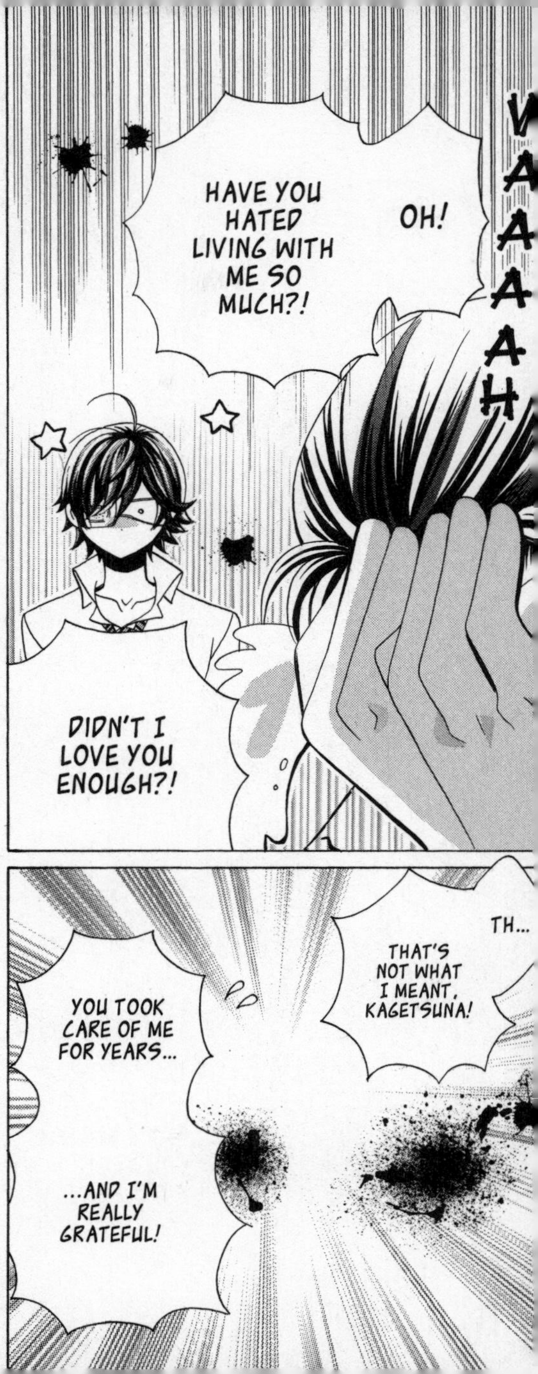
WAAAAH
OH!
HAVE YOU HATED LIVING WITH ME SO MUCH?!
DIDN'T I LOVE YOU ENOUGH?!
TH...
THAT'S NOT WHAT I MEANT, KAGETSUNA!
YOU TOOK CARE OF ME FOR YEARS...
...AND I'M REALLY GRATEFUL!

SPECIAL THANKS

Yuka Ito-sama,
Rieko Hirai-sama,
Kayoko Takahashi-sama,
Kawasaki-sama,
Nagisa Sato Sensei.

Rei Nanase Sensei,
Arisu Fujishiro Sensei,
Mumi Mimura Sensei,
Masayo Nagata-sama,
Naochan-sama,
Asuka Sakura Sensei
and many others.

Bookstore Dan Kinshicho Branch, Kinokuniya Shinjuku Branch, LIBRO Ikebukuro Branch, Kinokuniya Hankyu 32-bangai Branch.

Sendai Hachimonjiya Bookstore, Books HOSHINO Kintetsu Pass'e Branch, Asahiya Tennoji MiO Branch, Kurashiki Kikuya Bookstore.

Salesperson:
Mizusawa-sama

Previous salesperson:
Honma-sama

Previous editor:
Nakata-sama

Current editor:
Shoji-sama

I also sincerely express my gratitude to everyone who picked up this volume.

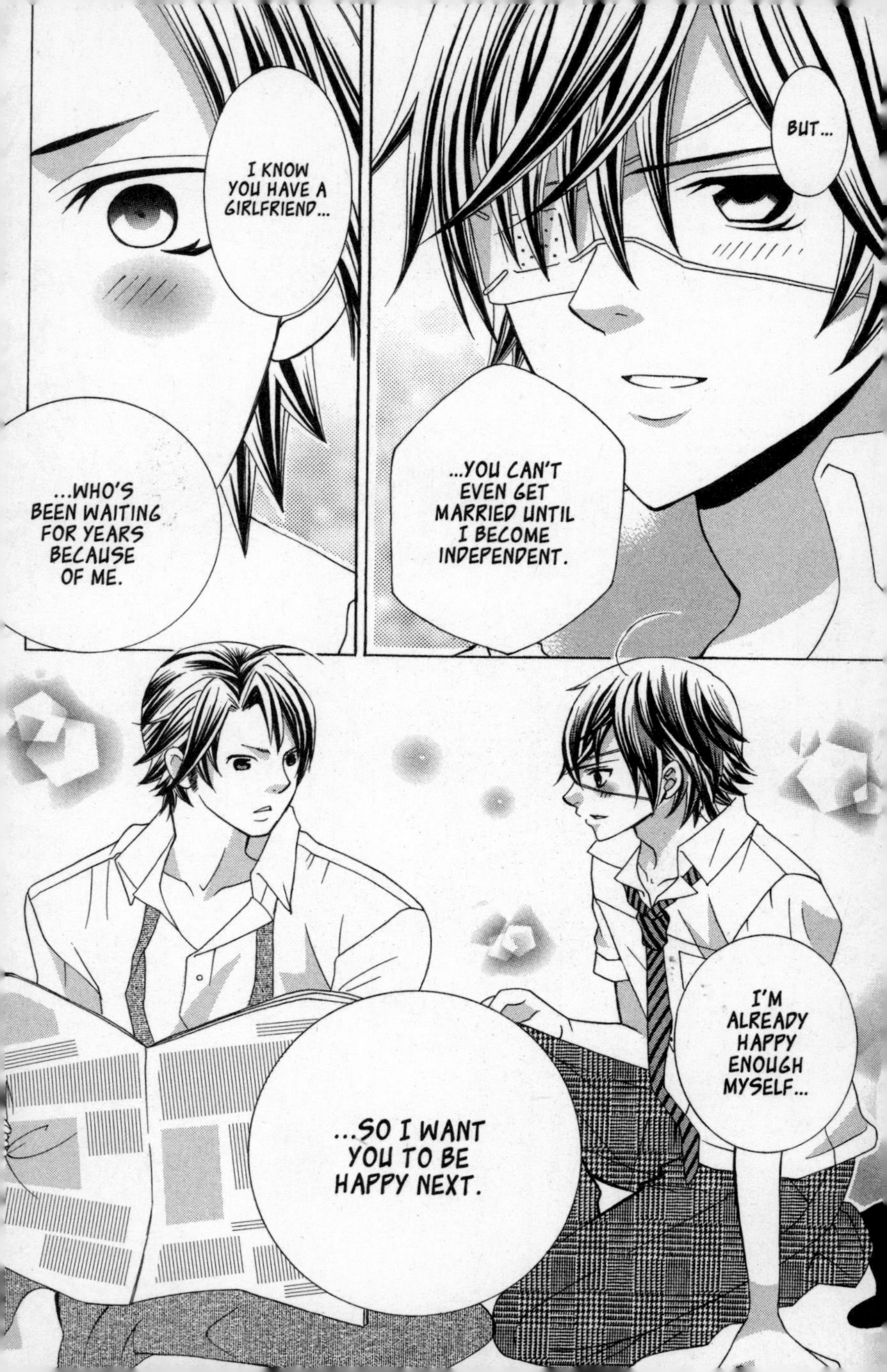
I KNOW YOU HAVE A GIRLFRIEND...
...WHO'S BEEN WAITING FOR YEARS BECAUSE OF ME.
BUT...
...YOU CAN'T EVEN GET MARRIED UNTIL I BECOME INDEPENDENT.
I'M ALREADY HAPPY ENOUGH MYSELF...
...SO I WANT YOU TO BE HAPPY NEXT.

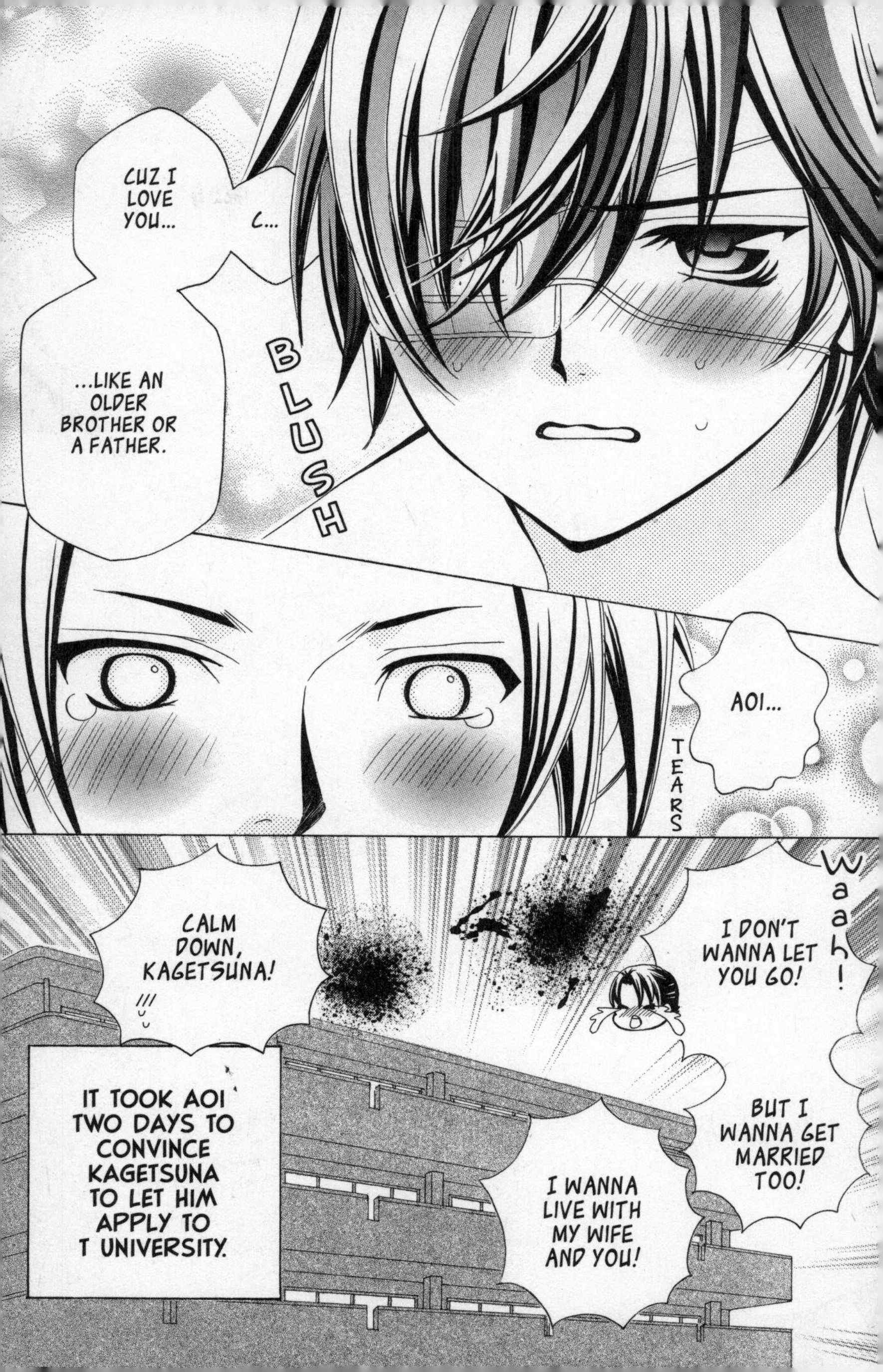
C...
CUZ I LOVE YOU...
...LIKE AN OLDER BROTHER OR A FATHER.
BLUSH
AOI...
TEARS
Waah!
I DON'T WANNA LET YOU GO!
BUT I WANNA GET MARRIED TOO!
I WANNA LIVE WITH MY WIFE AND YOU!
CALM DOWN, KAGETSUNA!
IT TOOK AOI TWO DAYS TO CONVINCE KAGETSUNA TO LET HIM APPLY TO T UNIVERSITY.

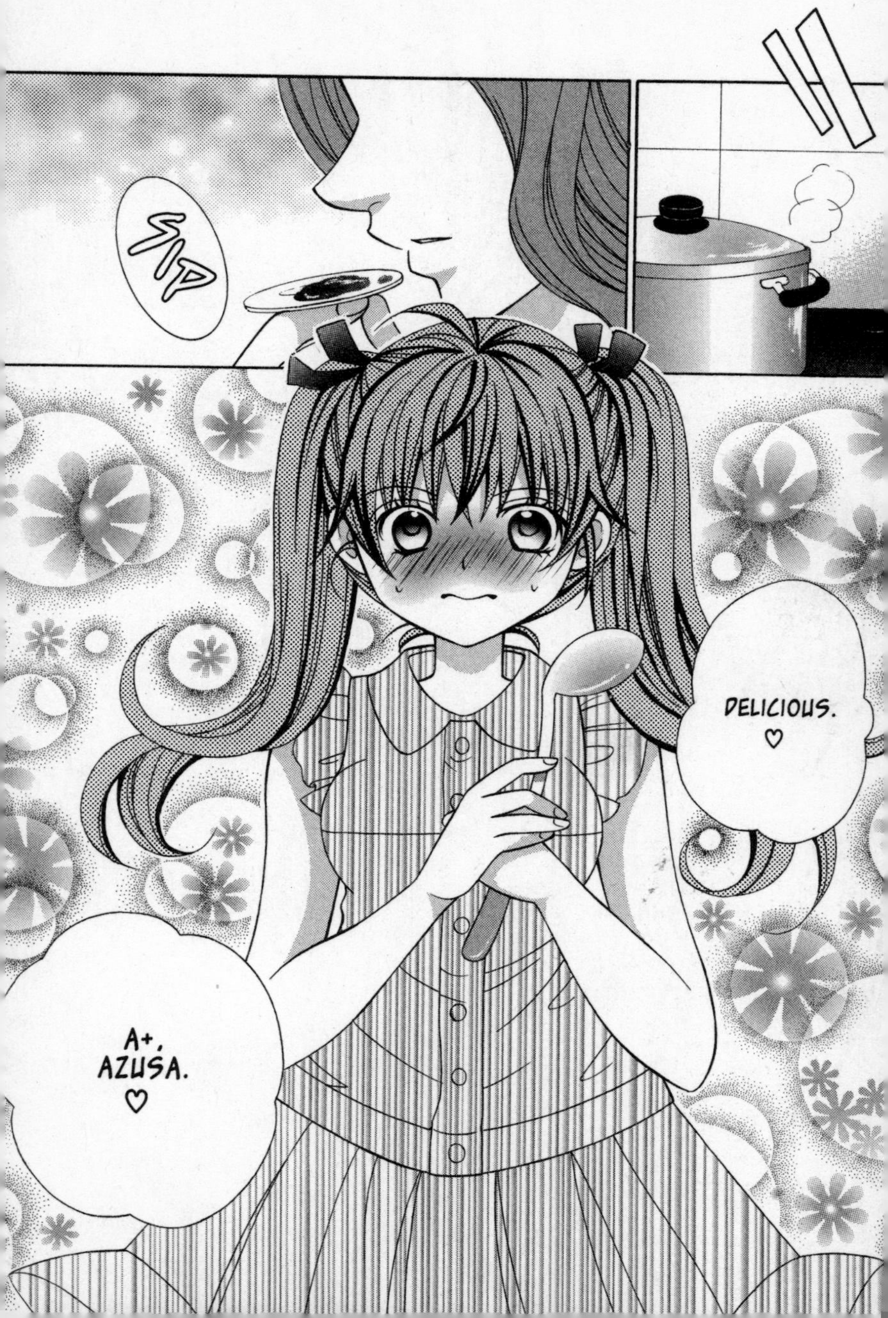
SIP
DELICIOUS. ♡
A+, AZUSA. ♡

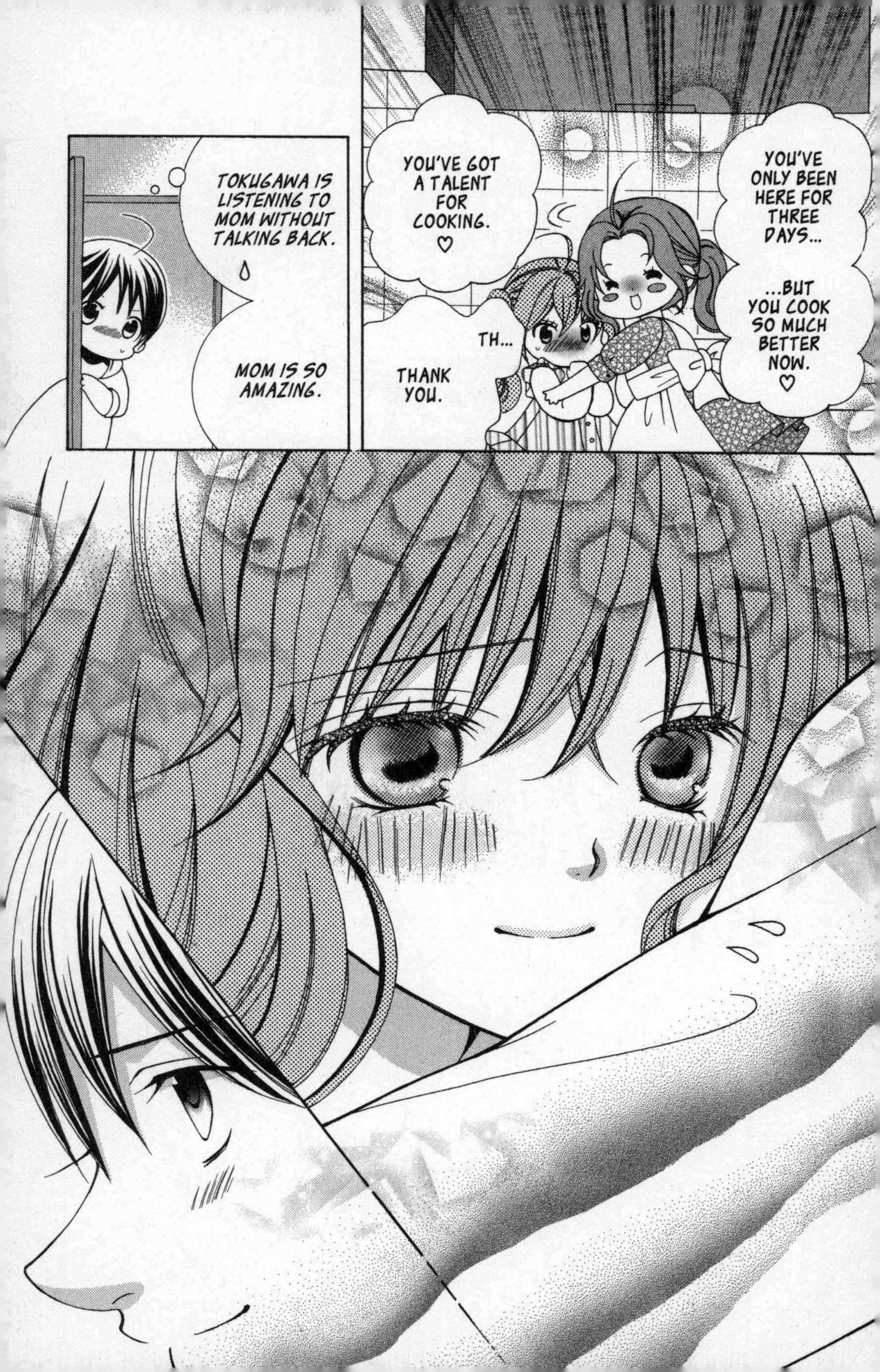
YOU'VE ONLY BEEN HERE FOR THREE DAYS...
...BUT YOU COOK SO MUCH BETTER NOW. ♡
YOU'VE GOT A TALENT FOR COOKING. ♡
TH...
THANK YOU.
TOKUGAWA IS LISTENING TO MOM WITHOUT TALKING BACK.
MOM IS SO AMAZING.

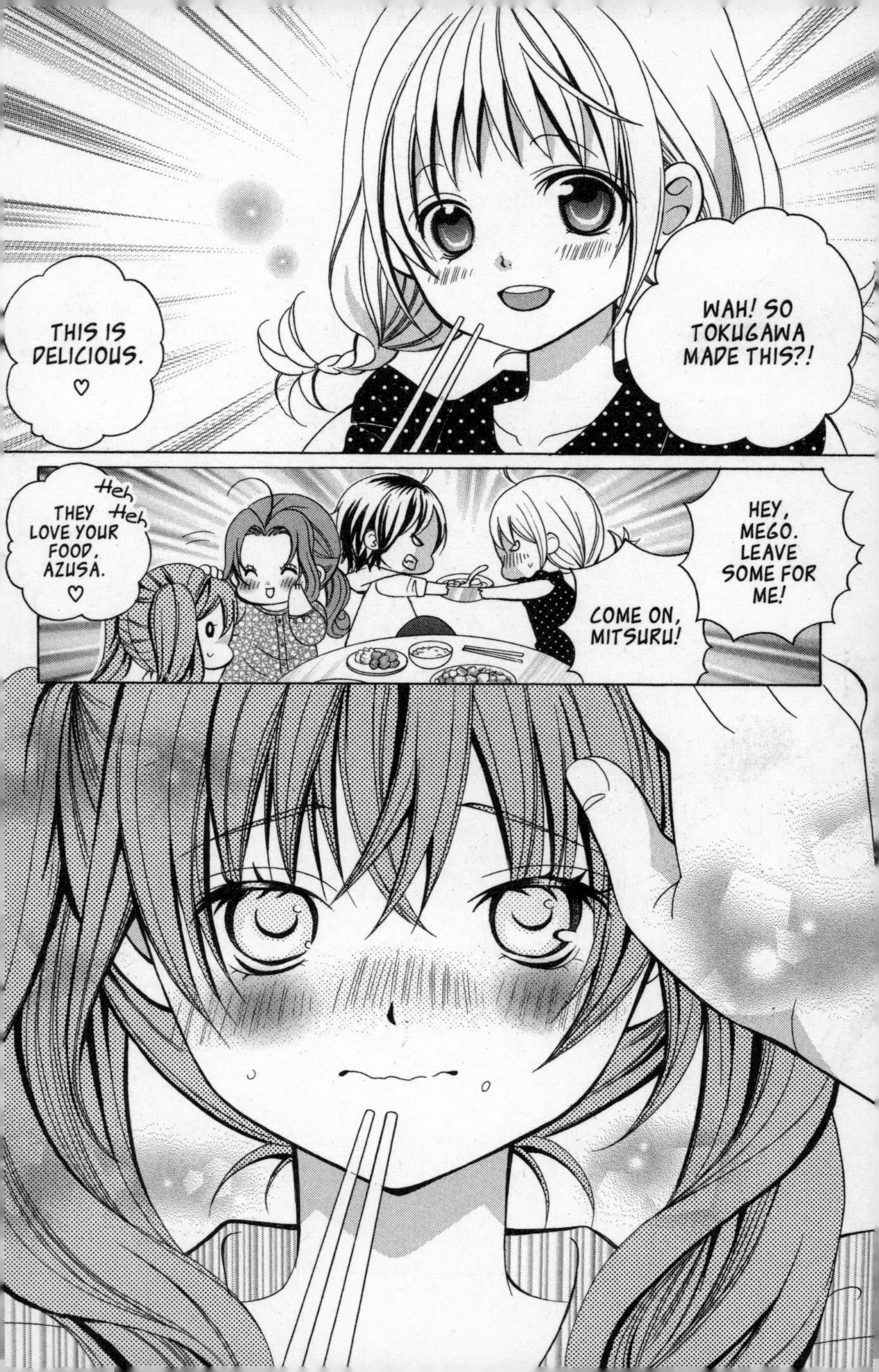
WAH! SO TOKUGAWA MADE THIS?!
THIS IS DELICIOUS. ♡
HEY, MEGO. LEAVE SOME FOR ME!
COME ON, MITSURU!
Heh Heh
THEY LOVE YOUR FOOD, AZUSA. ♡

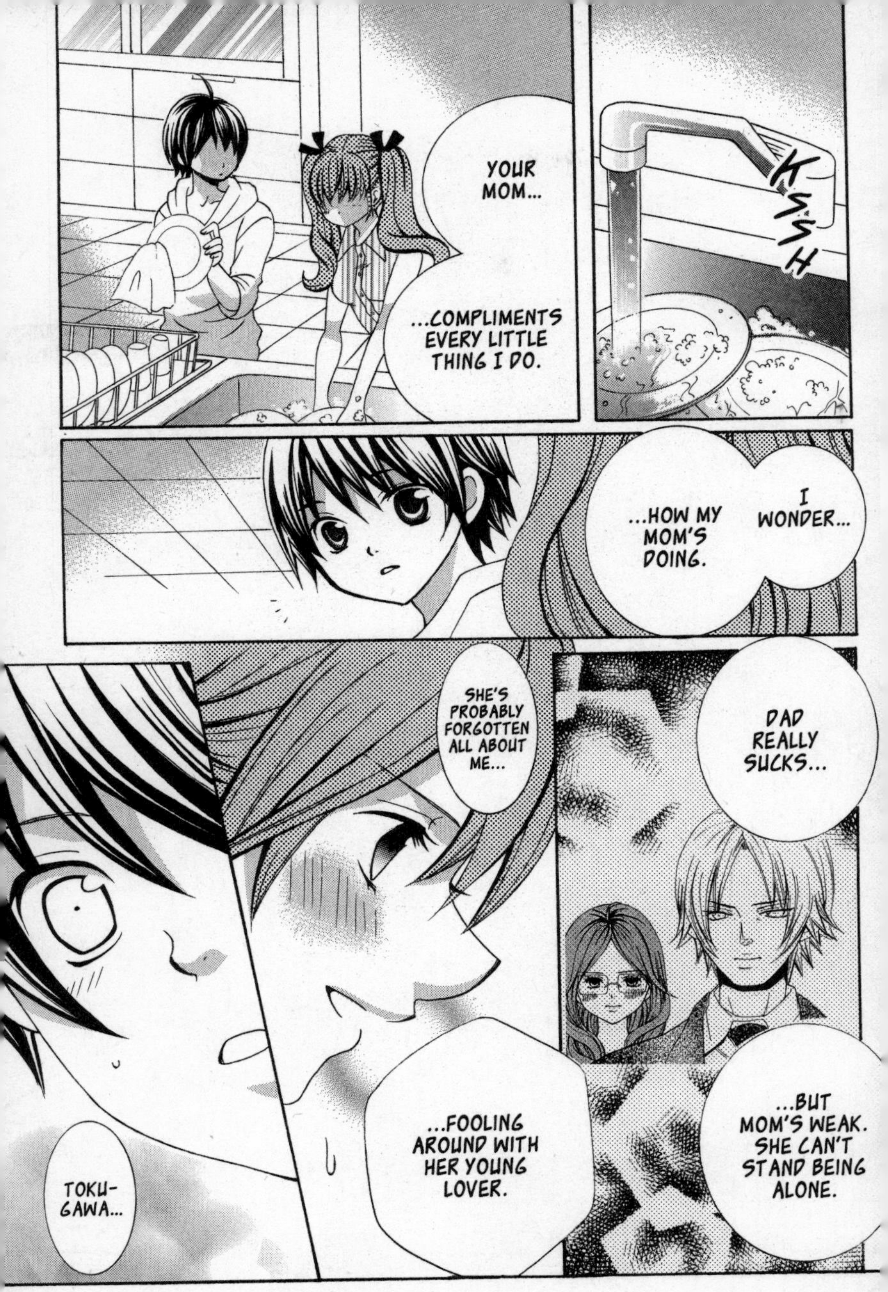
KSSH
YOUR MOM...
...COMPLIMENTS EVERY LITTLE THING I DO.
I WONDER...
...HOW MY MOM'S DOING.
DAD REALLY SUCKS...
...BUT MOM'S WEAK. SHE CAN'T STAND BEING ALONE.
SHE'S PROBABLY FORGOTTEN ALL ABOUT ME...
...FOOLING AROUND WITH HER YOUNG LOVER.
TOKU-GAWA...

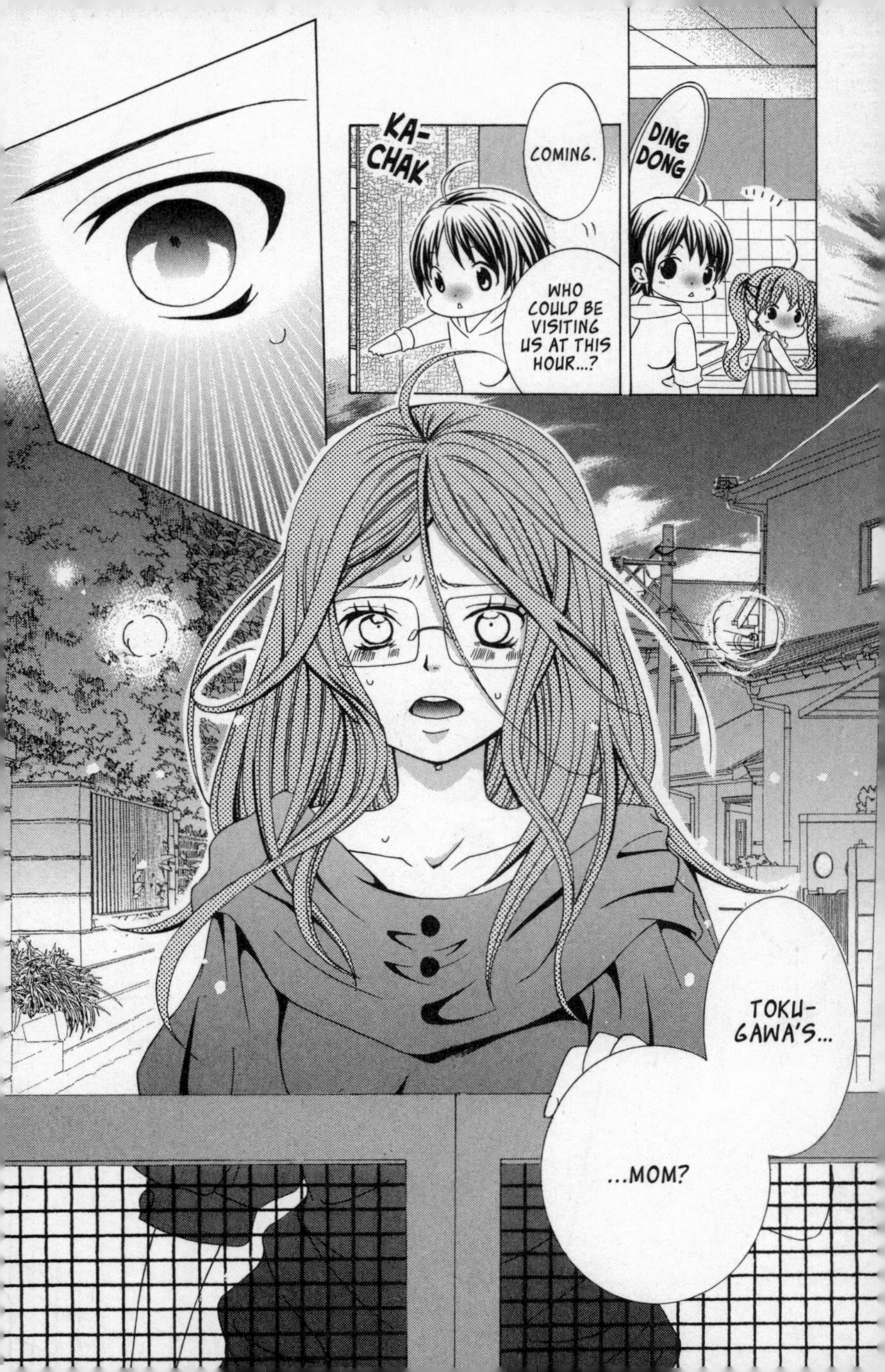
DING DONG
COMING.
KA-CHAK
WHO COULD BE VISITING US AT THIS HOUR...?
TOKU-GAWA'S...
...MOM?

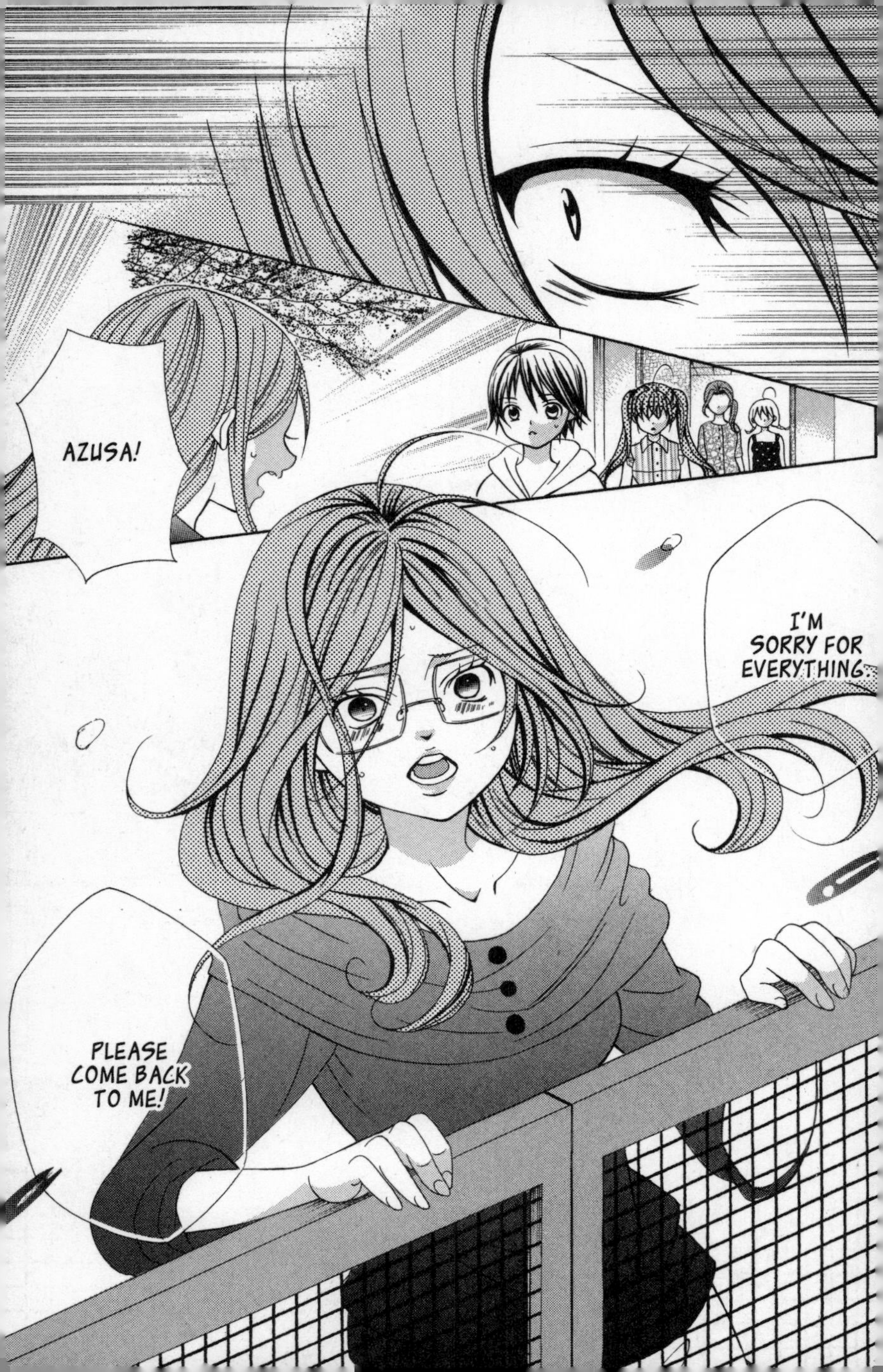
AZUSA!
I'M SORRY FOR EVERYTHING...
PLEASE COME BACK TO ME!

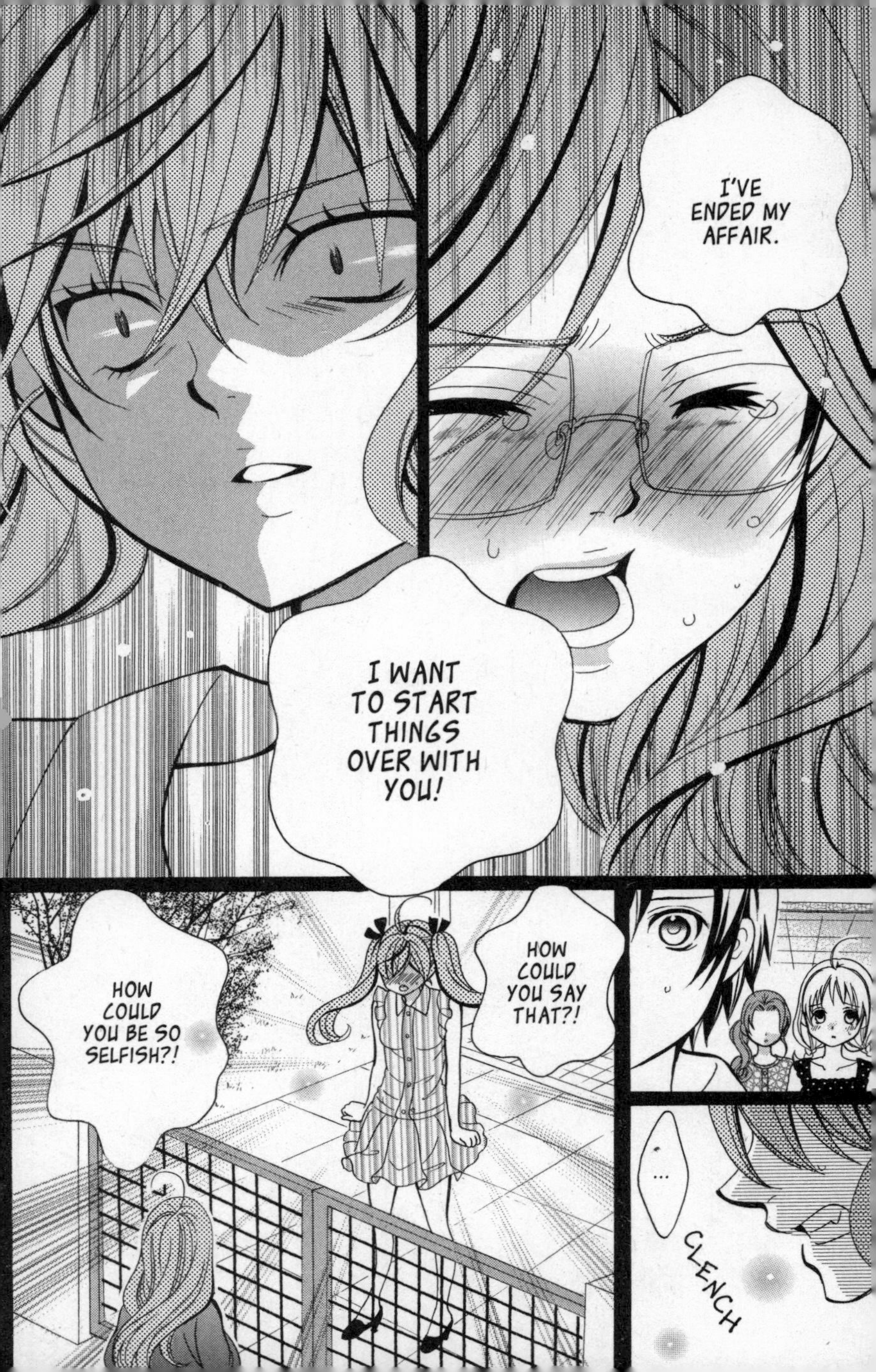
I'VE ENDED MY AFFAIR.
I WANT TO START THINGS OVER WITH YOU!
...
CLENCH
HOW COULD YOU SAY THAT?!
HOW COULD YOU BE SO SELFISH?!

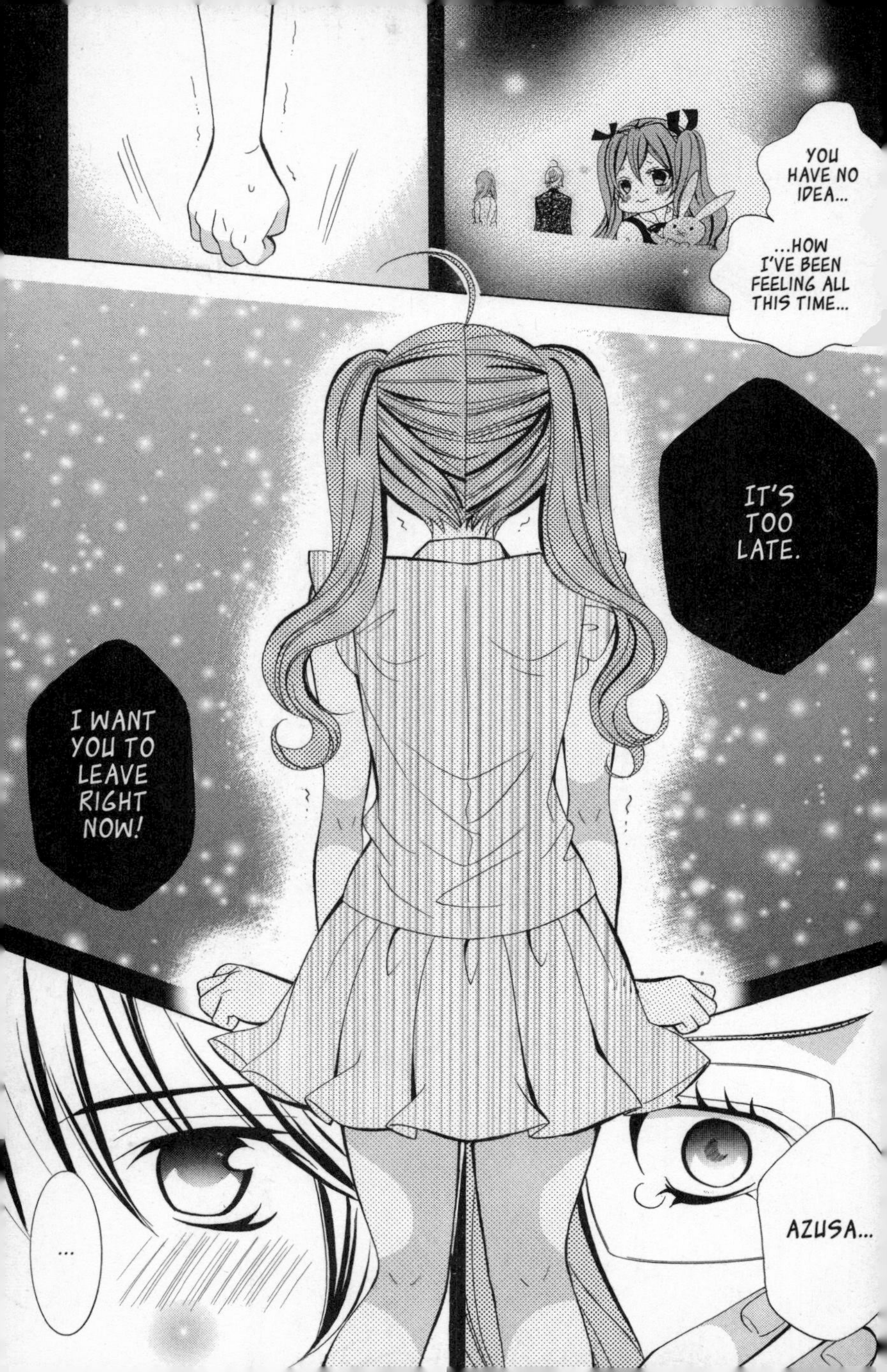
YOU HAVE NO IDEA...
...HOW I'VE BEEN FEELING ALL THIS TIME...
IT'S TOO LATE.
I WANT YOU TO LEAVE RIGHT NOW!
AZUSA...
...

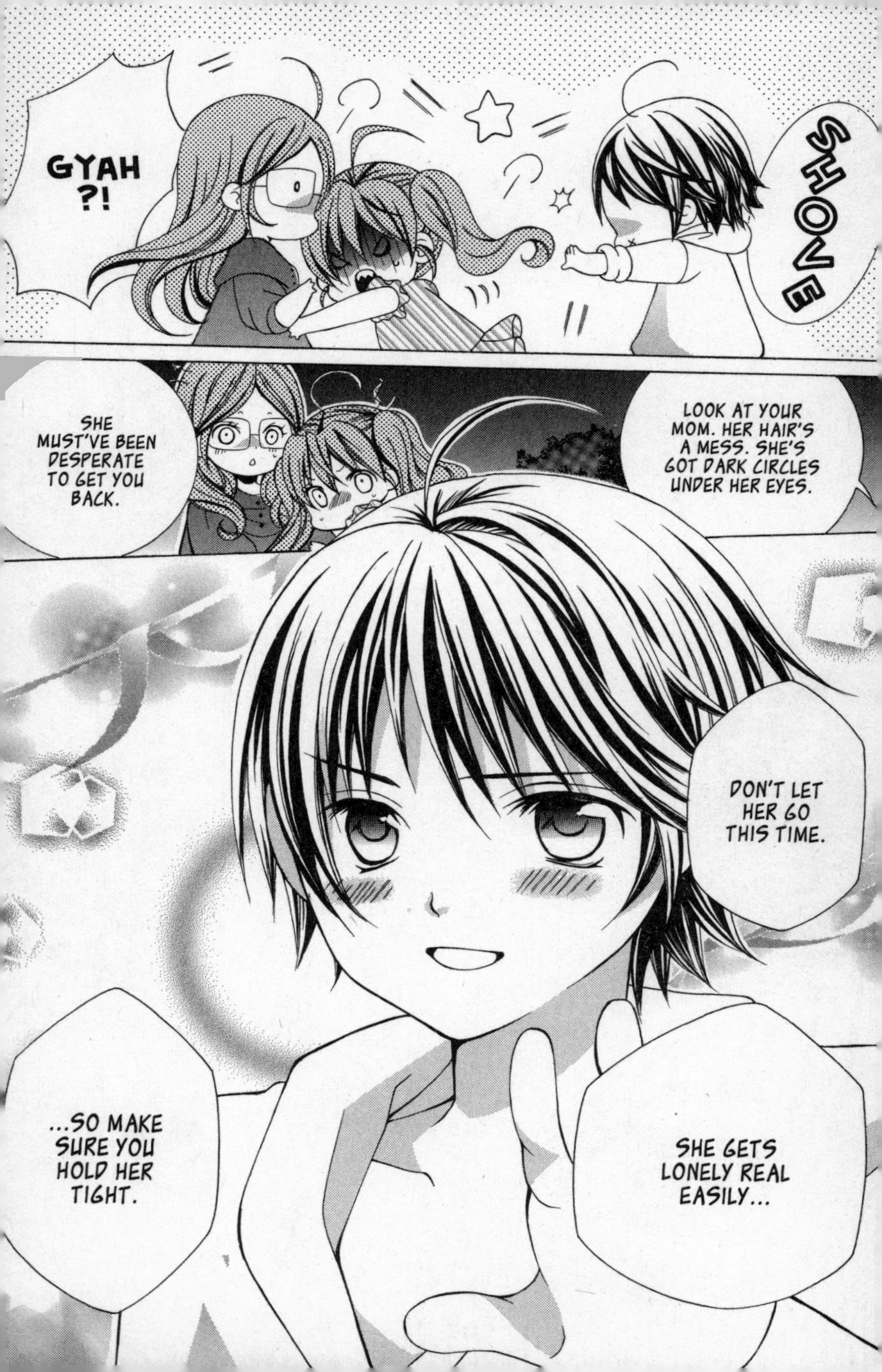
SHOVE
GYAH ?!
LOOK AT YOUR MOM. HER HAIR'S A MESS. SHE'S GOT DARK CIRCLES UNDER HER EYES.
SHE MUST'VE BEEN DESPERATE TO GET YOU BACK.
DON'T LET HER GO THIS TIME.
SHE GETS LONELY REAL EASILY...
...SO MAKE SURE YOU HOLD HER TIGHT.

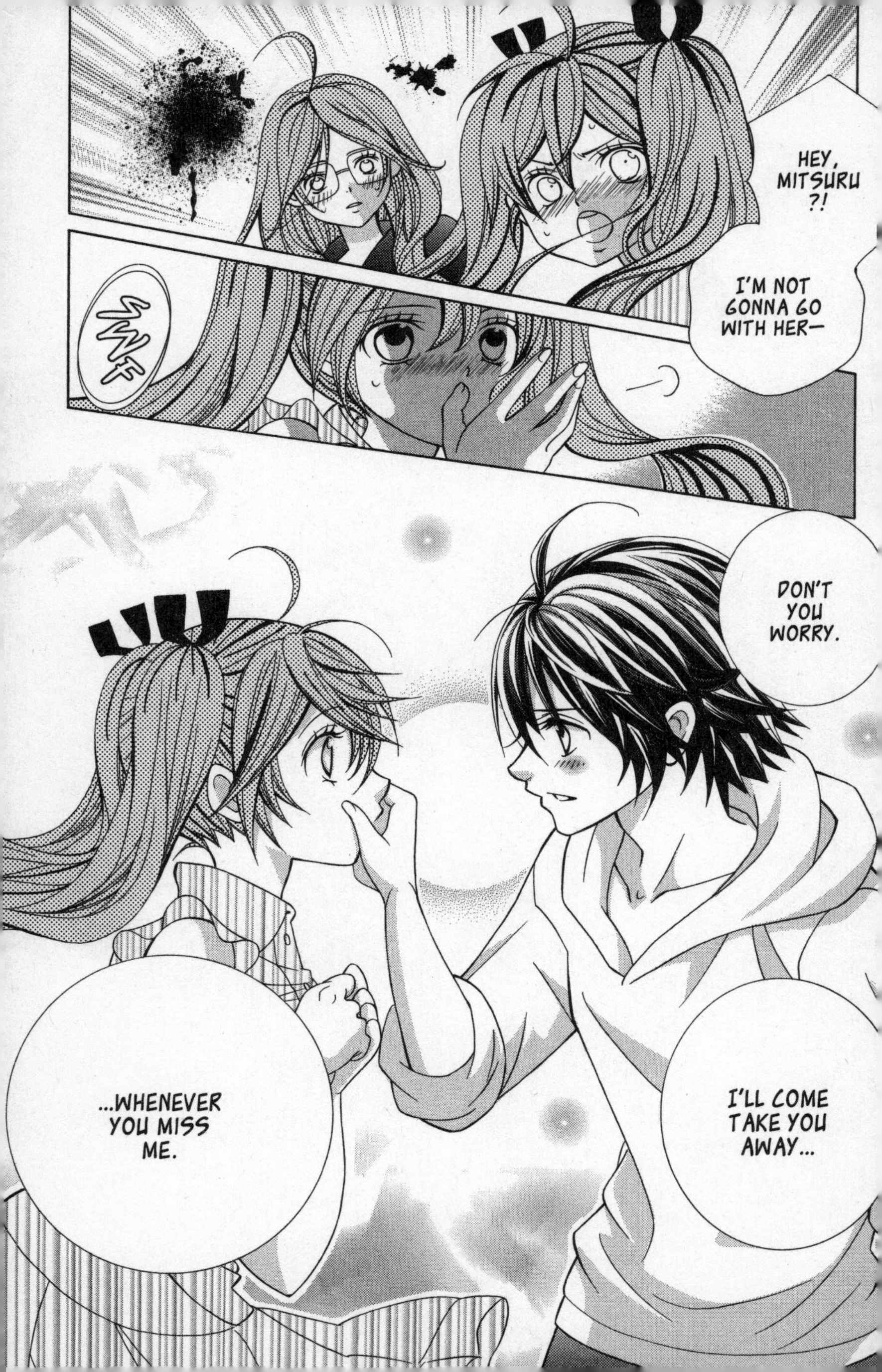
HEY, MITSURU ?!
I'M NOT GONNA GO WITH HER—
SNIF
DON'T YOU WORRY.
I'LL COME TAKE YOU AWAY...
...WHENEVER YOU MISS ME.

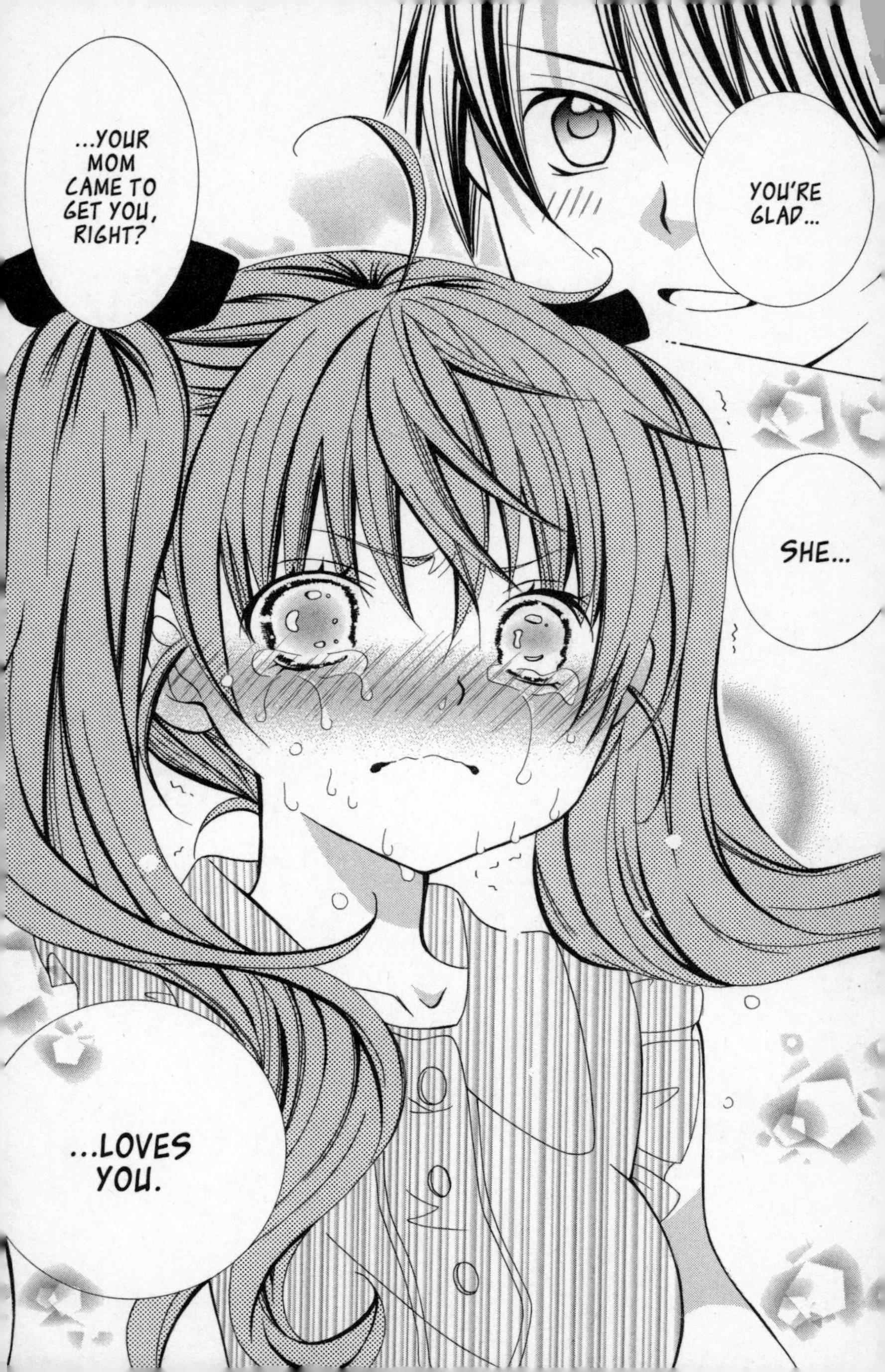
YOU'RE GLAD...
...YOUR MOM CAME TO GET YOU, RIGHT?
SHE...
...LOVES YOU.

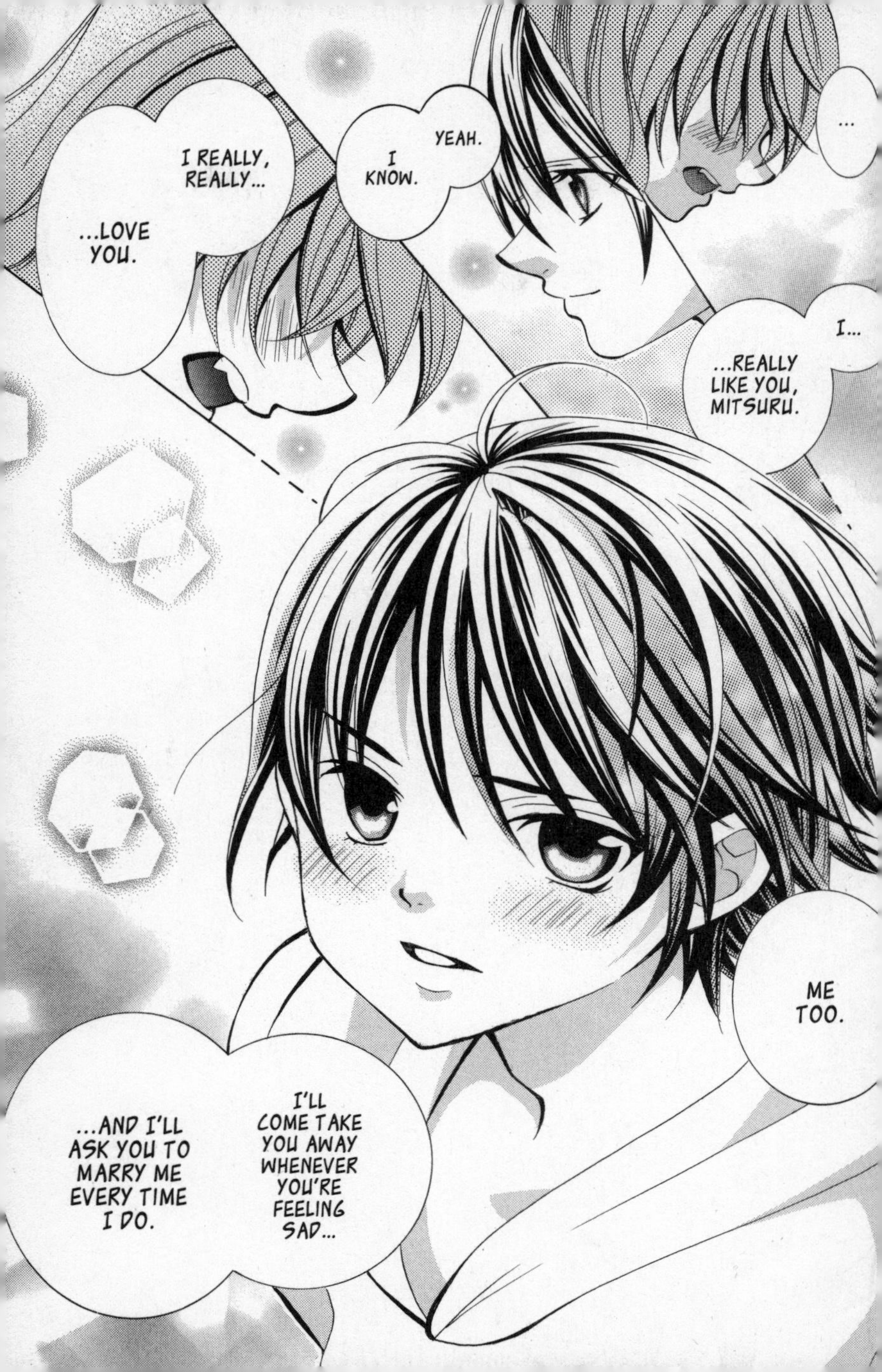
...
I... ...REALLY LIKE YOU, MITSURU.
YEAH. I KNOW.
I REALLY, REALLY... ...LOVE YOU.
ME TOO.
I'LL COME TAKE YOU AWAY WHENEVER YOU'RE FEELING SAD...
...AND I'LL ASK YOU TO MARRY ME EVERY TIME I DO.

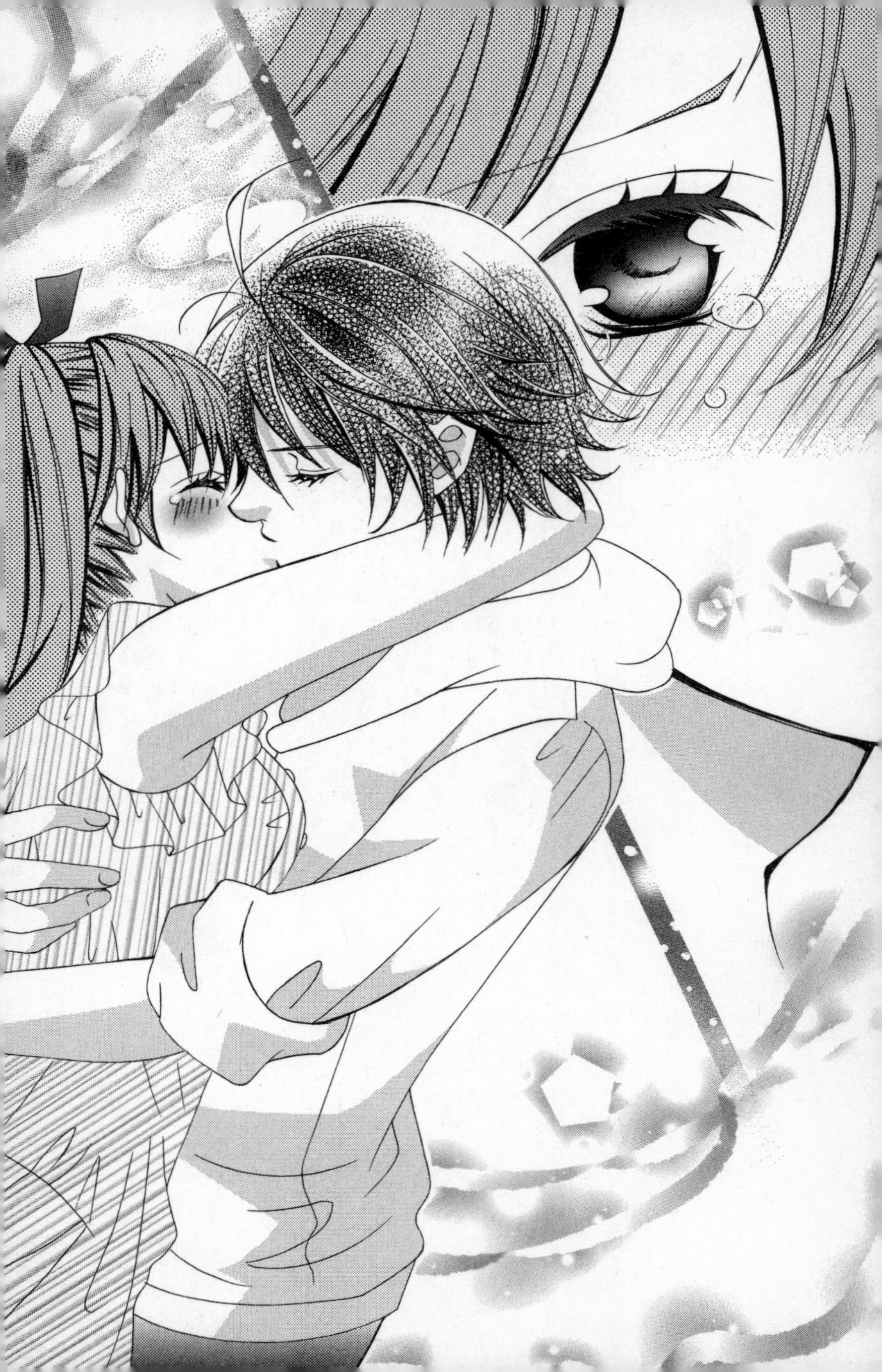

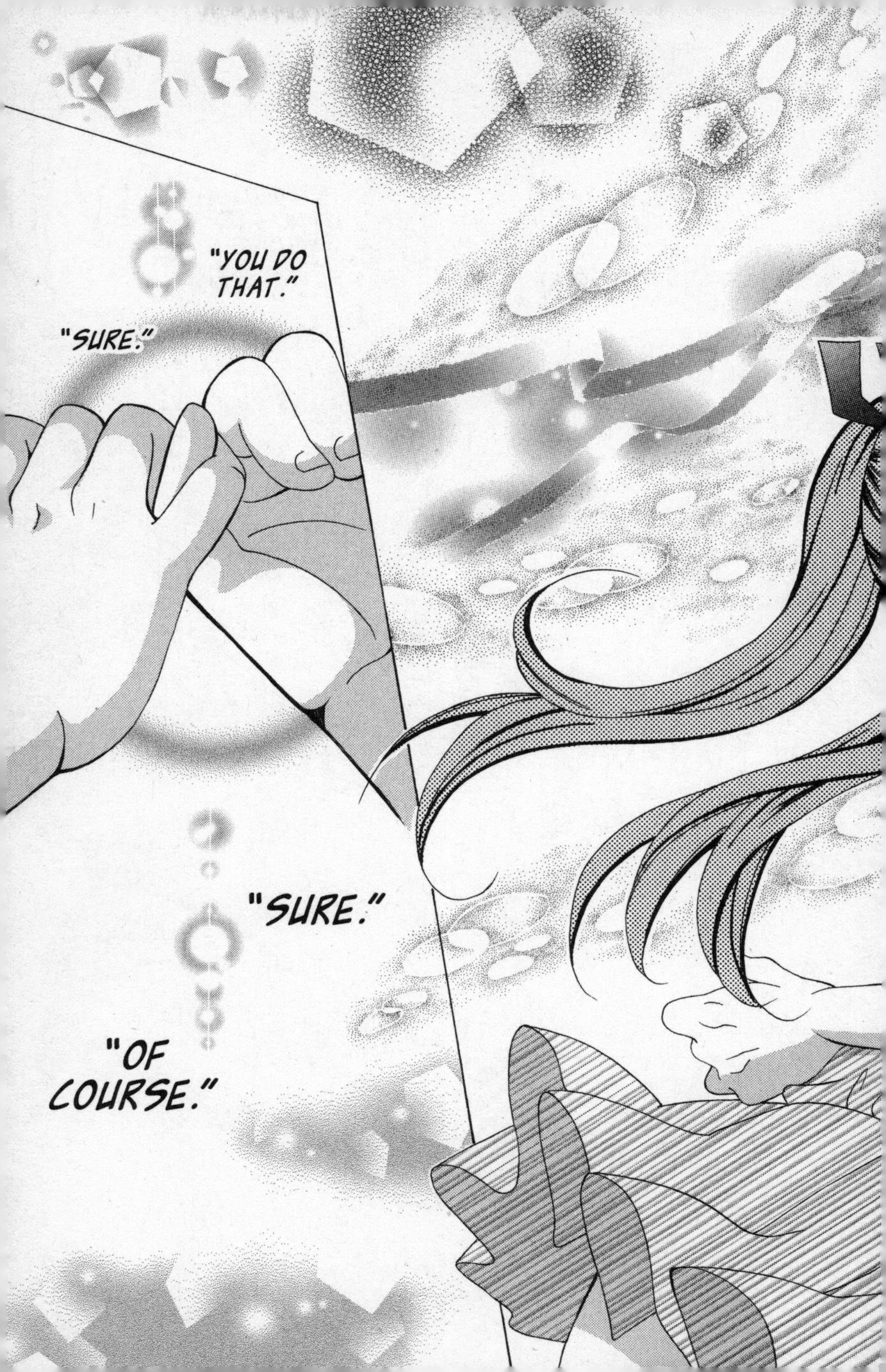
"YOU DO THAT."
"SURE."
"SURE."
"OF COURSE."

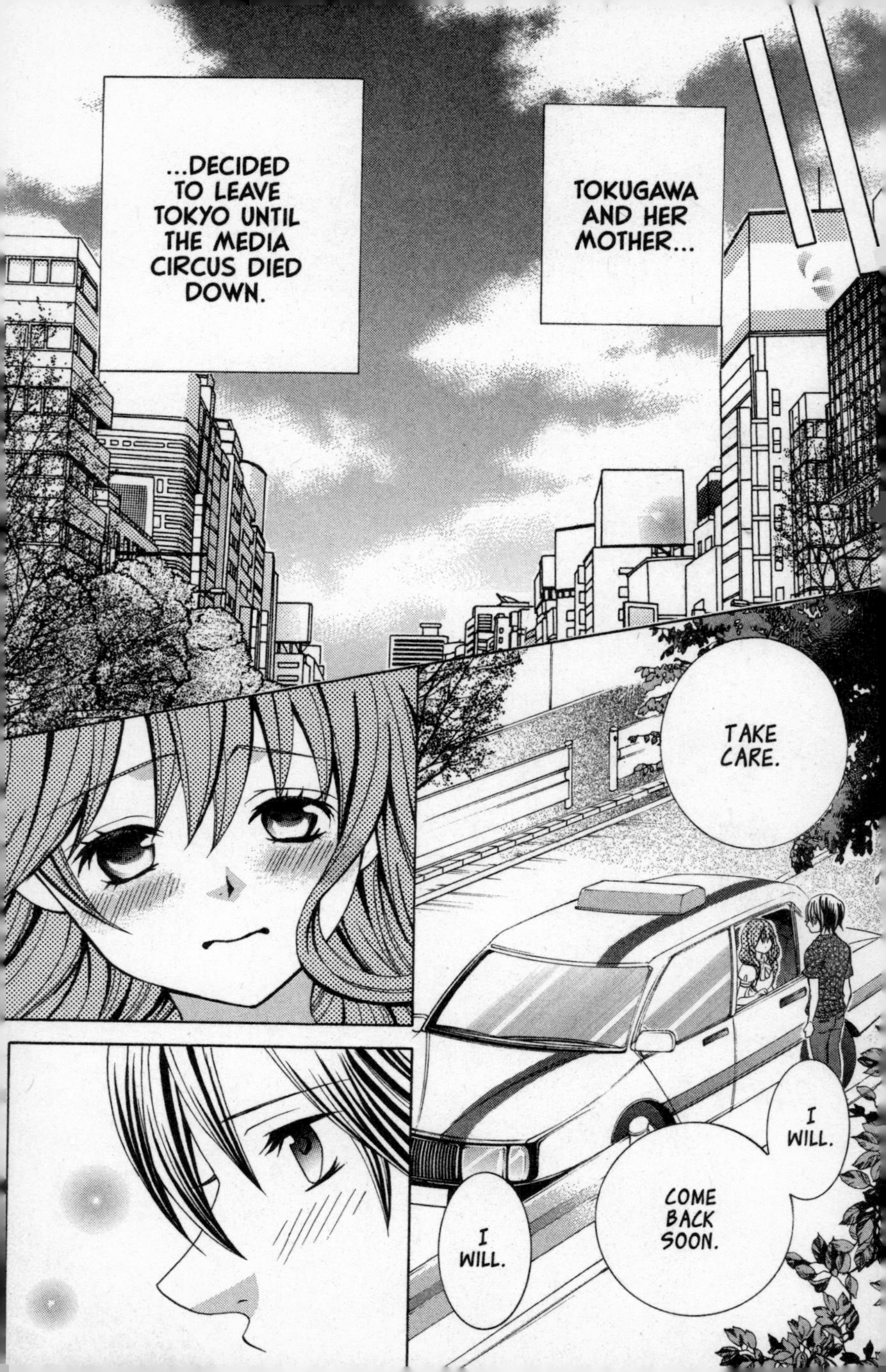
TOKUGAWA AND HER MOTHER...
...DECIDED TO LEAVE TOKYO UNTIL THE MEDIA CIRCUS DIED DOWN.
TAKE CARE.
I WILL.
COME BACK SOON.
I WILL.

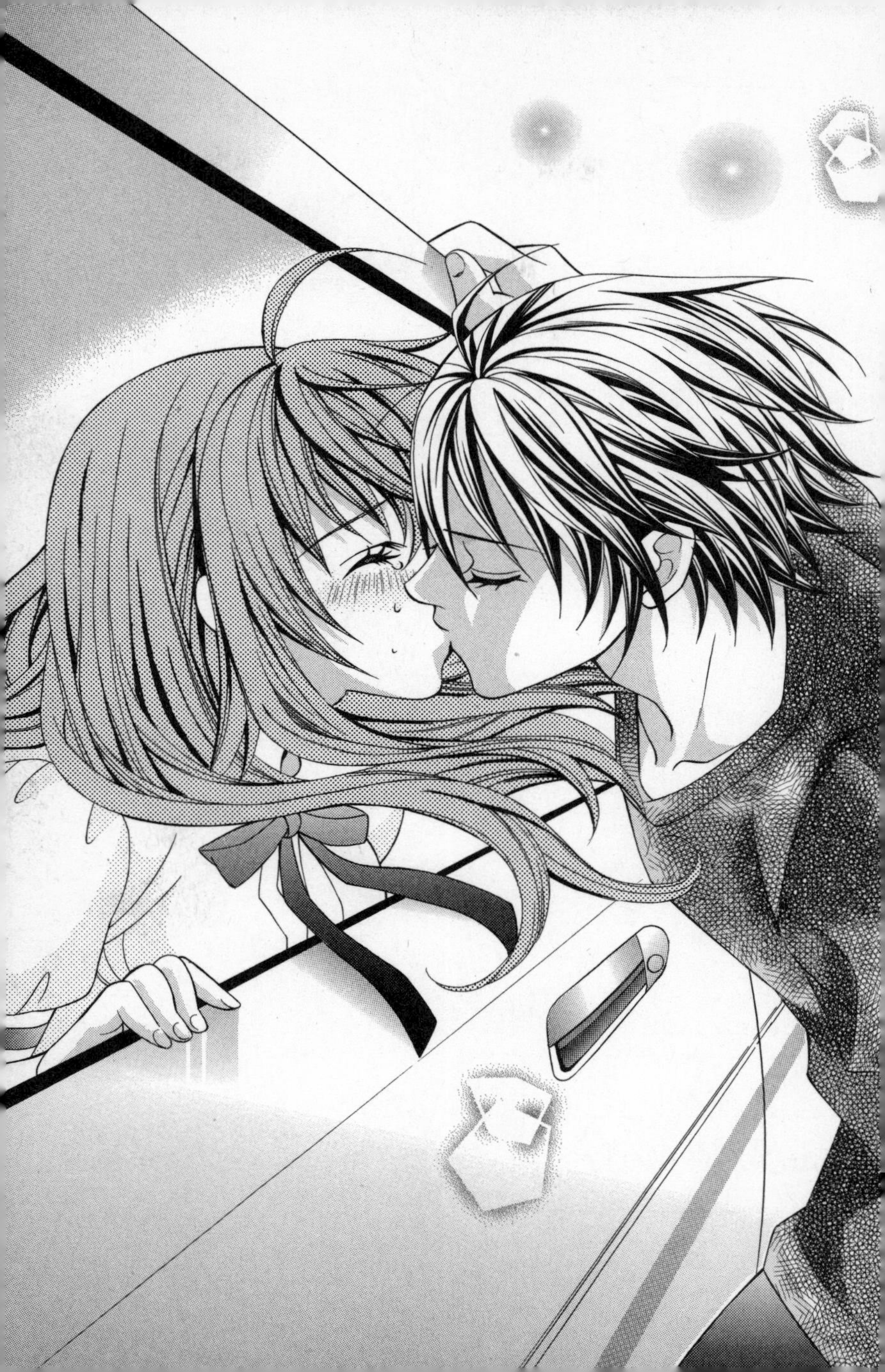

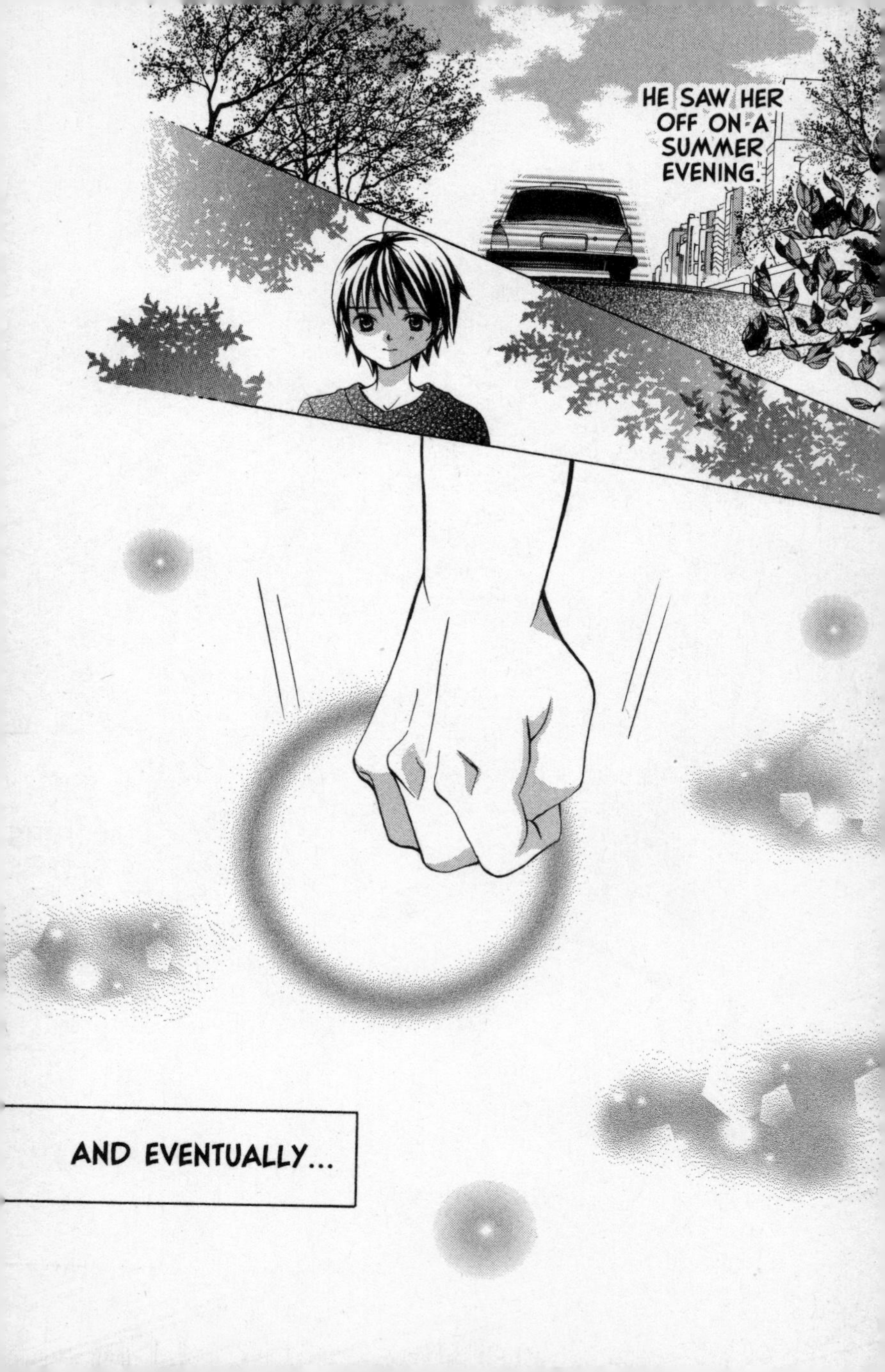
HE SAW HER OFF ON A SUMMER EVENING.
AND EVENTUALLY...

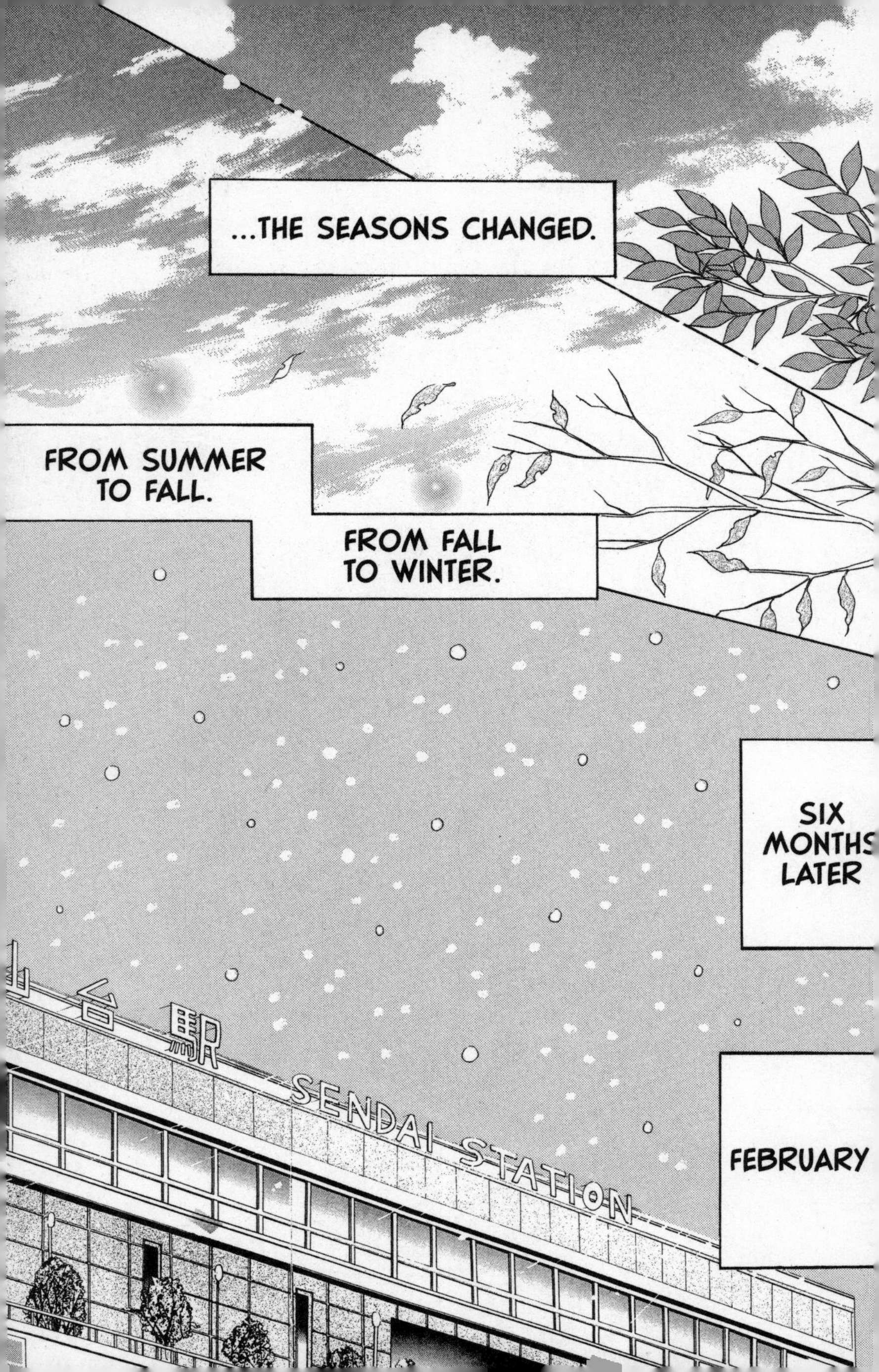
...THE SEASONS CHANGED.
FROM SUMMER TO FALL.
FROM FALL TO WINTER.
SIX MONTHS LATER
FEBRUARY
SENDAI STATION

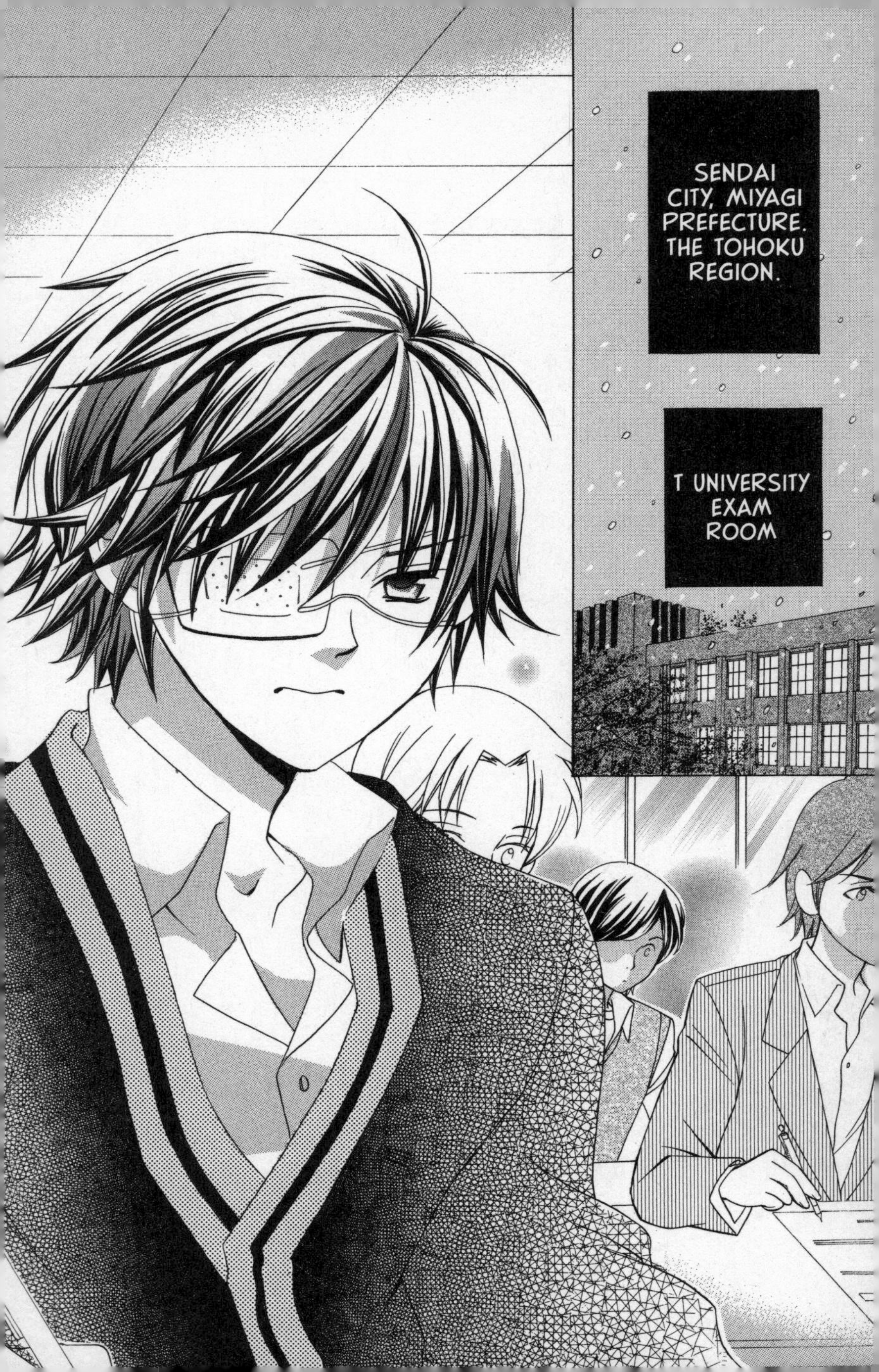
SENDAI CITY, MIYAGI PREFECTURE. THE TOHOKU REGION.
T UNIVERSITY EXAM ROOM

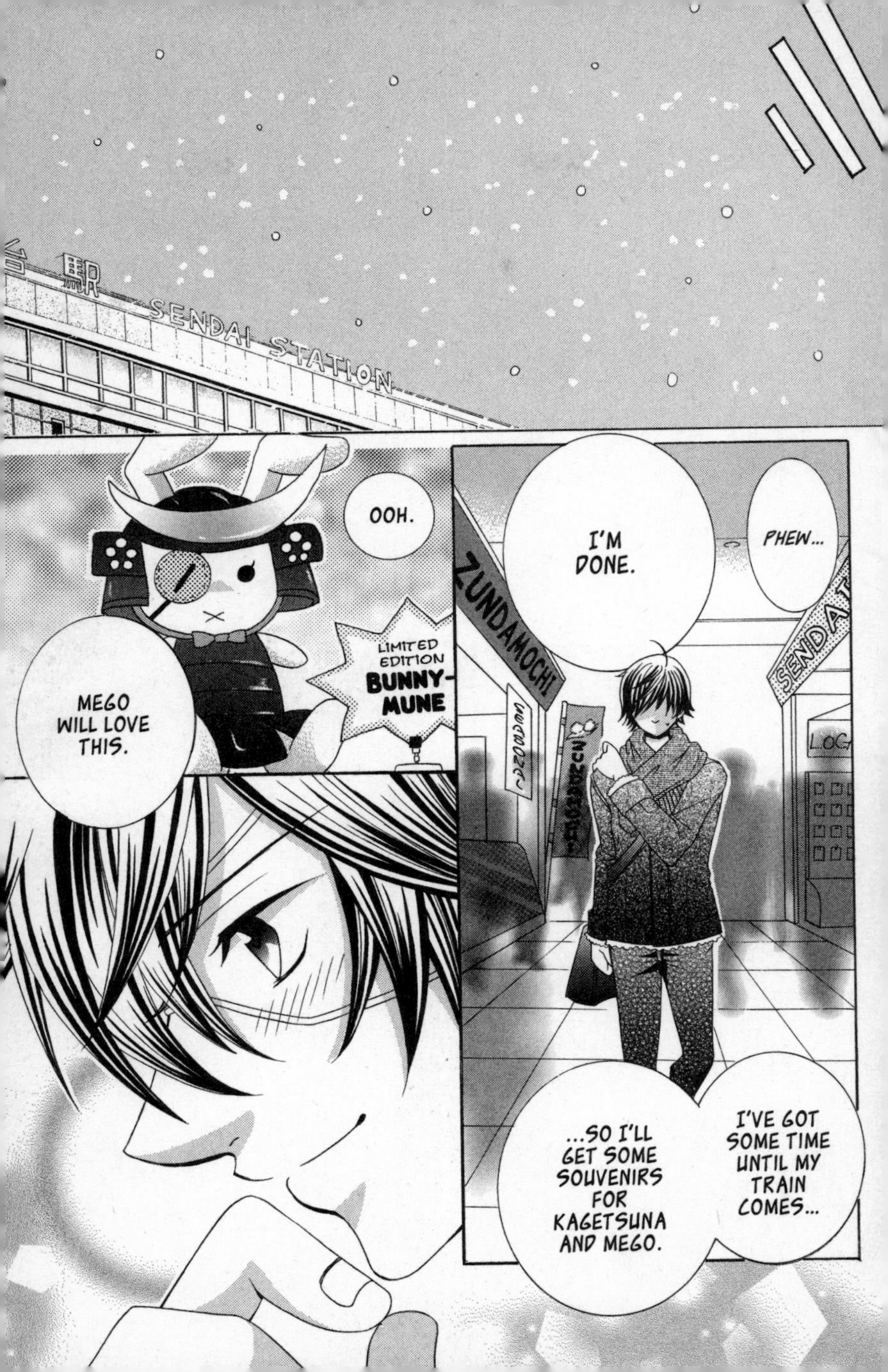
SENDAI STATION
ZUNDAMOCHI
PHEW...
I'M DONE.
I'VE GOT SOME TIME UNTIL MY TRAIN COMES...
...SO I'LL GET SOME SOUVENIRS FOR KAGETSUNA AND MEGO.
OOH.
LIMITED EDITION BUNNY-MUNE
MEGO WILL LOVE THIS.

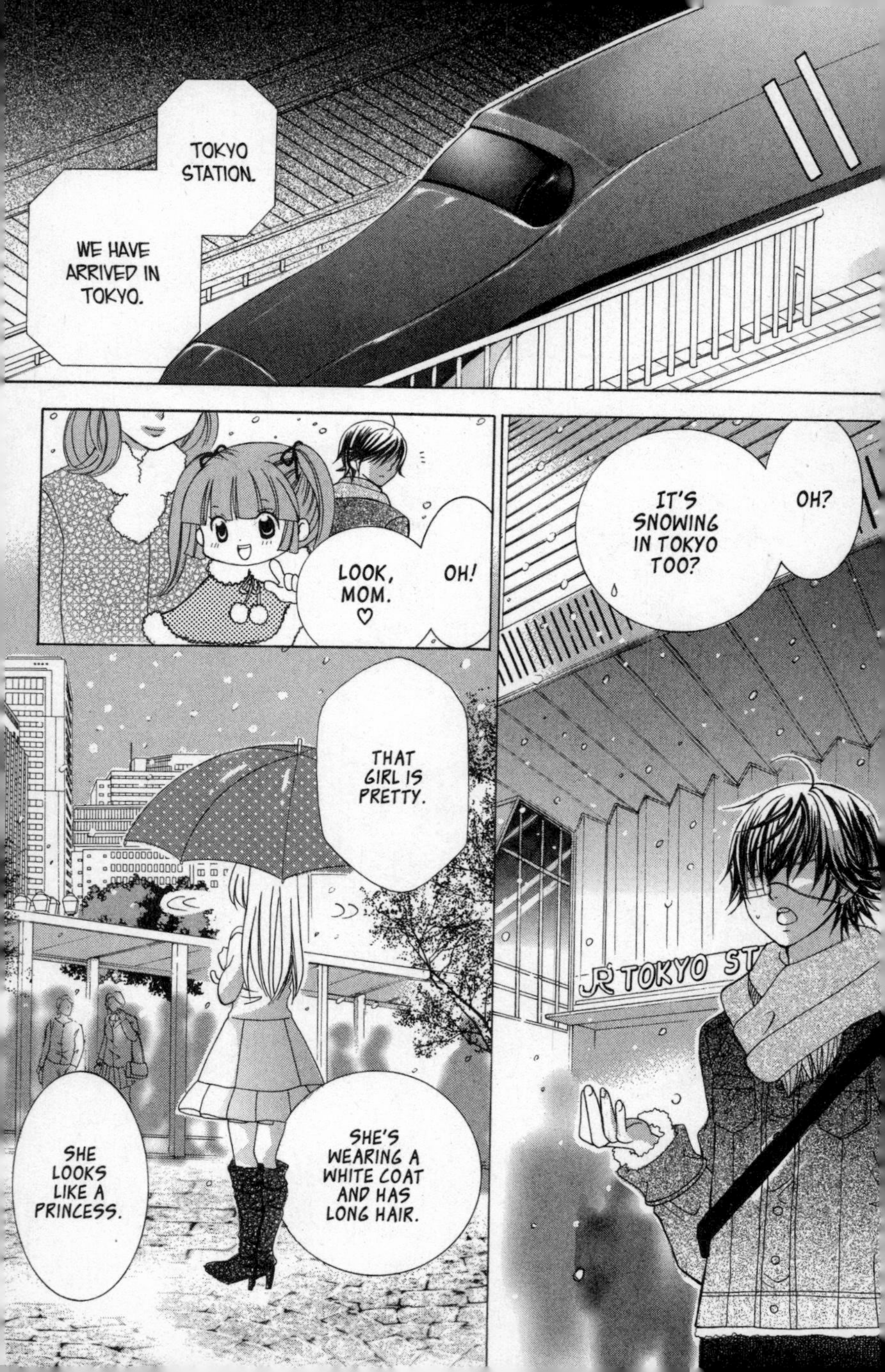
TOKYO STATION.
WE HAVE ARRIVED IN TOKYO.
OH?
IT'S SNOWING IN TOKYO TOO?
JR TOKYO ST
OH!
LOOK, MOM. ♡
THAT GIRL IS PRETTY.
SHE'S WEARING A WHITE COAT AND HAS LONG HAIR.
SHE LOOKS LIKE A PRINCESS.

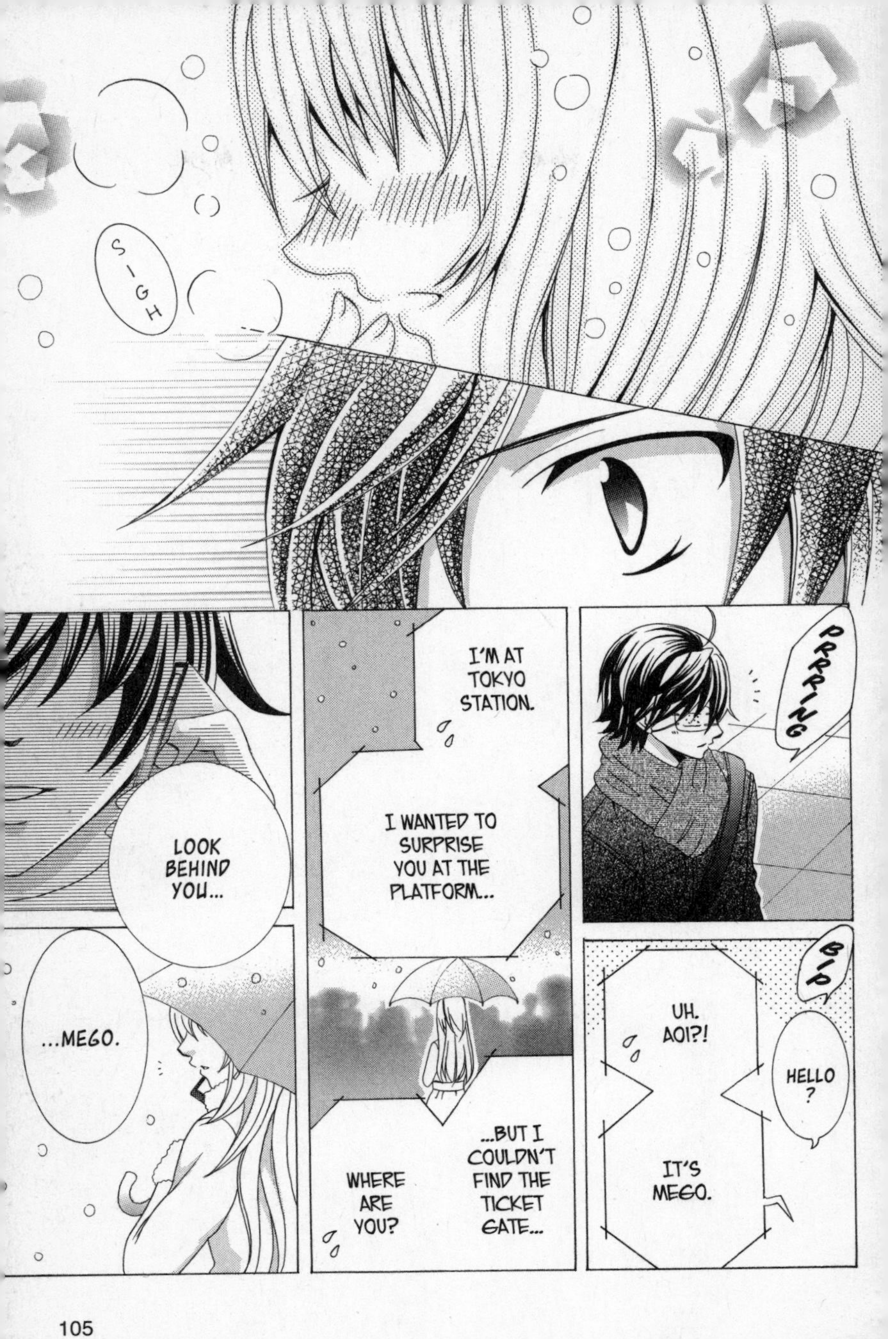
SIGH
PRRRING
BIP
HELLO?
IT'S MEGO.
UH. AOI?!
I'M AT TOKYO STATION.
I WANTED TO SURPRISE YOU AT THE PLATFORM...
...BUT I COULDN'T FIND THE TICKET GATE...
WHERE ARE YOU?
...MEGO.
LOOK BEHIND YOU...

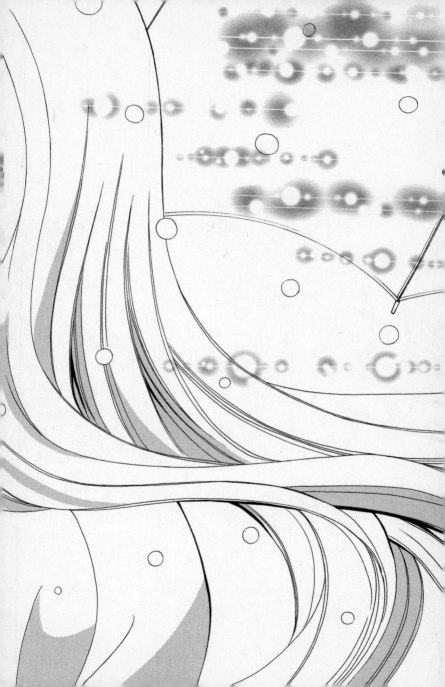

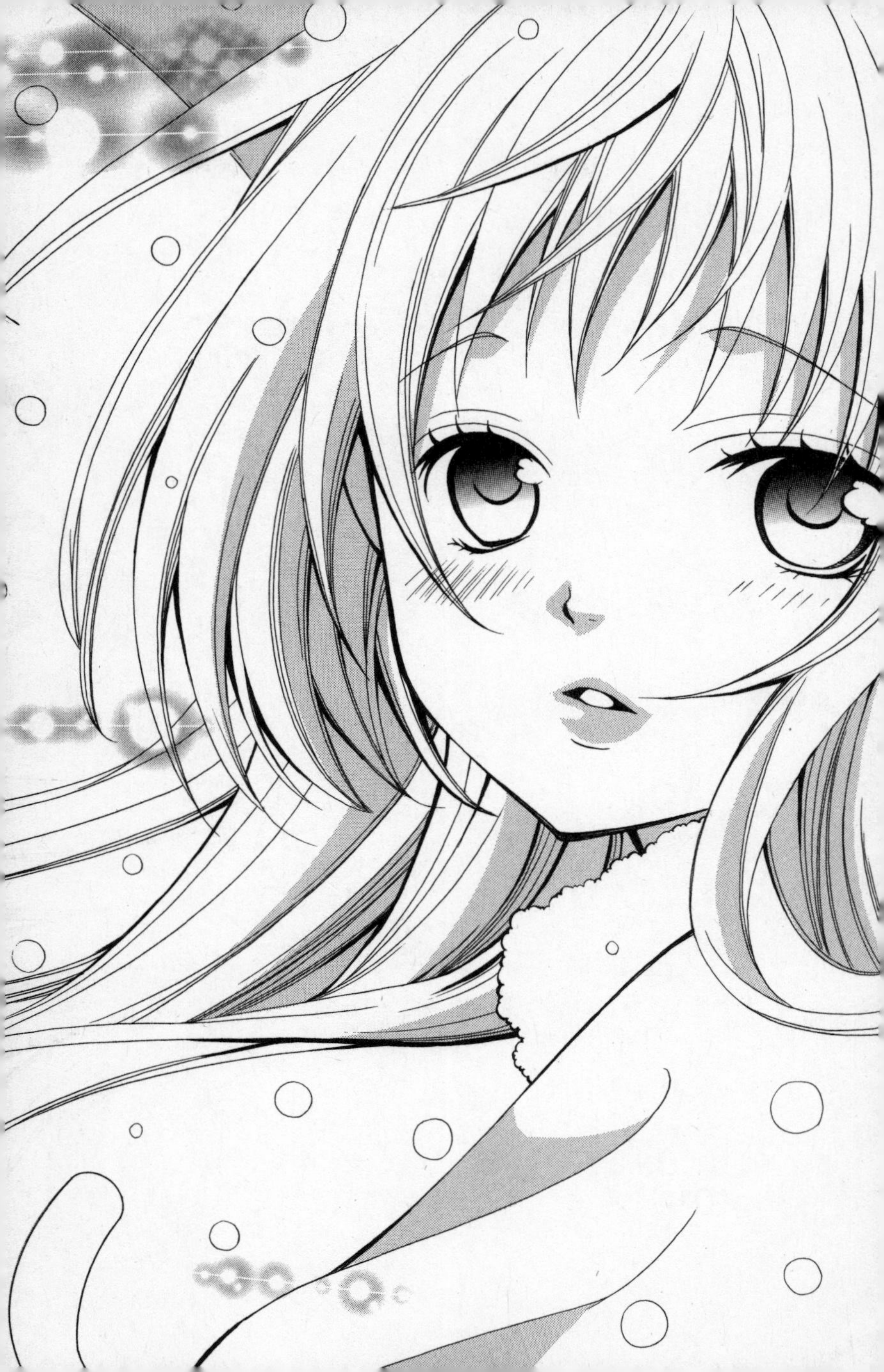

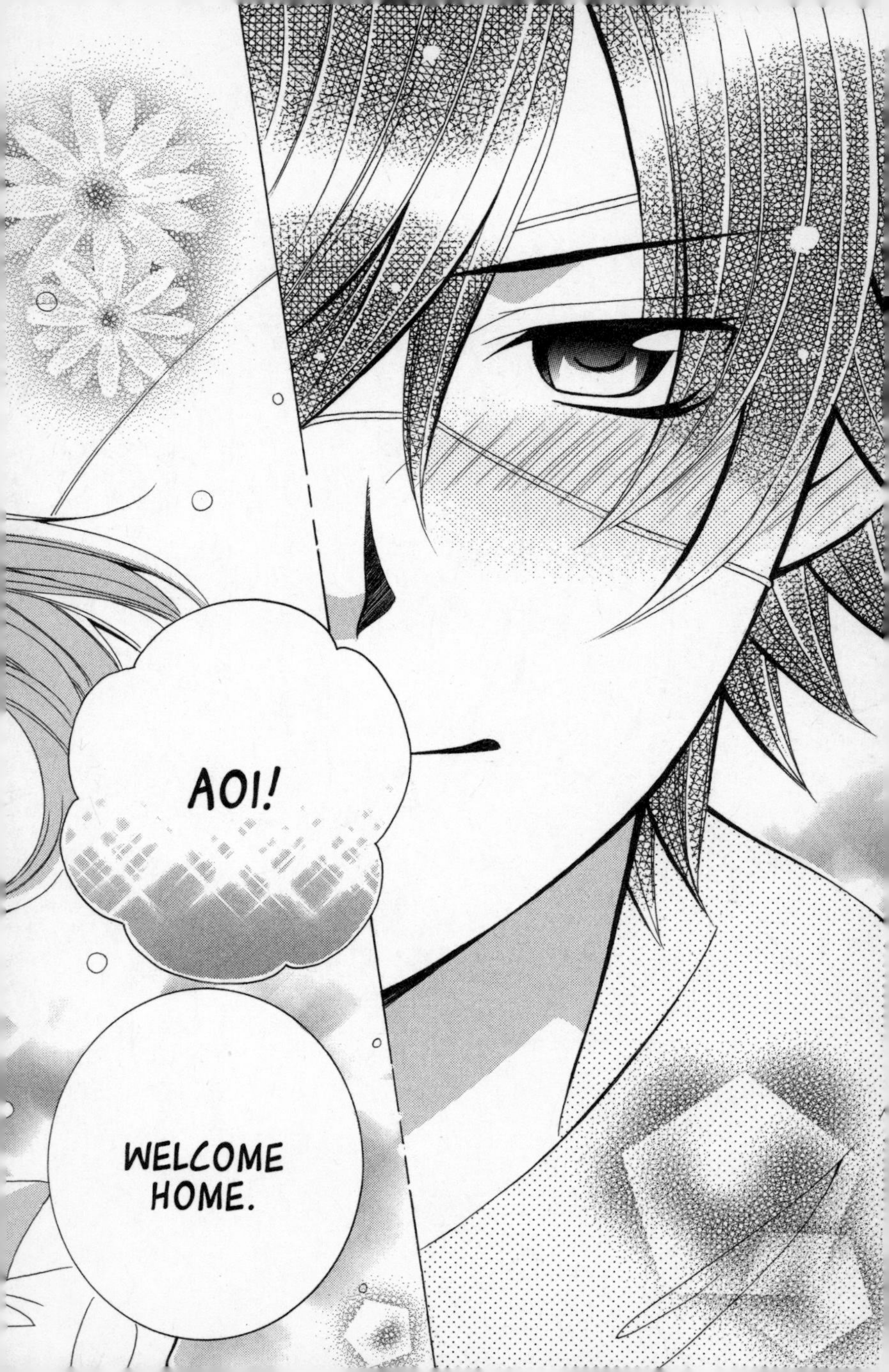
AOI!
WELCOME HOME.

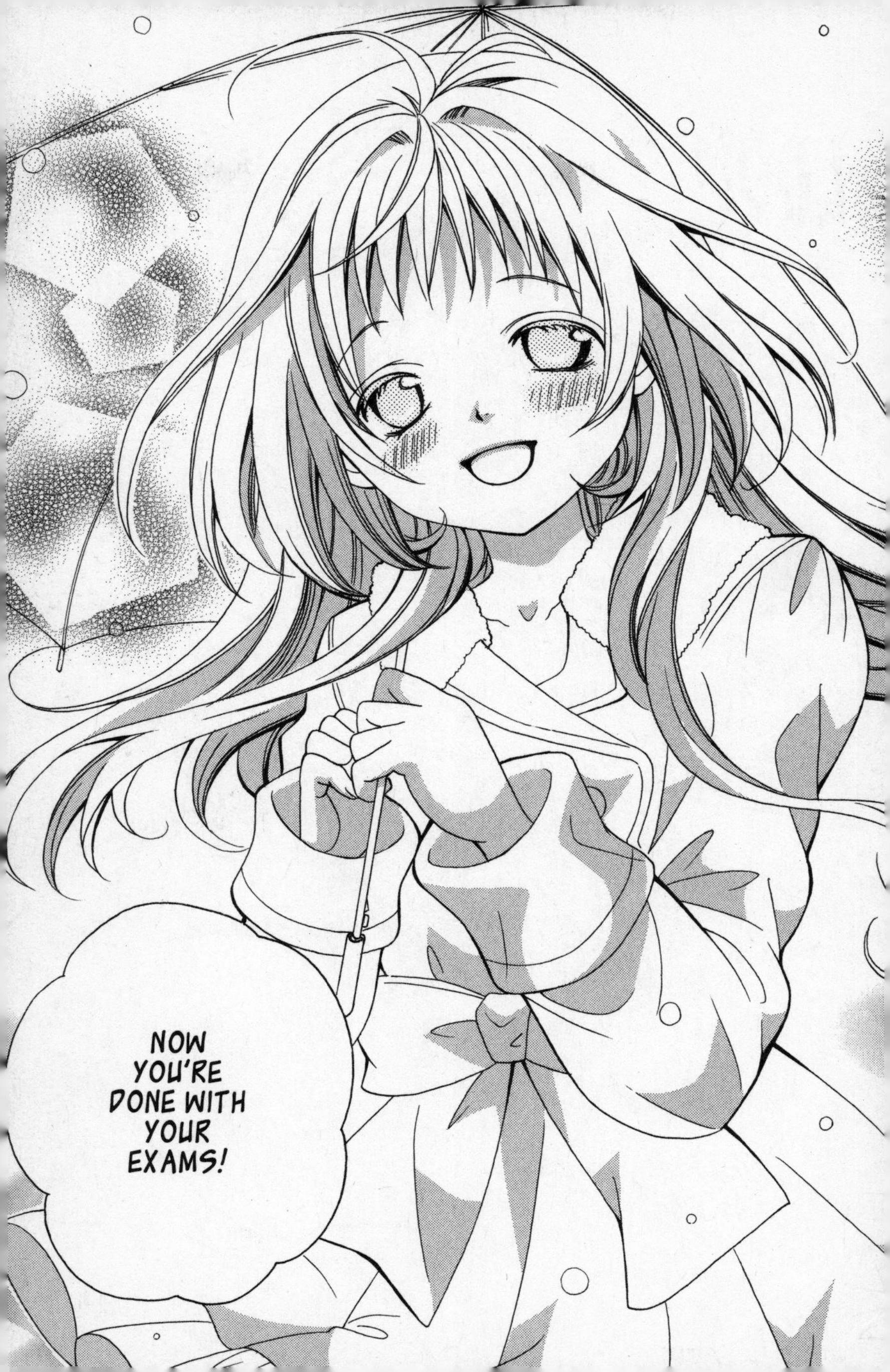
NOW YOU'RE DONE WITH YOUR EXAMS!

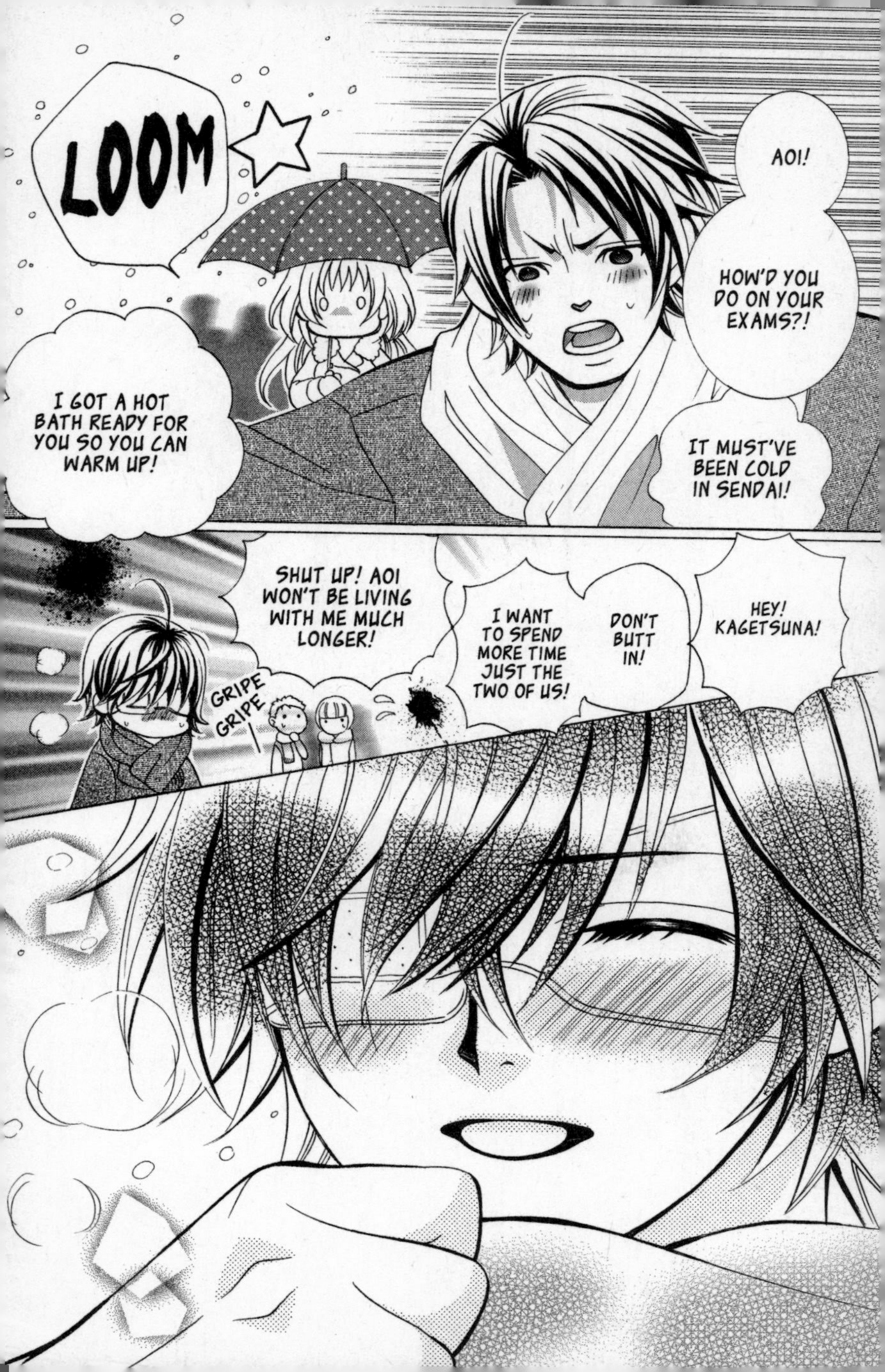
AOI!
HOW'D YOU DO ON YOUR EXAMS?!
IT MUST'VE BEEN COLD IN SENDAI!
LOOM
I GOT A HOT BATH READY FOR YOU SO YOU CAN WARM UP!
HEY! KAGETSUNA!
DON'T BUTT IN!
I WANT TO SPEND MORE TIME JUST THE TWO OF US!
SHUT UP! AOI WON'T BE LIVING WITH ME MUCH LONGER!
GRIPE GRIPE

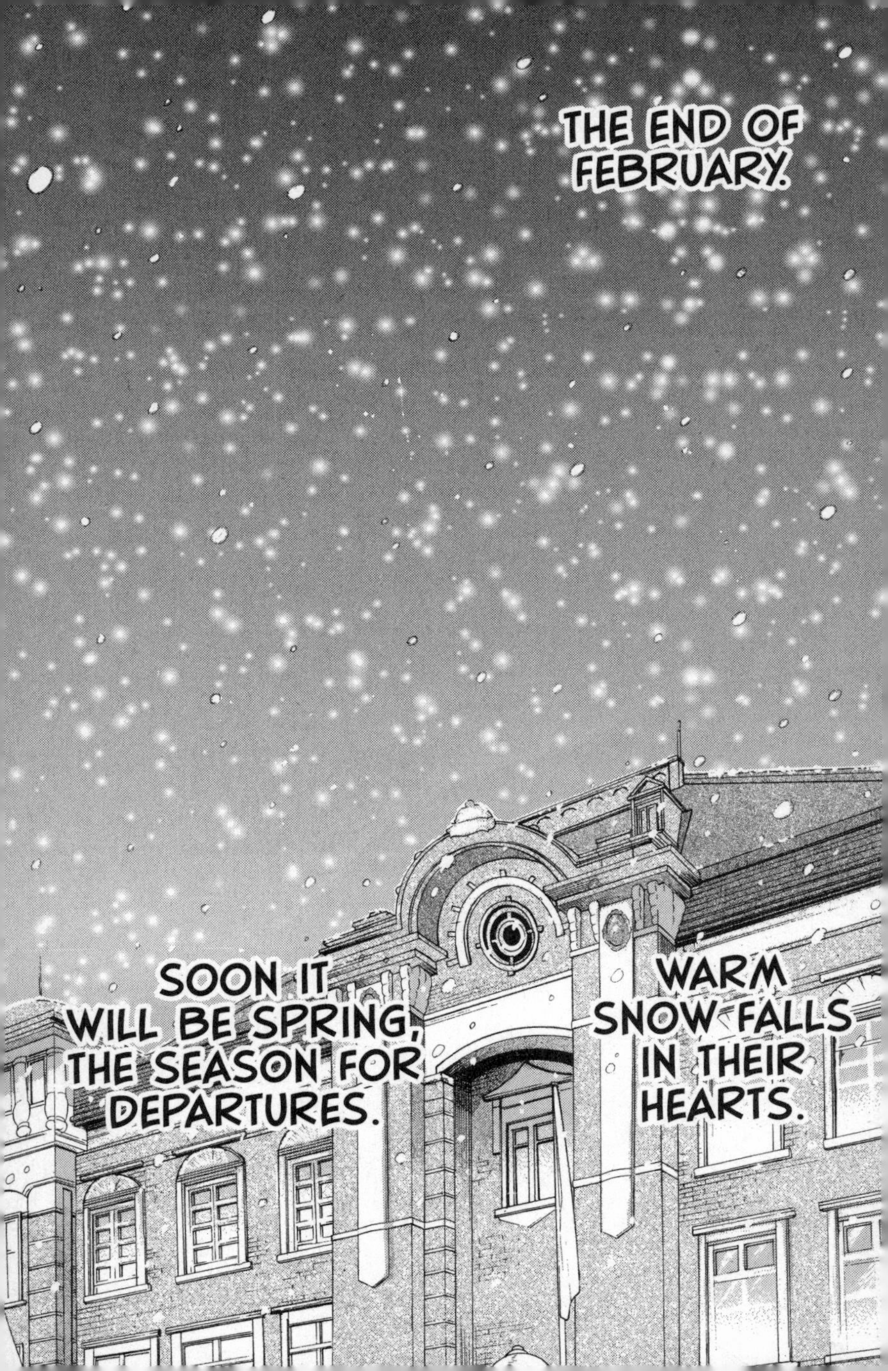
THE END OF FEBRUARY.
WARM SNOW FALLS IN THEIR HEARTS.
SOON IT WILL BE SPRING, THE SEASON FOR DEPARTURES.

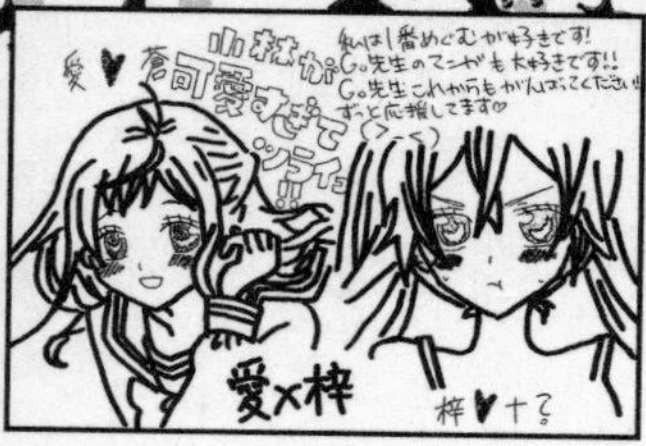
小林が可愛すぎてツライっ!!
愛×梓

Rion Matsubara (Hiroshima) ←
Ed.: I love this duo!!

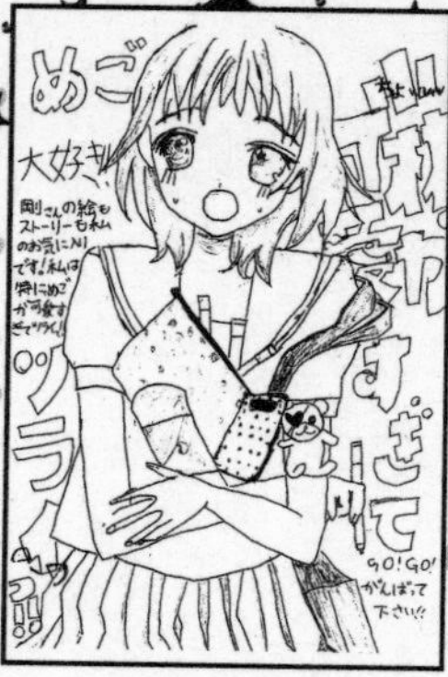

Toshimi Yoshida (Kanagawa) ←
Ed.: Gimme that eye-patch bear!!

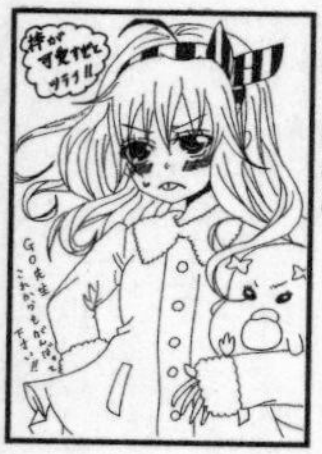

Suzu (Gunma) ←
Ed.: Azusa's cuteness explodes!!

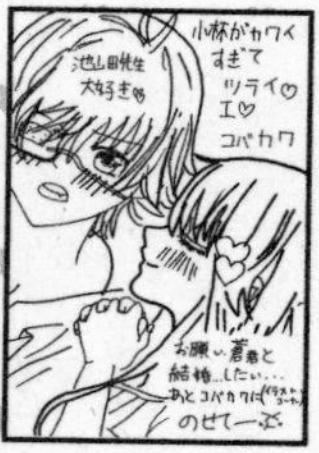
小林がカワイすぎてツライ♡

Rena Matsuzawa (Chiba) →
Ed.: Aoi! You gotta stay faithful!!

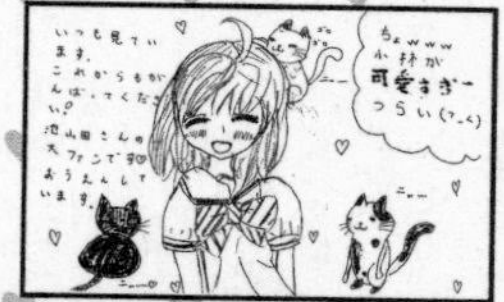

Honoka Utsuki (Tokyo) ↑
Ed.: Mego and the adorable cats. ♥

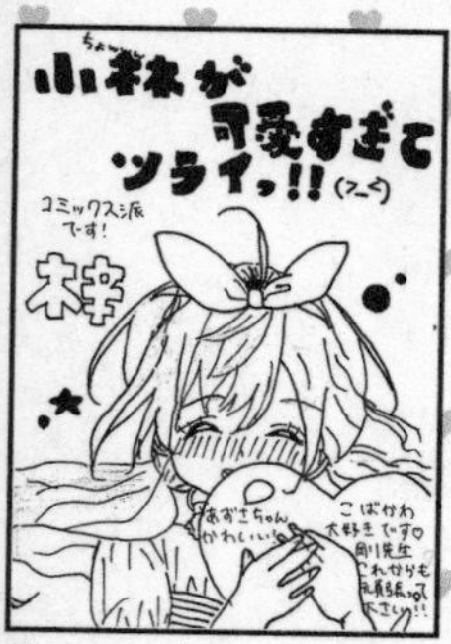
小林が可愛すぎてツライっ!!
梓

Sorara (Hokkaido) ←
Ed.: The blushing Azusa looks super cute!!

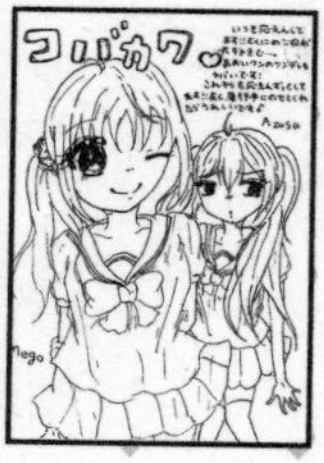
コバカワ

Yuka (Osaka) →
Ed.: Both Mego and Azusa look beautiful. ♥

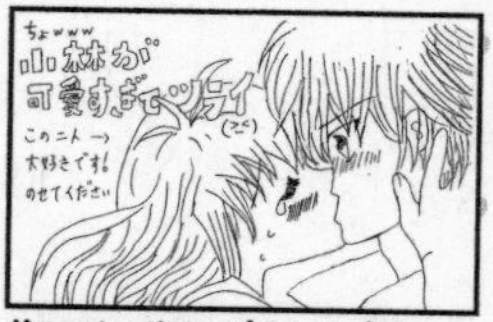

Manaka Yokoi (Osaka) ↑
Ed.: This is a memorable scene!!

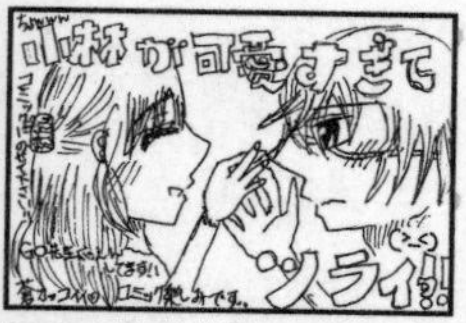
小林が可愛すぎて
ツライ!!

Asane Omori (Kanagwa) ↑
Ed.: They are lovey-dovey. ♥

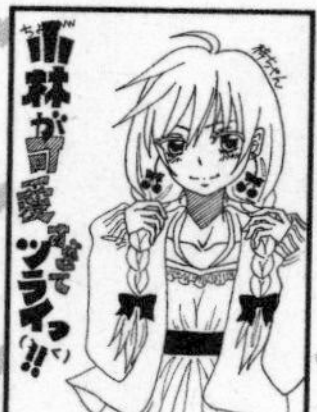

Azumoru (Okayama) ←
Ed.: The earrings look great on her!!

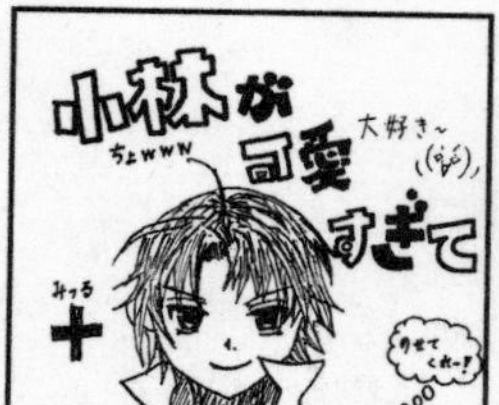
小林が可愛すぎて
ツライっ!!
Sho-Comiも単行本も読んでます!!!

Wakana Matsumoto ↑ (Miyazaki)
Ed.: I'll roll around too!!

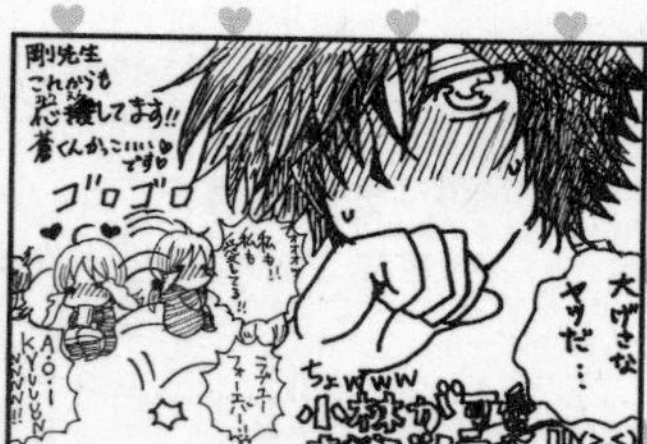
ゴロゴロ

Mitsuki Tsukamoto (Shizuoka) ←
Ed.: Mitsuru looks so manly! I love him!!

Chapter 54

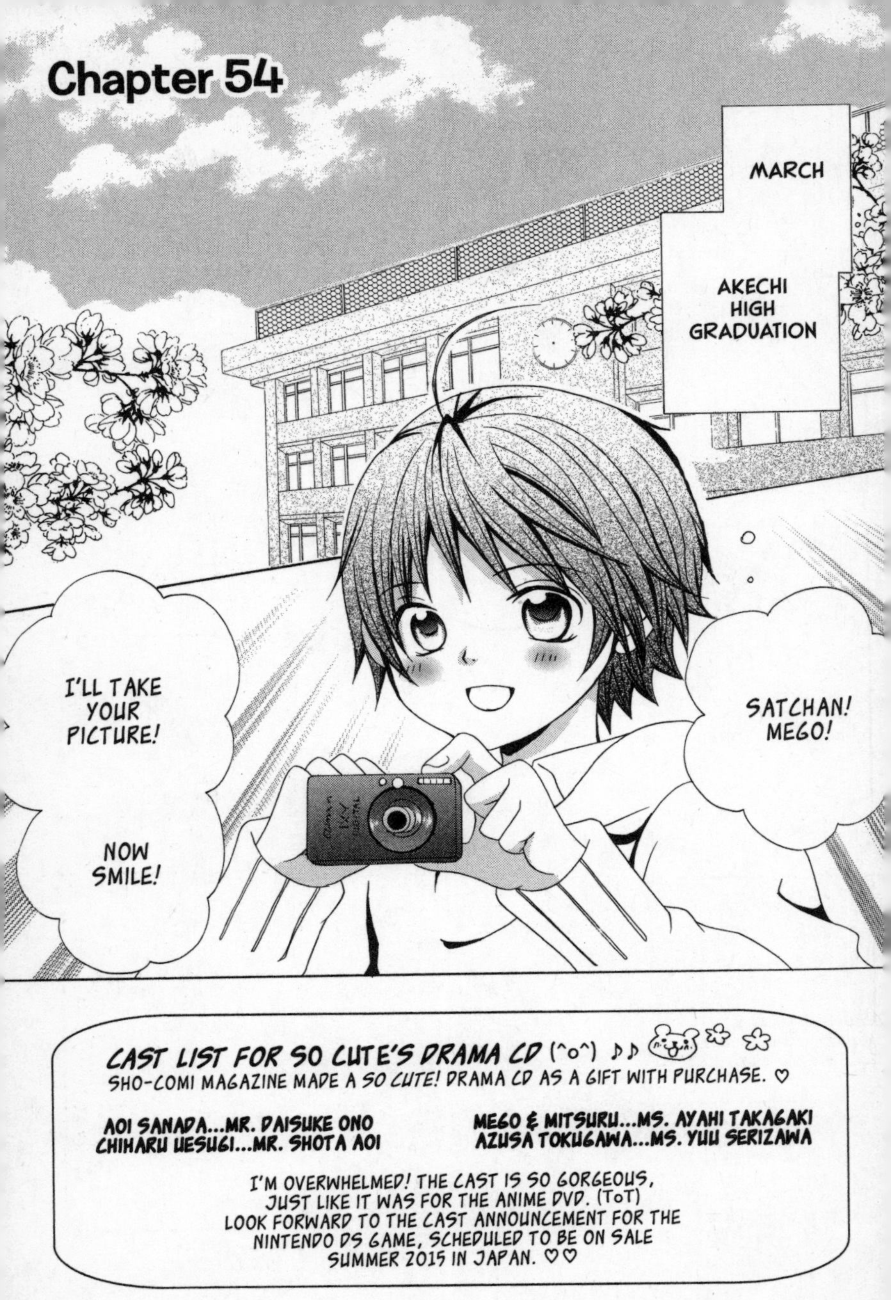
MARCH
AKECHI HIGH GRADUATION
SATCHAN! MEGO!
I'LL TAKE YOUR PICTURE!
NOW SMILE!

CAST LIST FOR SO CUTE'S DRAMA CD (^o^) ♪♪

SHO-COMI MAGAZINE MADE A *SO CUTE!* DRAMA CD AS A GIFT WITH PURCHASE. ♡

AOI SANADA...MR. DAISUKE ONO
CHIHARU UESUGI...MR. SHOTA AOI
MEGO & MITSURU...MS. AYAHI TAKAGAKI
AZUSA TOKUGAWA...MS. YUU SERIZAWA

I'M OVERWHELMED! THE CAST IS SO GORGEOUS, JUST LIKE IT WAS FOR THE ANIME DVD. (ToT) LOOK FORWARD TO THE CAST ANNOUNCEMENT FOR THE NINTENDO DS GAME, SCHEDULED TO BE ON SALE SUMMER 2015 IN JAPAN. ♡♡

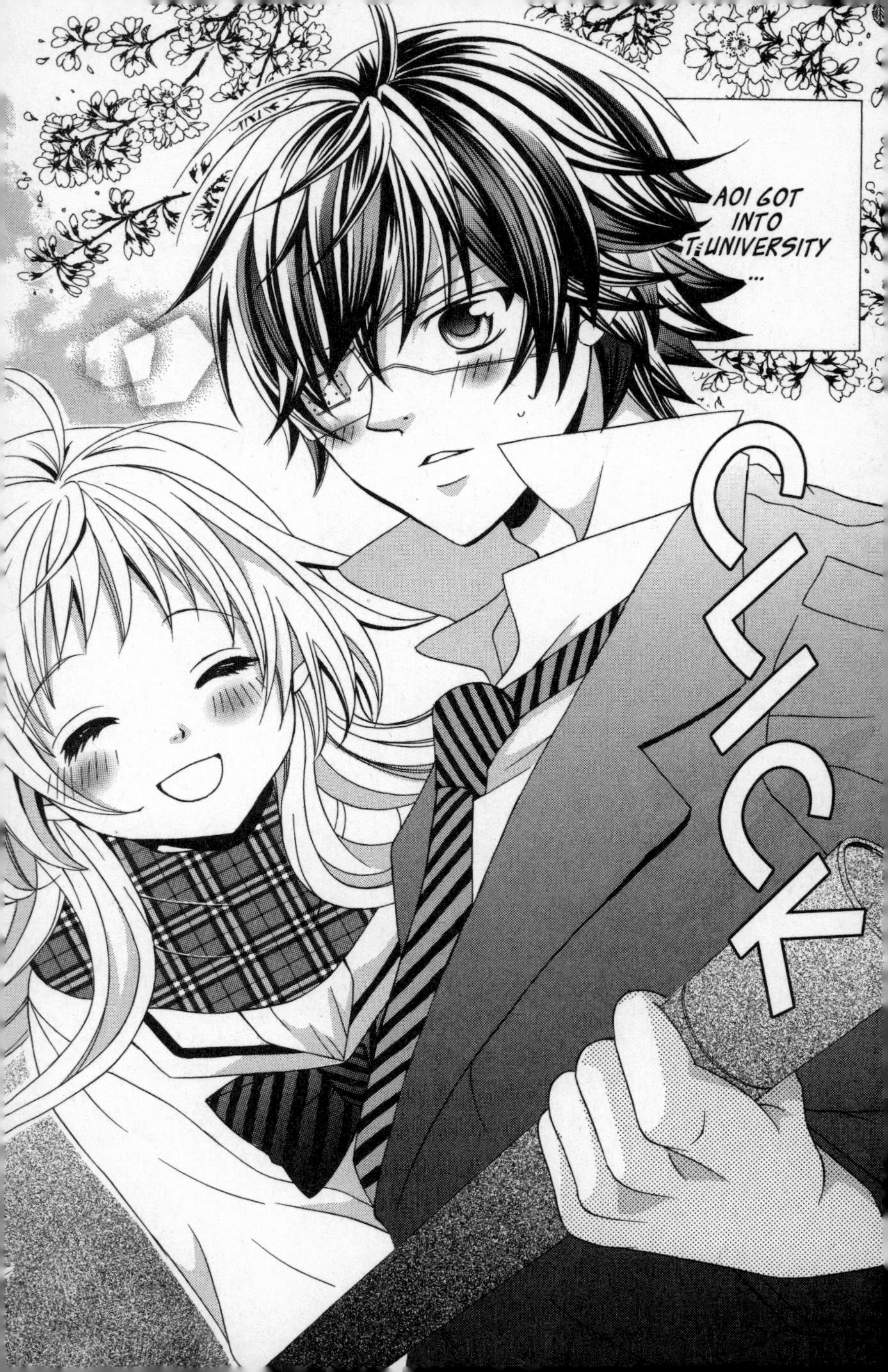
AOI GOT INTO T. UNIVERSITY ...
CLICK

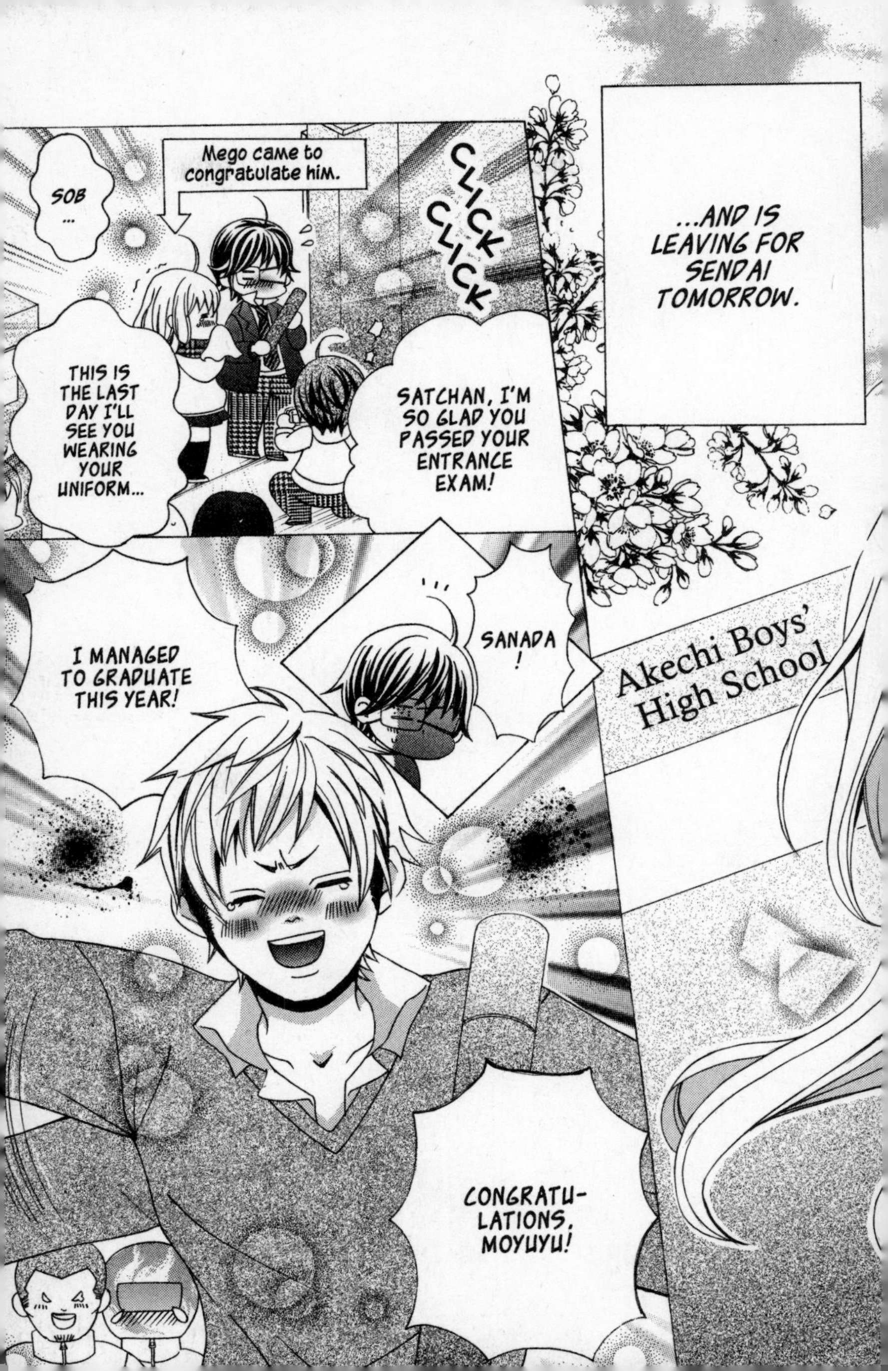
...AND IS LEAVING FOR SENDAI TOMORROW.
CLICK CLICK
Mego came to congratulate him.
SOB ...
SATCHAN, I'M SO GLAD YOU PASSED YOUR ENTRANCE EXAM!
THIS IS THE LAST DAY I'LL SEE YOU WEARING YOUR UNIFORM...
Akechi Boys' High School
SANADA!
I MANAGED TO GRADUATE THIS YEAR!
CONGRATU-LATIONS, MOYUYU!

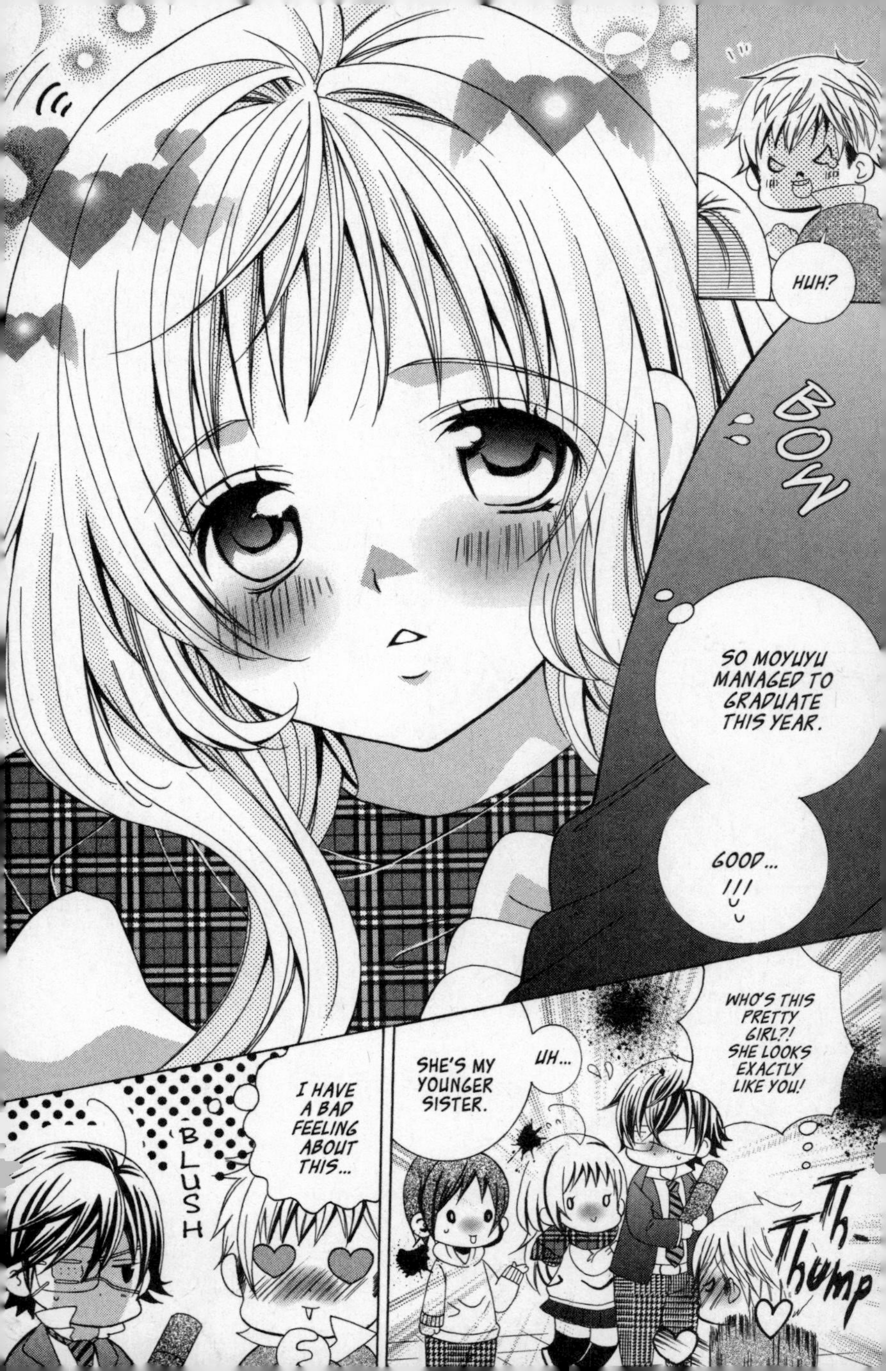
HUH?
BOW
SO MOYUYU MANAGED TO GRADUATE THIS YEAR.
GOOD...
WHO'S THIS PRETTY GIRL?! SHE LOOKS EXACTLY LIKE YOU!
UH...
SHE'S MY YOUNGER SISTER.
Th-Thump
I HAVE A BAD FEELING ABOUT THIS...
BLUSH

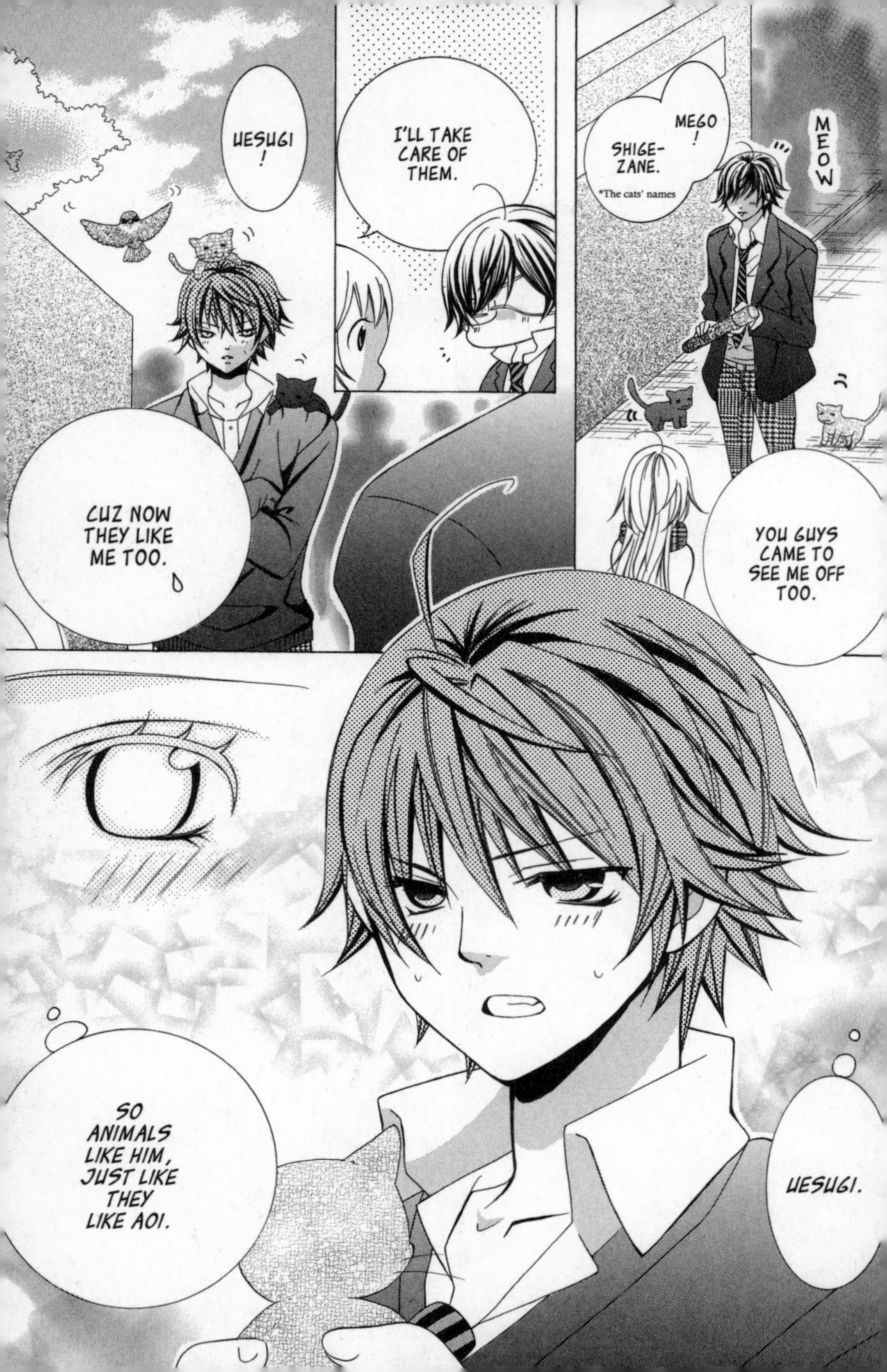
MEOW
MEGO!
SHIGE-ZANE.
*The cats' names
YOU GUYS CAME TO SEE ME OFF TOO.
I'LL TAKE CARE OF THEM.
UESUGI!
CUZ NOW THEY LIKE ME TOO.
UESUGI.
SO ANIMALS LIKE HIM, JUST LIKE THEY LIKE AOI.

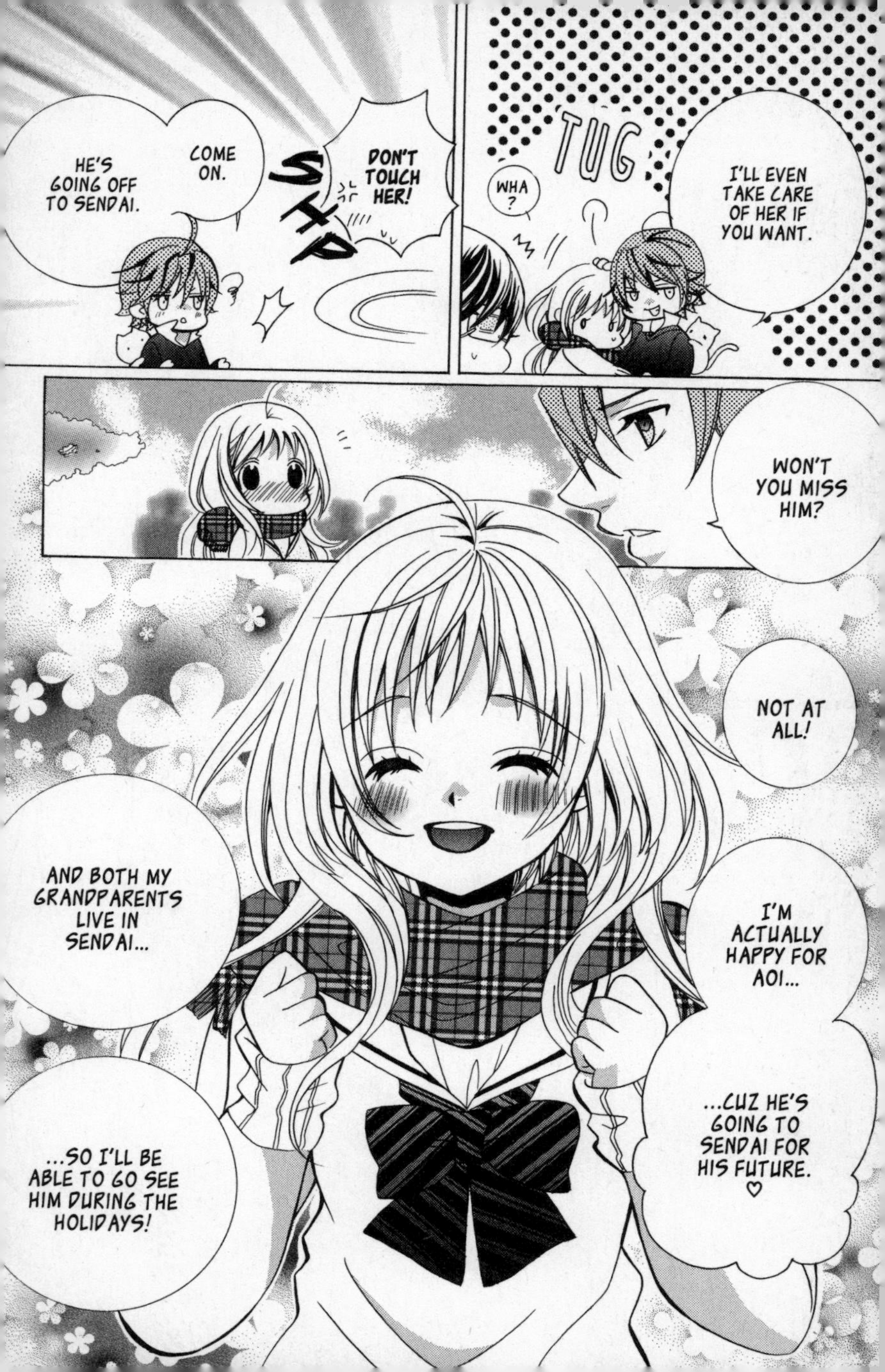
I'LL EVEN TAKE CARE OF HER IF YOU WANT.
TUG
WHA ?
DON'T TOUCH HER!
SHP
COME ON.
HE'S GOING OFF TO SENDAI.
WON'T YOU MISS HIM?
NOT AT ALL!
I'M ACTUALLY HAPPY FOR AOI...
...CUZ HE'S GOING TO SENDAI FOR HIS FUTURE. ♡
AND BOTH MY GRANDPARENTS LIVE IN SENDAI...
...SO I'LL BE ABLE TO GO SEE HIM DURING THE HOLIDAYS!

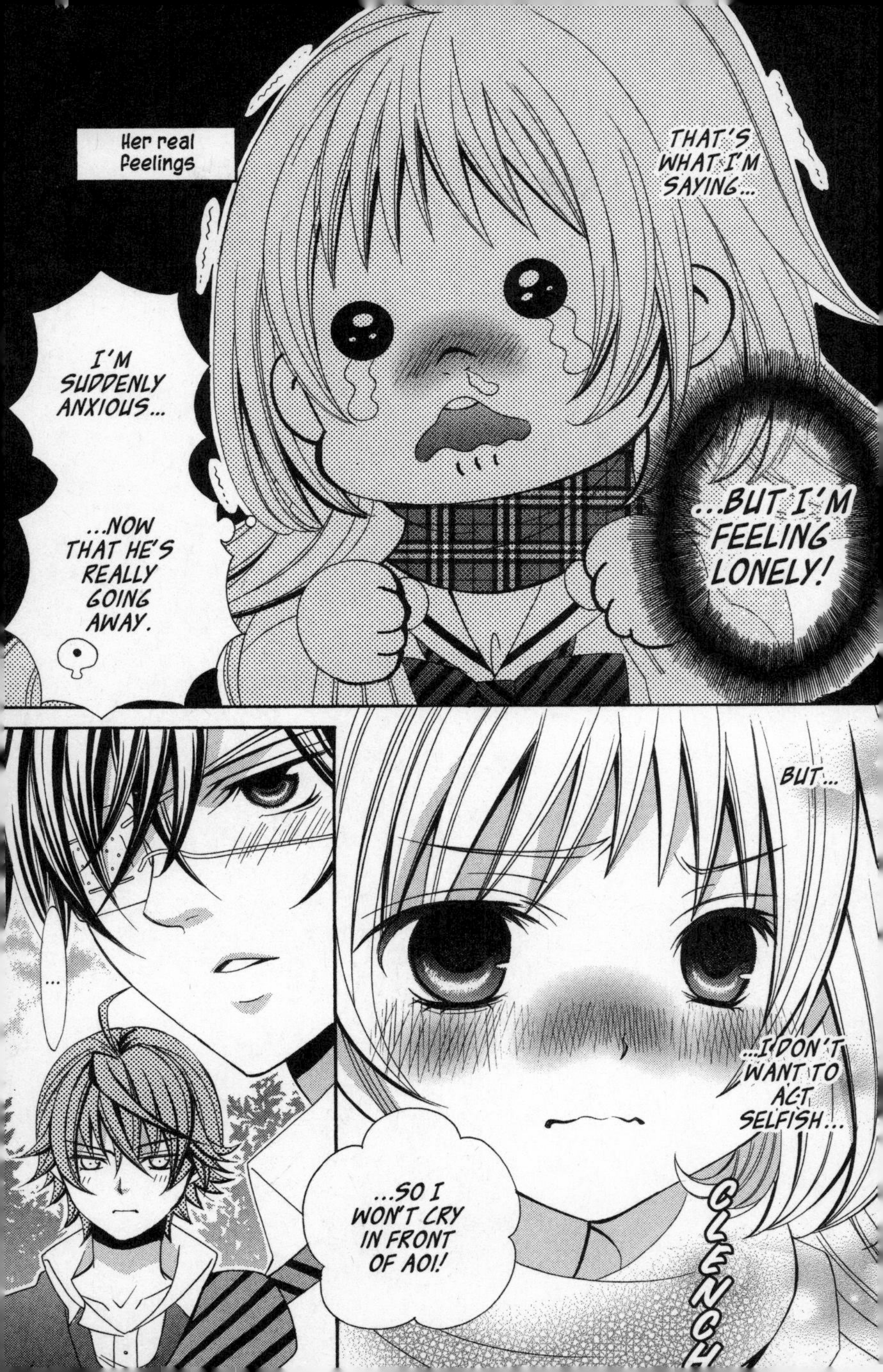
THAT'S WHAT I'M SAYING...
Her real feelings
I'M SUDDENLY ANXIOUS...
...BUT I'M FEELING LONELY!
...NOW THAT HE'S REALLY GOING AWAY.
BUT...
...I DON'T WANT TO ACT SELFISH...
...SO I WON'T CRY IN FRONT OF AOI!
CLENCH
...

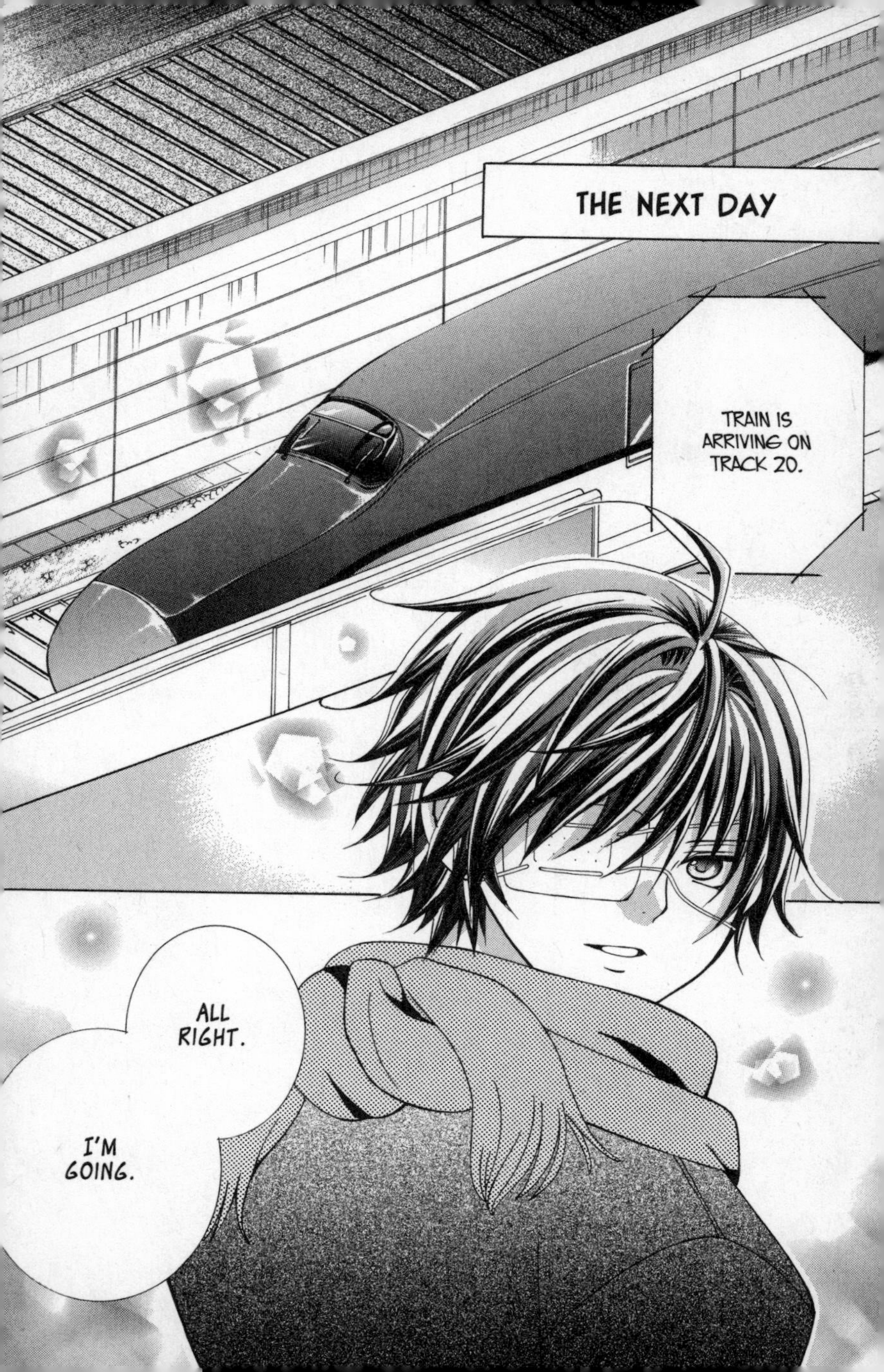
THE NEXT DAY
TRAIN IS ARRIVING ON TRACK 20.
ALL RIGHT.
I'M GOING.

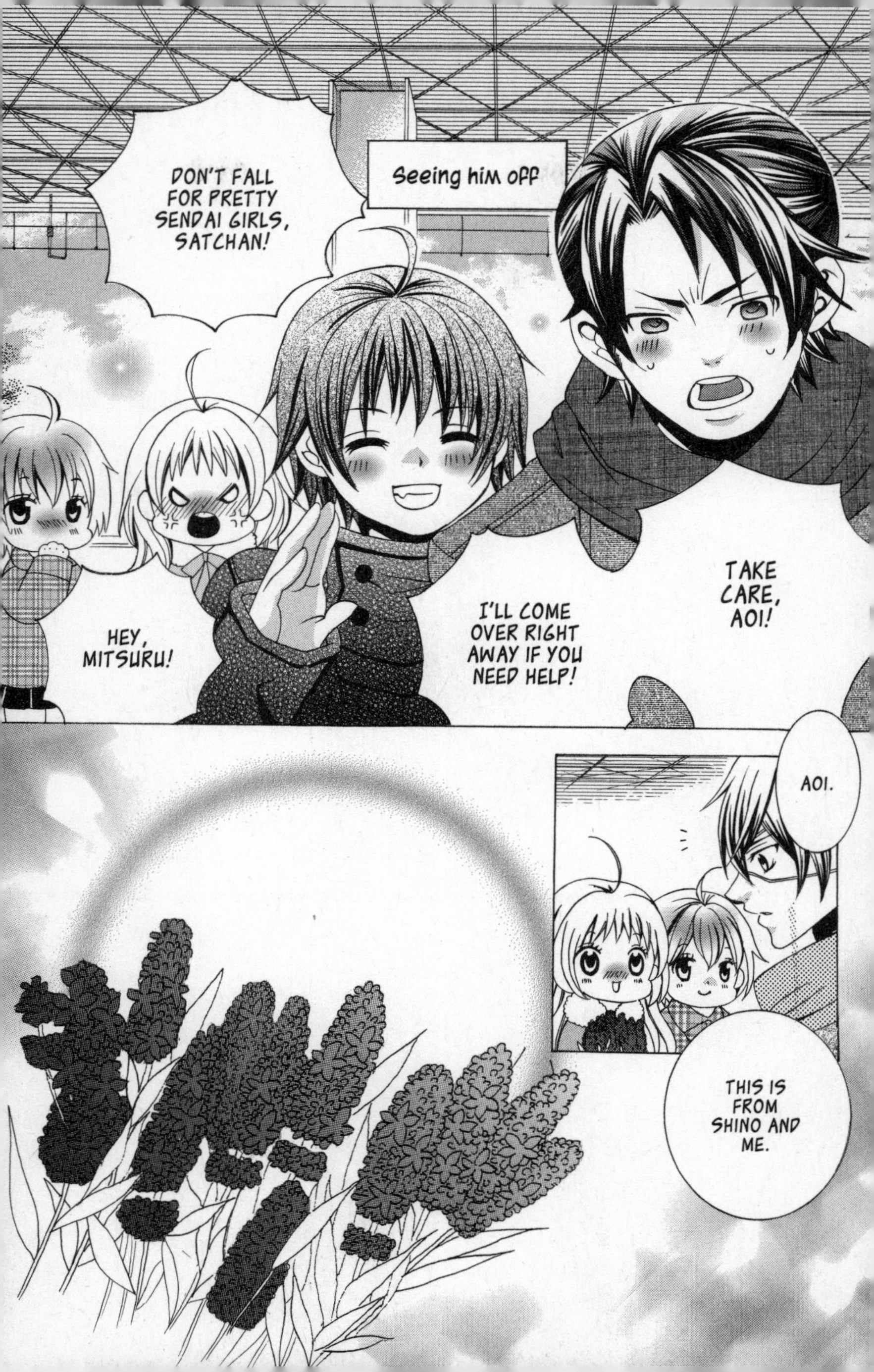

Seeing him off
TAKE CARE, AOI!
I'LL COME OVER RIGHT AWAY IF YOU NEED HELP!
DON'T FALL FOR PRETTY SENDAI GIRLS, SATCHAN!
HEY, MITSURU!
AOI.
THIS IS FROM SHINO AND ME.

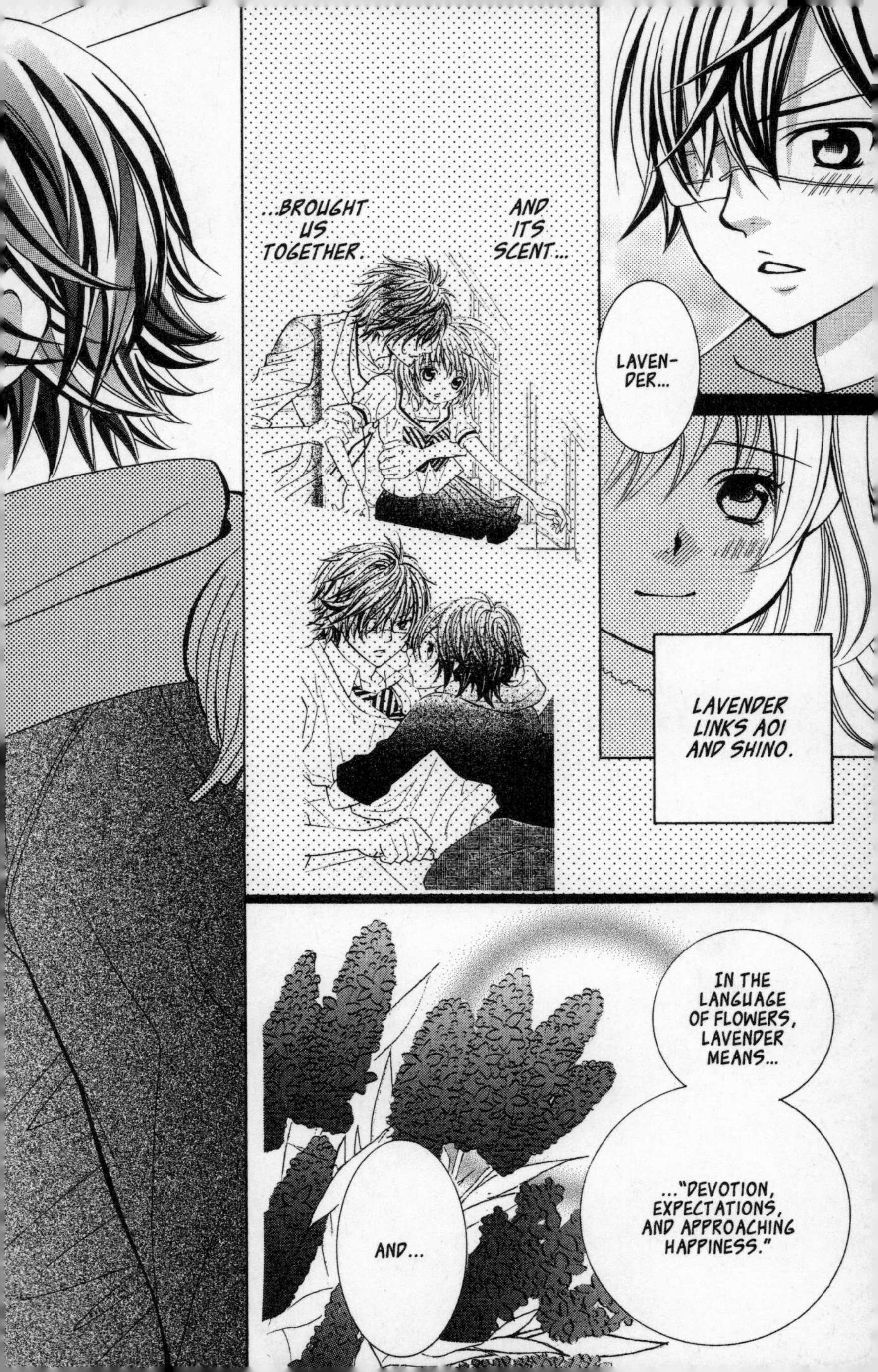
LAVEN-DER...
LAVENDER LINKS AOI AND SHINO.
AND ITS SCENT...
...BROUGHT US TOGETHER.
IN THE LANGUAGE OF FLOWERS, LAVENDER MEANS...
..."DEVOTION, EXPECTATIONS, AND APPROACHING HAPPINESS."
AND...

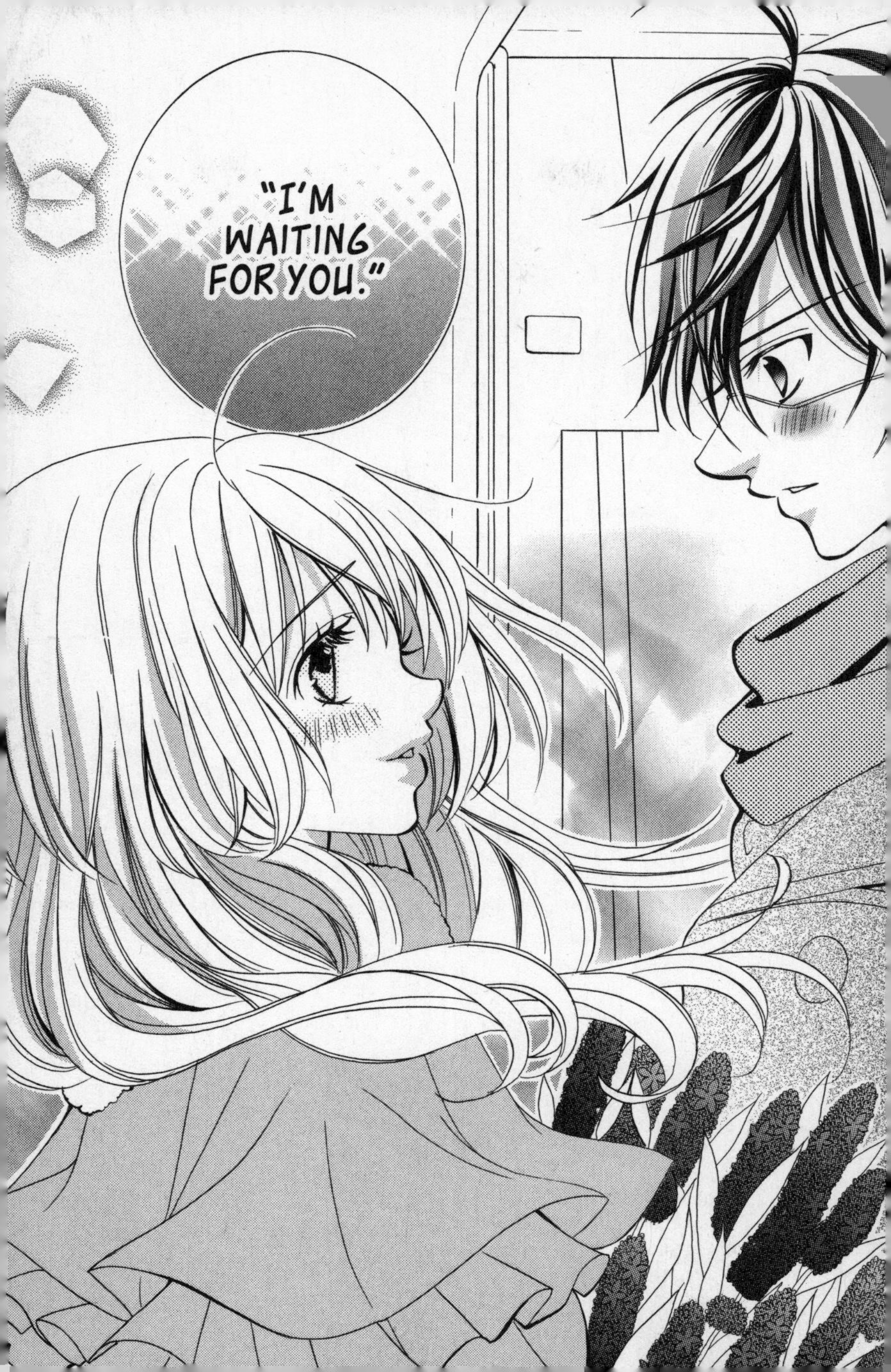
"I'M WAITING FOR YOU."

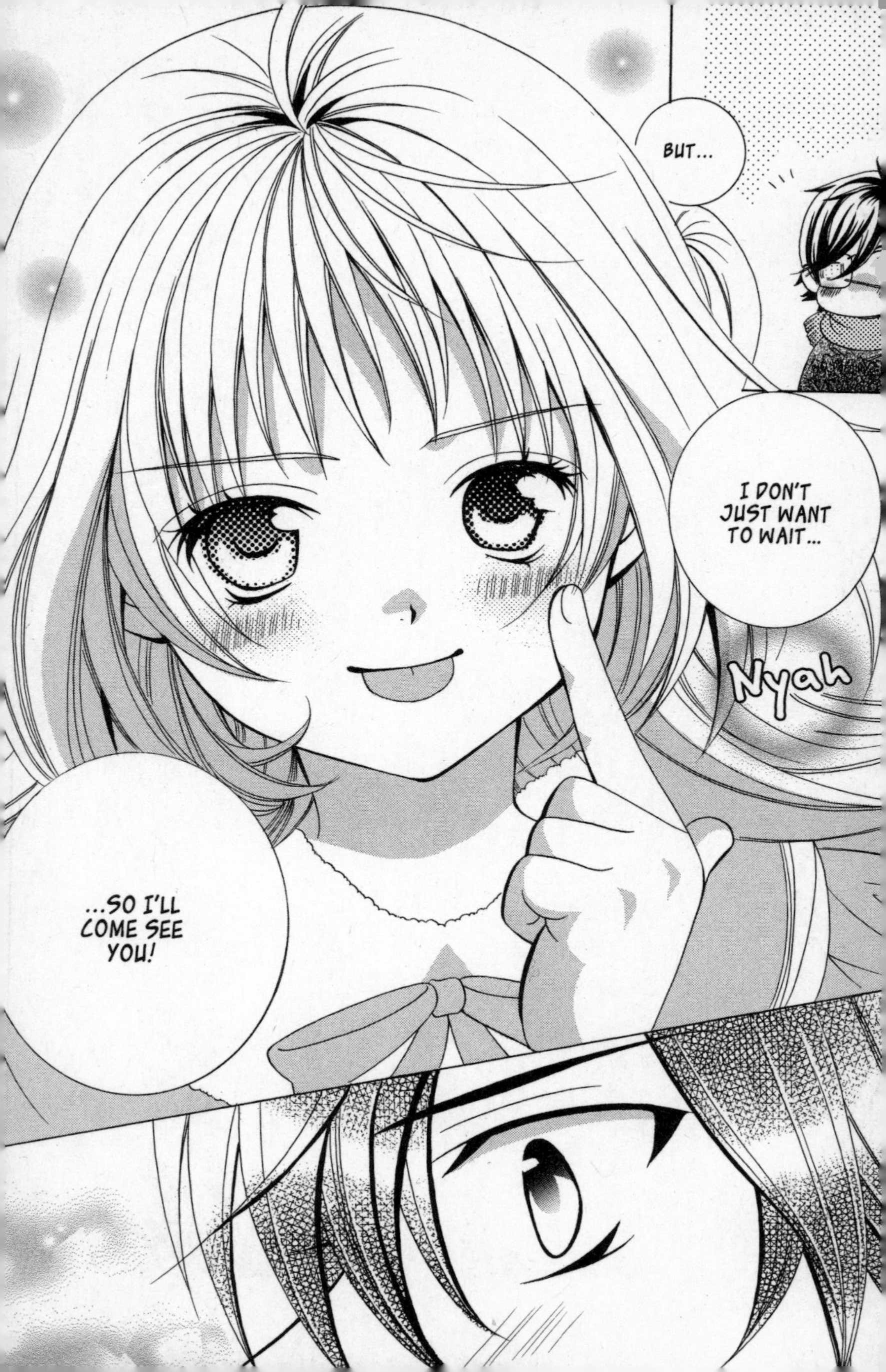
BUT...
I DON'T JUST WANT TO WAIT...
Nyah
...SO I'LL COME SEE YOU!

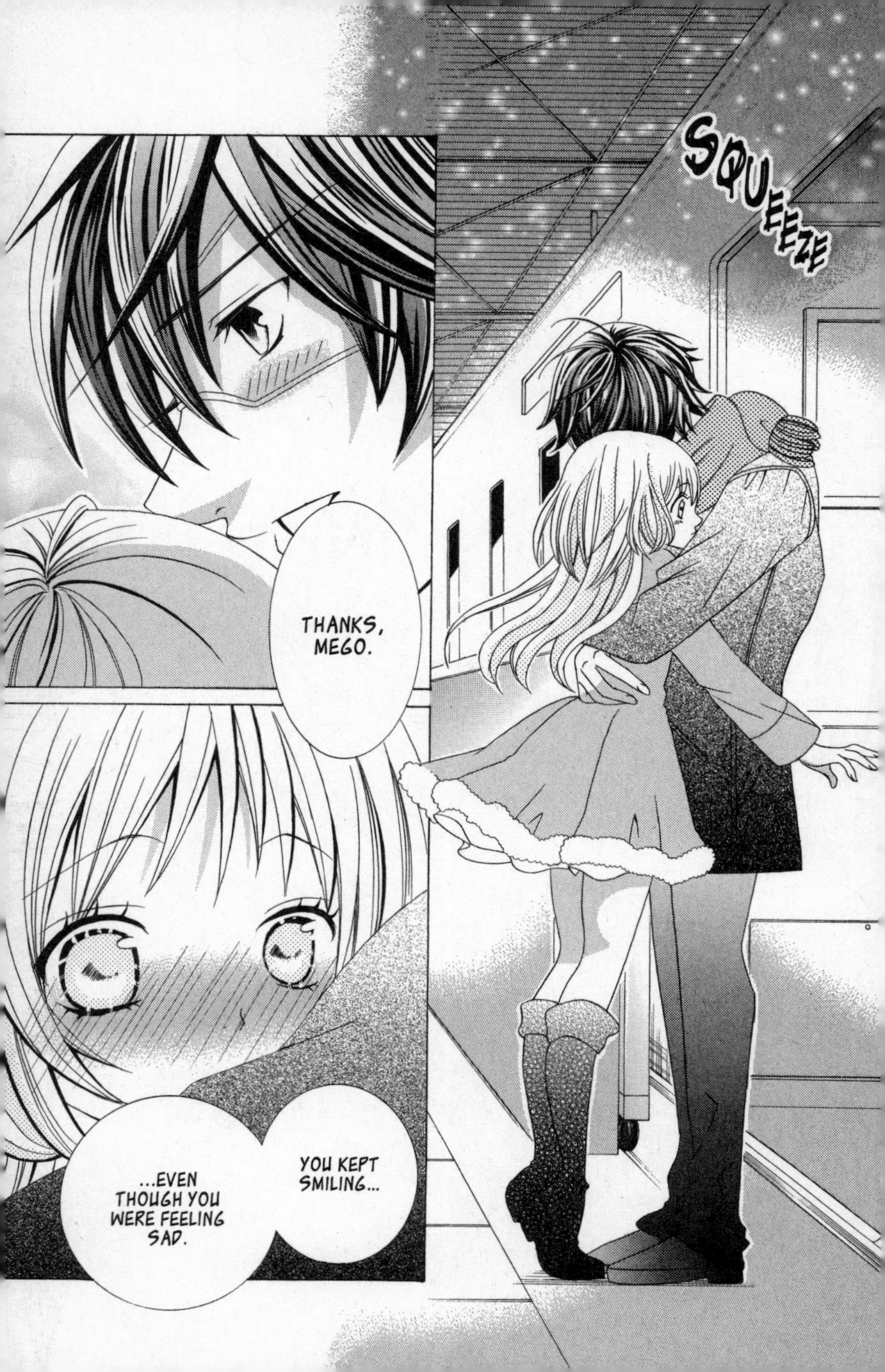
SQUEEEZE
THANKS, MEGO.
YOU KEPT SMILING...
...EVEN THOUGH YOU WERE FEELING SAD.

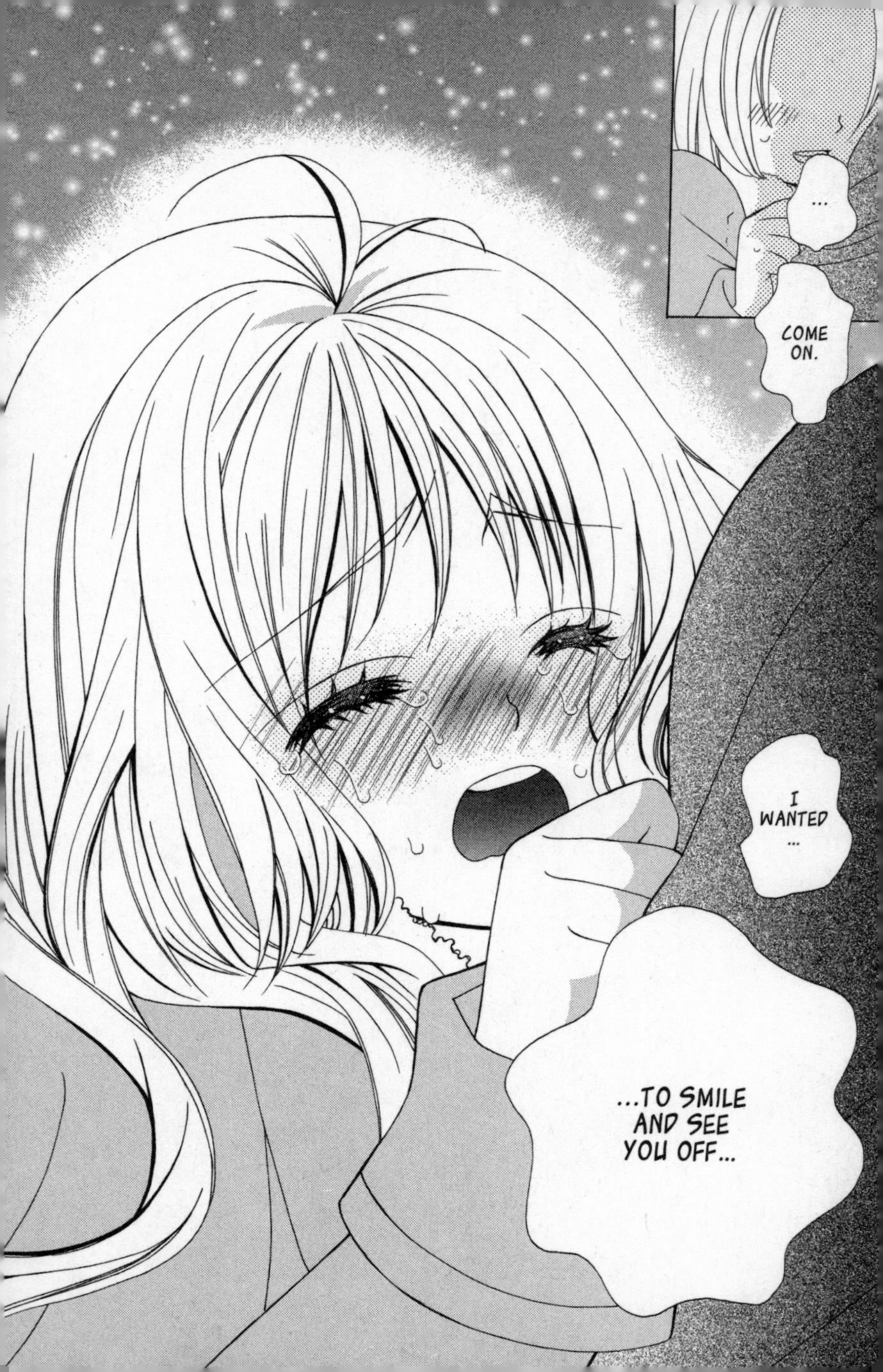
...
COME ON.
I WANTED ...
...TO SMILE AND SEE YOU OFF...

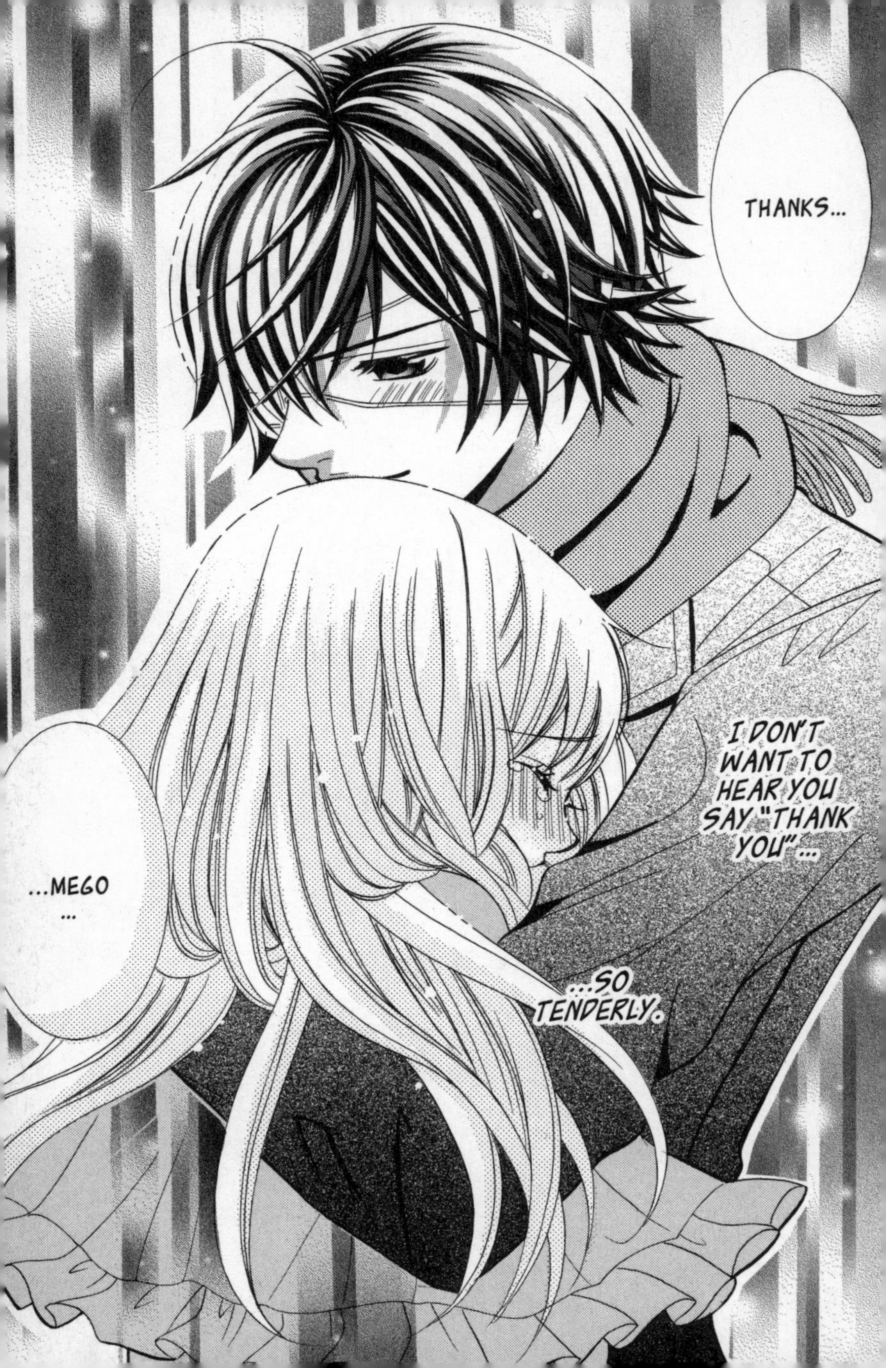
THANKS...
I DON'T WANT TO HEAR YOU SAY "THANK YOU"...
...MEGO ...
...SO TENDERLY.

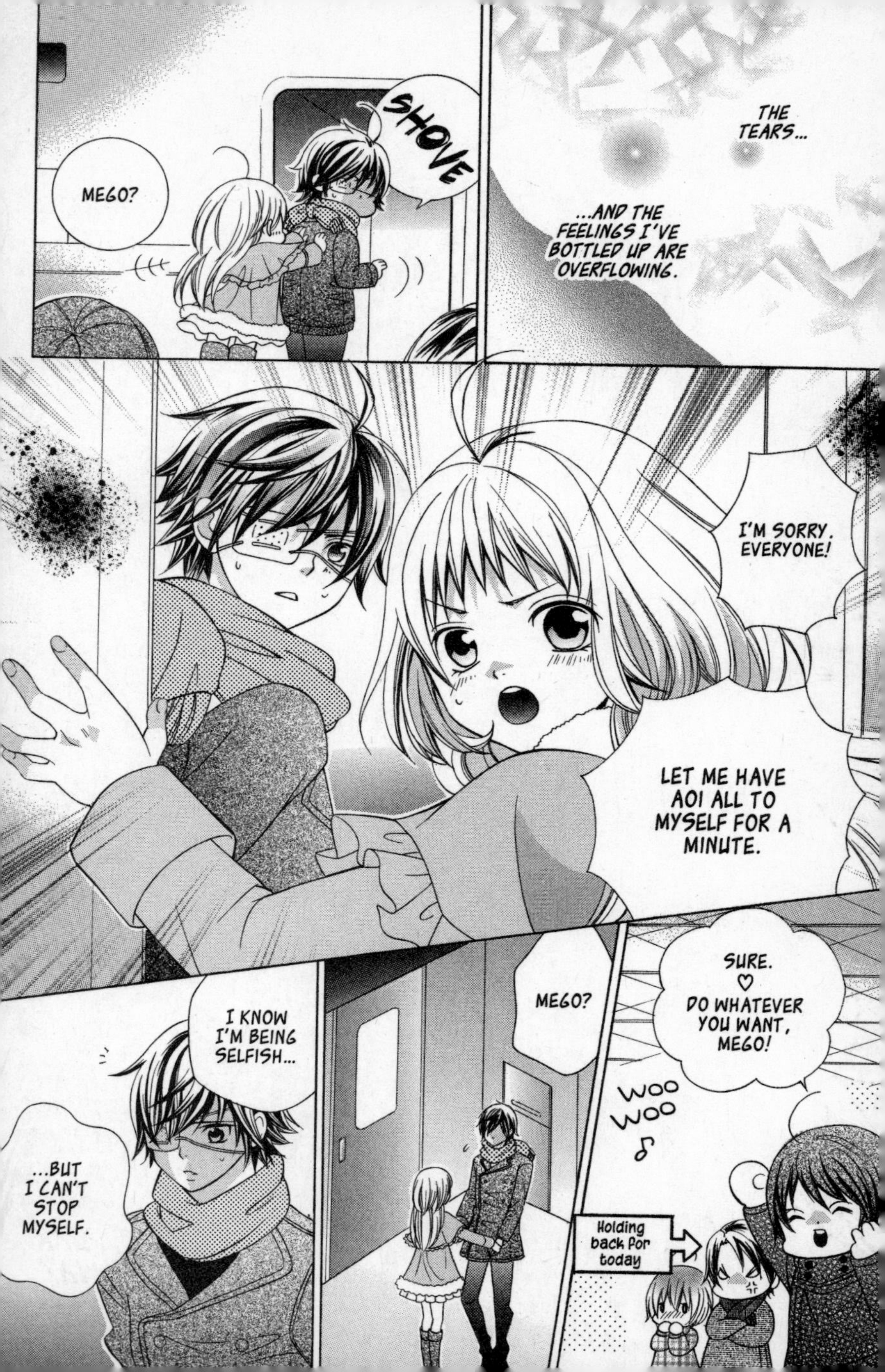
THE TEARS...
...AND THE FEELINGS I'VE BOTTLED UP ARE OVERFLOWING.
SHOVE
MEGO?
I'M SORRY, EVERYONE!
LET ME HAVE AOI ALL TO MYSELF FOR A MINUTE.
SURE. ♡ DO WHATEVER YOU WANT, MEGO!
MEGO?
WOO WOO ♪
Holding back for today
I KNOW I'M BEING SELFISH...
...BUT I CAN'T STOP MYSELF.

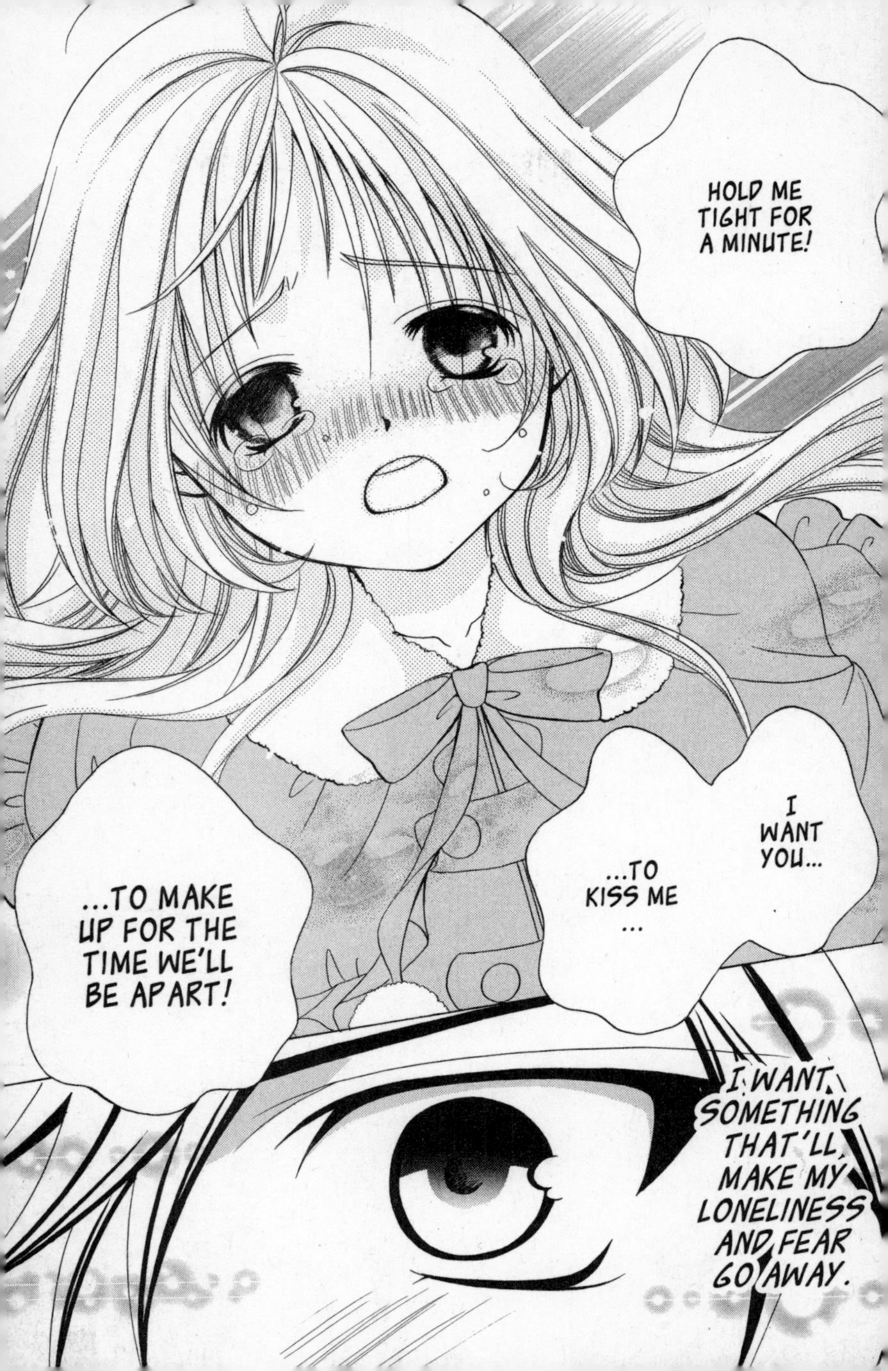
HOLD ME TIGHT FOR A MINUTE!
I WANT YOU...
...TO KISS ME ...
...TO MAKE UP FOR THE TIME WE'LL BE APART!
I WANT SOMETHING THAT'LL MAKE MY LONELINESS AND FEAR GO AWAY.

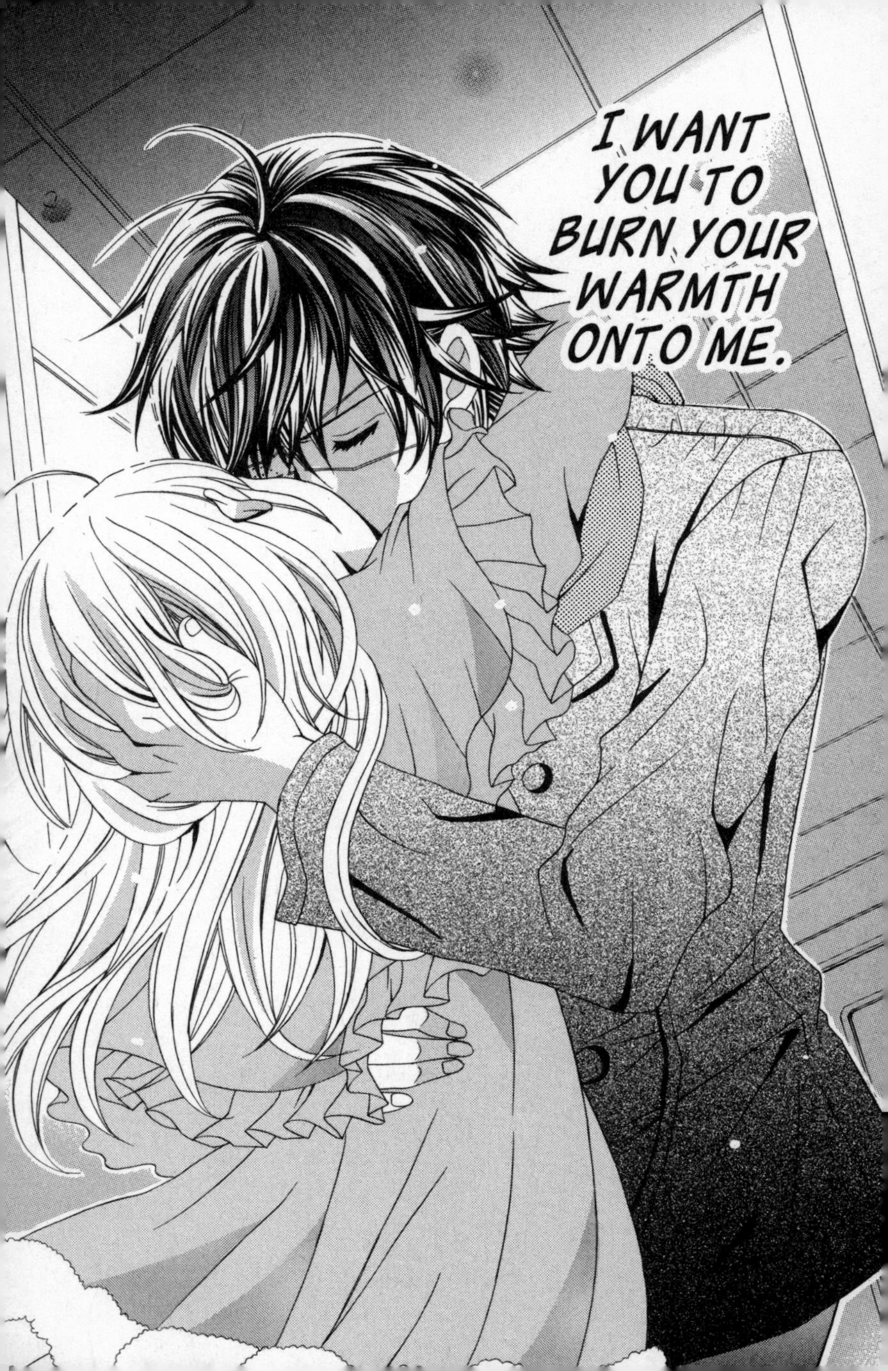
I WANT YOU TO BURN YOUR WARMTH ONTO ME.

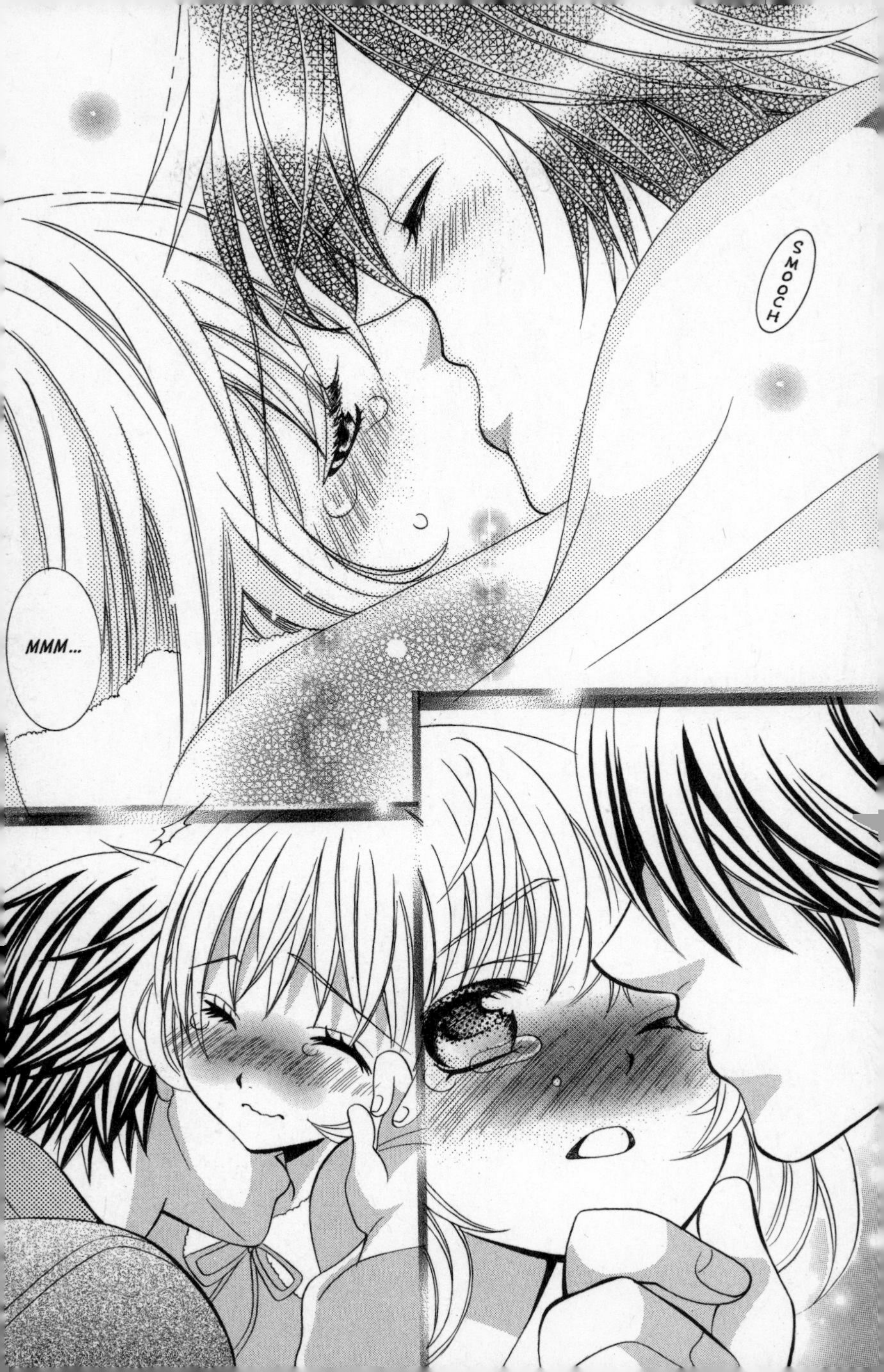
SMOOCH
MMM...

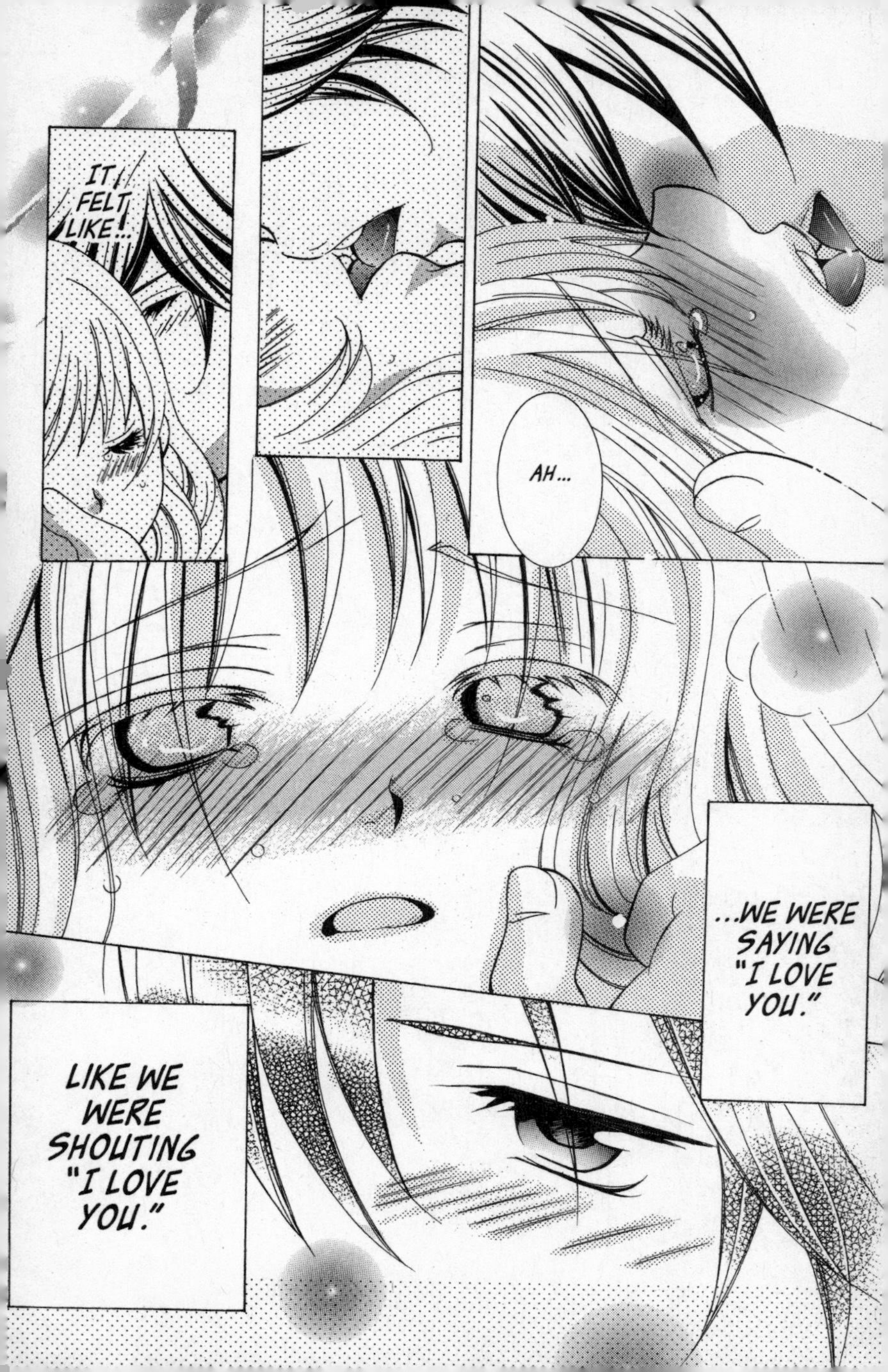
AH...
IT FELT LIKE...
...WE WERE SAYING "I LOVE YOU."
LIKE WE WERE SHOUTING "I LOVE YOU."

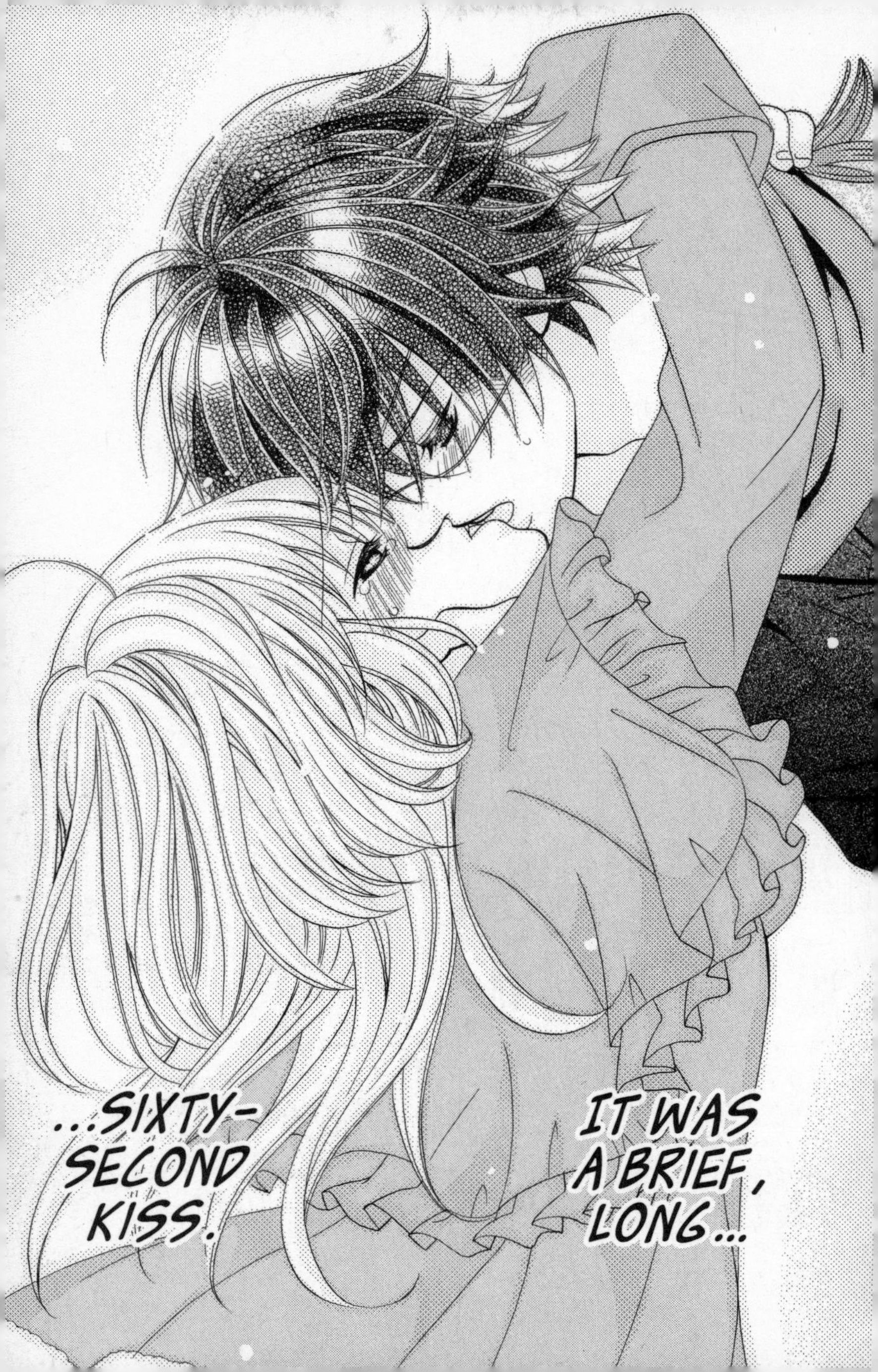
IT WAS A BRIEF, LONG...
...SIXTY-SECOND KISS.

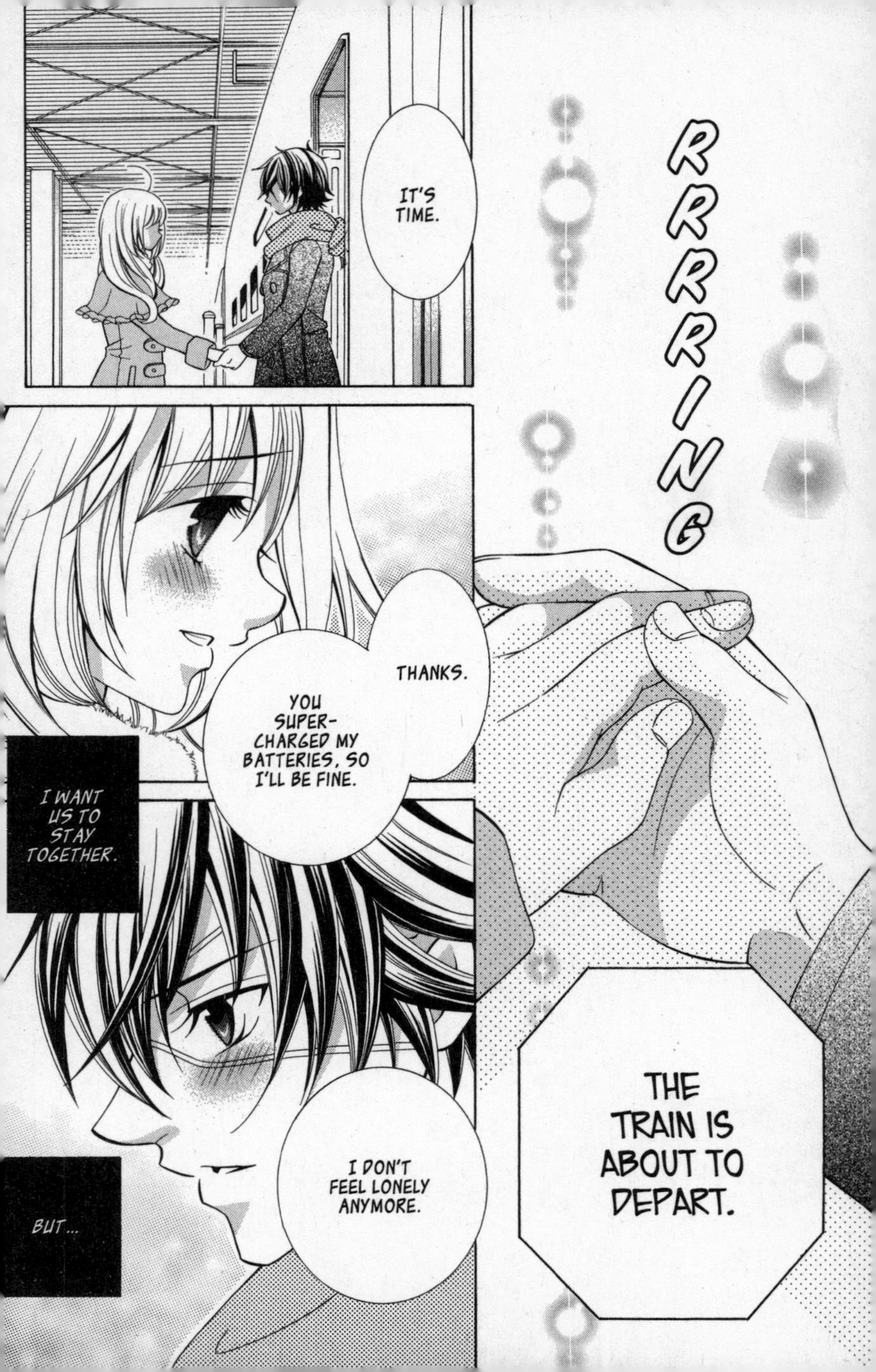
RRRRING
THE TRAIN IS ABOUT TO DEPART.
IT'S TIME.
THANKS.
YOU SUPER-CHARGED MY BATTERIES, SO I'LL BE FINE.
I WANT US TO STAY TOGETHER.
I DON'T FEEL LONELY ANYMORE.
BUT...

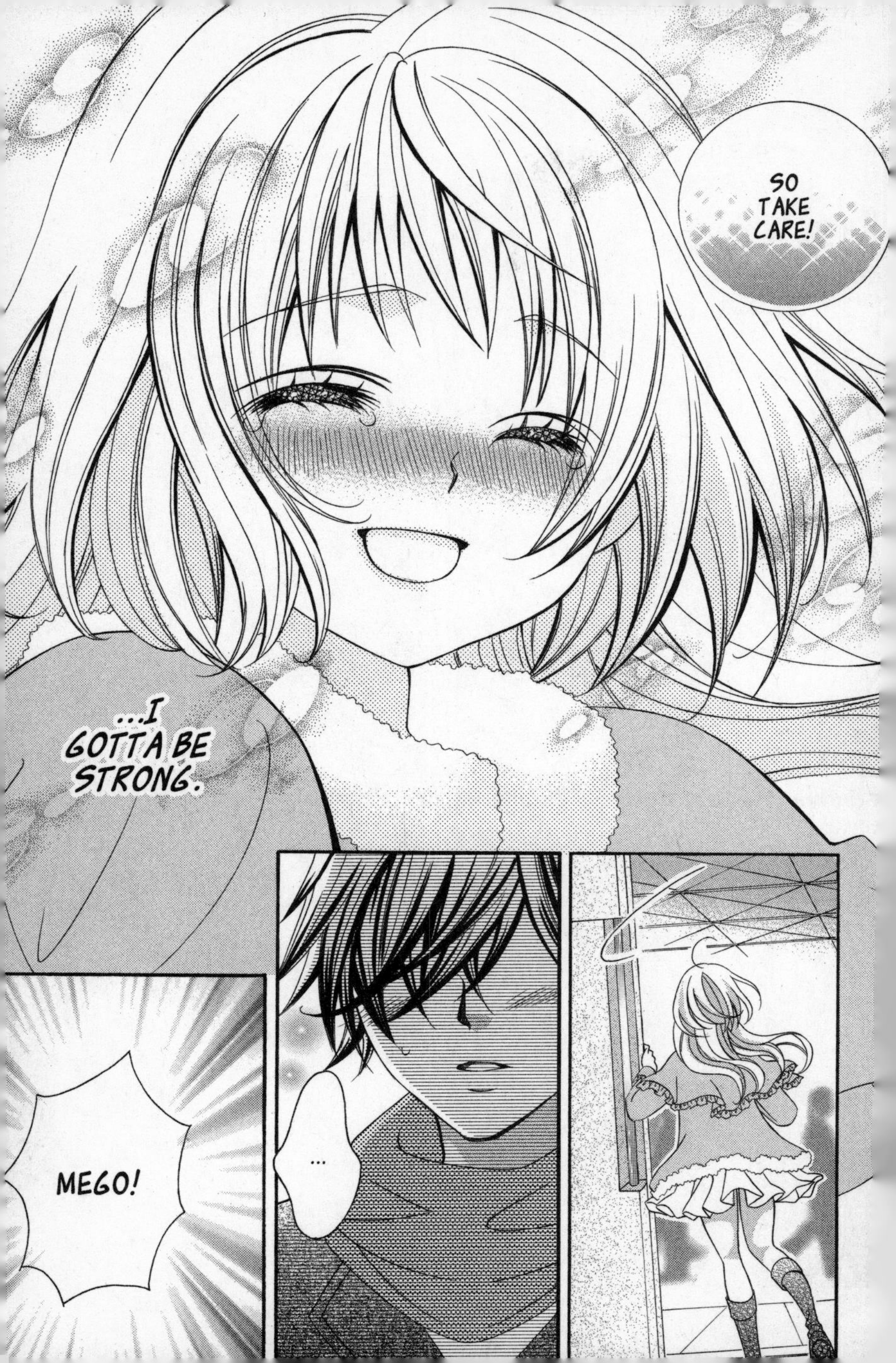
SO TAKE CARE!
...I GOTTA BE STRONG.
...
MEGO!

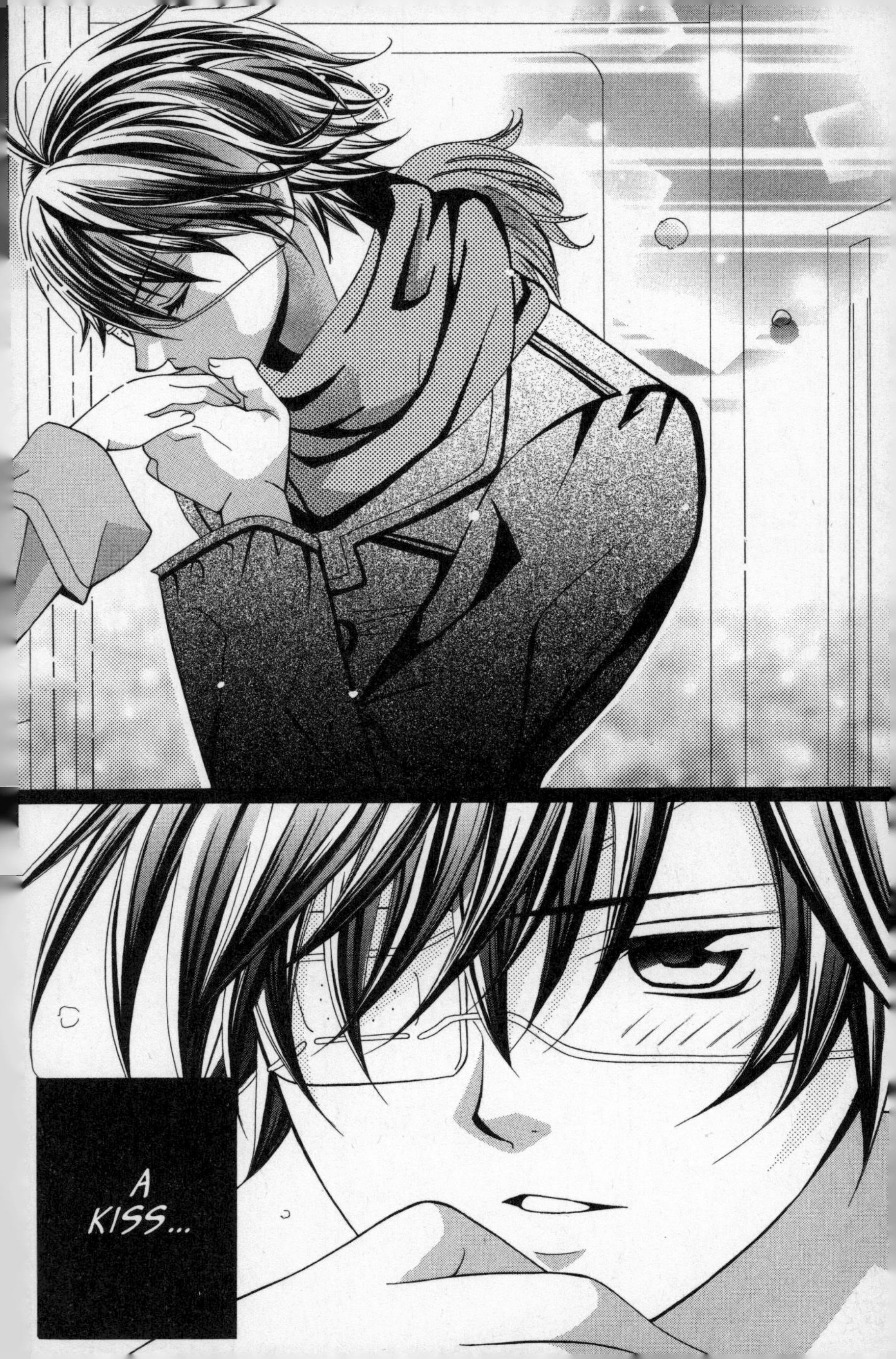
A KISS...

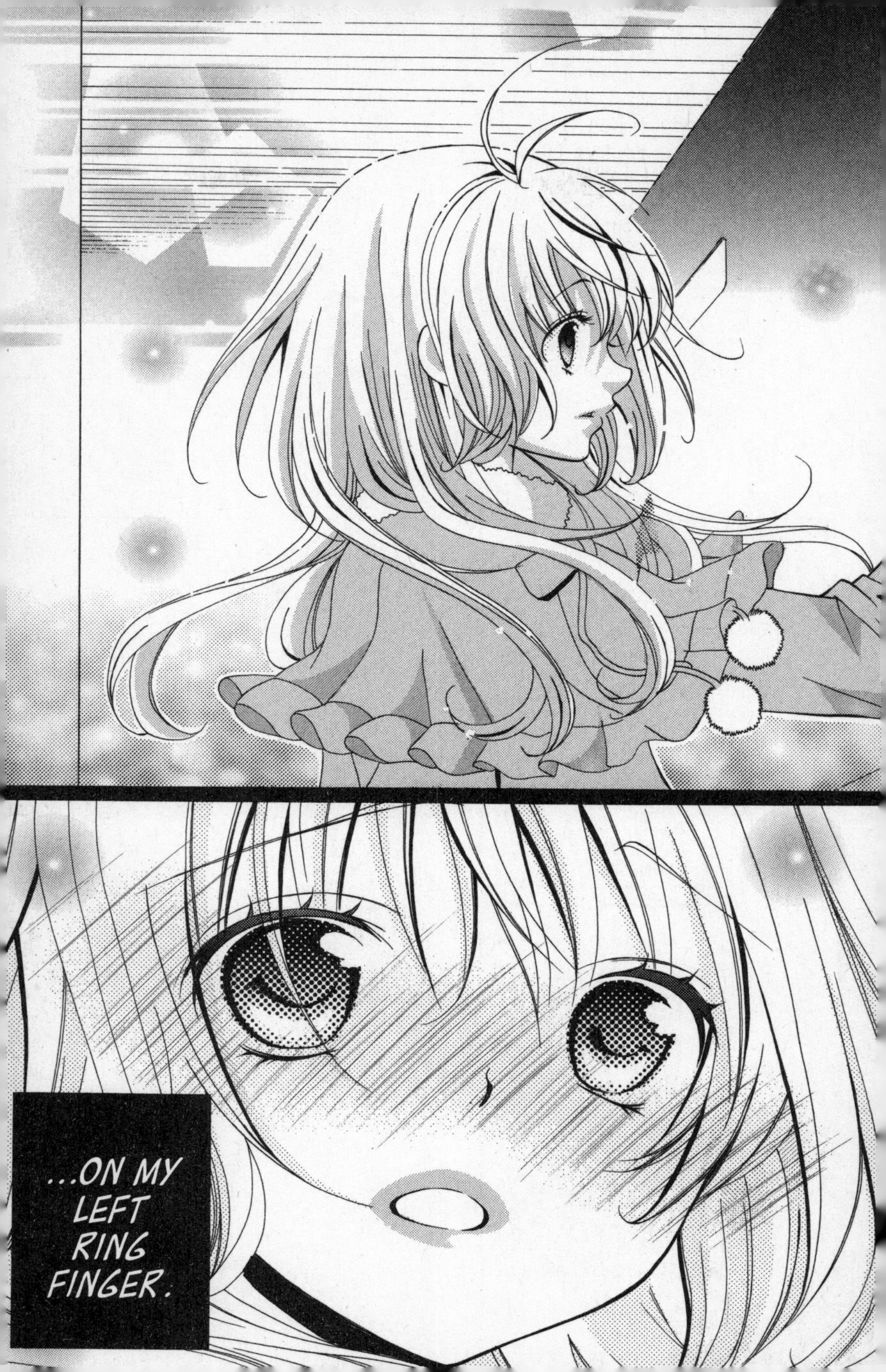
...ON MY LEFT RING FINGER.

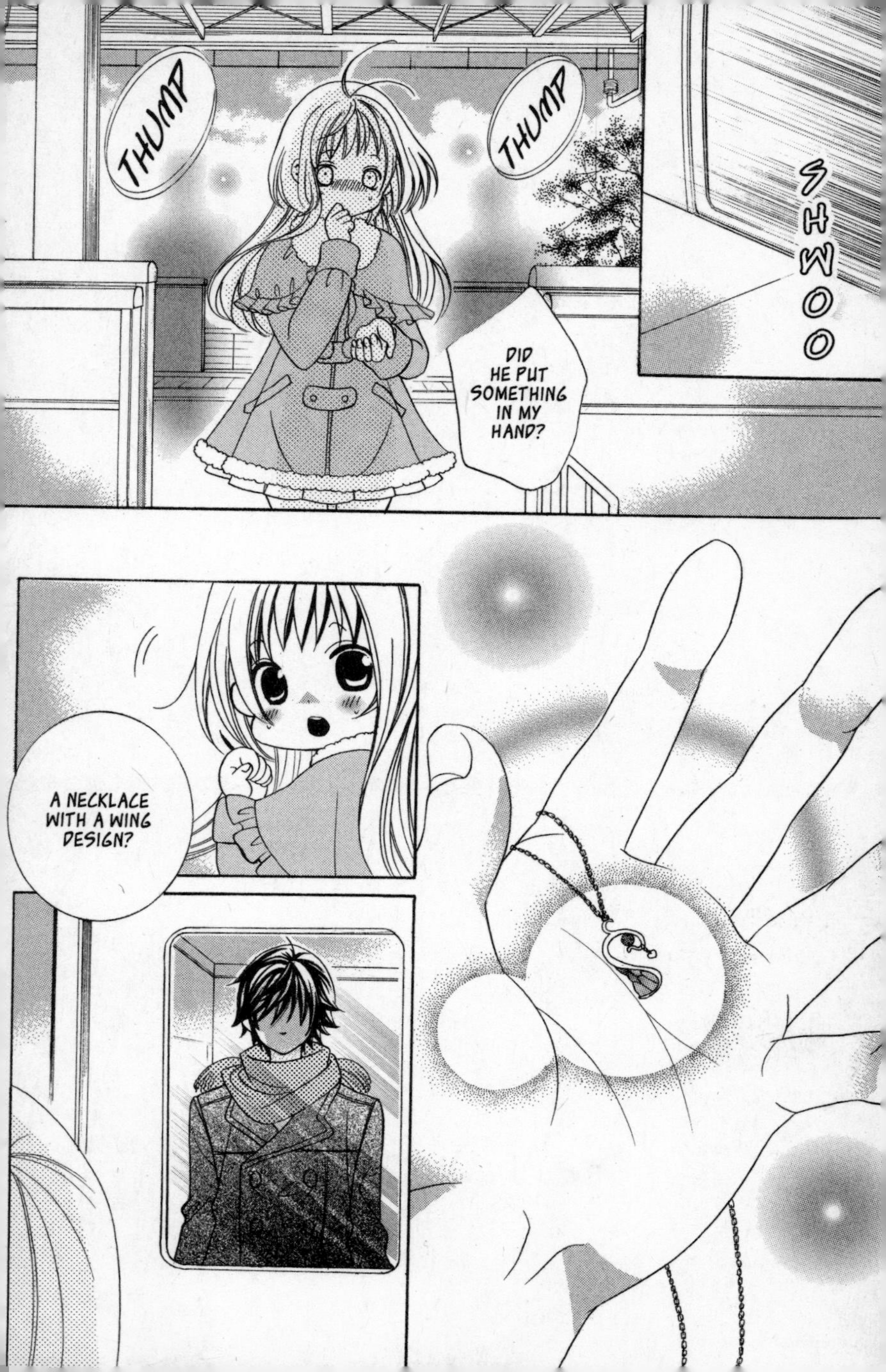
SHWOO
THUMP
THUMP
DID HE PUT SOMETHING IN MY HAND?
A NECKLACE WITH A WING DESIGN?

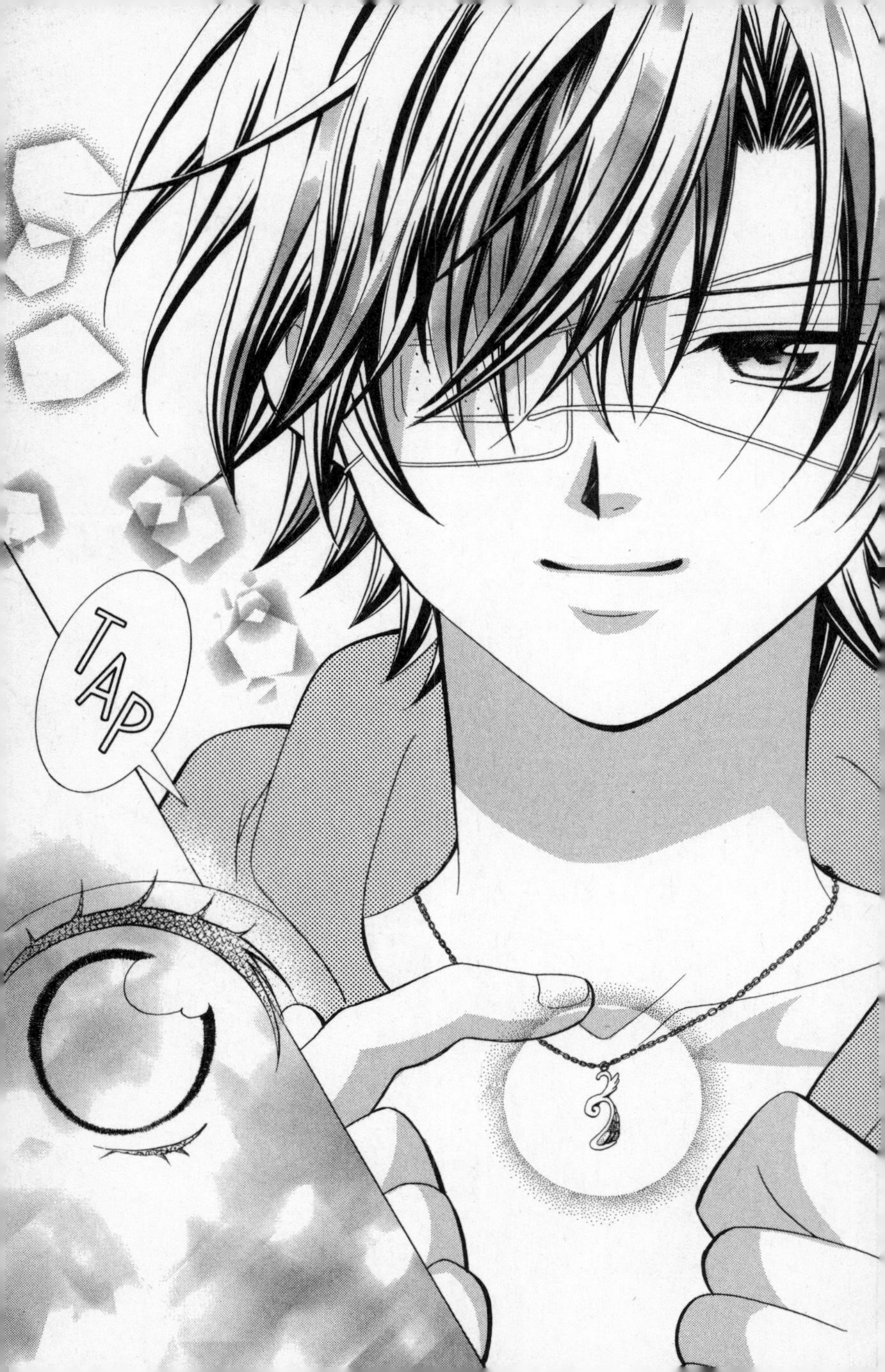
TAP

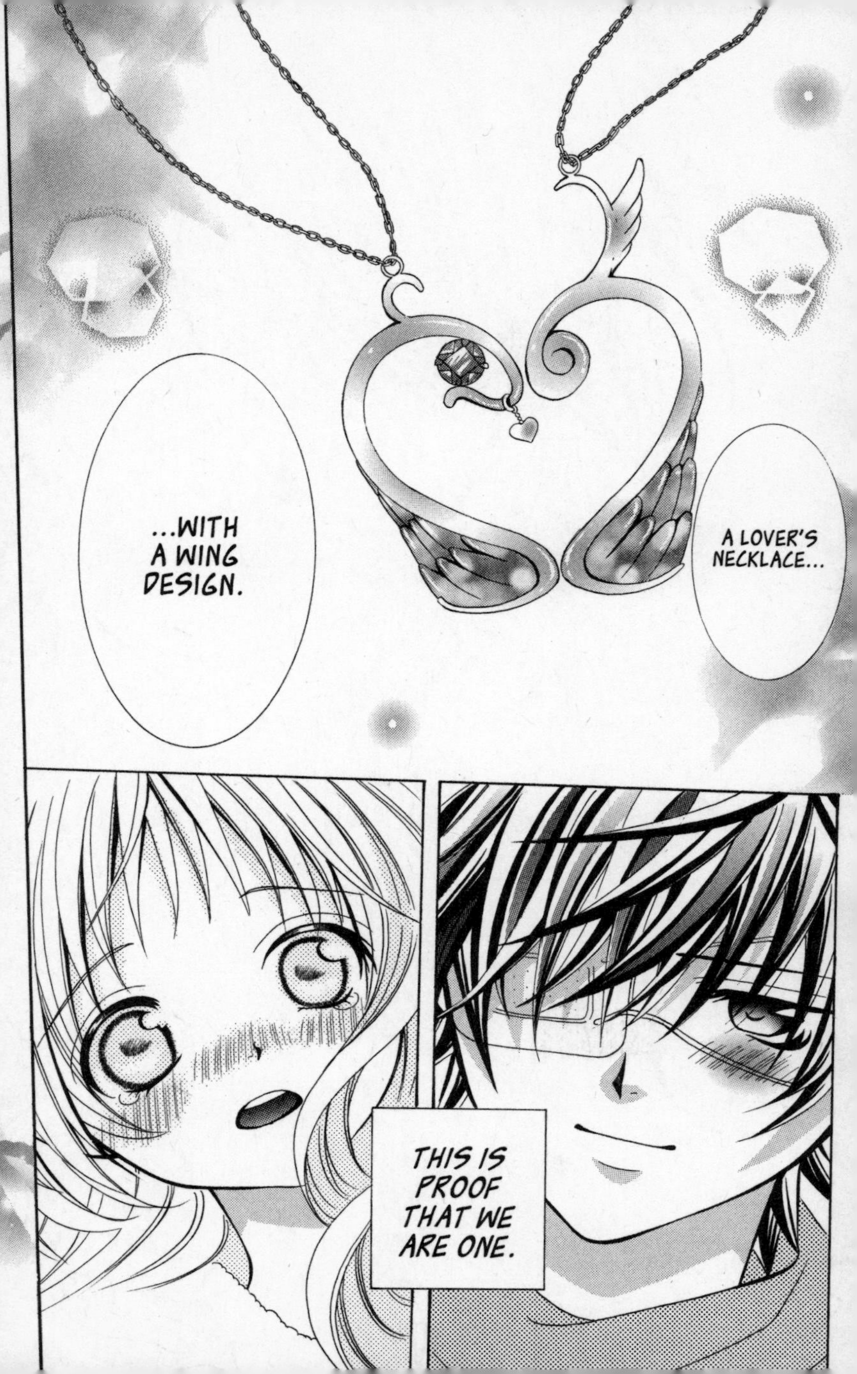
A LOVER'S NECKLACE...
...WITH A WING DESIGN.
THIS IS PROOF THAT WE ARE ONE.

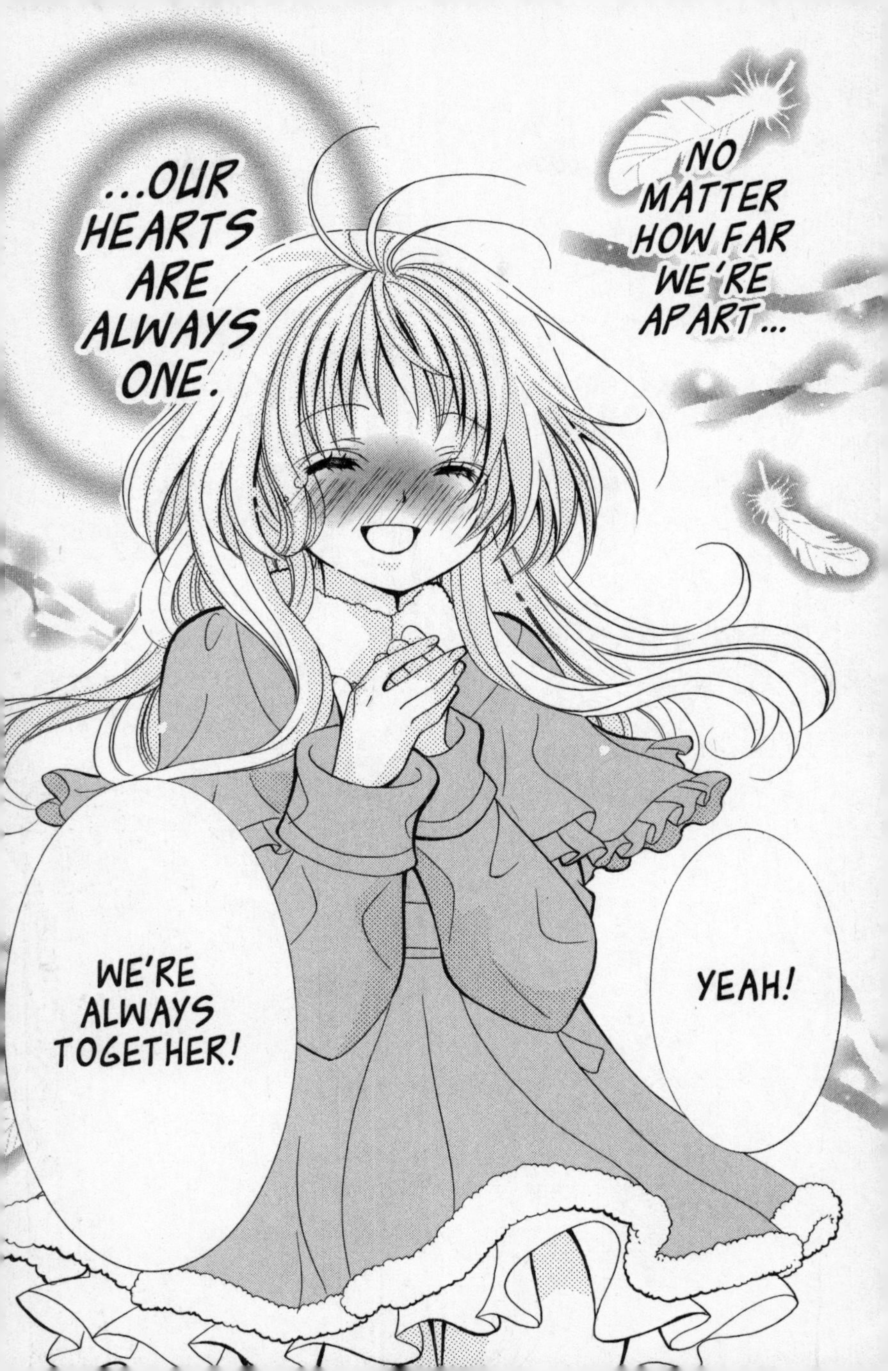
NO MATTER HOW FAR WE'RE APART...
...OUR HEARTS ARE ALWAYS ONE.
YEAH!
WE'RE ALWAYS TOGETHER!

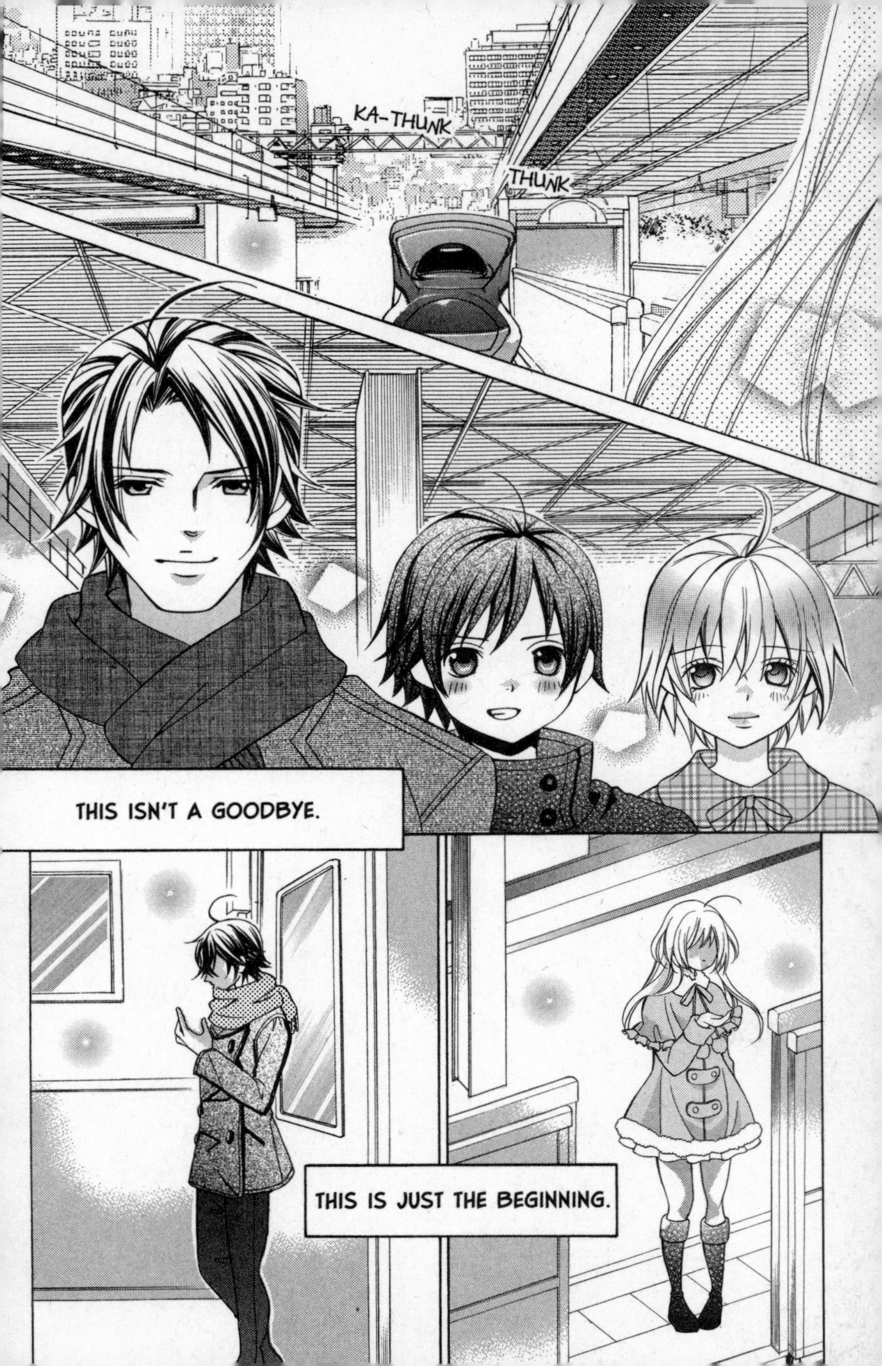
KA-THUNK
THUNK
THIS ISN'T A GOODBYE.
THIS IS JUST THE BEGINNING.

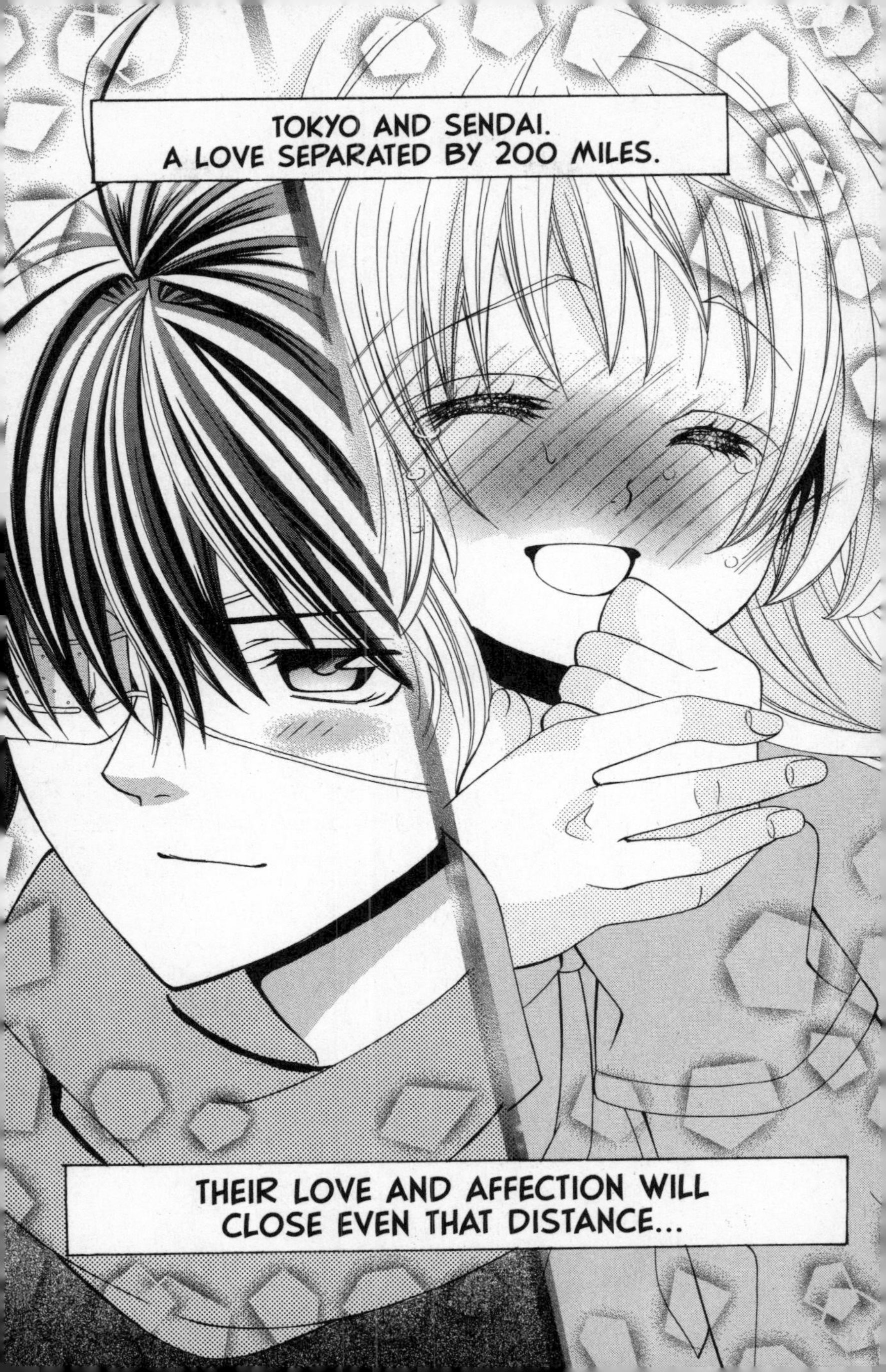
TOKYO AND SENDAI.
A LOVE SEPARATED BY 200 MILES.
THEIR LOVE AND AFFECTION WILL
CLOSE EVEN THAT DISTANCE...

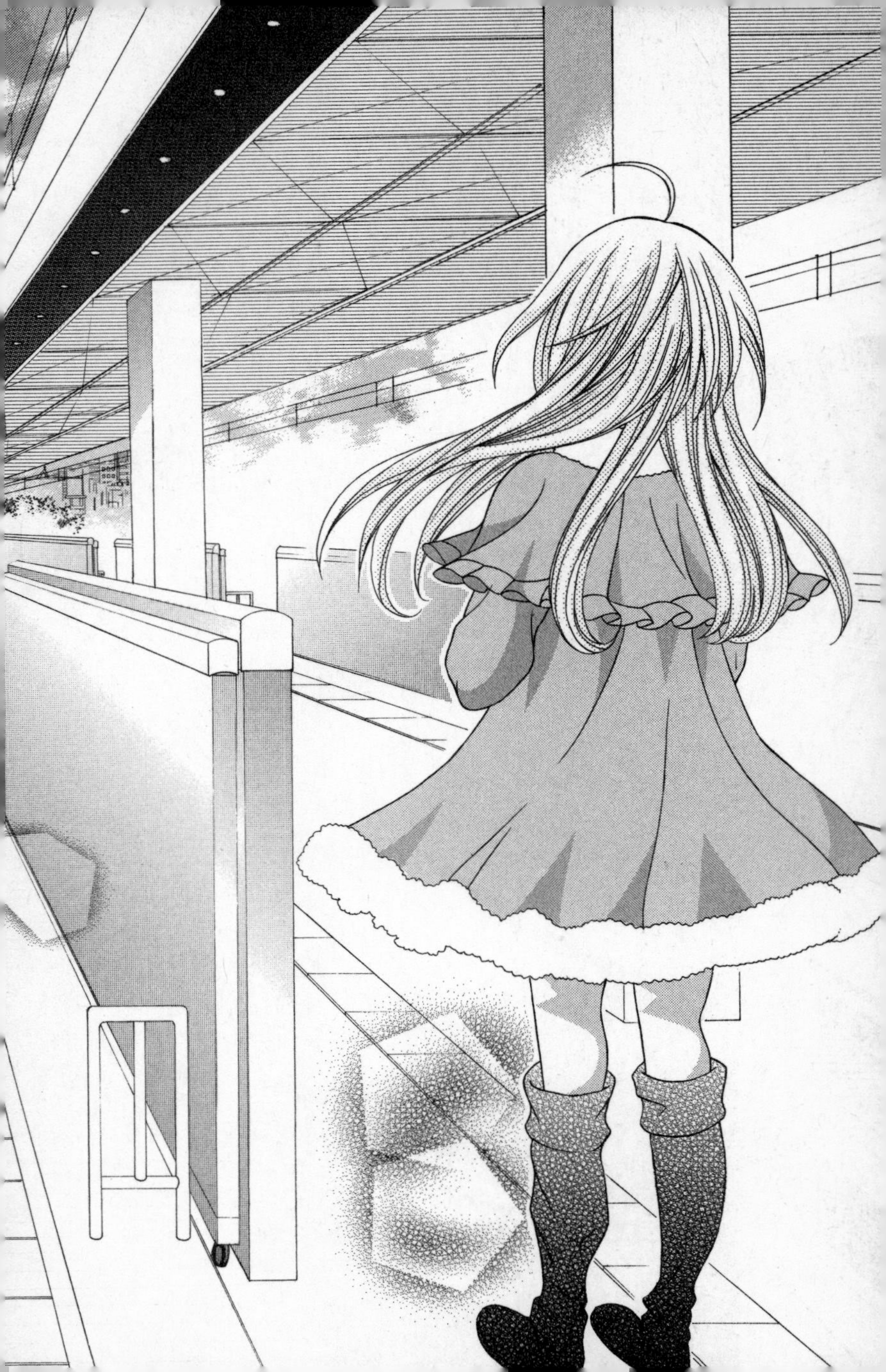

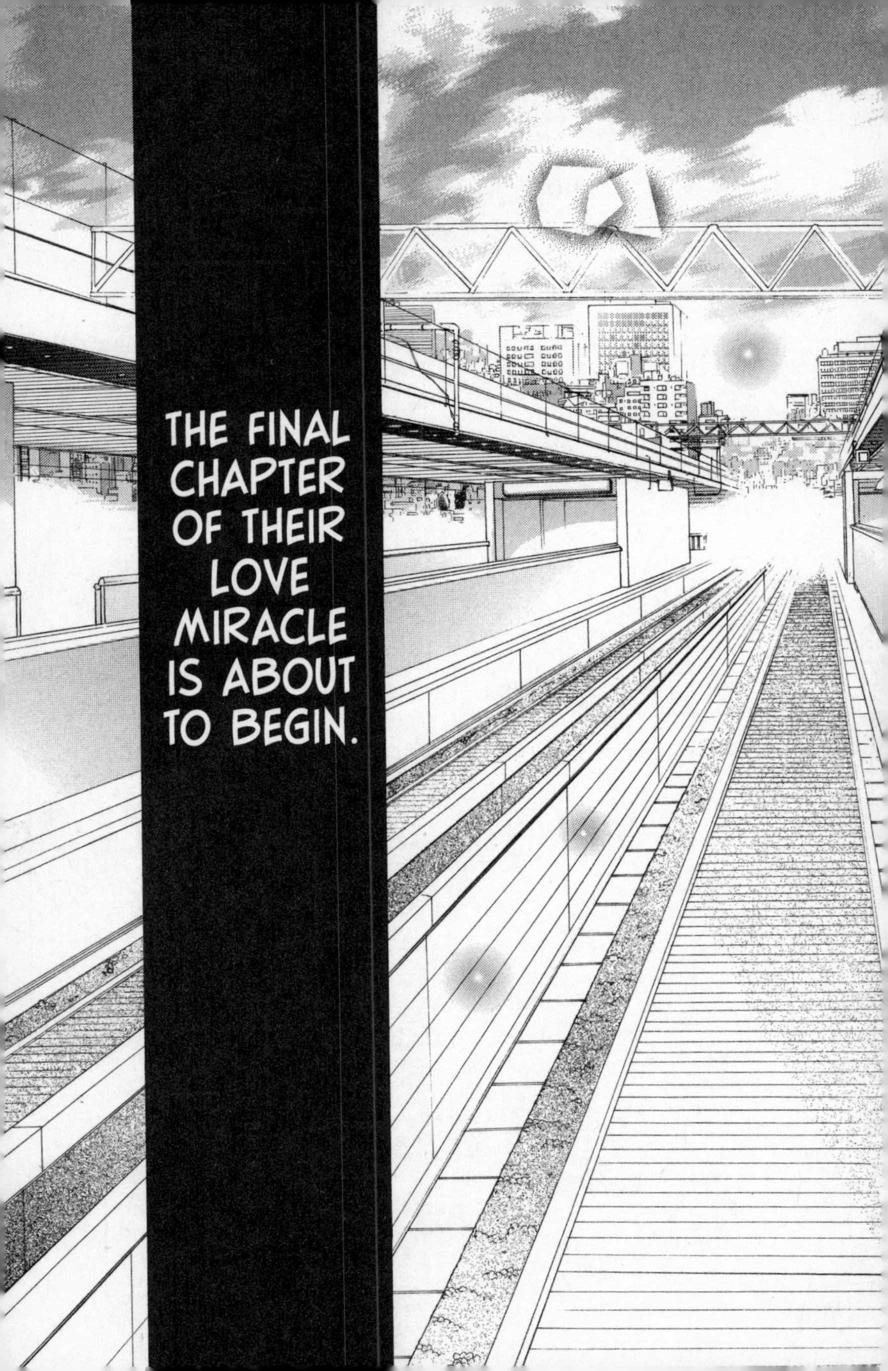
THE FINAL CHAPTER OF THEIR LOVE MIRACLE IS ABOUT TO BEGIN.

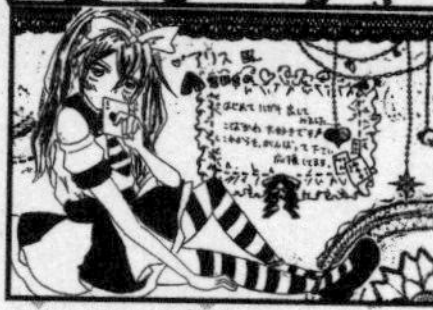

Sazanami (Shizuoka) ↑
Ed.: This Mego is unbelievably cute!!

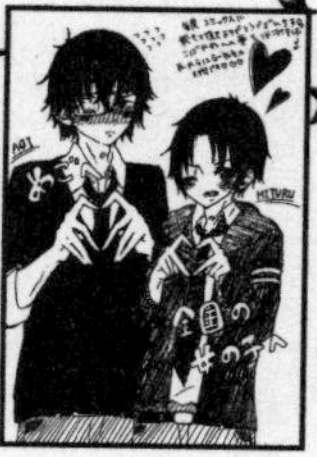

ZZZ... (Chiba) →
Ed.: Boys want them too!!

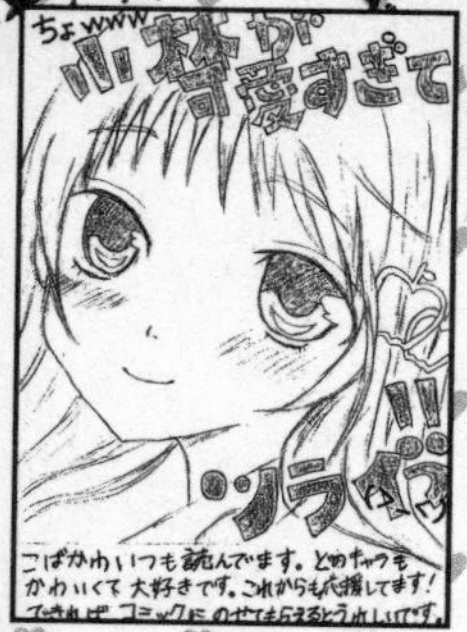
ちょwww
小林が可愛すぎて
!!ツライ
こばかわいつも読んでます。とめキャラもかわいくて大好きです。これからも応援してます!
できれば、コミックにのせてもらえるとうれしいです。

MANA (Shizuoka) ←
Ed.: This Mego's unbelievably cute!!

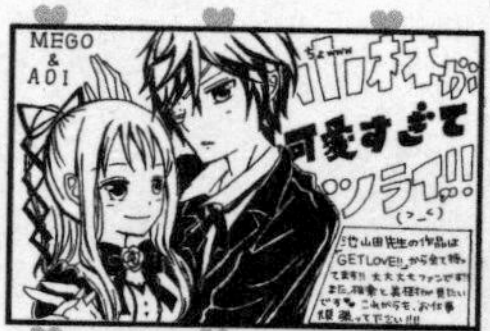
MEGO
AOI
小林が可愛すぎてツライ!!

Momoko Oda (Kagawa) ↑
Ed.: Classic duo.♥

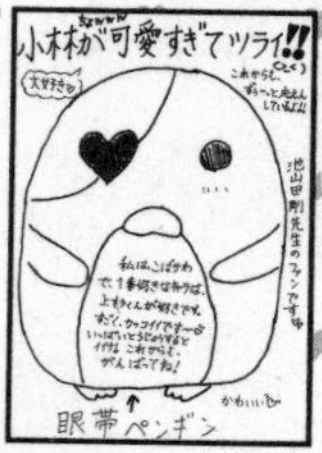
小林が可愛すぎてツライ!!
眼帯ペンギン

Panda (Mie) ←
Ed.: I'm jealous readers love the penguins so much!!

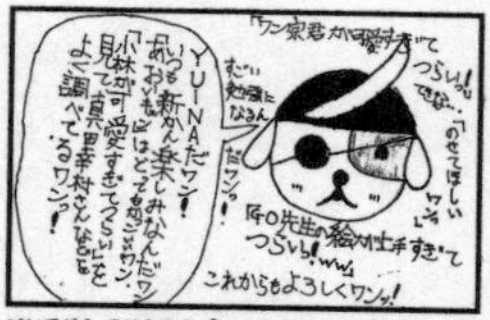
これからもよろしくワン!

YUINA INADA (Nagasaki) ↑
Ed.: Readers love Woof-mune too!!

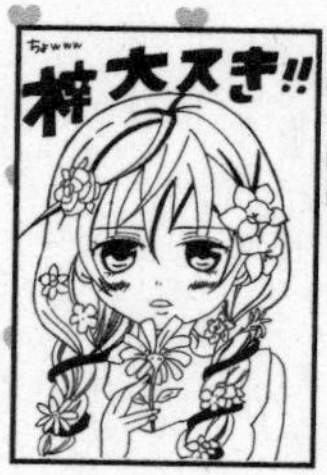
ちょwww
梓大スキ!!

Kazuki Yamauchi (Kumamoto) ←
Ed.: I love you forever, Azusa!!

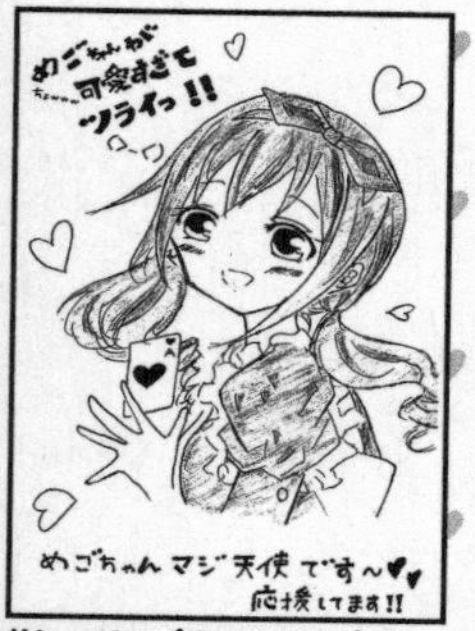
めごちゃんが
ちょ~~可愛すぎてツライっ!!
めごちゃんマジ天使です~♥
応援してます!!

Misomiso (Kanagawa) ↑
Ed.: Mego's really an angel!!

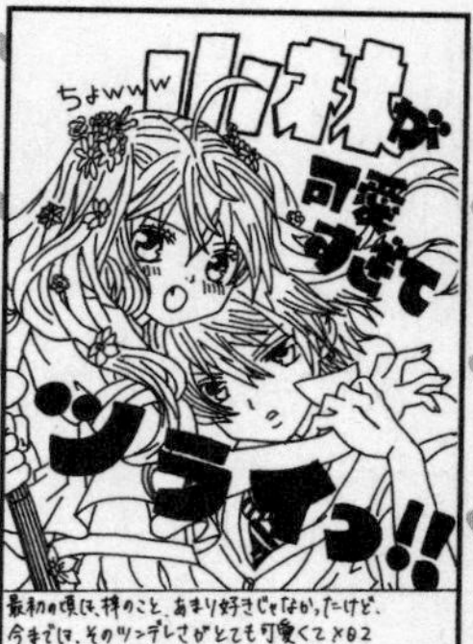
ちょwww
小林が可愛すぎてツライっ!!
最初の頃は、梓のこと、あまり好きじゃなかったけど、今までは、そのツンデレさがとても可愛くてメロメロ
毎回、楽しみです♪ 今年も、Go先生にとって良い年になりますように。

Anna Nakajima (Kumamoto) →
Ed.: I love Azusa's devil tooth!!

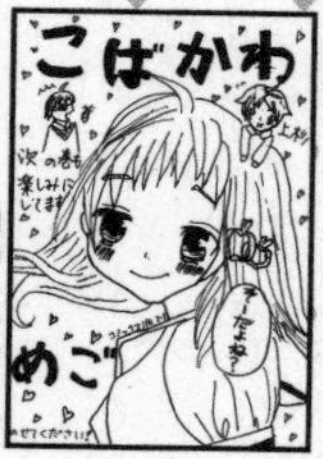
こばかわ
めご

Rio Sawada (Toyama) →
Ed.: Uesugi's fallen for Mego's cuteness?!

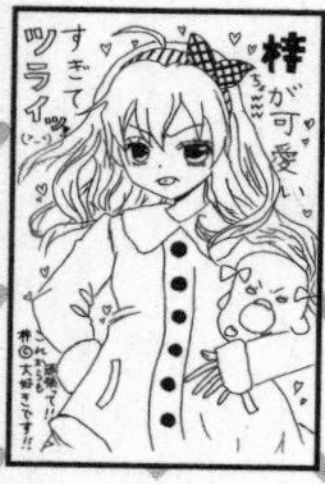
梓が可愛すぎてツライ

Marina Miyazaki (Kanagawa) ←
Ed.: I love Azusa being blunt!!

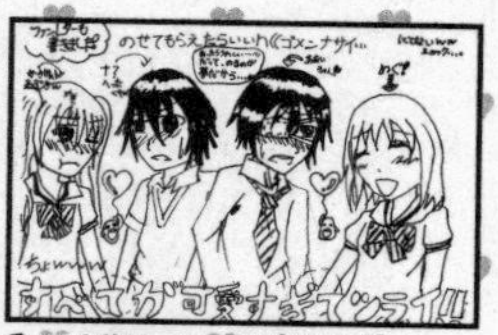

Inori Nakamura (Aichi) ↑
Ed.: This foursome is cute!!

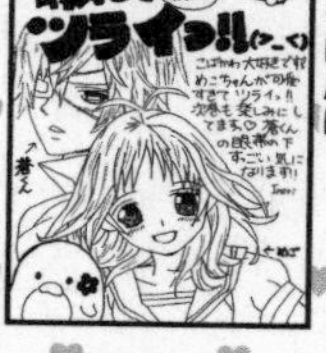
小林が可愛すぎてツライっ!!

Marina Miyazaki (Kanagawa) ←
Ed.: I love Azusa being blunt!!

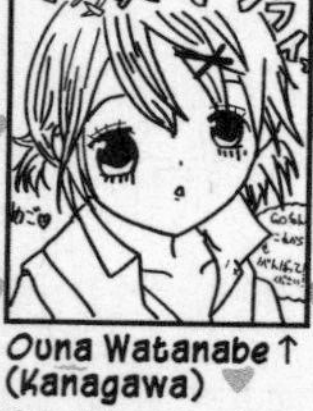
小林が可愛すぎてツライ!!

Ouna Watanabe ↑ (Kanagawa)
Ed.: I-I wanna take her home...

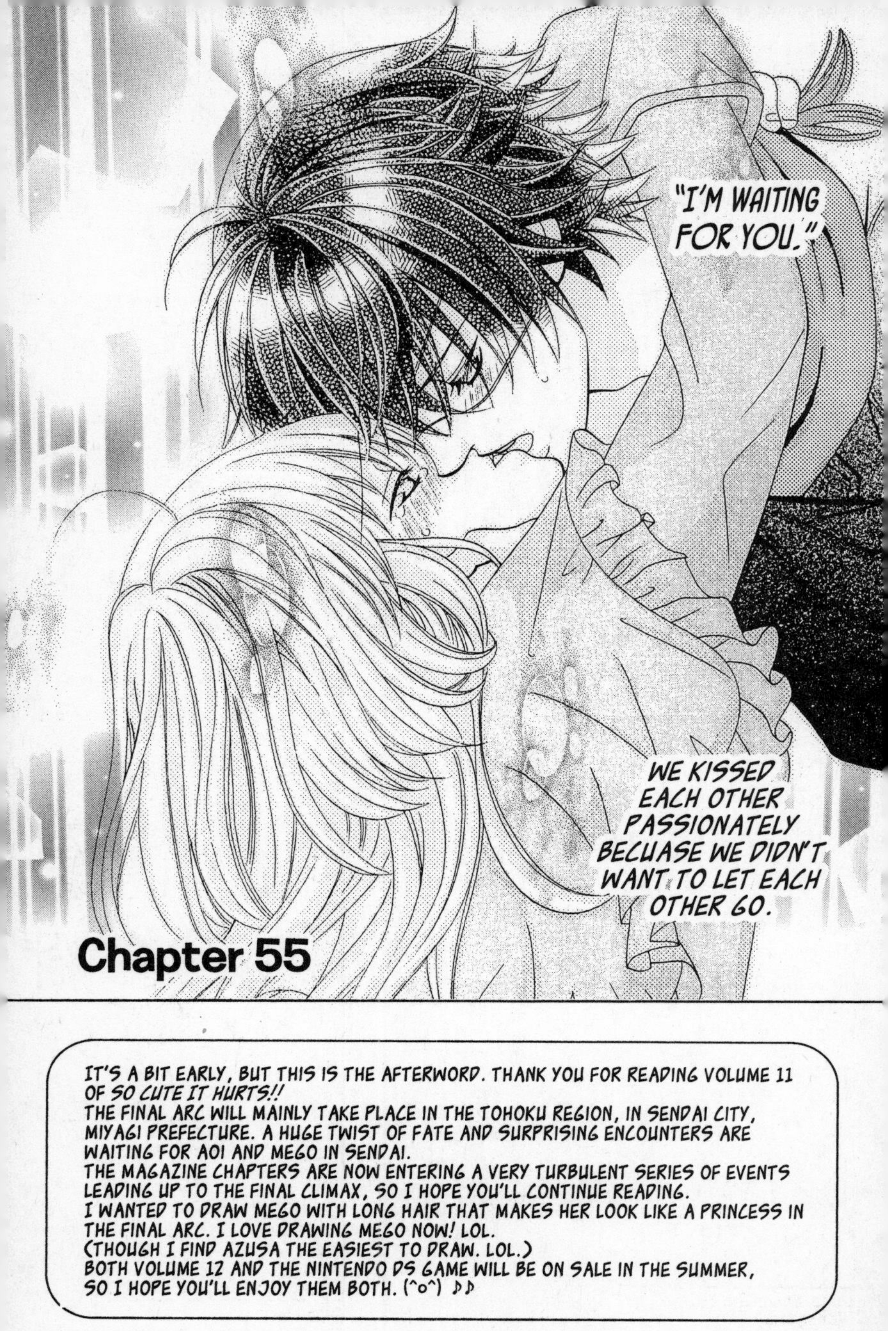
"I'M WAITING FOR YOU."
WE KISSED EACH OTHER PASSIONATELY BECUASE WE DIDN'T WANT TO LET EACH OTHER GO.

Chapter 55

IT'S A BIT EARLY, BUT THIS IS THE AFTERWORD. THANK YOU FOR READING VOLUME 11 OF *SO CUTE IT HURTS!!*
THE FINAL ARC WILL MAINLY TAKE PLACE IN THE TOHOKU REGION, IN SENDAI CITY, MIYAGI PREFECTURE. A HUGE TWIST OF FATE AND SURPRISING ENCOUNTERS ARE WAITING FOR AOI AND MEGO IN SENDAI.
THE MAGAZINE CHAPTERS ARE NOW ENTERING A VERY TURBULENT SERIES OF EVENTS LEADING UP TO THE FINAL CLIMAX, SO I HOPE YOU'LL CONTINUE READING.
I WANTED TO DRAW MEGO WITH LONG HAIR THAT MAKES HER LOOK LIKE A PRINCESS IN THE FINAL ARC. I LOVE DRAWING MEGO NOW! LOL.
(THOUGH I FIND AZUSA THE EASIEST TO DRAW. LOL.)
BOTH VOLUME 12 AND THE NINTENDO DS GAME WILL BE ON SALE IN THE SUMMER, SO I HOPE YOU'LL ENJOY THEM BOTH. (^o^) ♪♪

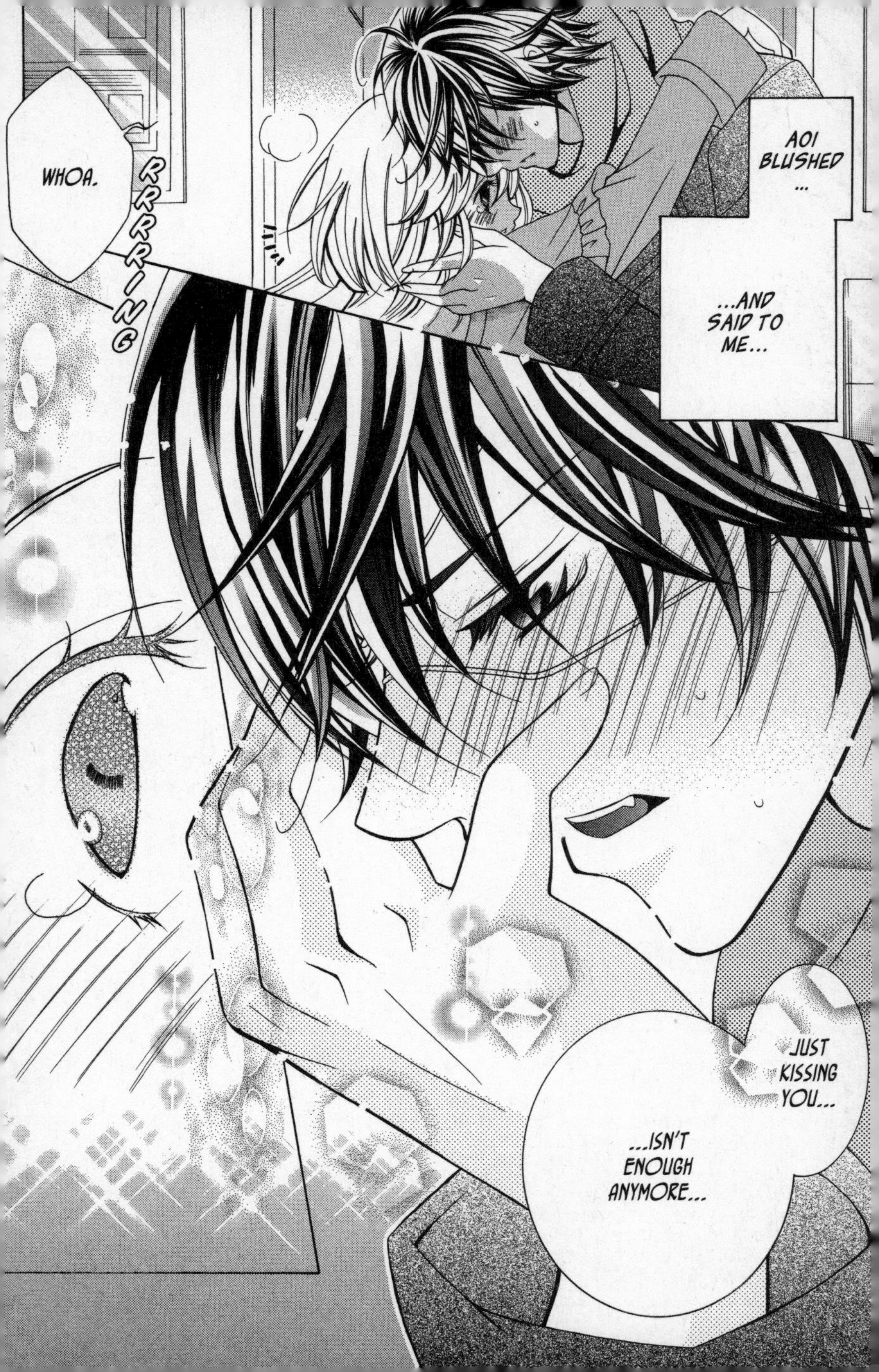
AOI BLUSHED...
...AND SAID TO ME...
JUST KISSING YOU...
...ISN'T ENOUGH ANYMORE...
RRRRING
WHOA.

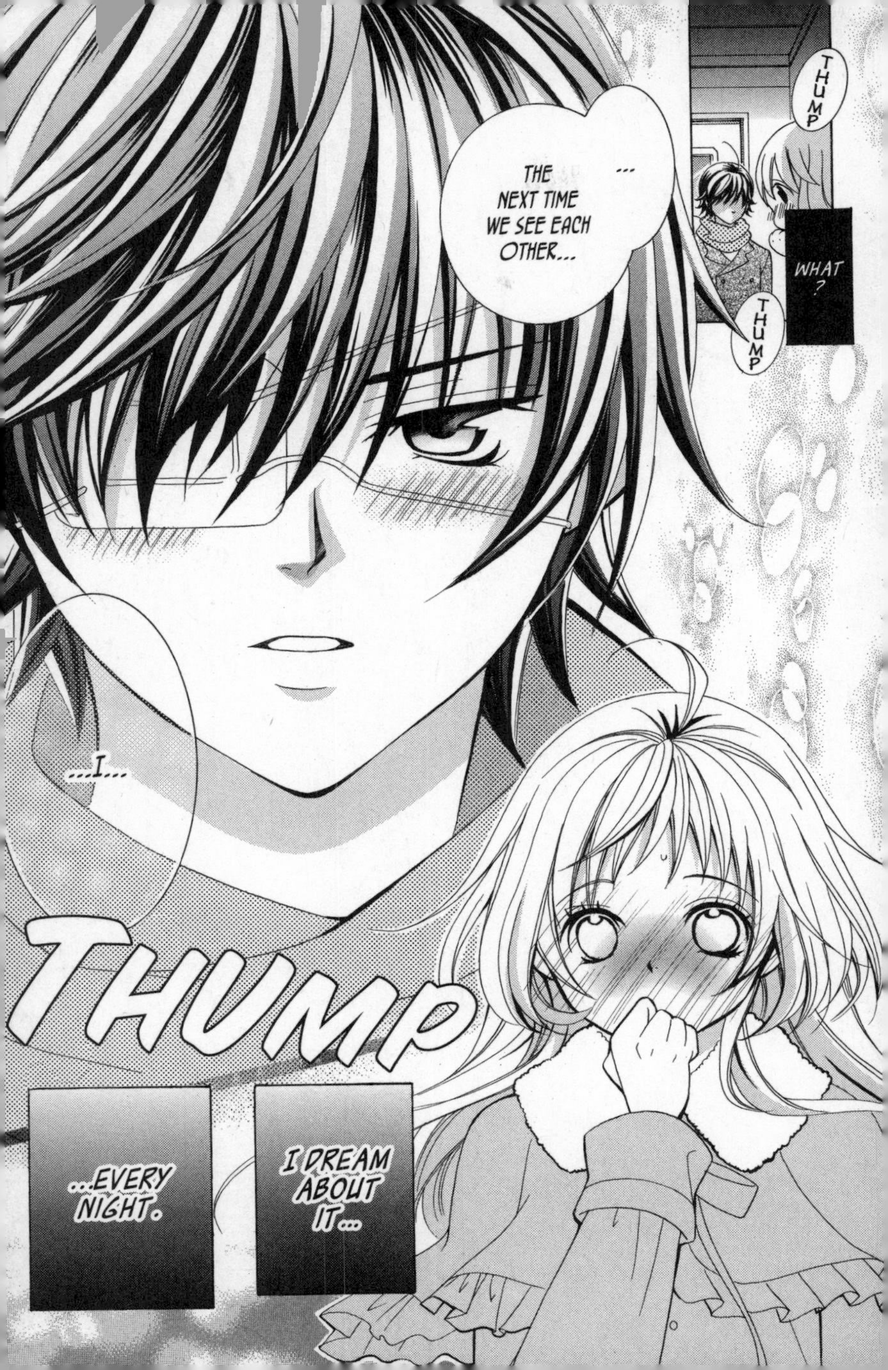
THUMP
WHAT?
THUMP
... THE NEXT TIME WE SEE EACH OTHER...
...I...
THUMP
I DREAM ABOUT IT...
...EVERY NIGHT.

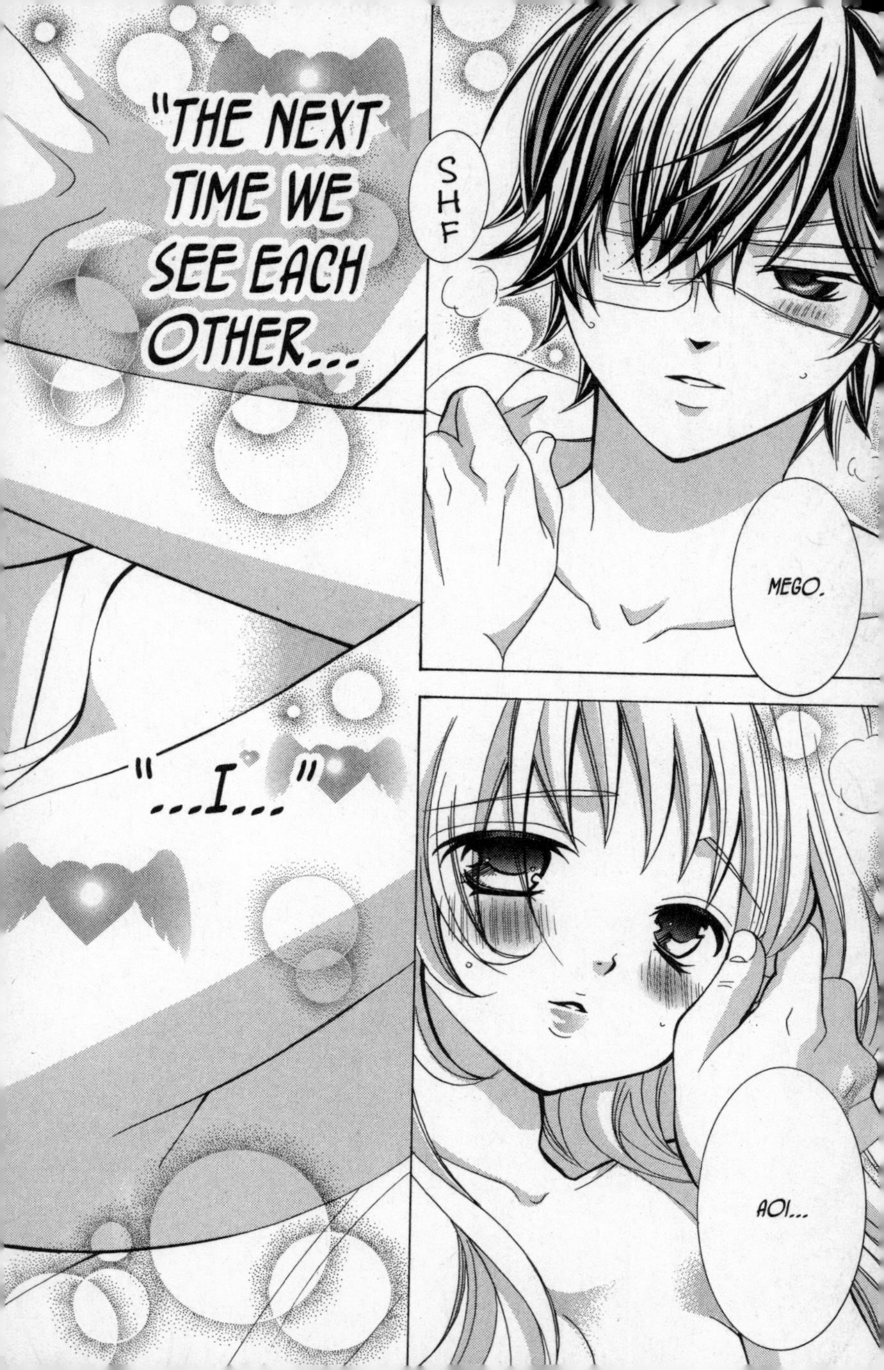
SHF
MEGO.
AOI...
"THE NEXT TIME WE SEE EACH OTHER...
"...I..."

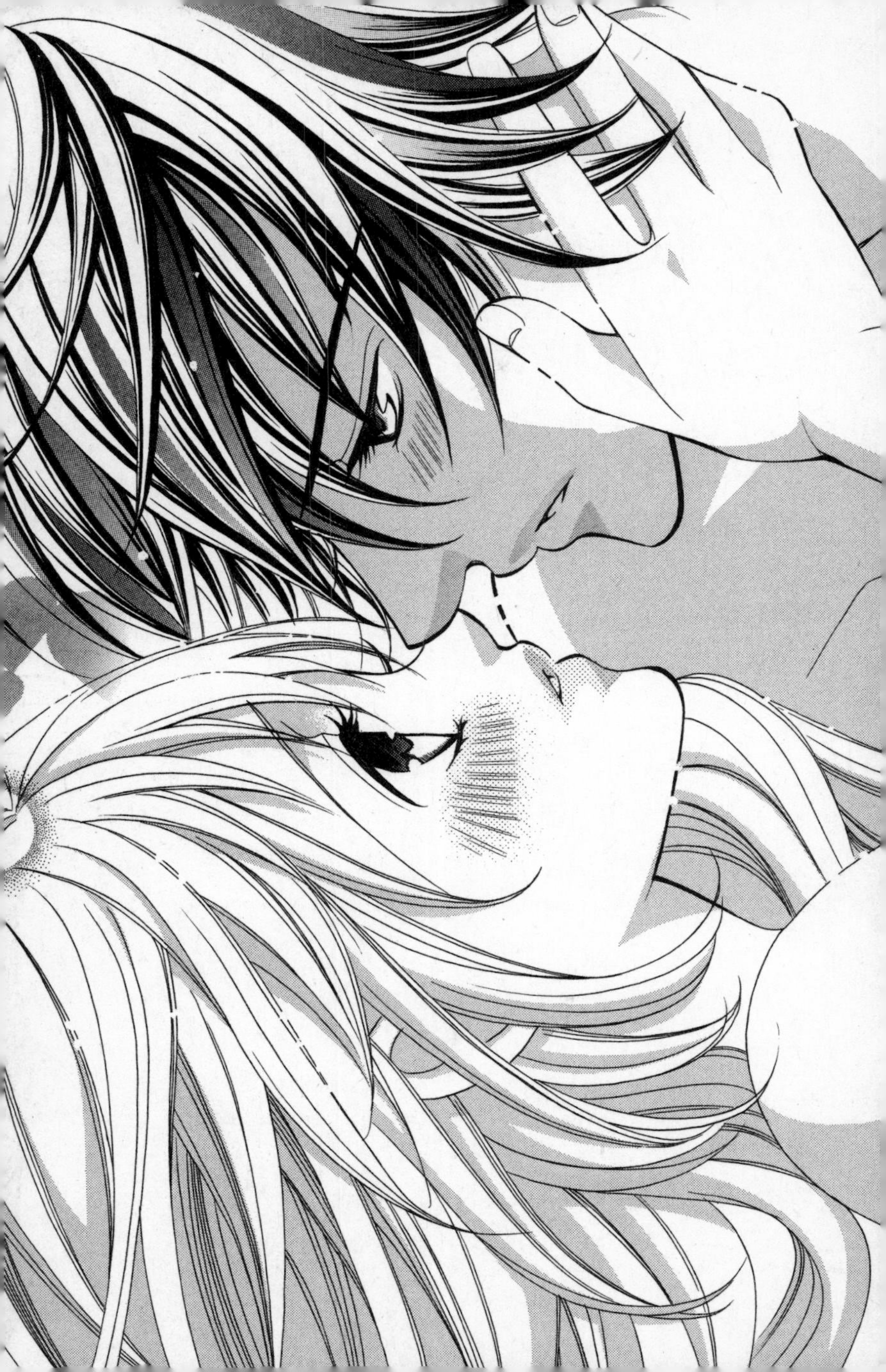

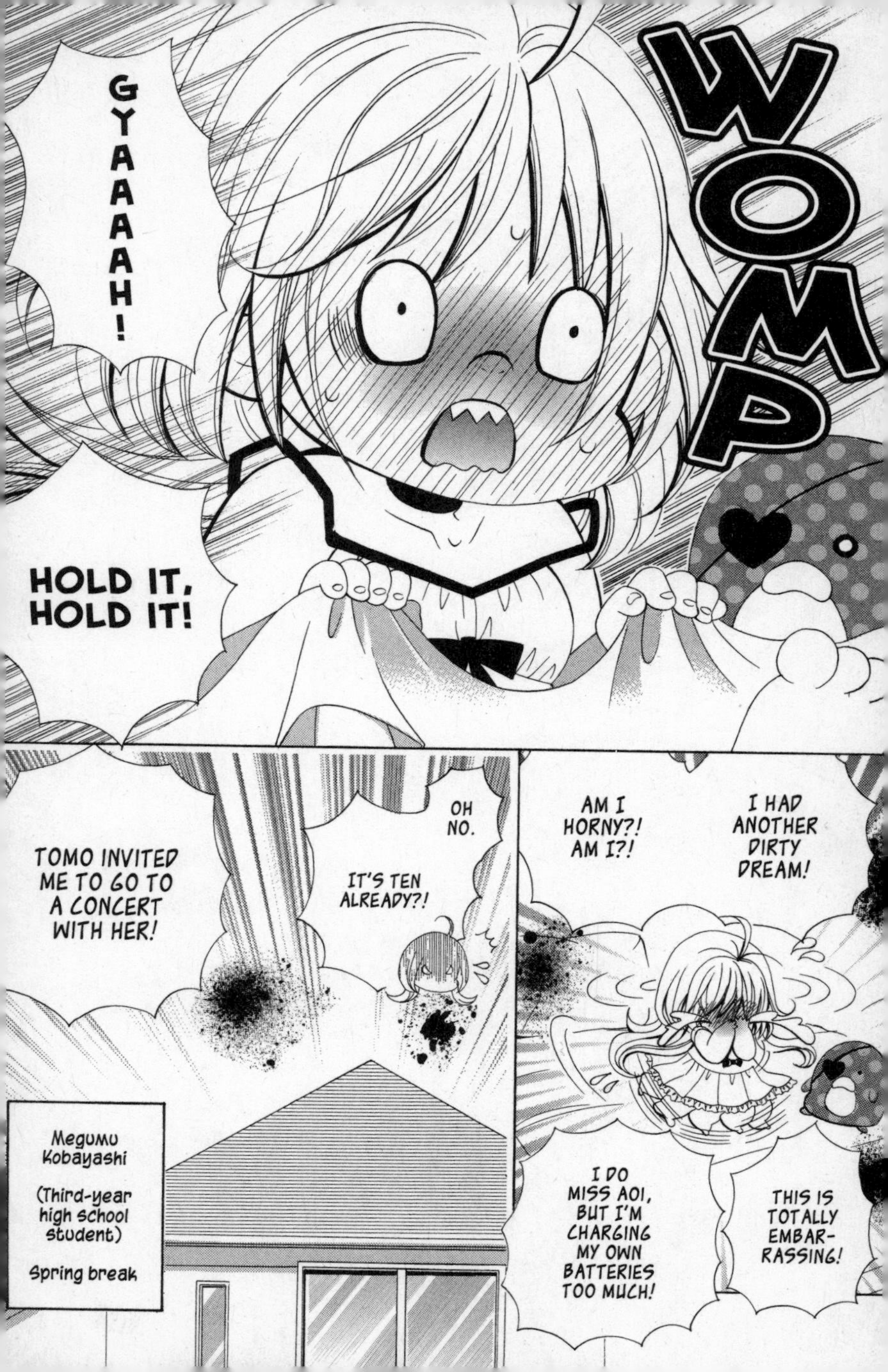
WOMP
GYAAAAAH!
HOLD IT, HOLD IT!
I HAD ANOTHER DIRTY DREAM!
AM I HORNY?! AM I?!
THIS IS TOTALLY EMBAR-RASSING!
I DO MISS AOI, BUT I'M CHARGING MY OWN BATTERIES TOO MUCH!
OH NO.
IT'S TEN ALREADY?!
TOMO INVITED ME TO GO TO A CONCERT WITH HER!
Megumu Kobayashi
(Third-year high school student)
Spring break

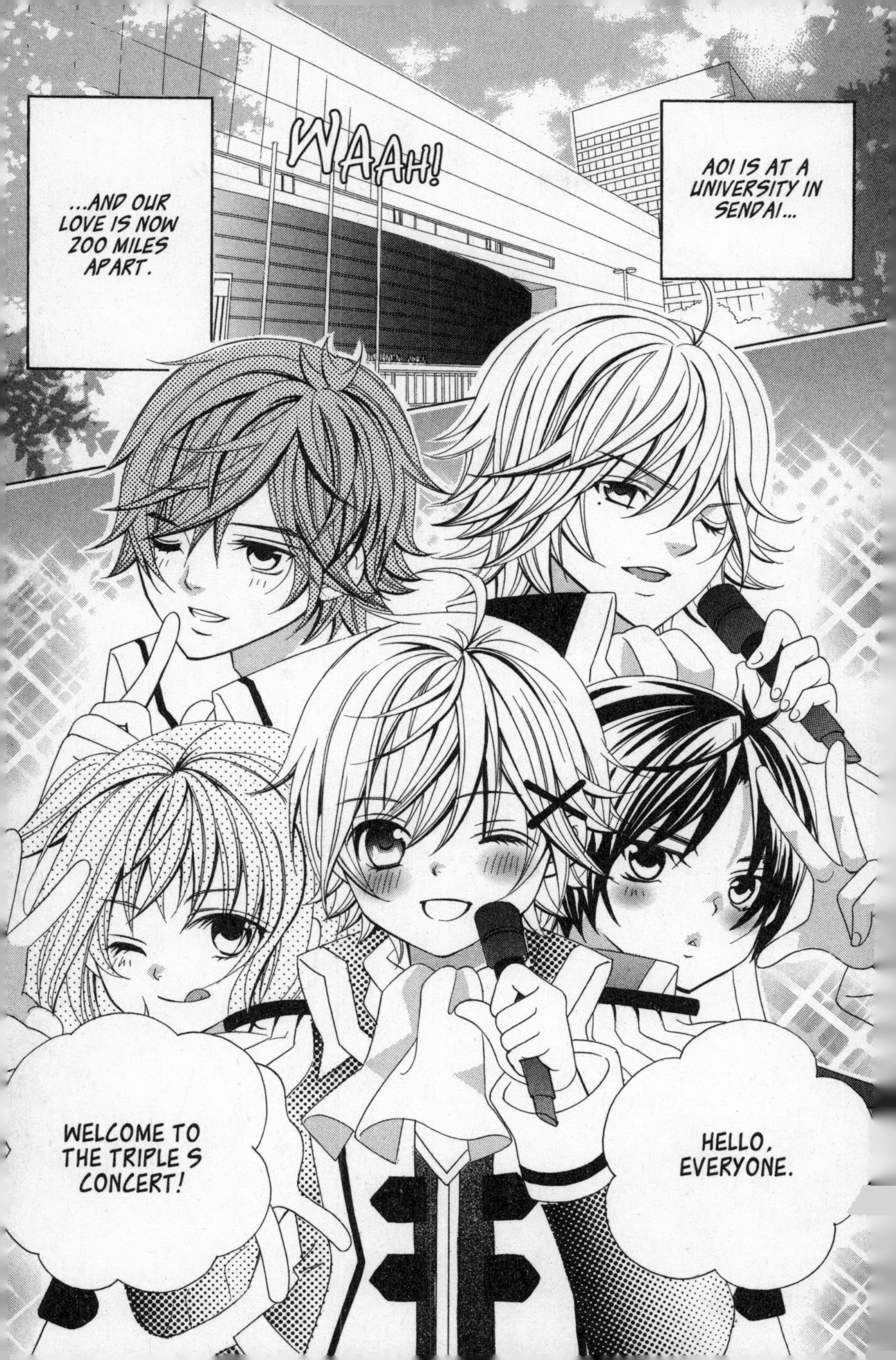
AOI IS AT A UNIVERSITY IN SENDAI...
WAAH!
...AND OUR LOVE IS NOW 200 MILES APART.
HELLO, EVERYONE.
WELCOME TO THE TRIPLE S CONCERT!

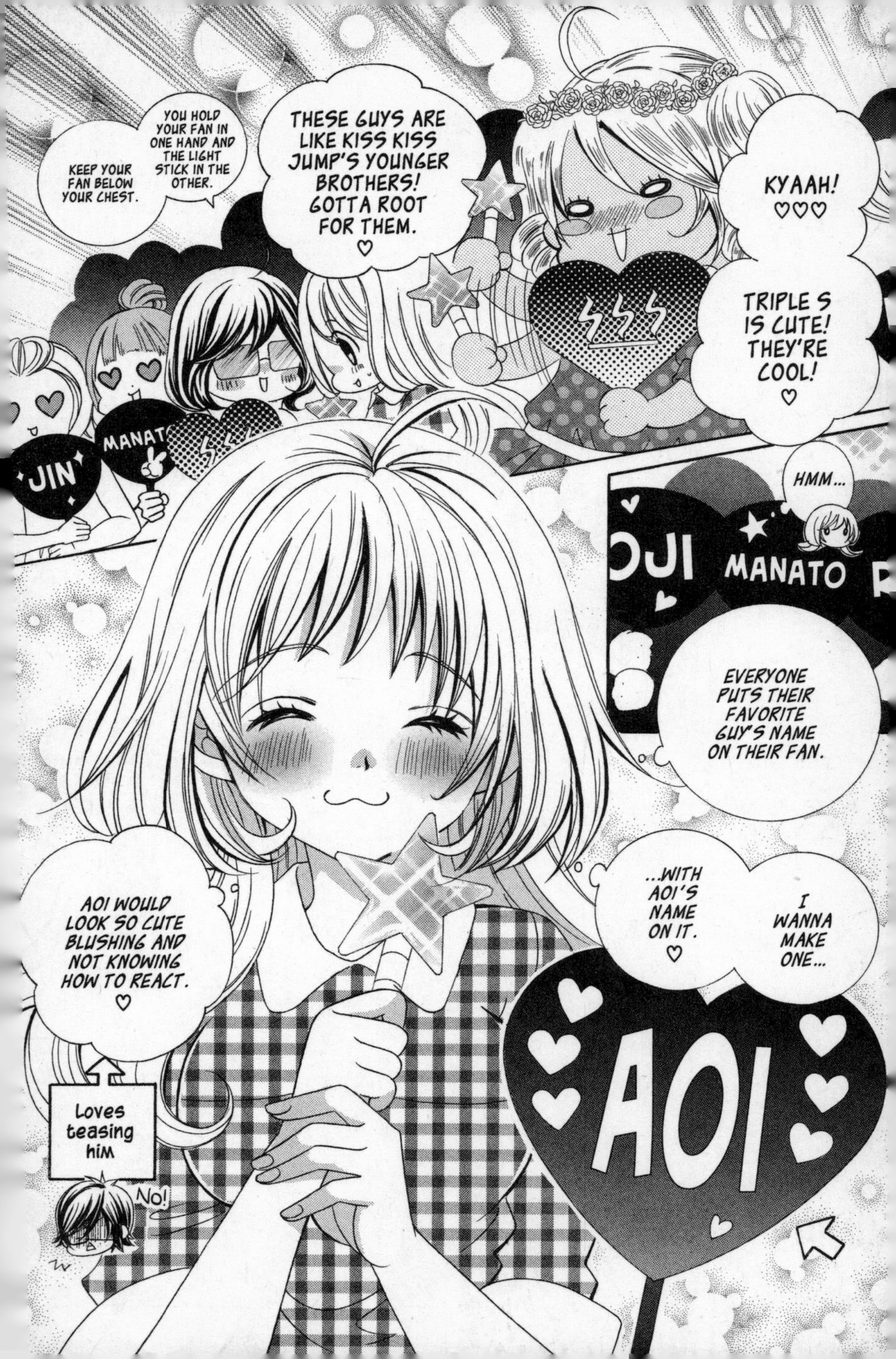
KYAAH! ♡♡♡
TRIPLE S IS CUTE! THEY'RE COOL! ♡
THESE GUYS ARE LIKE KISS KISS JUMP'S YOUNGER BROTHERS! GOTTA ROOT FOR THEM. ♡
YOU HOLD YOUR FAN IN ONE HAND AND THE LIGHT STICK IN THE OTHER.
KEEP YOUR FAN BELOW YOUR CHEST.
MANAT
JIN
HMM...
OJI
MANATO
EVERYONE PUTS THEIR FAVORITE GUY'S NAME ON THEIR FAN.
I WANNA MAKE ONE...
...WITH AOI'S NAME ON IT. ♡
AOI
AOI WOULD LOOK SO CUTE BLUSHING AND NOT KNOWING HOW TO REACT. ♡
Loves teasing him
No!

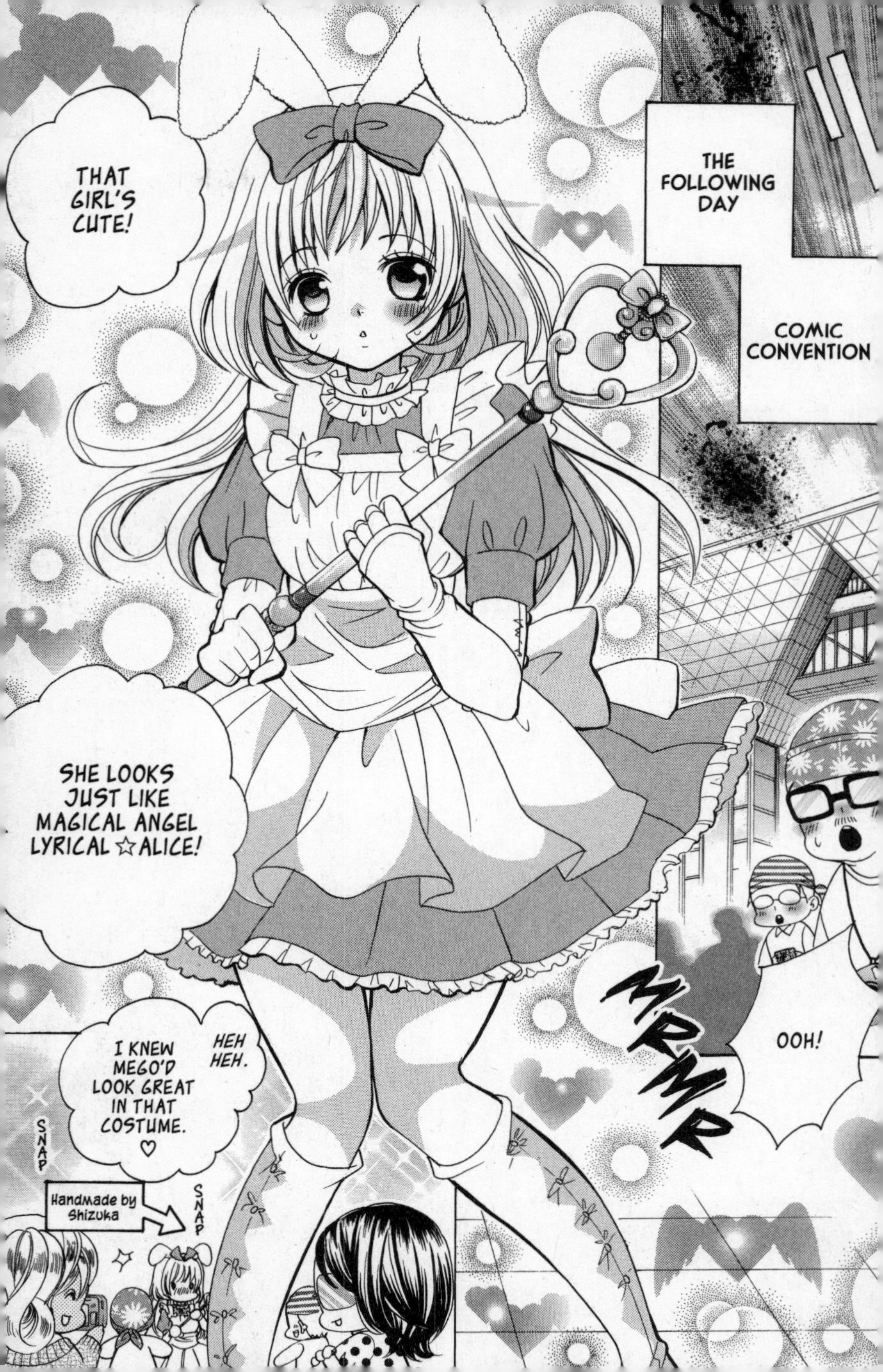
THE FOLLOWING DAY
COMIC CONVENTION
MRMR
OOH!
THAT GIRL'S CUTE!
SHE LOOKS JUST LIKE MAGICAL ANGEL LYRICAL☆ALICE!
HEH HEH.
I KNEW MEGO'D LOOK GREAT IN THAT COSTUME. ♡
SNAP
SNAP
Handmade by Shizuka

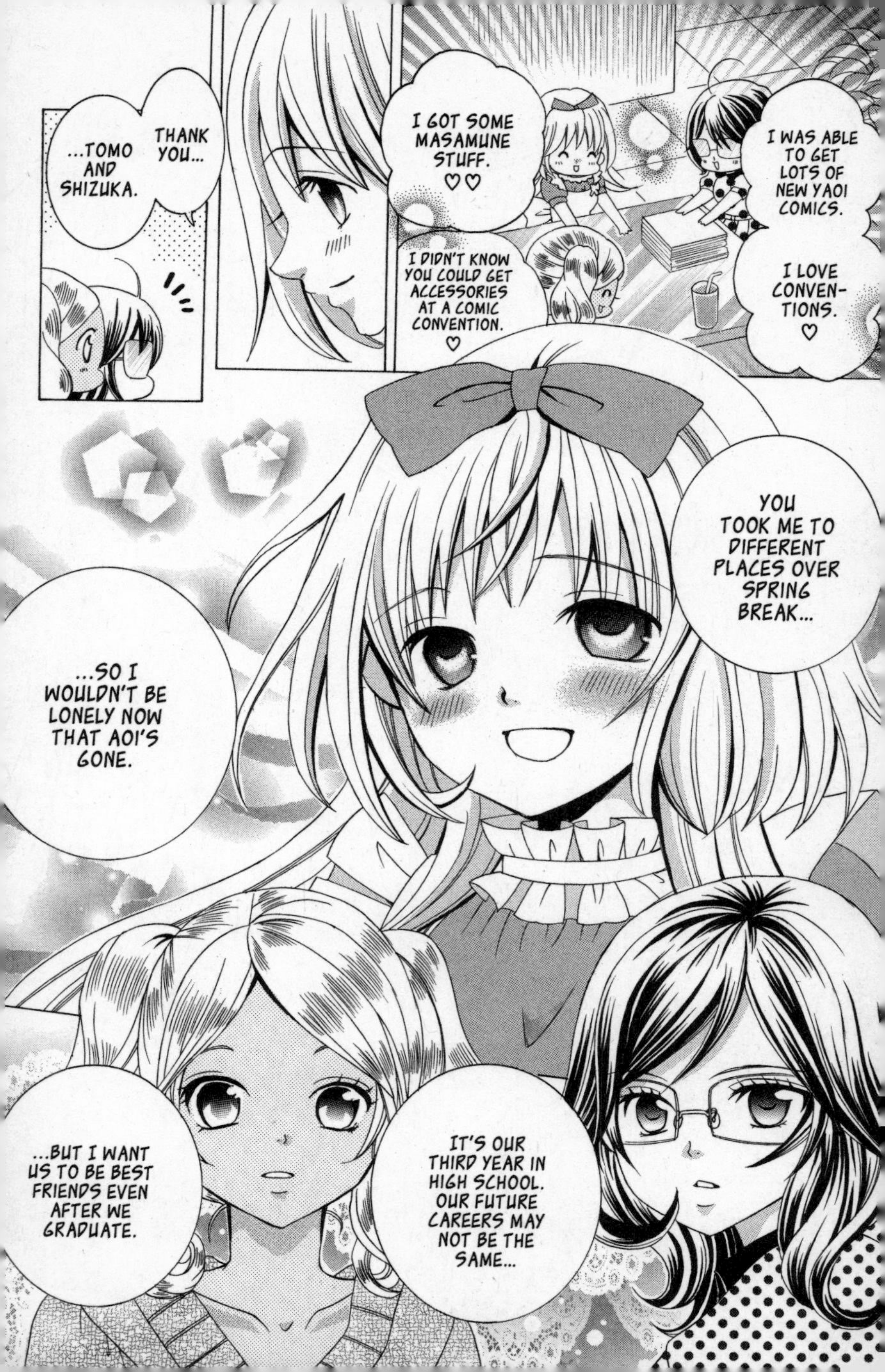

I WAS ABLE TO GET LOTS OF NEW YAOI COMICS.
I GOT SOME MASAMUNE STUFF. ♡♡
I LOVE CONVEN-TIONS. ♡
I DIDN'T KNOW YOU COULD GET ACCESSORIES AT A COMIC CONVENTION. ♡
THANK YOU...
...TOMO AND SHIZUKA.
YOU TOOK ME TO DIFFERENT PLACES OVER SPRING BREAK...
...SO I WOULDN'T BE LONELY NOW THAT AOI'S GONE.
IT'S OUR THIRD YEAR IN HIGH SCHOOL. OUR FUTURE CAREERS MAY NOT BE THE SAME...
...BUT I WANT US TO BE BEST FRIENDS EVEN AFTER WE GRADUATE.

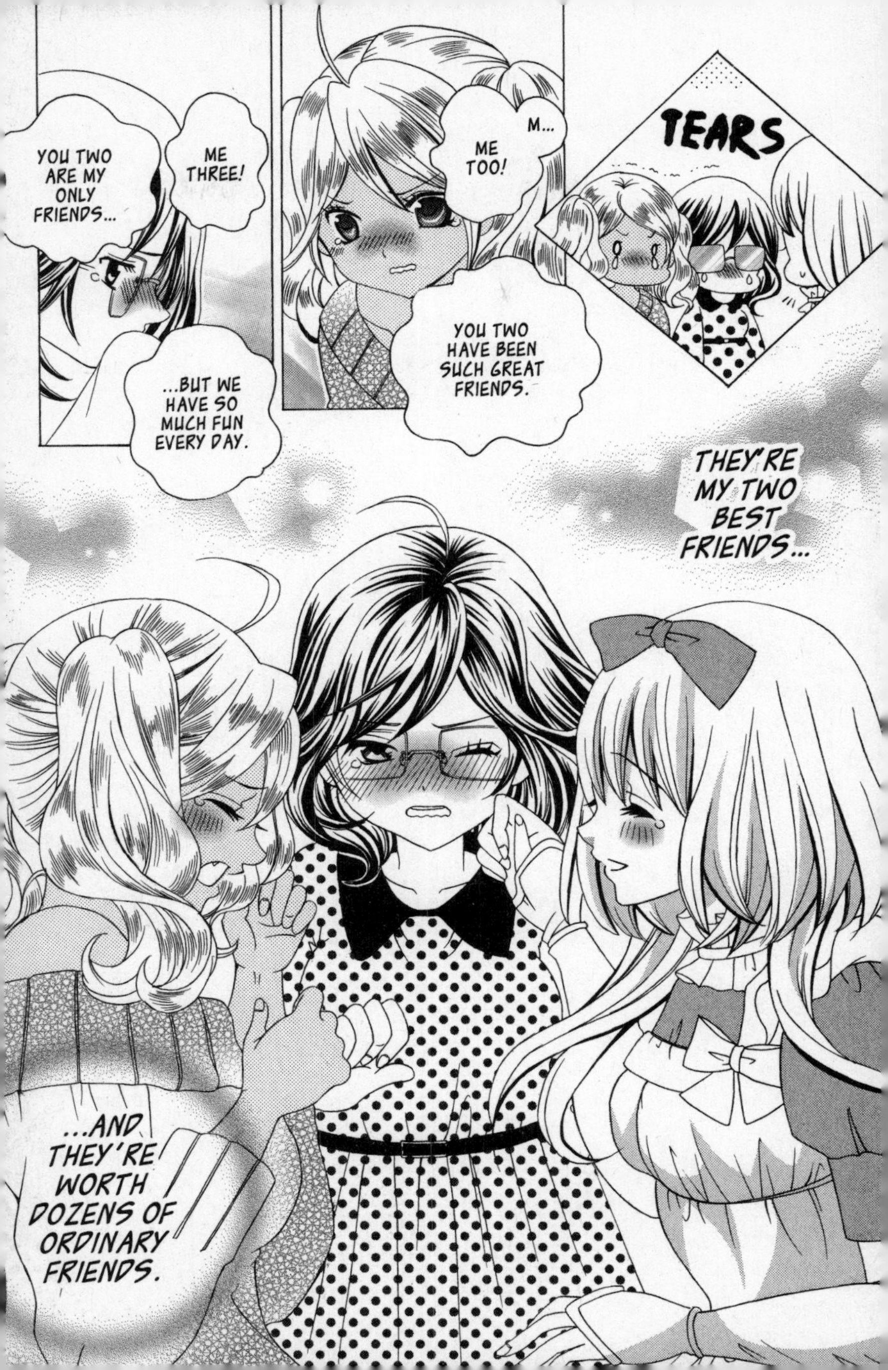
TEARS
M... ME TOO!
YOU TWO HAVE BEEN SUCH GREAT FRIENDS.
ME THREE!
YOU TWO ARE MY ONLY FRIENDS...
...BUT WE HAVE SO MUCH FUN EVERY DAY.
THEY'RE MY TWO BEST FRIENDS...
...AND THEY'RE WORTH DOZENS OF ORDINARY FRIENDS.

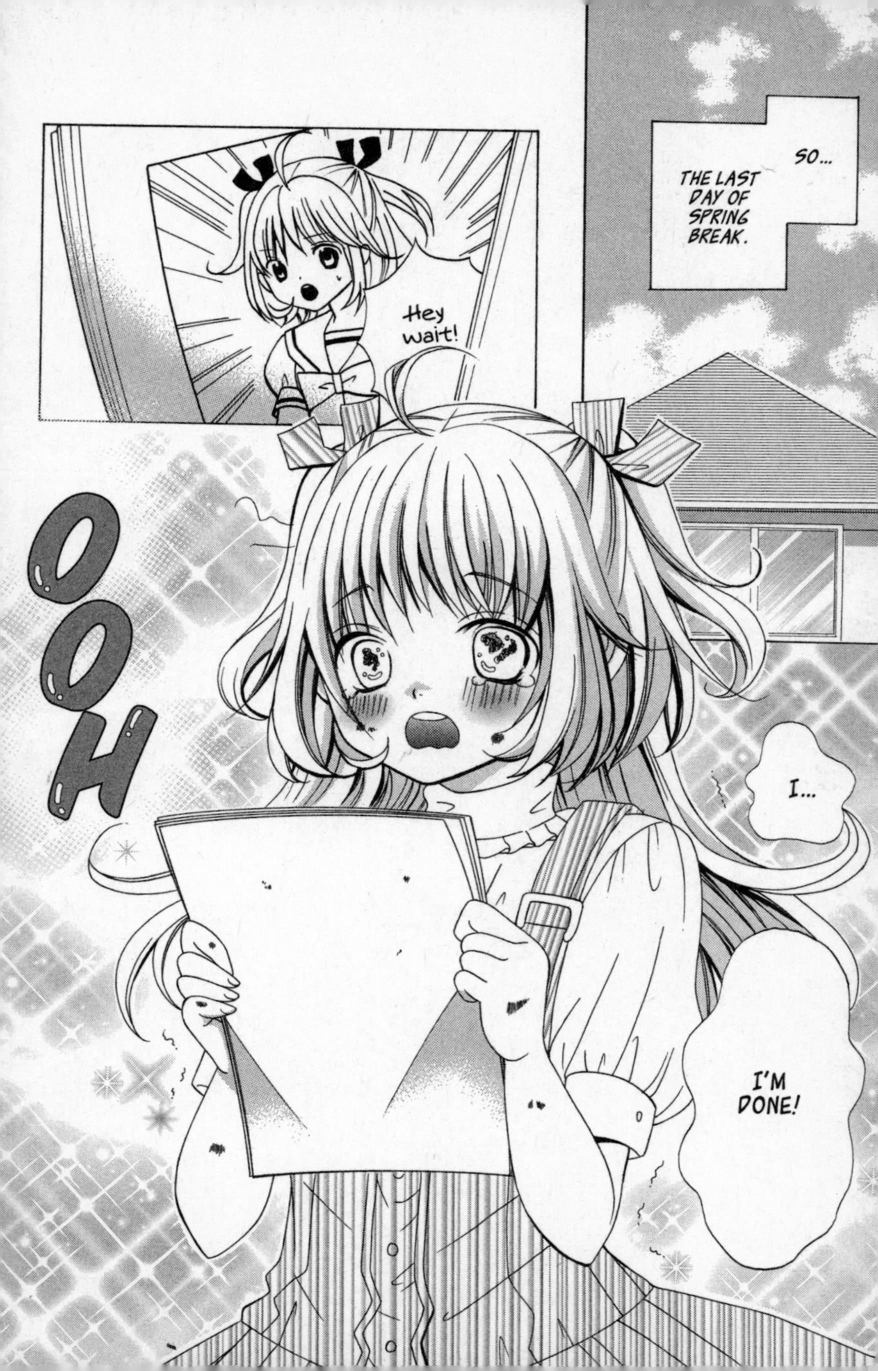
SO...
THE LAST DAY OF SPRING BREAK.
Hey wait!
OOH
I...
I'M DONE!

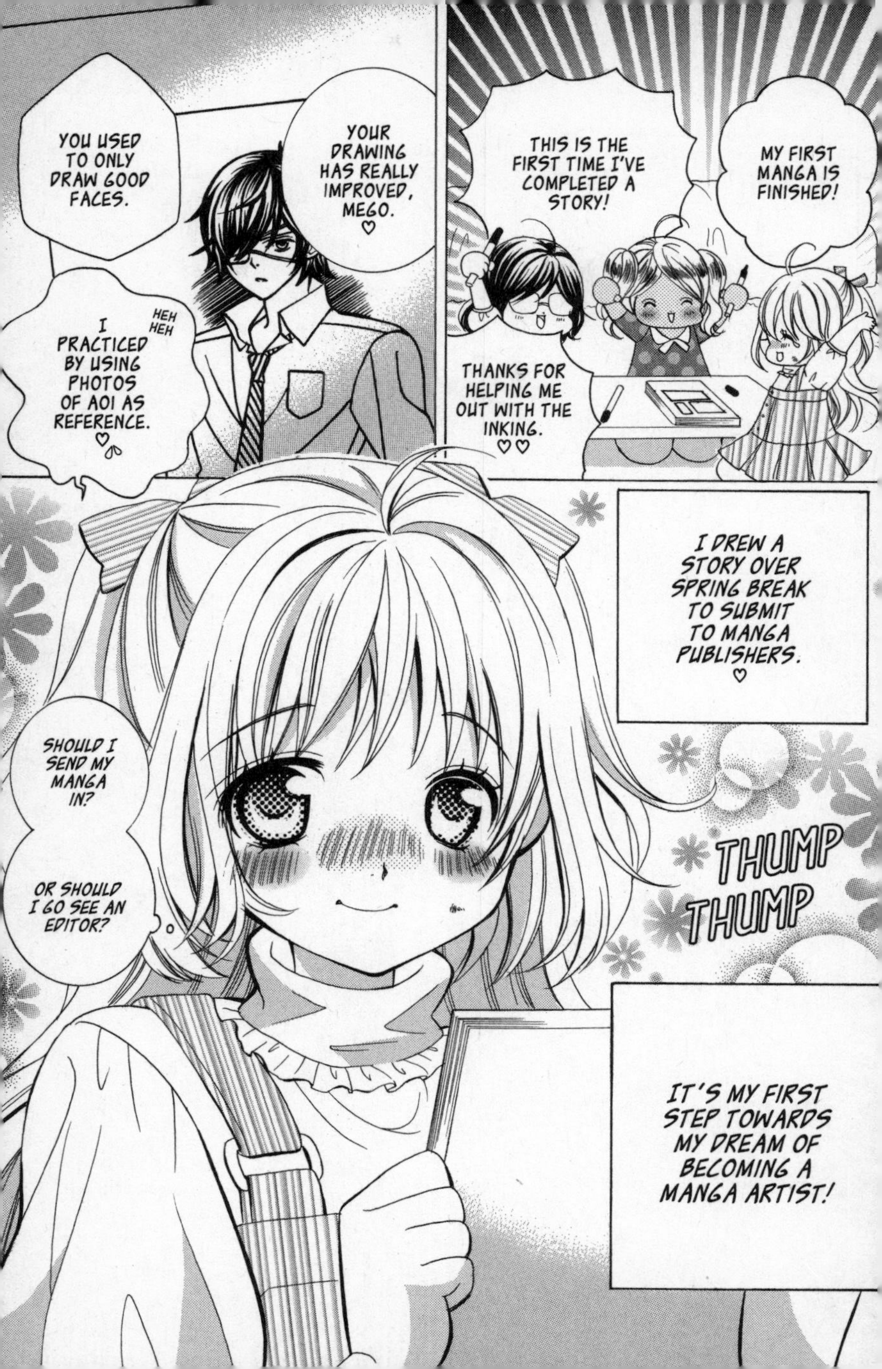
MY FIRST MANGA IS FINISHED!
THIS IS THE FIRST TIME I'VE COMPLETED A STORY!
THANKS FOR HELPING ME OUT WITH THE INKING.
YOUR DRAWING HAS REALLY IMPROVED, MEGO.
YOU USED TO ONLY DRAW GOOD FACES.
HEH HEH
I PRACTICED BY USING PHOTOS OF AOI AS REFERENCE.
I DREW A STORY OVER SPRING BREAK TO SUBMIT TO MANGA PUBLISHERS.
THUMP THUMP
SHOULD I SEND MY MANGA IN?
OR SHOULD I GO SEE AN EDITOR?
IT'S MY FIRST STEP TOWARDS MY DREAM OF BECOMING A MANGA ARTIST!

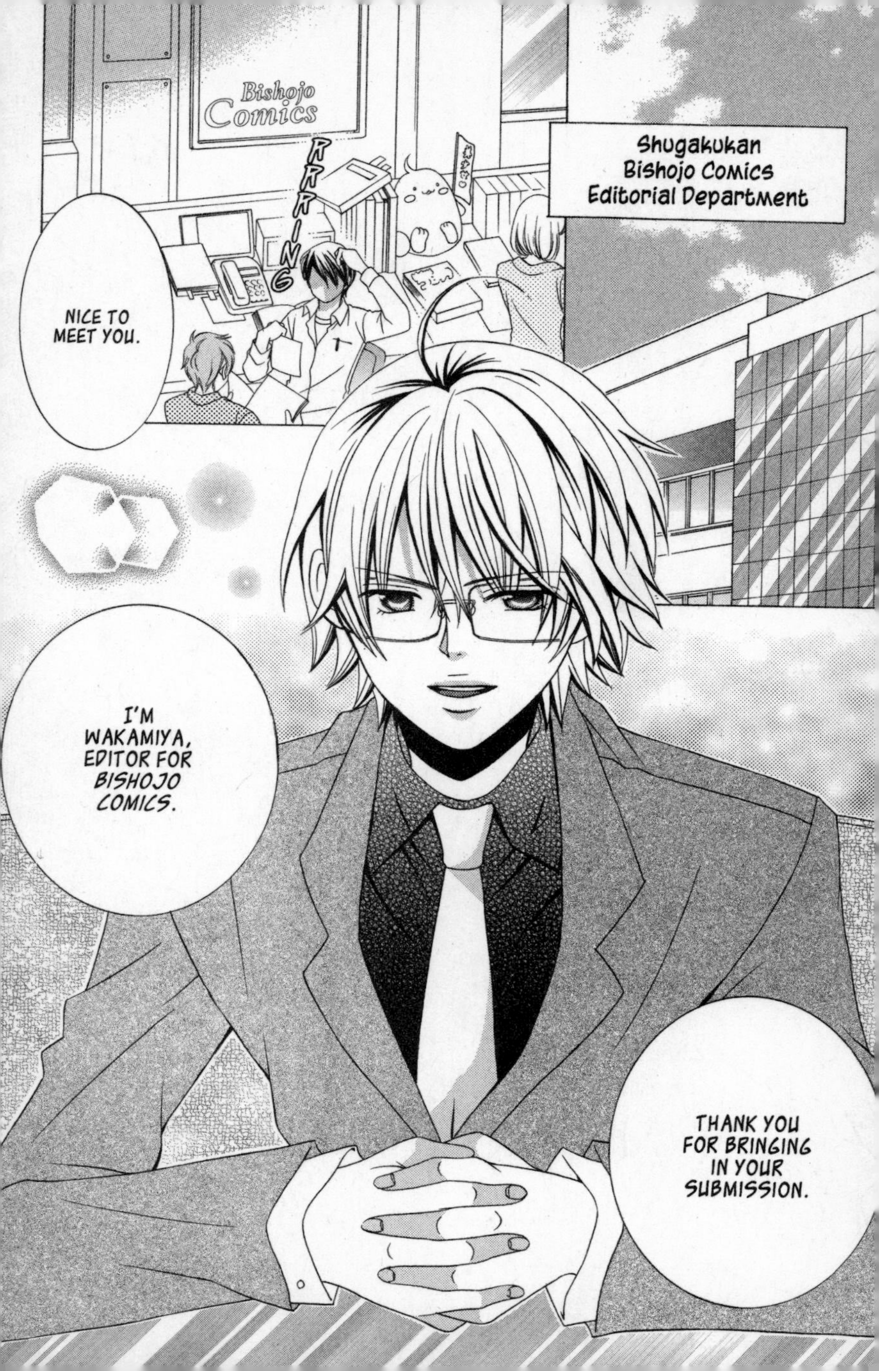
Shugakukan
Bishojo Comics
Editorial Department
Bishojo Comics
RRRING
NICE TO MEET YOU.
I'M WAKAMIYA, EDITOR FOR BISHOJO COMICS.
THANK YOU FOR BRINGING IN YOUR SUBMISSION.

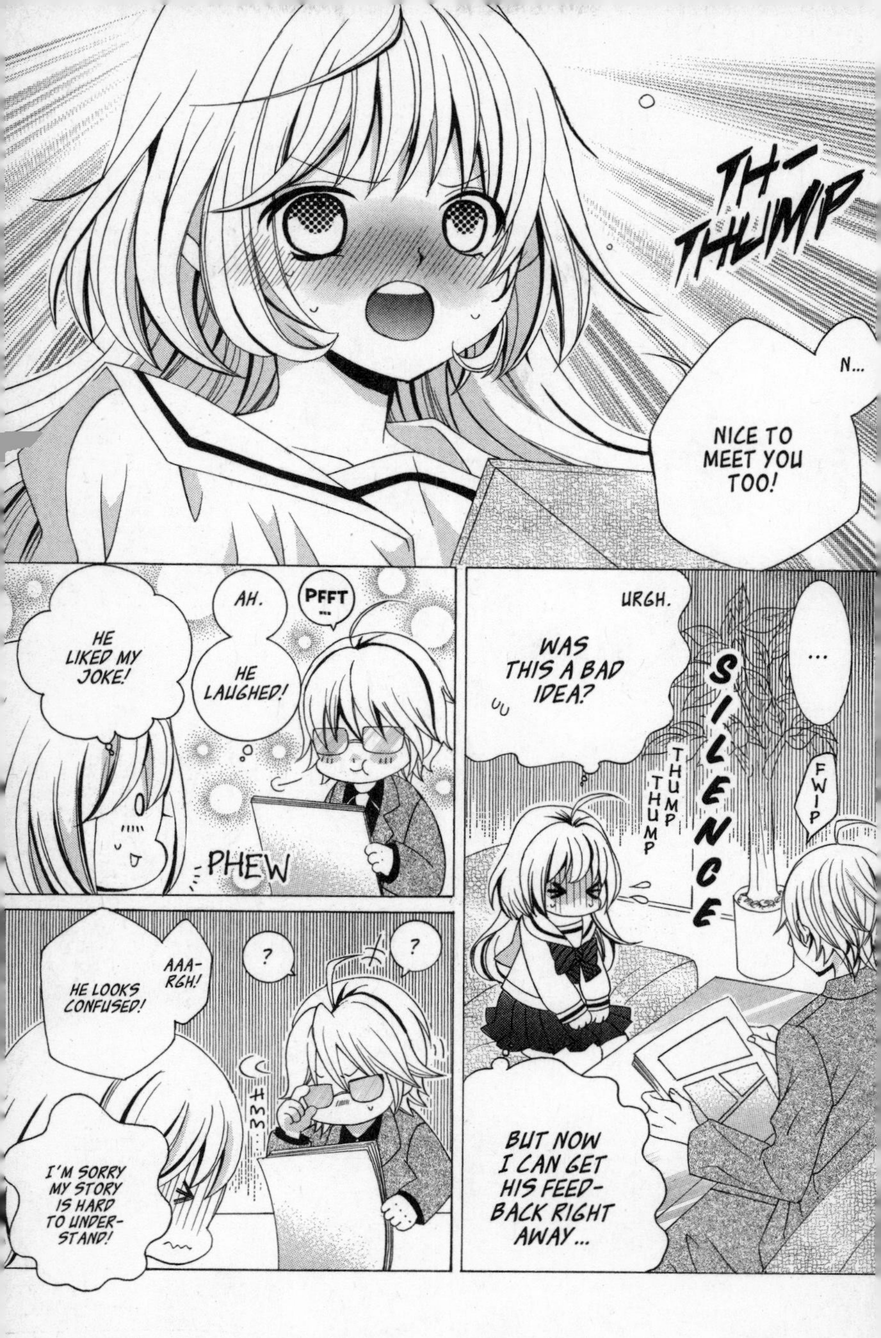
TH-THUMP
N...
NICE TO MEET YOU TOO!
...
FWIP
SILENCE
THUMP THUMP
URGH.
WAS THIS A BAD IDEA?
BUT NOW I CAN GET HIS FEED-BACK RIGHT AWAY...
PFFT...
AH.
HE LAUGHED!
HE LIKED MY JOKE!
PHEW
?
?
AAA-RGH!
HE LOOKS CONFUSED!
HMM...
I'M SORRY MY STORY IS HARD TO UNDER-STAND!

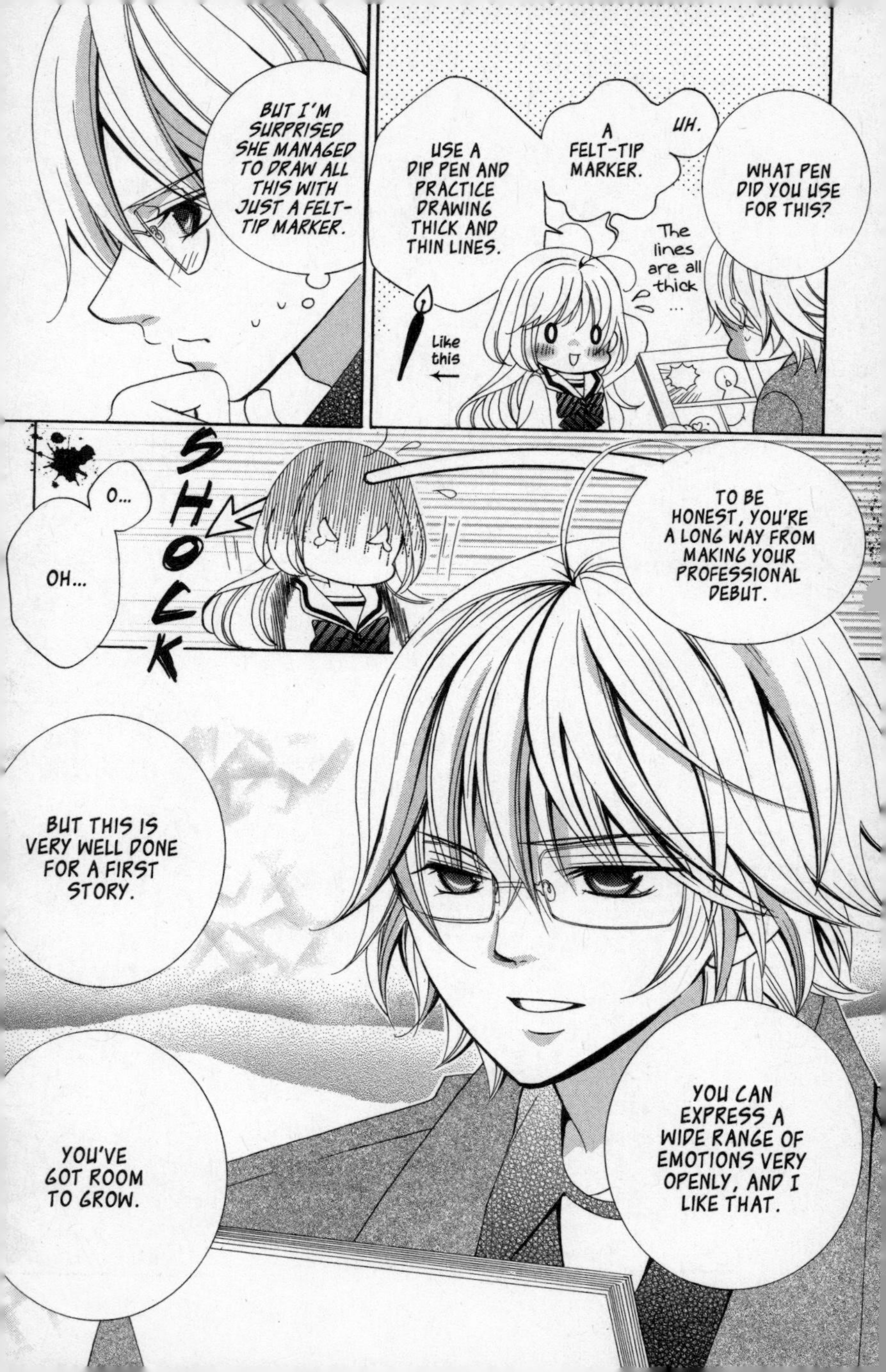
WHAT PEN DID YOU USE FOR THIS?
UH.
A FELT-TIP MARKER.
The lines are all thick ...
USE A DIP PEN AND PRACTICE DRAWING THICK AND THIN LINES.
Like this
BUT I'M SURPRISED SHE MANAGED TO DRAW ALL THIS WITH JUST A FELT-TIP MARKER.
TO BE HONEST, YOU'RE A LONG WAY FROM MAKING YOUR PROFESSIONAL DEBUT.
SHOCK
O...
OH...
BUT THIS IS VERY WELL DONE FOR A FIRST STORY.
YOU CAN EXPRESS A WIDE RANGE OF EMOTIONS VERY OPENLY, AND I LIKE THAT.
YOU'VE GOT ROOM TO GROW.

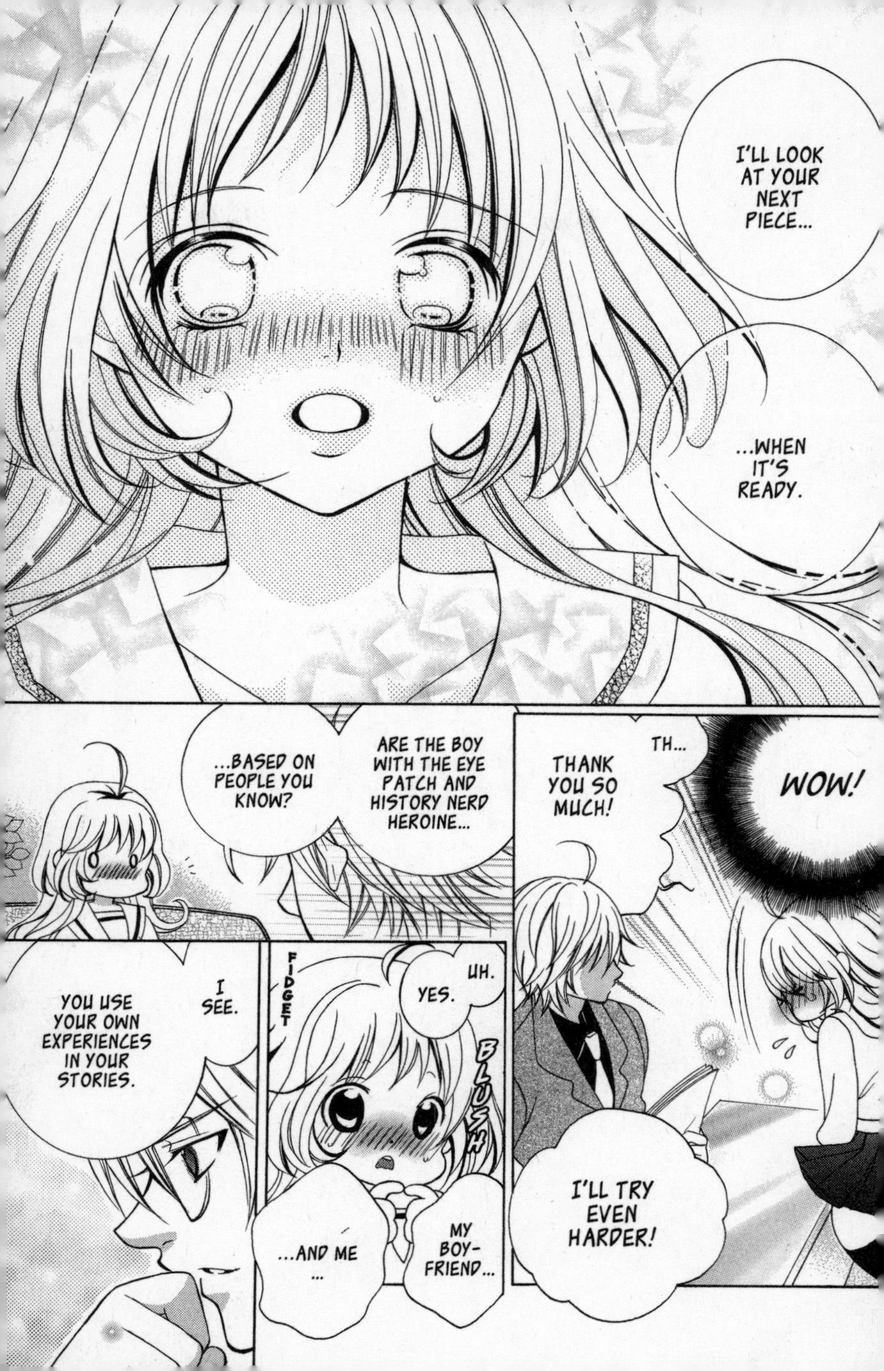
I'LL LOOK AT YOUR NEXT PIECE...
...WHEN IT'S READY.
WOW!
TH...
THANK YOU SO MUCH!
I'LL TRY EVEN HARDER!
ARE THE BOY WITH THE EYE PATCH AND HISTORY NERD HEROINE...
...BASED ON PEOPLE YOU KNOW?
UH.
YES.
FIDGET
BLUSH
MY BOY-FRIEND...
...AND ME ...
I SEE.
YOU USE YOUR OWN EXPERIENCES IN YOUR STORIES.

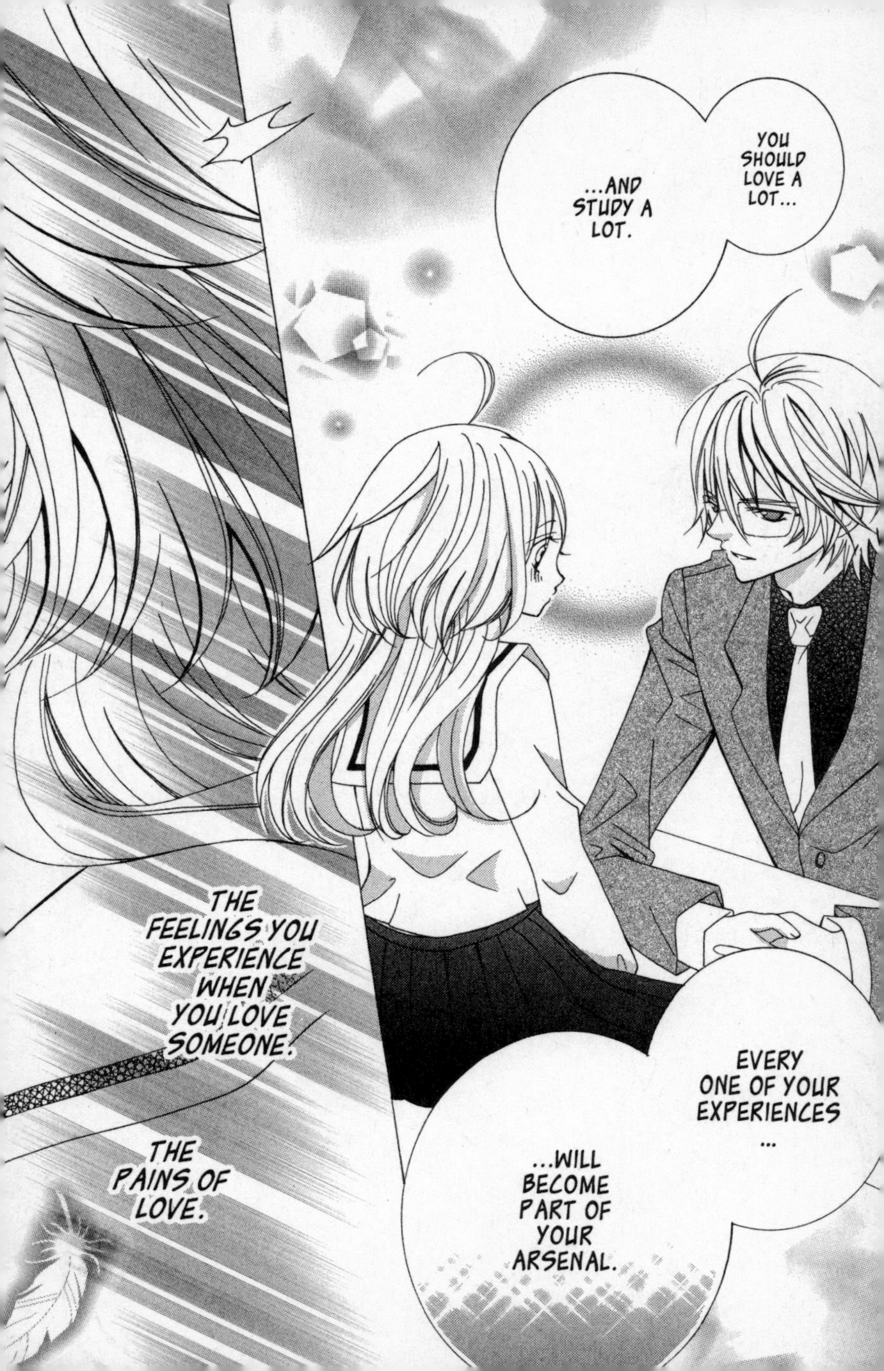
YOU SHOULD LOVE A LOT...
...AND STUDY A LOT.
EVERY ONE OF YOUR EXPERIENCES ...
...WILL BECOME PART OF YOUR ARSENAL.
THE FEELINGS YOU EXPERIENCE WHEN YOU LOVE SOMEONE.
THE PAINS OF LOVE.

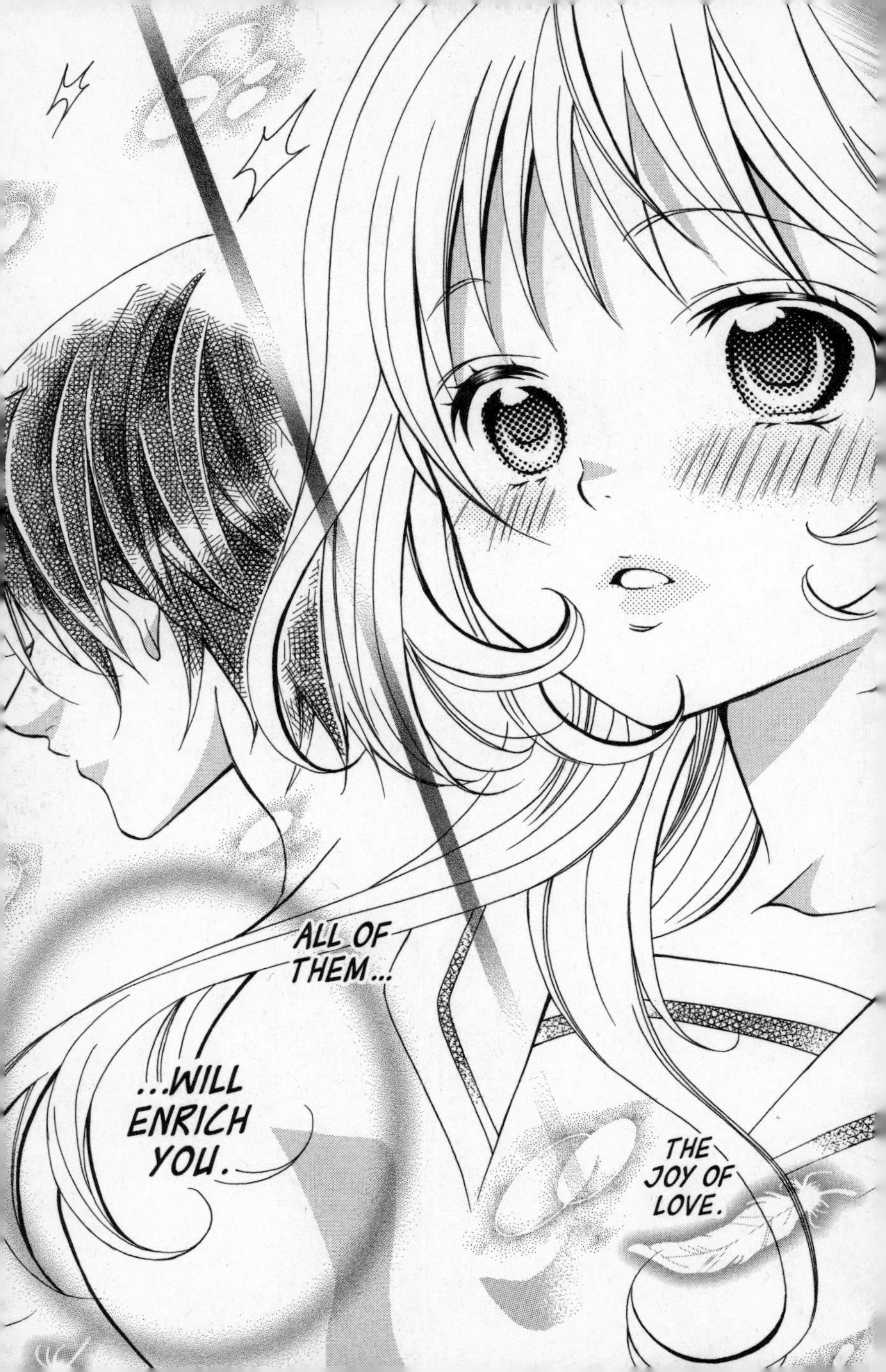
ALL OF THEM...
...WILL ENRICH YOU.
THE JOY OF LOVE.

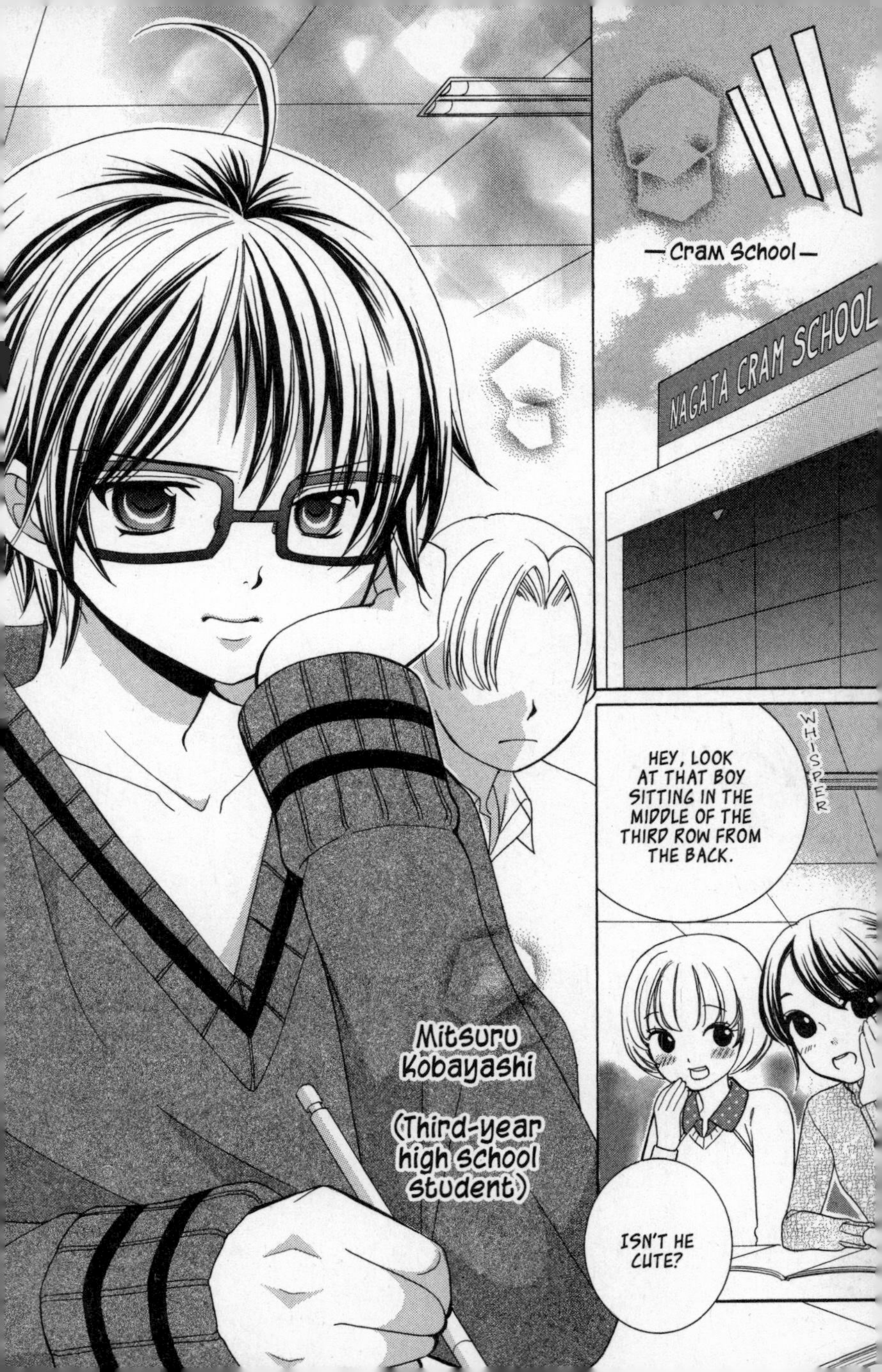
—Cram School—
NAGATA CRAM SCHOOL
WHISPER
HEY, LOOK AT THAT BOY SITTING IN THE MIDDLE OF THE THIRD ROW FROM THE BACK.
ISN'T HE CUTE?
Mitsuru Kobayashi
(Third-year high school student)

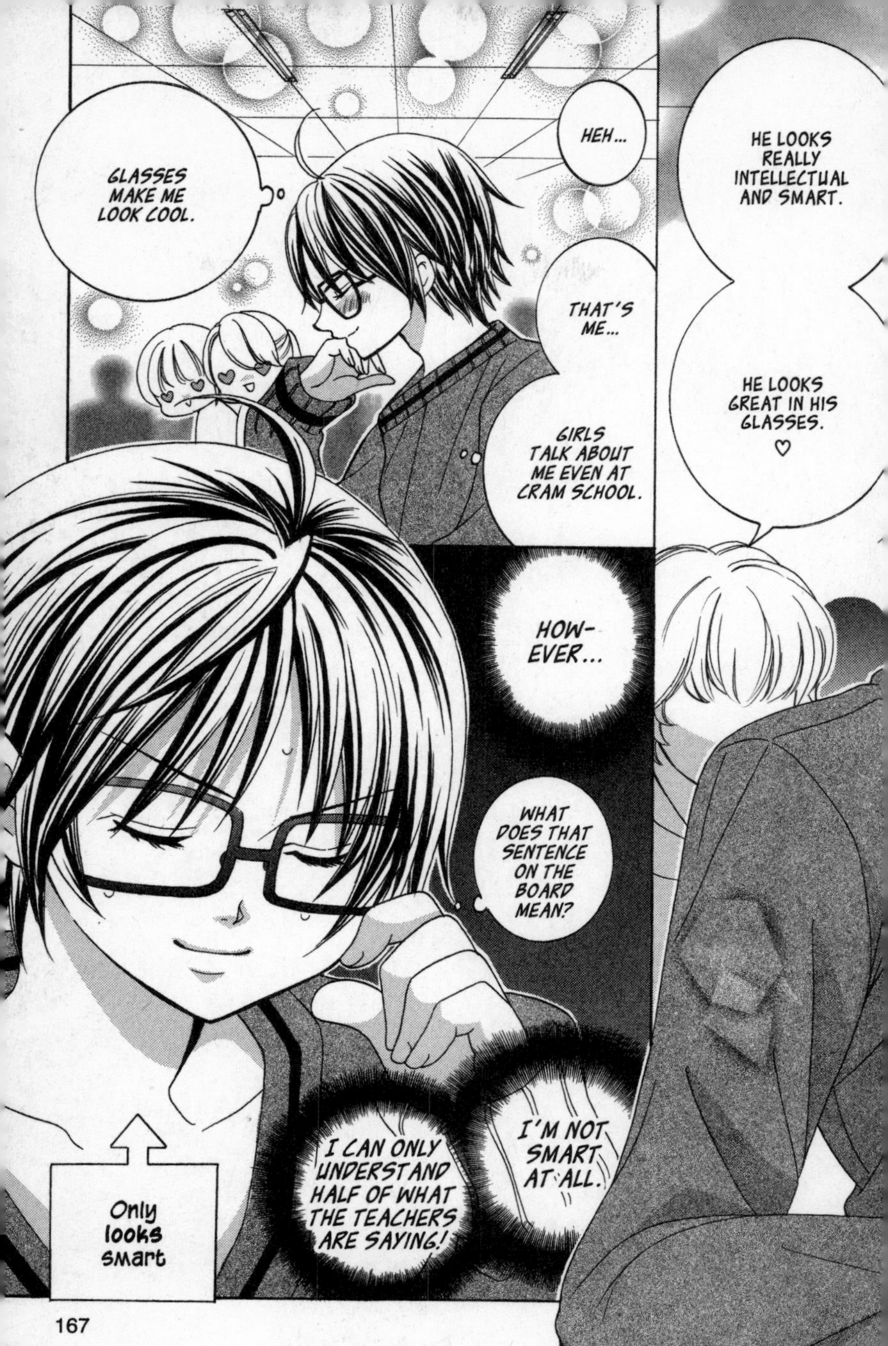
HE LOOKS REALLY INTELLECTUAL AND SMART.
HE LOOKS GREAT IN HIS GLASSES. ♡
HEH...
THAT'S ME...
GIRLS TALK ABOUT ME EVEN AT CRAM SCHOOL.
GLASSES MAKE ME LOOK COOL.
HOW-EVER...
WHAT DOES THAT SENTENCE ON THE BOARD MEAN?
I'M NOT SMART AT ALL.
I CAN ONLY UNDERSTAND HALF OF WHAT THE TEACHERS ARE SAYING!
Only looks smart

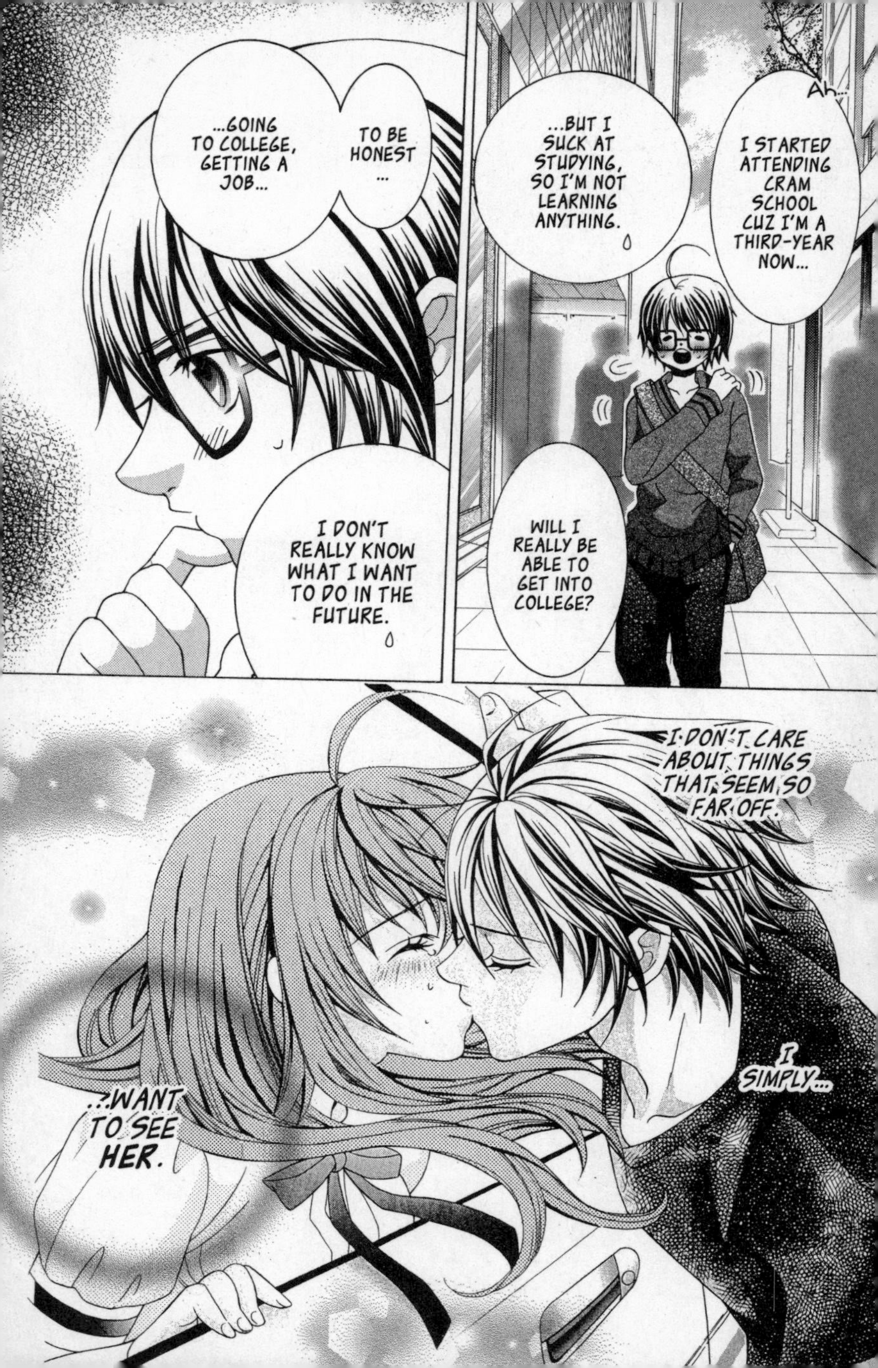
Ah...
I STARTED ATTENDING CRAM SCHOOL CUZ I'M A THIRD-YEAR NOW...
...BUT I SUCK AT STUDYING, SO I'M NOT LEARNING ANYTHING.
WILL I REALLY BE ABLE TO GET INTO COLLEGE?
TO BE HONEST...
...GOING TO COLLEGE, GETTING A JOB...
I DON'T REALLY KNOW WHAT I WANT TO DO IN THE FUTURE.
I DON'T CARE ABOUT THINGS THAT SEEM SO FAR OFF.
I SIMPLY...
...WANT TO SEE HER.

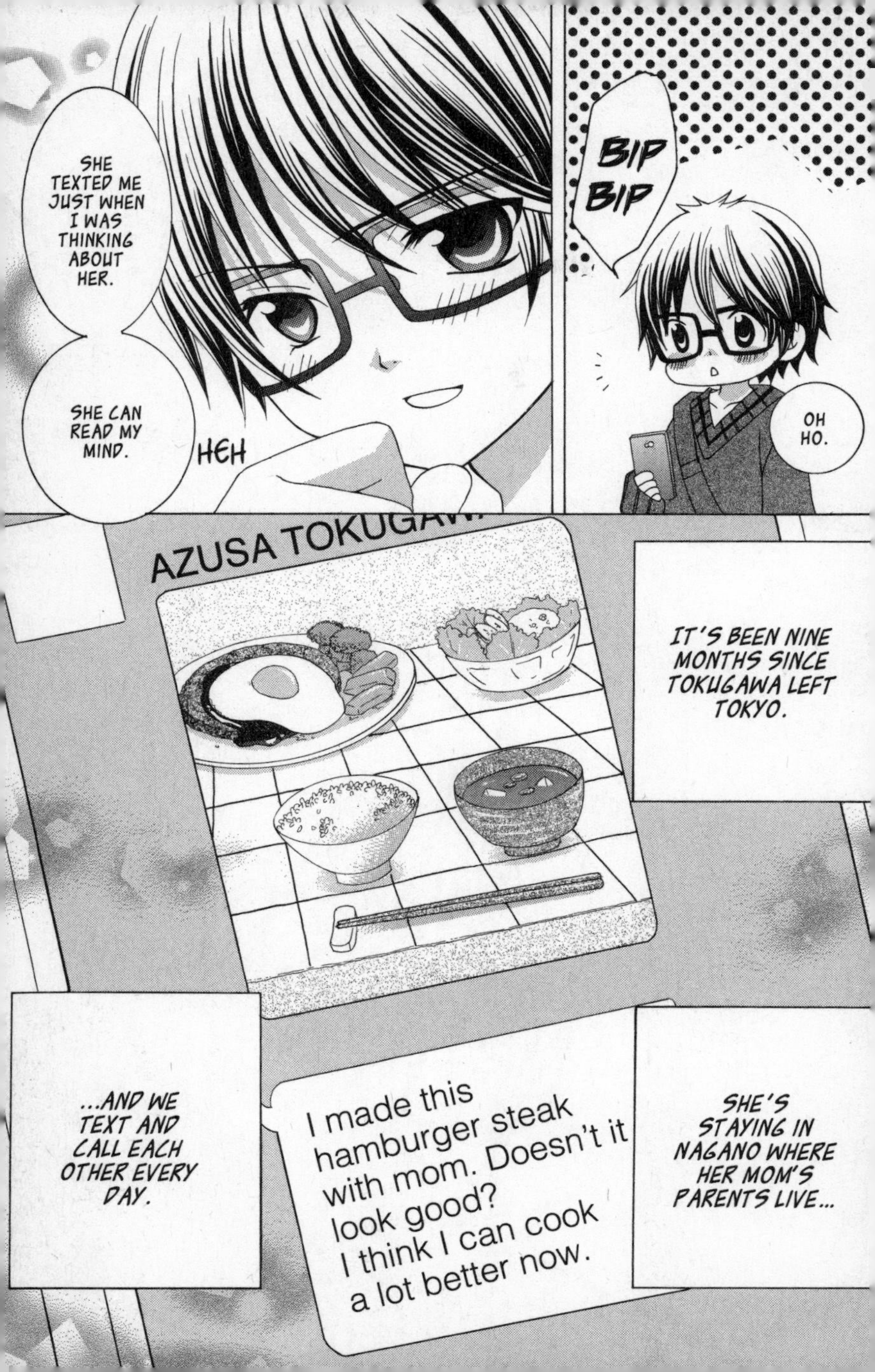
BIP BIP
OH HO.
SHE TEXTED ME JUST WHEN I WAS THINKING ABOUT HER.
SHE CAN READ MY MIND.
HEH
IT'S BEEN NINE MONTHS SINCE TOKUGAWA LEFT TOKYO.
AZUSA TOKUGAW
SHE'S STAYING IN NAGANO WHERE HER MOM'S PARENTS LIVE...
I made this hamburger steak with mom. Doesn't it look good? I think I can cook a lot better now.
...AND WE TEXT AND CALL EACH OTHER EVERY DAY.

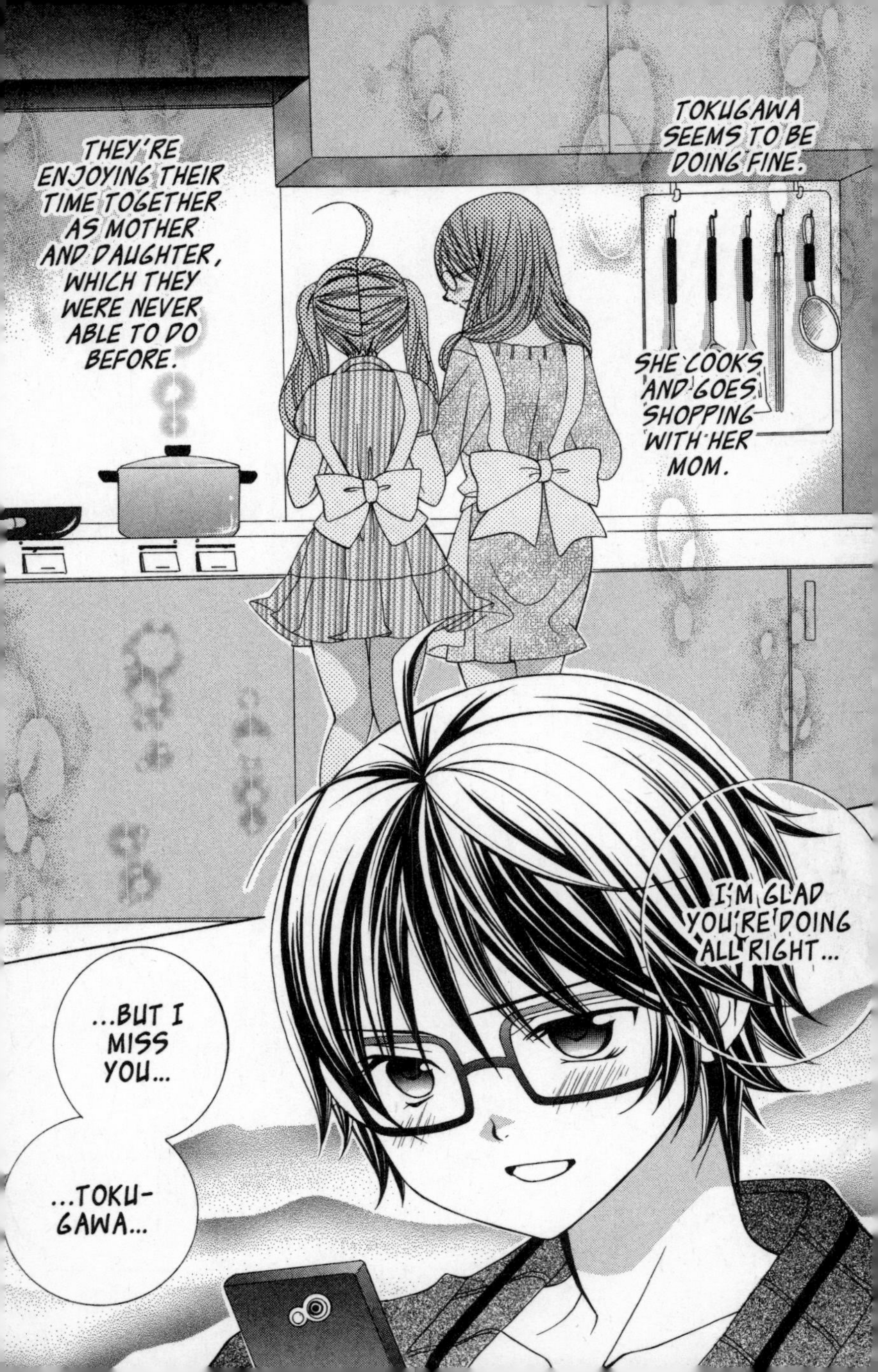
TOKUGAWA SEEMS TO BE DOING FINE.
SHE COOKS AND GOES SHOPPING WITH HER MOM.
THEY'RE ENJOYING THEIR TIME TOGETHER AS MOTHER AND DAUGHTER, WHICH THEY WERE NEVER ABLE TO DO BEFORE.
I'M GLAD YOU'RE DOING ALL RIGHT...
...BUT I MISS YOU...
...TOKU-GAWA...

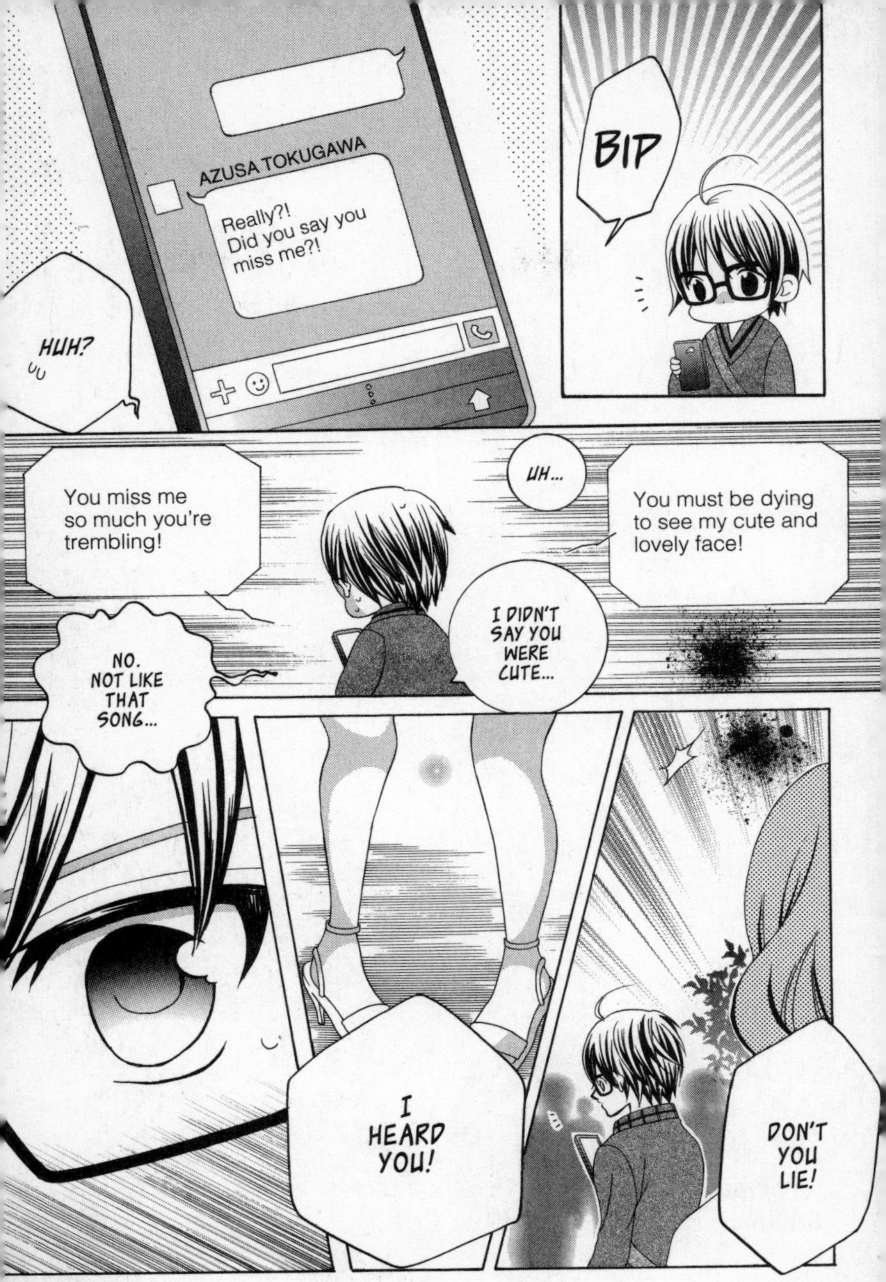
BIP
AZUSA TOKUGAWA
Really?! Did you say you miss me?!
HUH?
You must be dying to see my cute and lovely face!
UH...
You miss me so much you're trembling!
I DIDN'T SAY YOU WERE CUTE...
NO. NOT LIKE THAT SONG...
DON'T YOU LIE!
I HEARD YOU!

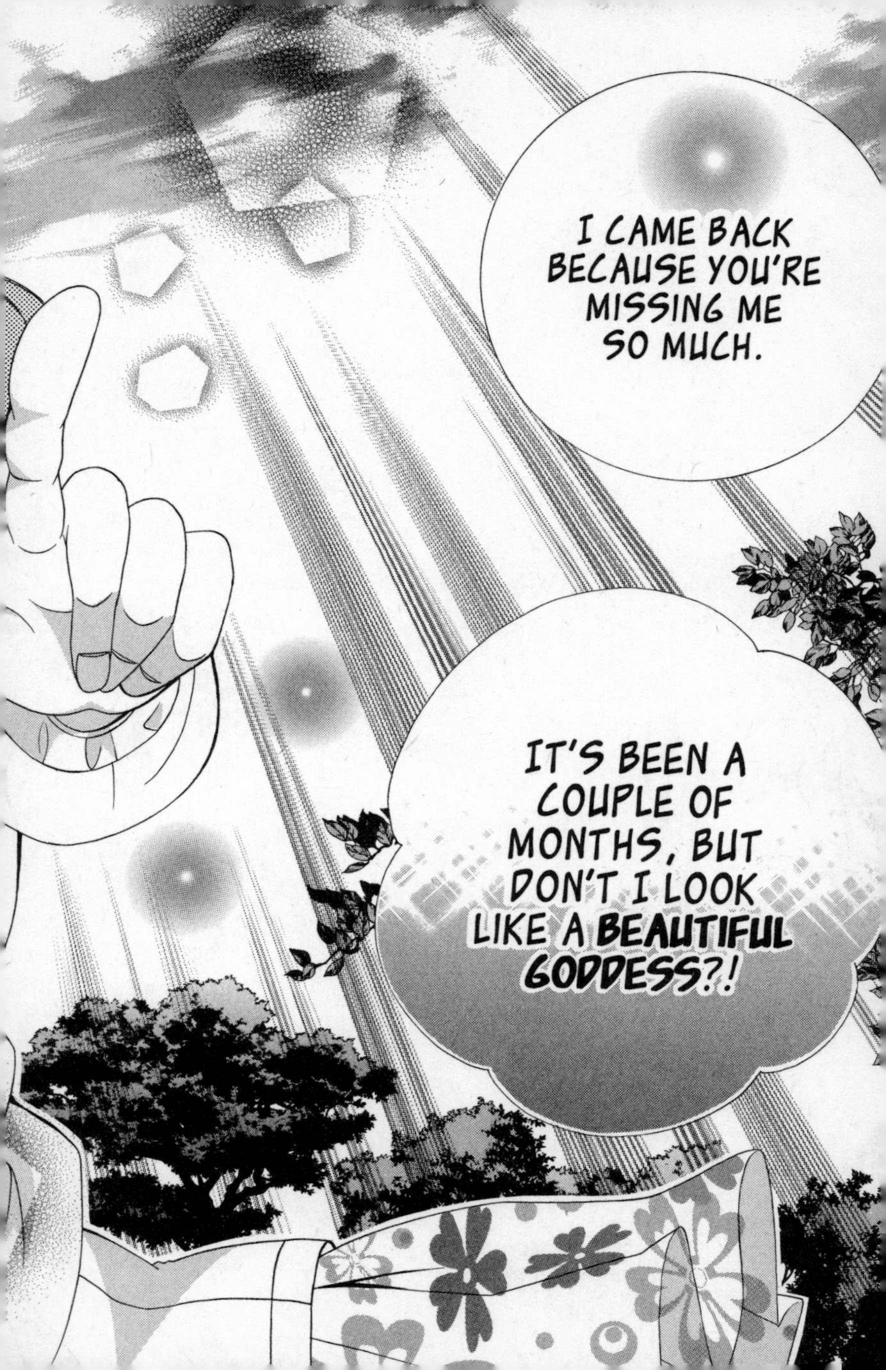
I CAME BACK BECAUSE YOU'RE MISSING ME SO MUCH.
IT'S BEEN A COUPLE OF MONTHS, BUT DON'T I LOOK LIKE A **BEAUTIFUL GODDESS**?!

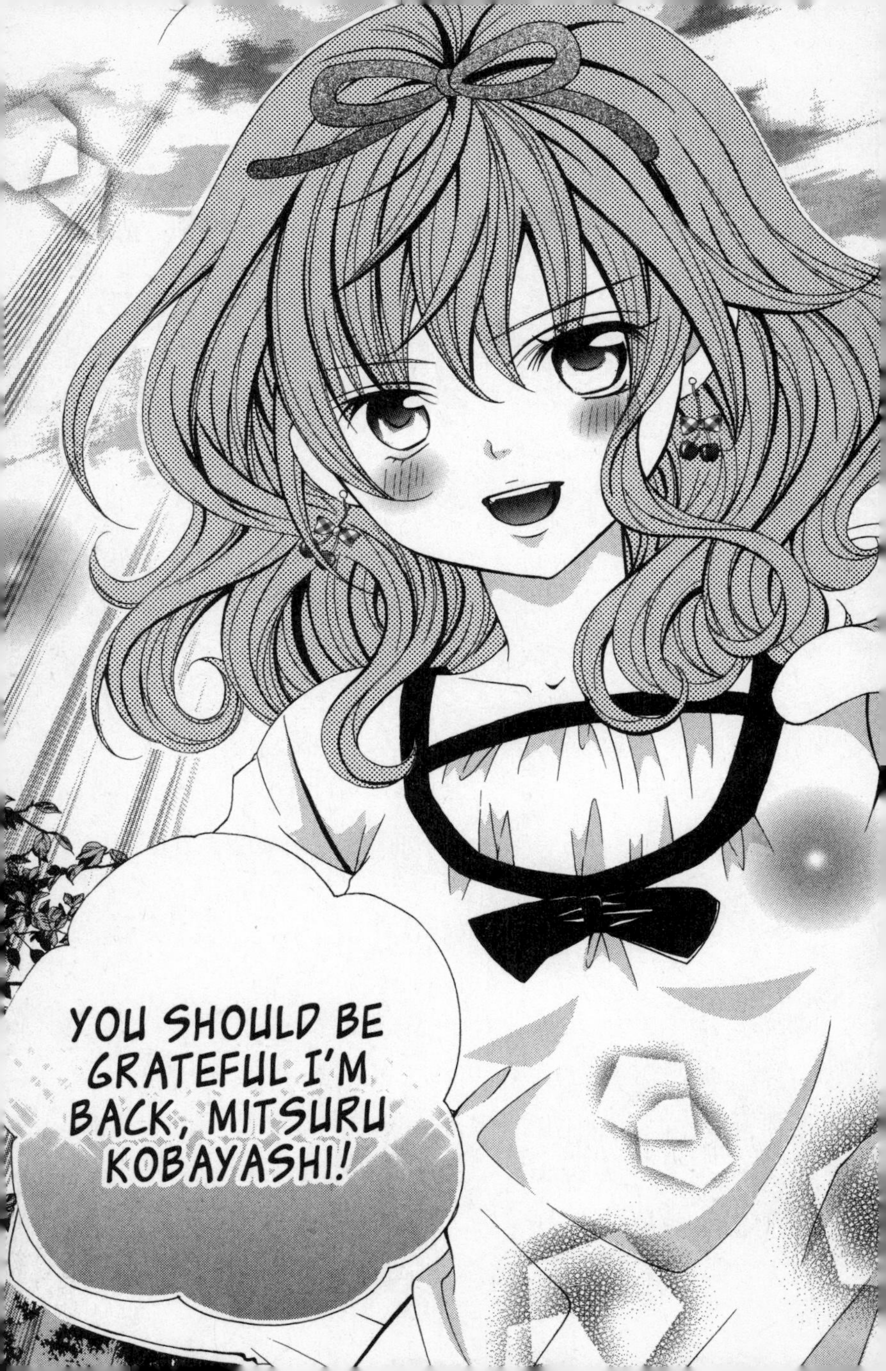
YOU SHOULD BE GRATEFUL I'M BACK, MITSURU KOBAYASHI!

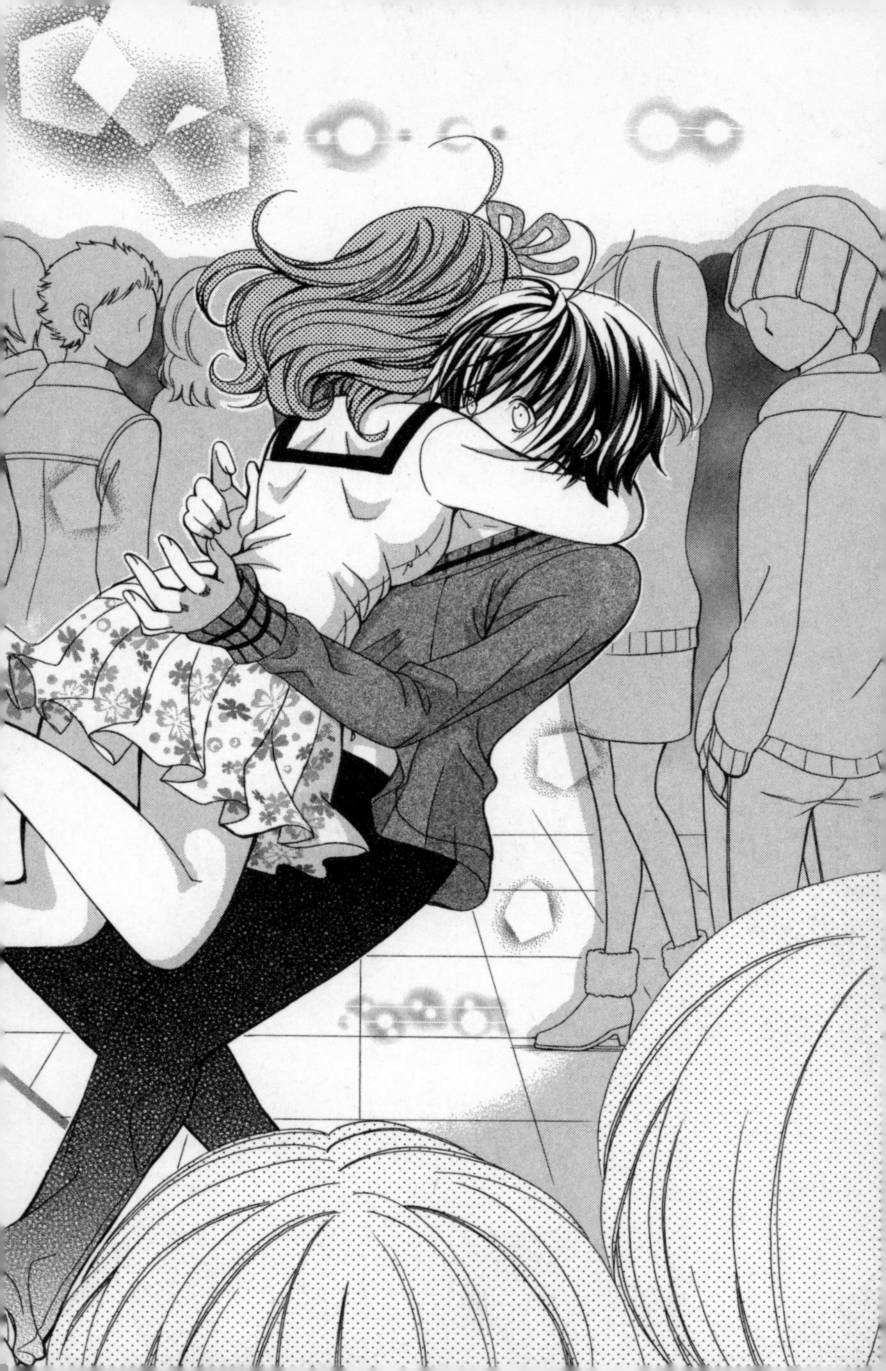

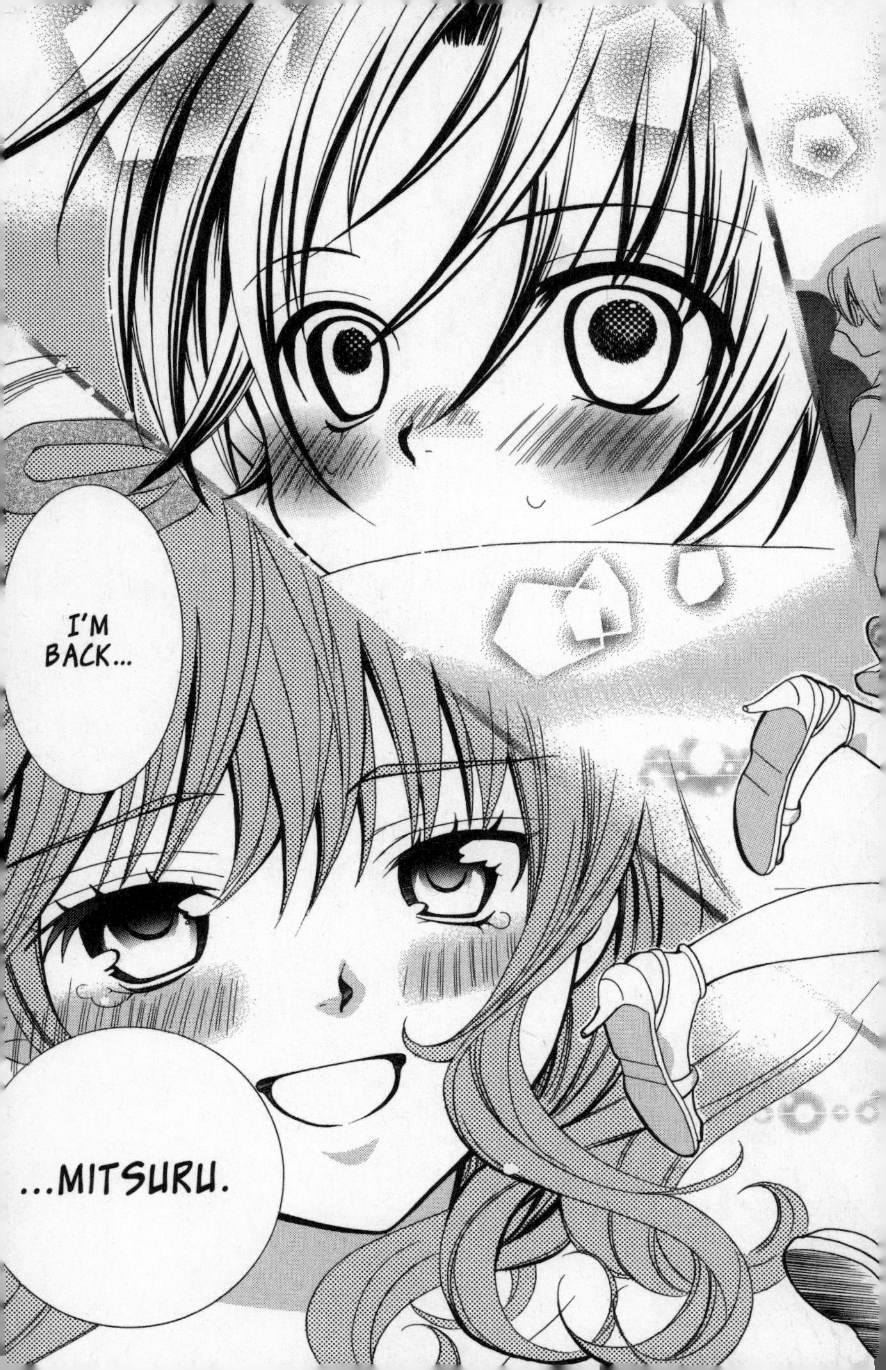
I'M BACK...
...MITSURU.

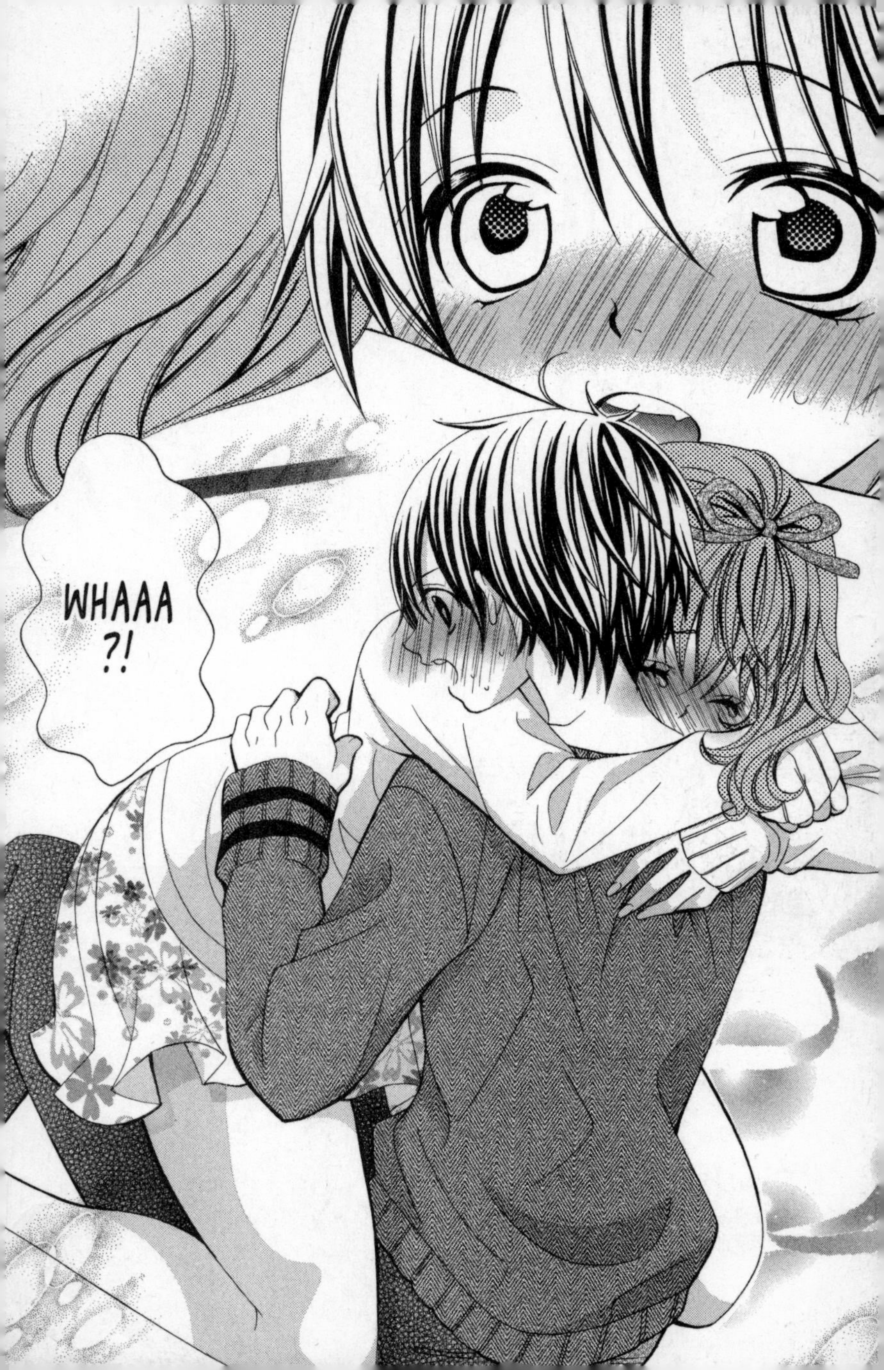
WHAAA
?!

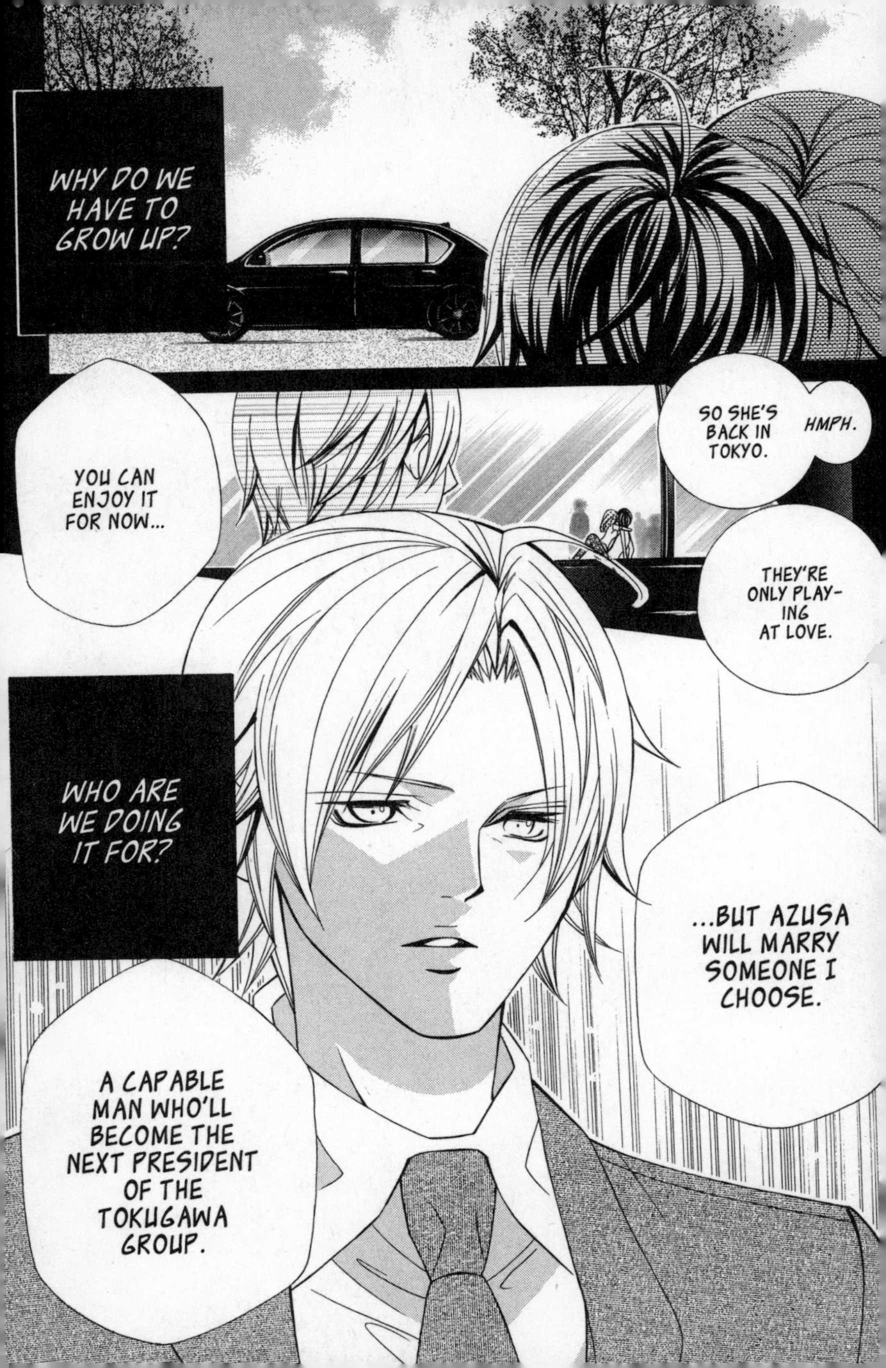
WHY DO WE HAVE TO GROW UP?
SO SHE'S BACK IN TOKYO.
HMPH.
THEY'RE ONLY PLAYING AT LOVE.
YOU CAN ENJOY IT FOR NOW...
WHO ARE WE DOING IT FOR?
...BUT AZUSA WILL MARRY SOMEONE I CHOOSE.
A CAPABLE MAN WHO'LL BECOME THE NEXT PRESIDENT OF THE TOKUGAWA GROUP.

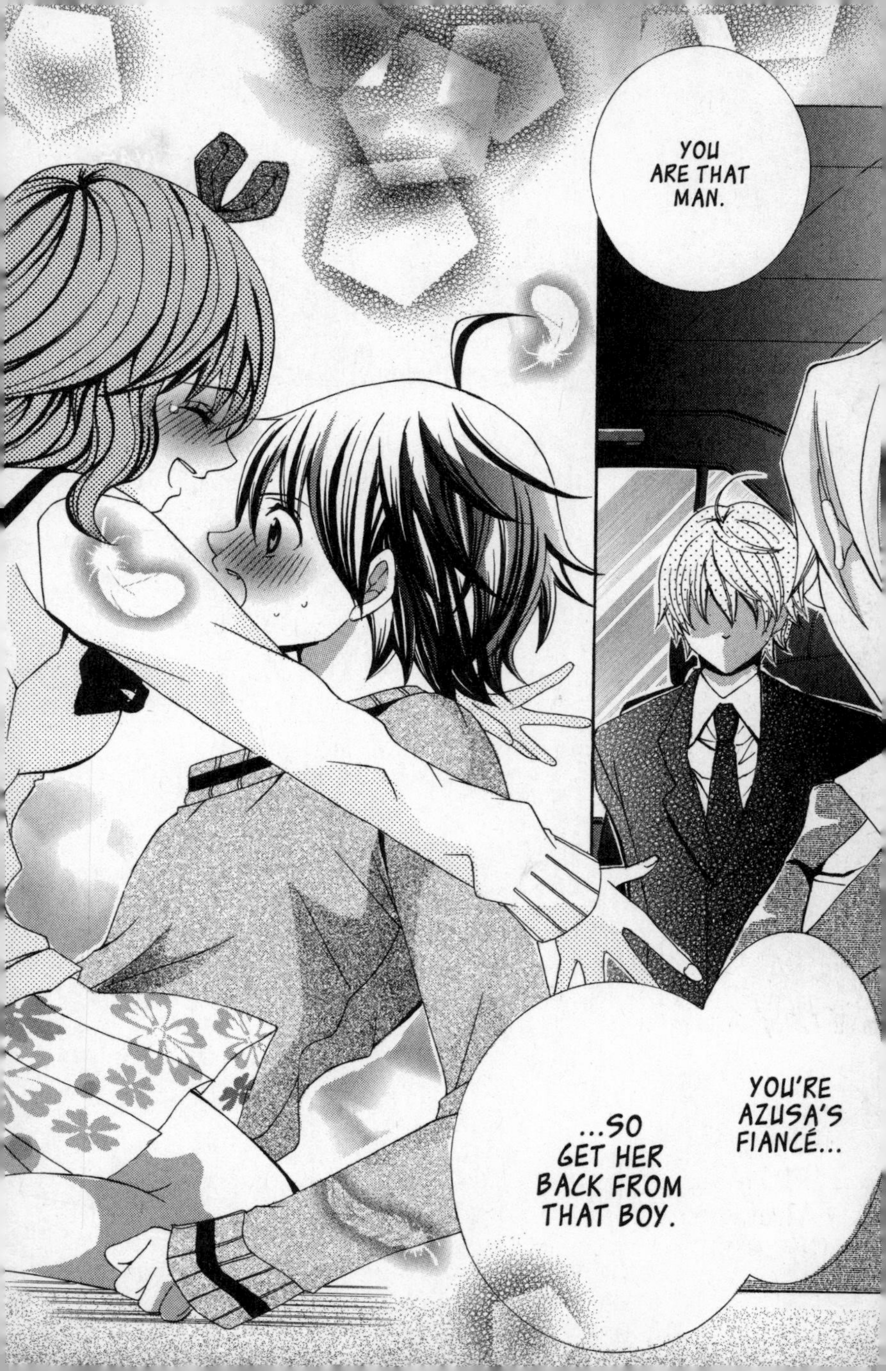
YOU ARE THAT MAN.
YOU'RE AZUSA'S FIANCÉ...
...SO GET HER BACK FROM THAT BOY.

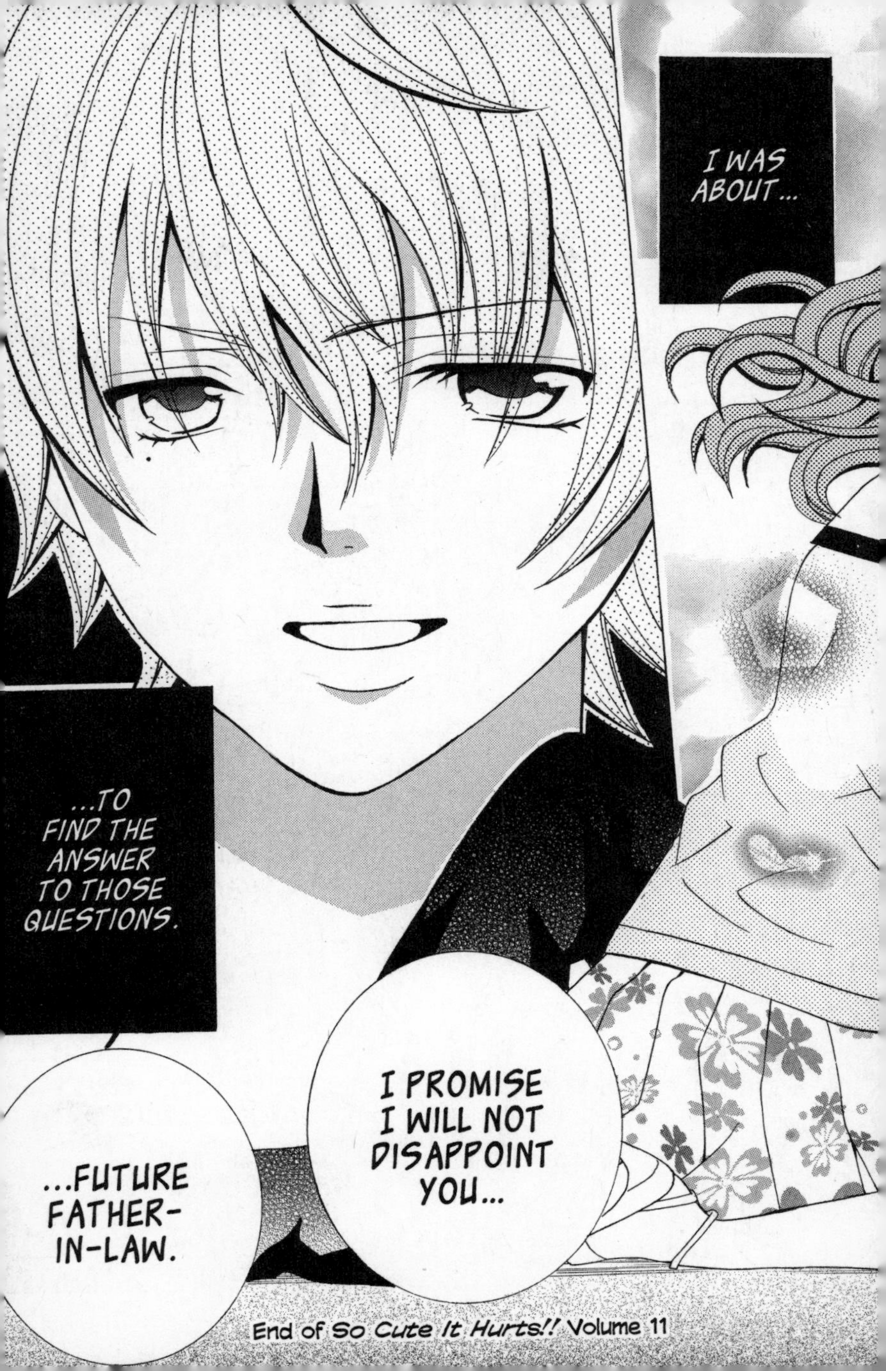
I WAS ABOUT...
...TO FIND THE ANSWER TO THOSE QUESTIONS.
I PROMISE I WILL NOT DISAPPOINT YOU...
...FUTURE FATHER-IN-LAW.

End of *So Cute It Hurts!!* Volume 11

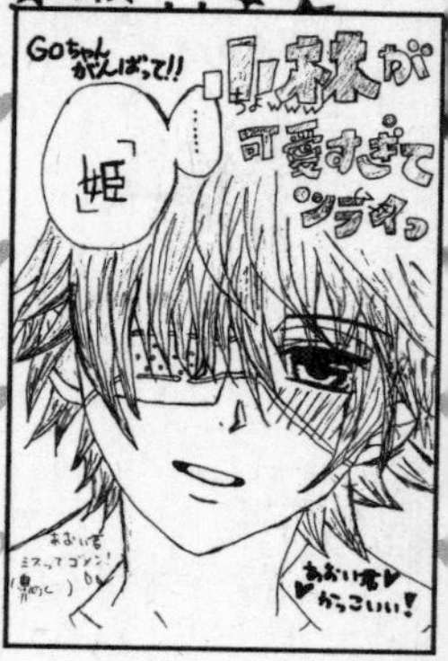
Goちゃんがんばって!!
姫
小林が可愛すぎてツラタンっ
あおい君♥かっこいい!

Chii-chan (Gifu) →
Ed.: Oh-ho!! Cool!!

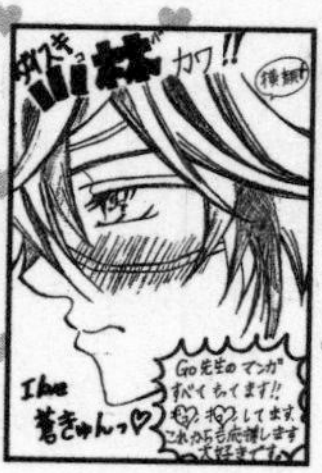

Nano-san (Hokkaido) ←
Ed.: His profile looks cool too!!

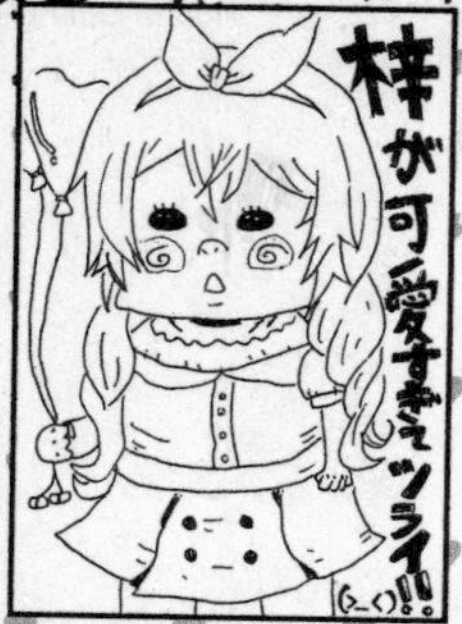
梓が可愛すぎてツライ!!
(>_<)

Nanaho Kai (Shizuoka) ←
Ed.: I love this ugly-but-cute Azusa!!

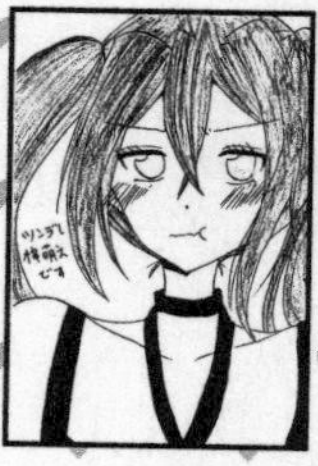

Yuki Kobayashi (Nagano) ←
Ed.: I wanna poke her cheeks.

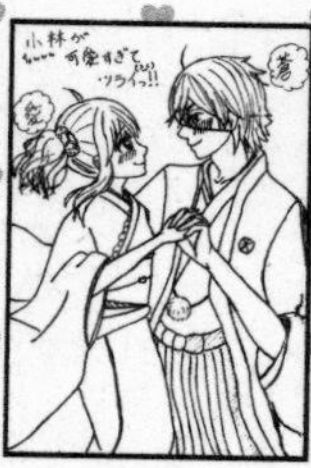
小林が ちょ〜 可愛すぎて ツライっ!!
蒼

Yui Koizumi (Saitama) ←
Ed.: They look cool in their kimono!!

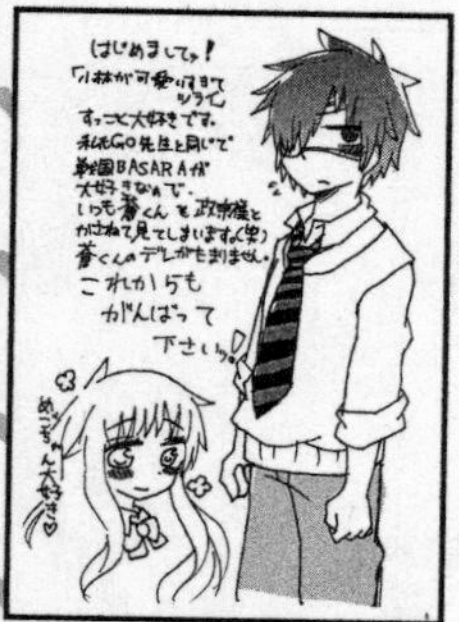
はじめまして!
これからも がんばって 下さいっ!!

Sai Miama (Okayama) ↑
Ed.: These two blushing look totally cute!!

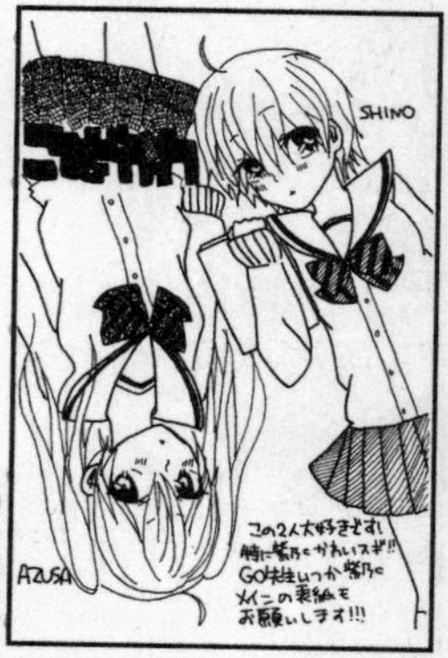
SHINO
AZUSA
この2人大好きです!!

Eirui (Gifu) →
Ed.: What a beautiful pair!!

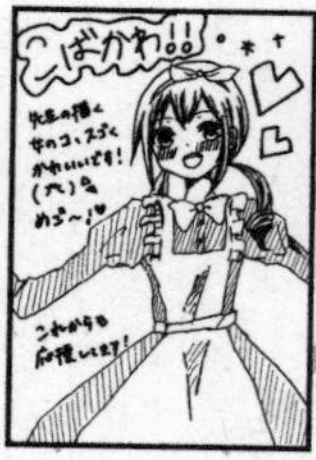
こばかわ!!

Mizuho Hirose (Osaka) ←
Ed.: Mego's cuteness is criminal!!

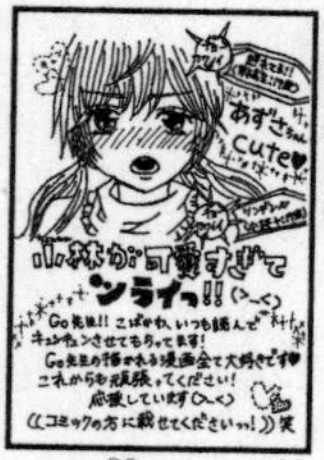
Cute♥
小林が可愛すぎてツライっ!!

Peach-hime (Kumamoto) ←
Ed.: Azusa's cuteness is killing me!!

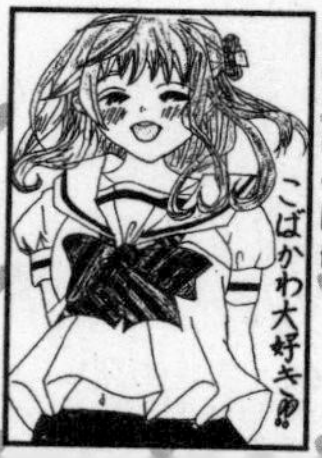

Atchan (Hyogo) ←
Ed.: I can see your belly button... You're too sexy. (><)

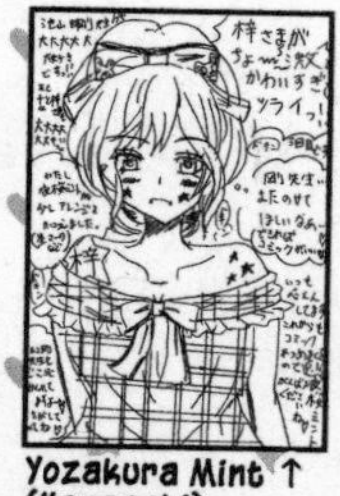

Yozakura Mint ↑ (Nagasaki)
Ed.: I find the 100 percent sweet Azusa so lovable!!

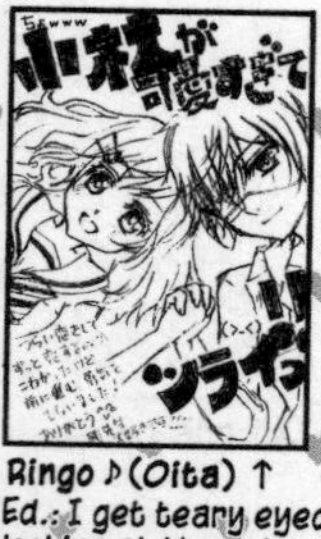
小林が可愛すぎて
ツライっ

Ringo♪ (Oita) ↑
Ed.: I get teary eyed looking at these two together...

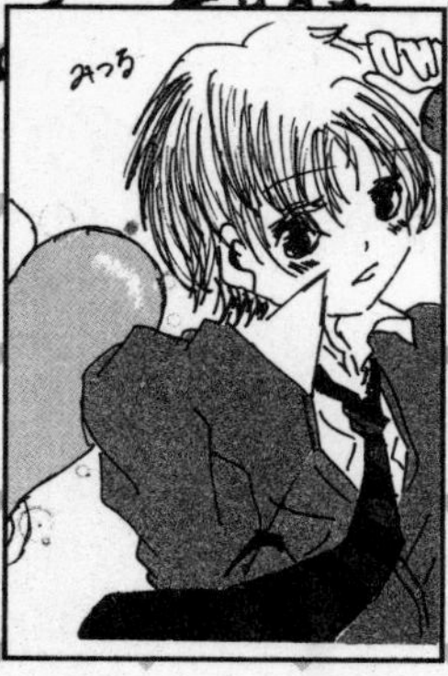

Juna Ooi (Tokyo) ←

Ed.: Ooh, cute!!

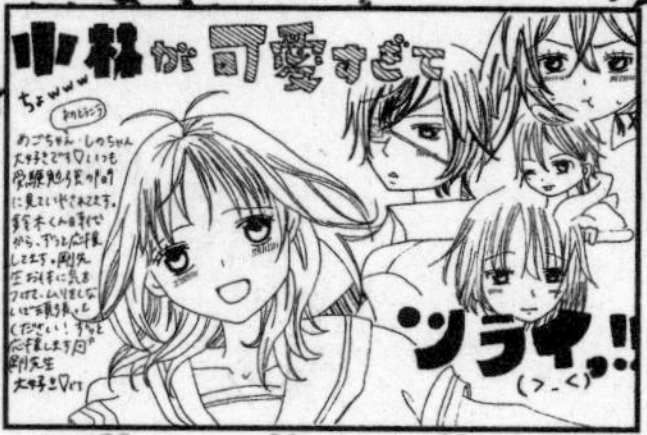

ツライ!!

Yuppi (Miyagi) ←

Ed.: I wanna hold them tight. ♥

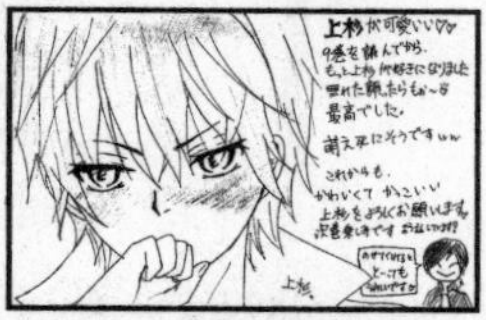

Seto Okami (Tokushima) ↑

Ed.: Heeeere's Uesugi!!

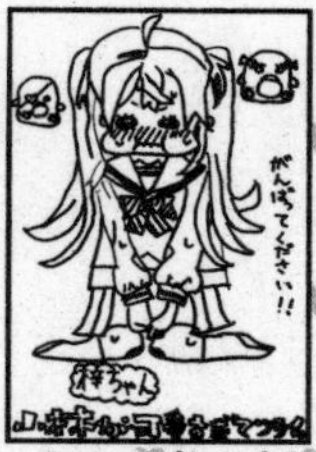

☆Budo☆ (Aichi) ↑

Ed.: Blushing Azusa looks so cute!!

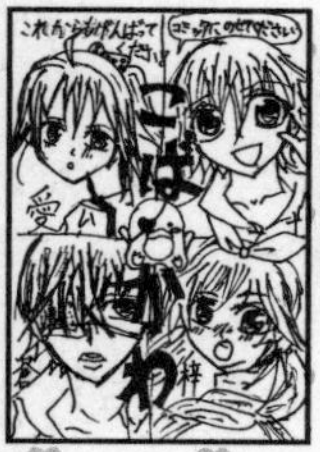

Saki Yoshida (Osaka) ←

Ed.: The foursome and the penguin!!

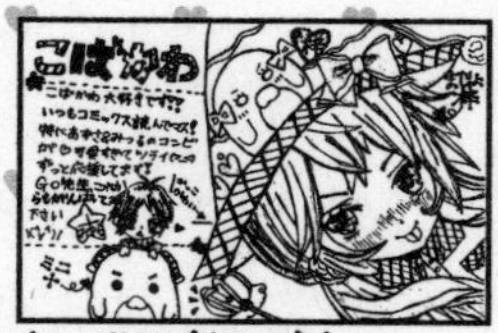

Azumitsu (Hyogo) ↑

Ed.: Yeah, Azusa's both cool and cute!!

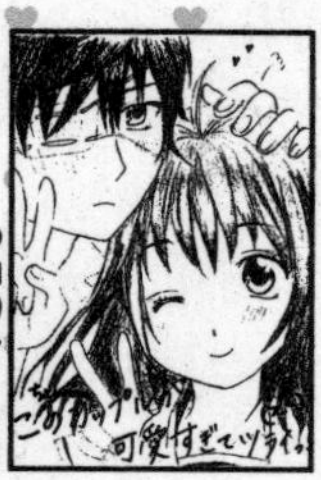

Tomoyo Takaoka (Ehime) →

Ed.: A victory sign!!

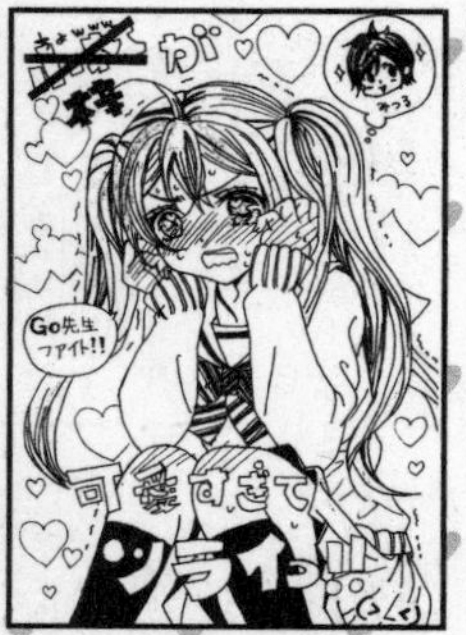

Go先生
ファイト!!
可愛すぎて
ツライっ!!

Himena Kurebayashi ↑ (Aichi)

Ed.: Yeah, Azusa's so cute it hurts!!

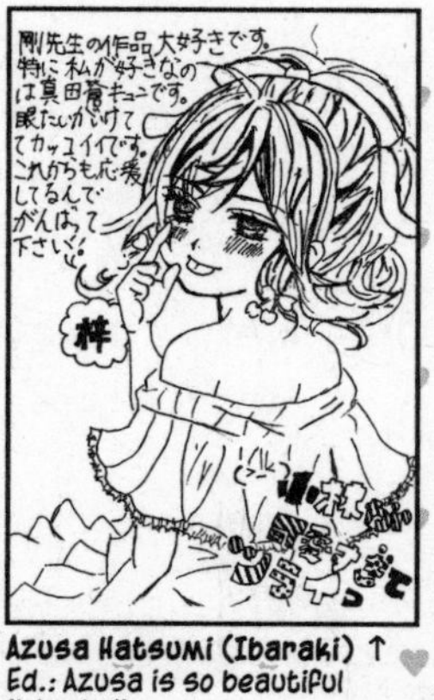

Azusa Hatsumi (Ibaraki) ↑

Ed.: Azusa is so beautiful it hurts!!

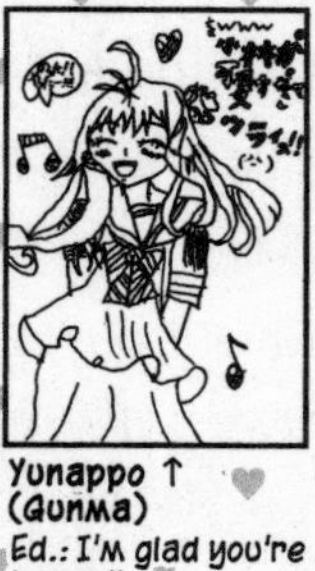

Yunappo ↑ (Gunma)

Ed.: I'm glad you're happy!!

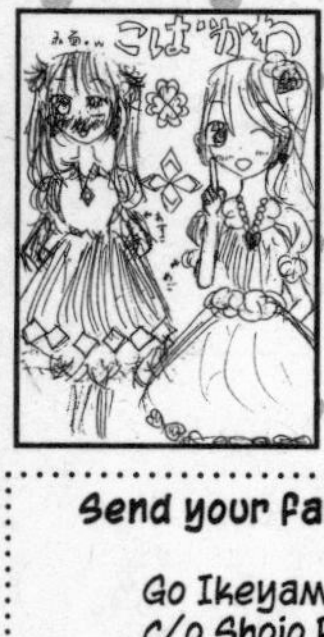

こばかわ

Noan (Toyama) ←

Ed.: Both Mego and Azusa are super cute!!

Send your fan mail to:

Go Ikeyamada
C/o Shojo Beat
VIZ Media, LLC
P.O. Box 77010
San Francisco, CA 94107

AUTHOR BIO

A *So Cute!* Nintendo DS game will be released in Japan in the summer of 2015!

This is the third time my manga has become a game, and I'm very, very happy!! *Uwasa no Midori-kun!!* and *Suki desu Suzuki-kun!!* were the first two to become games.

The voice cast for the game is gorgeous, so keep an eye out for the cast announcement. (^O^) The production staff paid attention to even the smallest details, and I'm very much looking forward to the finished product. (^O^) ♪♪

Go Ikeyamada is a Gemini from Miyagi Prefecture whose hobbies include taking naps and watching movies. Her debut manga *Get Love!!* appeared in *Shojo Comic* in 2002, and her current work *So Cute It Hurts!!* (*Kobayashi ga Kawai Suguite Tsurai!!*) is being published by VIZ Media.

SO CUTE IT HURTS!!
Volume 11

Shojo Beat Edition

STORY AND ART BY
GO IKEYAMADA

English Translation & Adaptation/Tomo Kimura
Touch-Up Art & Lettering/Joanna Estep
Design/Izumi Evers
Editor/Pancha Diaz

KOBAYASHI GA KAWAISUGITE TSURAI!! Vol.11
by Go IKEYAMADA
© 2012 Go IKEYAMADA
All rights reserved.
Original Japanese edition published by SHOGAKUKAN.
English translation rights in the United States of America, Canada,
the United Kingdom and Ireland arranged with SHOGAKUKAN.

Printed in the U.S.A.

Published by VIZ Media, LLC
P.O. Box 77010
San Francisco, CA 94107

10 9 8 7 6 5 4 3 2 1
First printing, February 2017

www.viz.com   www.shojobeat.com

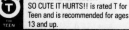

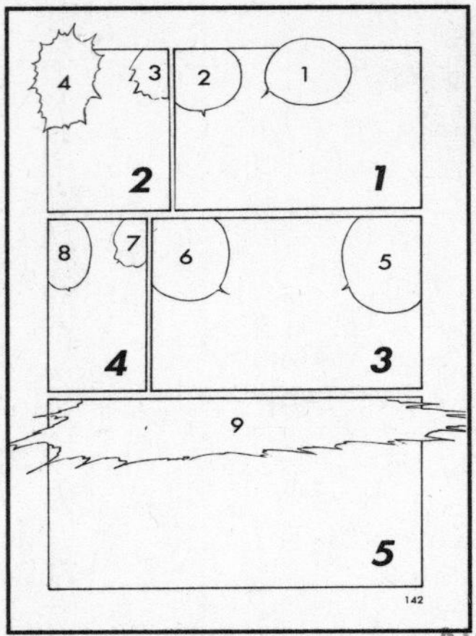
1
2
1
3
4
2
5
6
3
7
8
4
9
5
142

This is the last page.

In keeping with the original Japanese comic format, this book reads from right to left—so action, sound effects and word balloons are completely reversed. This preserves the orientation of the original artwork—plus, it's fun! Check out the diagram shown here to get the hang of things, and then turn to the other side of the book to get started!

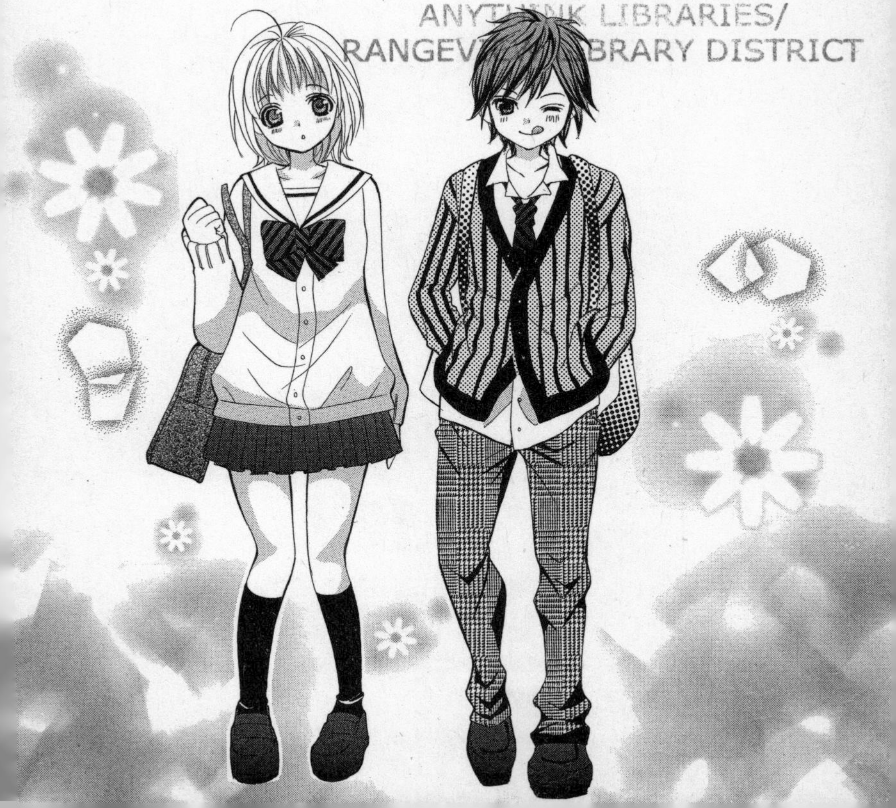